Rhapsody in Red

Rhapsody in Red

How Western Classical Music
Became Chinese

Sheila Melvin and Jindong Cai

Algora Publishing
New York

ISBN: 0-87586-179-2 (softcover)
ISBN: 0-87586-180-5 (hardcover)
ISBN: 0-87586-186-5 (ebook)

Library of Congress Cataloging-in-Publication Data

Melvin, Sheila.
 Rhapsody in red : how classical music became Chinese / by Sheila Melvin &
Jindong Cai.
   p. cm.
  ISBN 0-87586-179-2 (softcover : alk. paper) — ISBN 0-87586-180-6 (hardcov-
er : alk. paper) — ISBN 0-87586-186-5 (ebook)
 1. Music—China—20th century—History and criticism. 2. Music—China—
European influences. I. Cai, Jindong. II. Title.

 ML366.5M45 2004
 781.6'8'0951—dc22

                        2004011185

Front Cover: From top left clockwise:
1. The violinist Ma Sicong, president of the Central Conservatory, performing
for Chinese soliders at the front during the Korean War.
2. Shanghai Symphony Orchestra dressed in army uniform for a performance
of the revolutionary symphony Shajiabang in the late 1960s.
3. Focused Violinist © Strauss/Curtis/CORBIS Photographer: Strauss/Curtis
4. Classical Musicians Play at Ming Tombs © Dean Conger/CORBIS

Printed in the United States

For Sebastian and Cecilia, with love.

TABLE OF CONTENTS

PRELUDE

Classical music today is increasingly the turf of musicians from China. Indeed, so many of the world's top composers and performers of classical music are Chinese-born and educated that their success has been labeled a "huge phenomenon." So, too, are many of the rank-and-file orchestra musicians, music school professors, private violin and piano teachers, and students who are classical music's backbone and future. Although it is less remarked upon, even the production of instruments like pianos, violins, and cellos is ever more a Chinese specialty.

But China is not just an exporter of classical music, musicians, and instruments — it is also a voracious consumer. Classical music has become so deeply embedded in urban China that the performance of a Western opera may draw a bigger audience than that of a Peking opera. Major cities like Shanghai and Beijing have several symphony orchestras that regularly perform works from the standard classical repertoire as well as compositions by Chinese composers. Beijing is now the site of an international music festival that draws top orchestras and soloists from around the world. The piano is immensely popular throughout the country; some estimates suggest as many as 38 million Chinese children are currently learning to play piano.

And yet, China also has its own rich, varied and ancient musical traditions. How and why did Western classical music develop such deep roots? This is a question that we have often asked ourselves — and been asked — and it is this that we set out to answer in writing *Rhapsody in Red: How Western Classical Music Became Chinese.*

Rhapsody in Red is not a history of classical music in China, except of the incidental sort. Rather, like its musical equivalent, it is a series of linked sections

1

that revolve around a common theme. Our approach is people-centered, rather than academic, with each chapter built around one or two key figures or events. It starts in Shanghai in the early 20th century when the all-foreign Shanghai Municipal Orchestra was building a reputation as "the best orchestra in the Far East." From Shanghai, it leaps back in time to the turn of the 17th century when the Jesuit Matteo Ricci presented a clavichord to the emperor, a gift that eventually led to a remarkable tradition of Western classical music study and performance in the Forbidden City. It then progresses forward through the tumult and triumphs of the 20th century — the May 4th Movement, World War II, the Communist victory, the establishment of the People's Republic, the Cultural Revolution, and the re-opening to the outside world that followed it.

Our tale is anchored to several key musicians who devoted their lives to helping classical music take hold and develop. We have chosen this approach because it gives life to a story that until now has remained largely untold. But, it does mean that there are dedicated, talented and important musicians who have gone unnamed or been mentioned only in passing. This is not a reflection of their contributions, but of the demands of building a cogent and compelling narrative. Likewise, because our focus is on classical music in China itself, we have discussed only briefly the Chinese composers and performers who are currently triumphant in concert halls and opera houses around the world — the story of their successes and influence on classical music internationally is, perhaps, the subject for another book.

It took us much longer to write this book than we ever envisioned. This was partly due to the births of our children, Sebastian and Cecilia, who naturally took priority. But, equally significant was the unexpected amount of information we managed to find. Having been ignored for many decades, the subject of Western classical music in China has recently been the focus of scholarly attention and several important academic books have been published by Chinese historians and musicologists. Many of the old guard Chinese musicians have agreed to be the subjects of authorized biographies. Music publishing houses have compiled and published the complete writings of famous musicians. However, because China does not yet have a single comprehensive source for books, finding these works required perseverance, good luck, and many trips to bookstores, libraries, and even flea markets in different cities. So far as we know, the complete works of Xian Xinghai can only be found at the Central Conservatory bookstore in Beijing; for a selection of works on Ma Sicong, it is necessary to go to the Ma Sicong Memorial in Guangzhou; several important books on Xiao Youmei are out of print and we could only find them by going directly to the publisher in Shanghai.

There is also a considerable amount of English-language information on the subject of classical music in China. Articles on the contemporary era are easy to find, but historic information tends to be spread through books and periodicals on a variety of unrelated subjects. We found biographies and autobiographies of Jesuits, musicians, artists, military leaders, and politicians who had some contact with China to be especially useful sources for small — but fascinating — parts of our story.

However, unearthing the relevant paragraphs in such works required much digging and many inter-library loan requests to the Louisiana State University Library. Similarly, the Shanghai Library has well preserved and easily accessible archives of the city's pre-liberation English language newspapers but they are not indexed, so finding articles about the Shanghai Municipal Orchestra required us to page through every day, month and year of the yellowing newspapers. The potential for distraction from eye-catching articles or advertisements aside, this is a time-consuming process.

Throughout the writing of this book, we have grappled with our use of the term "classical music." It is a phrase that we find to be deeply flawed and woefully inexact, but largely unavoidable. Because it had not yet been coined during most of the time period covered in Chapter 2, we have substituted "European music" instead. But in writing about the missionaries who used music as a tool of conversion and education in the 19th and early 20th centuries, we switch to "Western music" since many of them were American and the music they taught was not strictly-speaking "European" or "classical." However, as we got deeper into the 20th century, we were largely forced to drop "Western music" because by then the term could include jazz, pop, rock, disco, and rap, none of which we discuss. So, for the title of our book and through many of its chapters, we have been obliged to use the phrase "classical music" to refer to a broad range of music that was originally brought to China from the West and includes the clavichord, the military march, opera, the symphony, the piano concerto, and more. If the phrase and our use of it are far from perfect, we at least find comfort in the fact that even The Oxford Dictionary of Music defines classical music as a "term which, applied to music, has vague rather than specific meaning."

We have used pinyin romanization for Chinese names except in cases where an alternate romanization is standard or official — as with Chiang Kai-shek or Peking University — and in the citation of sources that use different romanizations.

We are deeply indebted to the musicians, composers and scholars in China who took the time to talk with us. Tan Shuzhen shared tea and conversation with Sheila many times over several years and also provided us with valuable written materials. Li Delun and Li Jue welcomed us into their home twice for long conversations, despite Mr. Li's poor health. Zhou Xiaoyan took time from a demanding schedule to share her life story with Sheila. Some of the many other people who helped us figure prominently in this book, while others do not, but all provided us with important and useful information. They include Dai Penghai; Guo Wenjing; He Yuanyuan; He Zhanhao; Hu Yongyan; Huang Feili; Li Ling; Li Zhang; Lu Zaiyi; Luo Zhongrong and his family; Qu Xiaosong; Wang Xilin; Wu Zuqiang; Xiao Bai; Ye Xiaogang; Yu Long, Xu Bozeng; and Zhu Jianer. Although we did not formally interview Chinese composers who live in the US, Jindong has conducted many of their pieces and we have benefited from many informal conversations with Tan Dun, Chen Yi and Zhou Long, whose friendships we value, and also from briefer conversations with Bright Sheng, Ge Ganru and Jin Xiang.

Many people at the Shanghai Symphony assisted us in some way, especially Maestro Chen Xieyang, Chen Guangxian, Wen Tan and Yang Zhaoying. Chen

Guangxian was kind enough to invite Sheila to the Shanghai Symphony's 120th anniversary celebration and to put her in touch with Tan Shuzhen afterwards. The Shanghai Symphony's archives were of great value to us, especially the programs from the Paci era which Wen Tan kindly had copied for us. He also shared his own experiences as a member of the orchestra for many decades and directed us to other valuable research materials.

Floria Paci Zaharoff contacted us after seeing a *New York Times* story that we wrote about the Shanghai Symphony. She then gave us a wealth of information that brought her father Mario Paci to life for us and — we hope — for our readers. She also introduced us to Dong Guangguang. Ms. Dong and her husband Ma Sihong were kind enough to welcome us into their New York State home where they shared some memories with us and also let us see the Steinway that once belonged to Maestro Paci. Jacob Avshalomov spoke to Jindong by phone and directed us to the book that he wrote about his father's life in China. Peter Tcherepnin spoke to Sheila by phone and helped clear up several questions about the lives and careers of both his parents. Nancy Bradburd and Clinton F. Nieweg of the Philadelphia Orchestra promptly answered several questions related to the Eugene Ormandy's communications with Li Delun.

Although we had no institutional support in writing this book, we had considerable encouragement from family and friends for which we will always be grateful. We would like to thank our families in the United States for providing us not only with moral support, but with practical assistance by helping to care for our children whenever they came to visit, so we could have extra time to write. They are Jinliang, Lyta, Anna and Sarah Cai; Nei dal Bem; Sarah Campbell; Sheila Campbell; Don Melvin; Michelle Melvin; and Catherine Visocky. Our families in China provided us with equal encouragement and also welcomed us into their homes for many months of research and writing. They are Jinyong, Isabella, Sophia and Eva Cai; Jinqing Cai; Lilan, Ashley and Natalie Cheng; Dawn Vermilya; and Zhang Shuhua. Sheila owes extra thanks to her parents — Sarah Campell and Donald Melvin — for supporting her love of reading and writing throughout her life and Jindong to his — Zhang Shuhua and the late Cai Zeyi — for supporting his love of music.

We appreciate the interest of all our friends, particularly Pam Baldinger; Mike Bruhn; Kathy Chen; Shi-zheng Chen; Alex Clegg; Nigel Dawn; Marya Gwadz; Jane Huang; Tom and Elsa Katana; Corina Larkin; Zhang Lijia; Calum Macleod; Tacy Paul; Tacy Paul Roby; Anne Stevenson-Yang; Melana Zyla Vickers; Nick Viorst; Rebecca Weiner; Peter Wilson; Shirley Young; and Judith Zeitlin. Michelle Garnaut and Bruno van der Burg welcomed us into their home on several research trips to Shanghai, including when our son was only a few weeks old. Ashley Grayson and Erica Dillon each baby-sat Sebastian several mornings a week for a year so Sheila could write. Maestro Gerhard Samuel helped with several French translations and Doris Michaels gave us early encouragement.

We are appreciative of the editors who have supported Sheila's writing and published many articles that she wrote on arts and culture in China, several coauthored with Jindong. They are Hugo Restall, formerly of *The Asian Wall Street Journal* and now of *The Wall Street Journal*; Ray Sokolov, formerly of *The Wall Street Journal*; John Rockwell, of *The New York Times*; and Katherine Knorr of *The International Herald Tribune*. Sheila would also like to thank Lyman Miller, now of the Hoover Institute, and Robert Kapp, of The United States-China Business Council, for sharing their vast knowledge of China with her over the years. Jindong would like to thank Nie Zhongming, who led him to a career in conducting; Lorna Cooke deVaron and Carl St. Clair, who taught him at the New England Conservatory; and his mentor Gerhard Samuel, his professor at the College-Conservatory of Music in Cincinnati. Finally, we would like to thank our editor Andrea Secara and Algora Publishing for their patience and professionalism in working with us.

Above: The Shanghai Symphony Orchestra dressed in army uniform for a performance of the revolutionary symphony *Shajiabang* in the late 1960s.

Below: An army orchestra of Chinese traditional instruments formed in imitation of the Western symphony orchestra.

Above: The all-foreign Shanghai Municipal Orchestra and
Maestro Mario Paci (on podium) in 1936

Below: Tan Shuzhen, the first Chinese musician to play in the
Shanghai Municipal Orchestra, and its Italian concertmaster Arrigo Foa in 1929.

Above: The composer Ding Shande revising the last movement of his symphony, *The Long March*.

Below: A scene from the opera *The White-Haired Girl*, performed by the Central Opera and Ballet Theater in the early 1950s.

Nie Er, the composer of
China's national anthem,
in a publicity photo
taken in Shanghai
in the early 1930s.

A photo of rising young pianists taken in the late 1950s or early 1960s.
Liu Shikun is seated at the piano; Gu Shengying stands to his right;
and Yin Chengzong stands behind her on the far right.

The Italian Jesuit
Matteo Ricci,
who presented
a clavichord to
Emperor Wan Li
in 1601.

Xiao Youmei,
founder of the
Shanghai Conservatory,
circa 1927.

Xian Xinghai,
the "People's Composer,"
in the late 1930s.

Mao Zedong
giving a lecture at
Yanan's Lu Xun
Academy for Arts
and Literature in
1938.

Above: The violinist Ma Sicong, president of the Central Conservatory, performing for Chinese soliders at the front during the Korean War.

Below: Maestro Li Delun conducting the Central Philharmonic Society orchestra in a performance for the masses. The photo is undated, but was probably taken in the late 1960s.

Above: Mao Zedong (far left), Lin Biao (center) and Jiang Qing (far right) with performers of the revolutionary model Peking opera *The Red Lantern.* Everyone except for Mao is waving a copy of *Quotations from Chairman Mao.*

Below: Richard Nixon and Jiang Qing chatting at a performance of the revolutionary ballet *The Red Detachment of Women* during Nixon's 1972 visit to China.

Left:
"The hard-boned musician,"
He Luting,
in 1998.

Below: Li Delun and Isaac Stern at their 1999 reunion concert to mark the 20th anniversary of the film *From Mao to Mozart*.

Chapter 1. The Best Orchestra in the Far East

An Italian Pianist in Shanghai

Three days after Christmas in the winter of 1918, a P & O steamer from Hong Kong sailed up the Huangpu River toward Shanghai. The most dangerous part of the journey lay behind — more than one P& O ship had been lost to a typhoon or wrecked on the rocks of the China Sea — but the sheer number of junks, tugs and barges that crowded the shallow Shanghai harbor required extra caution and concentration. Indeed, on this particular day, with heavy, wet snowflakes falling from the leaden sky, navigation was almost entirely dependent on sound. Only when each sharp burst of the foghorn had called forth a chorus of mournful whistles from the over-sized conch shells blown aboard the junks did the captain maneuver his ship onward. Despite his caution, a junk would every now and then loom up close, specter-like in the mist, its square brown sails billowing as the wide, heavy-lashed eyes painted on its bow almost appeared to blink.

The P & O's cautious maneuvering into port must have seemed an eternity to its passengers, most of whom were no doubt straining their eyes to catch a glimpse of the Bund, Shanghai's famous waterfront esplanade that was lined with such landmarks as the Shanghai Club, with its renowned Long Bar, and the flower-filled Public Gardens, entry to which was banned to all Chinese except those employed as servants of the city's growing population of white residents. But for one passenger, a short, dark-eyed man named Mario Paci, these last hours of the journey were sheer agony.[1]

A Florentine by birth and a musician by calling, Paci was traveling from his home in Batavia, capital of the Dutch East Indies, to Shanghai where he had been invited to give a series of piano recitals in the city's Olympic Theater. For most of the three-day journey, he had been at the heart of shipboard social life, a lively

17

participant in countless conversations, card games, and drinking sessions. But, as luck would have it, the unholy combination of two major sea journeys, the endless Christmas revelries, and the unexpectedly biting cold of the East China winter combined to fell him just as he neared his destination. Instead of having a final cocktail or conversation with his many newfound friends, he had spent the last hours of the journey sweating and shivering in his berth.

By the time the P& O finally cast anchor and the tender chugged out to meet it, Paci was in such a bad state that it was deemed necessary to call for assistance. So, as his fellow passengers tumbled ashore clutching their hat-boxes and valises, shouting for coolies in pidgin English and bidding one another goodbye in a babble of European tongues, Paci was hoisted onto a stretcher. For illness to strike him down just at this moment was unthinkable — he had a tight schedule to adhere to, with his Shanghai engagement followed by more recitals in Tokyo and a very important premiere performance tour in the United States that was set to last for several weeks. But, unthinkable or no, Paci slipped into unconsciousness as the coolies trotted through the crowded streets and deposited him, inert, at Shanghai General Hospital.

When he awoke much later, it was in a clean white hospital room where he was informed that he had a serious case of pneumonia and would be bed-ridden for some time. Equally bad — perhaps even worse — was the news that his beloved Steinway concert grand that had been built especially for him in New York with tropicalized hardwood, and with which he always travelled, had been improperly stowed and was damaged by sea water. Paci's recitals in Shanghai were postponed, and those in Japan and the United States cancelled; the fiery pianist so accustomed to trotting around the globe at full throttle was forced to turn his focus to recovering his health.

Fortunately, though Paci had travelled to Shanghai alone, he was not a complete stranger to the city. In fact, he had visited once before, stopping for a single night in 1904 to give a recital at the German Club. This time around he had made the journey at the behest of Avray Strok, a Russian-Jewish businessman who was a prominent figure in Shanghai's growing international community and the city's top musical impresario, described by the pianist Artur Rubinstein as "the only one who arranged tours in Japan, China and the Philippine Islands."[2]

Like Paci, Strok loved music passionately and was known for his insistence on quality. "No use playing badly,"[3] was his favorite expression, which he repeated any time he set out to organize a concert. Although the two had never met, Strok had been impressed enough by Paci's reputation to bring him all the way to Shanghai and he did

---

1. Paci gives a brief account of his journey, illness and involuntary stay in Shanghai in an autobiographical essay called "Maestro Mario Paci (born 1878), conductor Shanghai Municipal Orchestra 1919-1942," which is published in *Souvenir Programme of Farewell Concert*, Shanghai Municipal Orchestra, May 31, 1942. He also discusses it in Ho Chia-Shui (1946). Paci gives highlights of life in last interview. *The China Press*, October 20. The interview was first published in Chinese in *Wen Wei Pao (Wen Hui Bao)*.

2. Rubinstein, A. (1980). *My Many Years*. New York: Alfred A. Knopf: 355.

3. Conversation with Paci's daughter, Floria Paci Zaharoff, New York, July 2000.

not give up on him simply because he was sick. On the contrary, he looked after Paci during the two months he was in hospital and the pair soon became good friends.

Mr. Strok worked in cooperation with Moutries, the all-around music store where Shanghai residents booked concert tickets, bought sheet music and instruments, and, quite serendipitously, got their pianos repaired.[4] Moutries thus took charge of fixing Paci's Steinway while Strok made plans to reschedule the postponed recitals and Paci convalesced.

Once he was released from hospital, Paci's recovery was rapid. Though still technically ill, he was soon reacquainting himself with people he had met aboard the P & O, striking up new friendships courtesy of Strok's introductions, and getting to know the exhilarating city in which he found himself stranded. As it happened, his forced recuperation in Shanghai coincided with the city's own recovery from the effects of World War I. Highly dependent on shipping, Shanghai had been left isolated from the outside world during the war years. Its economy had fallen into a minor recession and relations between foreign residents whose nations were battling each other had become severely strained. With the end of hostilities, the city regained its former spirit and, as one resident of the time put it, "Shanghai broke out into an unparalleled round of festivity, marked by collective and individual extravagance."[5] This extravagance and gaiety must have been both enticing and inspiring for the pleasure-loving but ambitious pianist.

Like most foreigners, Paci split his time between the International Settlement, where he had been hospitalized, and the French Concession, which was famous for its cafes, cabarets, restaurants and dance halls. Both the Settlement and the Concession had been founded in the wake of the Opium War, which broke out in 1839 after the Chinese confiscated, burnt and flushed out to sea 3 million pounds of raw opium belonging to British traders in a desperate effort to end the destructive opium trade and make the British see the error of their ways. This bold move backfired when the traders — determined to keep selling opium despite its devastating effect on millions of Chinese — convinced the British government to declare war. The British were victorious and in 1842 demanded as part of the price of peace the right for British traders to live and do business in five "treaty ports," including Shanghai. Other industrial nations quickly jumped on the band wagon, demanding that the Chinese extend to them the same privileges they had given the British. The United States pushed even further, insisting that Americans who lived in these treaty ports be subject to US laws, rather than those of China. This privilege — known as extraterritoriality — was in turn granted to citizens of many European nations and, eventually, to the Japanese. Its result was the creation in Shanghai of the British Settlement, the American Settlement and the French Concession, although the British

---

4. Moutries also assembled pianos from kits — as many automobiles are nowadays assembled in China — and was thus most likely the first piano producer in China.

5. Pott, F.L.H. (1928). *A Short History of Shanghai*. Shanghai: Kelly & Walsh, Limited: 237.

and Americans soon merged their separate settlements to create the International Settlement.

The International Settlement and French Concession began to attract not just traders, but missionaries, adventure-seekers and others for whom the opportunity to live in China — but outside the jurisdiction of its laws — proved too tempting to resist. The two areas were governed separately — the Settlement by a Municipal Council elected by foreign "Ratepayers," or those who paid land taxes, the Concession by a Conseil d'Administration — but were in reality closely linked. Drivers needed separate licenses for each area, but everyone else moved freely back and forth and social life spilled over the boundaries.

Despite their close links, the Settlement and the Concession differed considerably in physical appearance and culture. The orderly roads of the International Settlement were dominated by buildings of industry and commerce, like the banks and insurance companies that line the Bund to this day. Indeed, when the Hong Kong and Shanghai Bank opened its fabulous domed headquarters on the Bund in 1923, it was acknowledged as one of the biggest and finest bank buildings in the world. The architectural gems of the French Concession, on the other hand, were clubs — like the beautiful Cercle Sportif Français, now part of the Garden Hotel — and cathedrals. Life in the French Concession was more leisurely and languid than in the comparatively uptight International Settlement; the French did not worry themselves over little things like opium smuggling or prostitution, and their Concession eventually became a comfortable home base for powerful Chinese criminal gangs. As the saying went: In the International Settlement, the British will teach you how to do business; in the French Concession, the French will teach you how to live.

Paci knew how to do business — at least the business of his art — and he also knew how to live, and he spent his recuperation doing both. He wiled away many an evening in the cafes and restaurants of the French Concession, indulging his love of good food, sipping his favorite Marsala cocktails, smoking the cigarettes he could never give up, and chatting with new friends. But, even as he reveled in Shanghai's more hedonistic delights, he was listening to the live dance and jazz music that was a regular part of Shanghai nightlife, and thinking. At some moment during one of these nights, he determined that he would organize a grand orchestral concert for Shanghai's music lovers, forming his very own orchestra and conducting it himself — a realization of his life-long dual dreams of being both a conductor and a pianist.

First, however, he had to give his long-postponed recitals, which Avray Strok rescheduled for early February of 1919. Thanks to the long delay, Strok's public relations work, and Paci's own socializing about town, there was considerable buzz about the recitals and audience expectations were high. Aware of this, Paci chose a challenging program of Beethoven, Chopin, Debussy, and Liszt for his debut. The review that appeared in the next day's *North China Daily News* was unstinting in its praise of both Paci and his Steinway, the reviewer first bemoaning the fact that attendance at the recital had not been greater:

> It is, alas, tragically true that if there is any distraction in Shanghai in which the entertainment of the audience is the primary factor on the same day as a concert, the concert invariably suffers, however great a treat the concert may be both intellectually and musically. To hear Paci play the "Waldstein" Sonata was a revelation as well as a great treat.... Paci is a most interesting musician and plays with great freedom and wonderful command of tone.[6]

The word "magnificent" appeared repeatedly in the review, as adjective and adverb, applied to everything from Paci's Steinway to his interpretation of Debussy. The reviewer then concluded:

> There was such a variety of touch and tone colouring, such poetry and such perfect crispness and clearness of fingerwork, that the audience was charmed and Paci was enthusiastically recalled...Paci is a magnificent pianist and possesses all that a great pianist needs: musical interpretation, a beautiful singing touch, great power and wonderful technique, and all music lovers will look forward to his next concert.[7]

In light of these generous reviews, and given that he was performing for the first time in many months, Paci must have looked forward to his second recital as much as his audience, and the performance was praised even more lavishly than the first. Buoyed by this enthusiastic reception, and completely recovered from his illness, he proceeded with his plan to organize an orchestra. Mr. Strok put him together with two well-known soloists — the violinist Mr. Piastro and the pianist Mr. Mirovitch — booked the Lyceum Theater for the night of March 31, and set his promotion machine in motion. Meanwhile, Paci headed out to the cafes and clubs with a mission to recruit the best musicians he could find. As soon as he had secured a full complement of 40 musicians from the Philippines, Russia and Europe, he plunged them into a strenuous rehearsal schedule.

The rave reviews Paci had received for his piano recitals, the popularity of the soloists Mr. Strok had introduced, and the novelty of a concert pianist prowling cafes and dance halls in order to build an orchestra all combined to create a good deal of anticipation in advance of the concert. Tickets sold steadily and on the evening of March 31st crowds of Shanghai's foreign residents stepped out of their rickshaws and automobiles and entered the Lyceum in a flurry of cologne and chatter, the ladies perhaps holding handkerchiefs to their noses to ward off the foul stench of nearby Suzhou Creek. Shanghai audiences dressed to the nines for such events and must have made a colorful spectacle, the men in tuxedoes and the women in the latest fashions from Europe, purchased in Shanghai's Parisian boutiques or copied from fashion magazines by adept Chinese tailors. The concert-goers' glamour, however, would have

---

6. Mr. Paci's piano recital. *North China Daily News*, February 6, 1919.
7. *Ibid.*

stood in striking contrast to the lives of residents of the neighborhood, which was home to countless famine refugees who lived on the creek in dilapidated sampans, cooking and bathing with the same fetid water that served as their toilet and garbage dump.

As the audience members filed into the hall and settled into their seats, the members of Paci's pick-up orchestra thumbed through their parts, shifted in their chairs and practiced snippets from the evening's program. Paci emerged from his green room and stood quietly in the wings while the concertmaster, a Miss Macleod, stepped on stage to lead the musicians in tuning their instruments. After a suitably dramatic pause, Paci strode confidently onto the stage and was greeted by loud applause. Stopping beside his Steinway to savor the sight of the full, cheering house, he bowed slightly and then sat down at his piano. With a curt nod to the orchestra — some of whose members could barely see him — he then plunged into Mozart's Piano *Concerto No. 26 in D Major*, the wondrous *Coronation Concerto*. As the April 1 *Shanghai Times* described it,

> Besides playing the Solo instrument Mr. Paci prompted the orchestra as well. The concerto was delightfully rendered, the phrasing being perfect in finish and the delicate passages showing to advantage Mr. Paci's brilliant, aerial touch. Perhaps this revealed more than anything else the extent of Mr. Paci's usual attainments, and the high efficiency of the orchestra.[8]

The performance was met with loud ovations, to which Paci responded by playing the *Harmonious Blacksmith* variations of Handel.

For the next piece, Paci took up the baton to lead the orchestra in accompanying Mr. Piastro in Beethoven's *Violin Concerto*, a performance that *The China Press* said "cannot be spoken of with too much praise."[9] Paci next inserted a composition of his own, *Alla Menuetto* for strings, which was "well received" with a "pleasing melody."[10] Two more pieces for strings only — Grieg's *To the Spring* and Dvorak's *Nocturne* — were followed by Grieg's *Piano Concerto in A Minor*, with Mr. Mirovitch as soloist. While *The China Press* mildly rebuked Paci for conducting parts of the Grieg in a manner more suited to Wagner's *Ring* or Tchaikovsky's *1812* overture,[11] the *North China Daily News* labeled the orchestral accompaniment as "splendid."

With the Grieg, the concert came to a "triumphal close"[12] and the audience roared. Newspapers of the following day were unanimous in their praise for both Paci the pianist and Paci the maestro. Declared *The North China Daily News*:

> Signor Paci is a born conductor and he had his orchestra splendidly in hand. They played with wonderful unanimity throughout, which was a great achievement considering they were playing together for the first time...As a pianist, we have already

---

8. Lyceum Theater. *Shanghai Times*, April 1, 1919.
9. The symphony. *The China Press*, April 1, 1919.
10. Lyceum Theater. *Shanghai Times*, April 1, 1919.
11. The symphony. *The China Press*, April 1, 1919.
12. Grand orchestral concert. *North China Daily News*, April 1, 1919.

had opportunities of enjoying Signor Paci's splendid musicianship, and last night he again delighted us all.[13]

The elated reviewer further expressed the hope that the concert would be but the first of many:

> Ever since the announcement of this concert, expectation has been raised to the highest pitch. The packed house, the tremendous enthusiasm of the audience were a fitting tribute to the popularity of the three artists — Mirovitch, Piastro, and Paci — and at the same time showed how very ready we all are to greet the revival of an orchestra in our midst. We can only hope that it may be possible to reconstruct a permanent orchestra, so that Shanghai can once more have its symphony concerts, and even from a musical point of view have some right to be called, "The Paris of the East."[14]

MUSIC IN THE FOREIGN CONCESSIONS

"Paris of the East" was just one of the many sobriquets that had been given Shanghai over the years. Shanghai was a city so full of life — and of itself — that it seemed to demand sensational descriptions that could be capitalized, set off in quotation marks and spread around the world. Way back in 1869, Britain's Duke of Somerset had bestowed upon it the rather unflattering title "Sink of Iniquity" in a speech before the House of Lords. Many similarly colorful designations had followed, among them "The Far Country of the Prodigal Son," "Paradise of Adventurers," "The Sodom of China," and "The Whore of the East."

Given the less-than-complimentary nature of most these appellations, "Paris of the East" was understandably the one most preferred by the city's foreign residents and overseas boosters, not to mention the many Chinese intellectuals who looked to France as a beacon of culture and democratic ideals. Moreover, Paris at the time was on the brink of becoming the musical capital of the West, a city in which new works by Prokofiev, Stravinsky, Ravel, and Berg would delight — or enrage — audiences; where such operas as *Carmen, Tales of Hoffmann, Manon, Lakme,* and *Pelleas et Mellisande* would premiere; where princesses would commission works from Stravinsky and host salons at which Falla and Ravel would perform for the guests.[15] Even the most ardent of Shanghai supporters would likely have hesitated before calling the city a "musical Paris of the East."

Shanghai of course had music. Indeed, anyone who lived there was aware that it produced its own music, a distinctive sound track that propelled its residents forward as they worked, played, and dreamt grandiose dreams of their futures in a city whose greatness they knew to be predestined. No matter where you went in Shanghai, the

---

13. *Ibid.*
14. *Ibid.*
15. See Simeone, Nigel, French without fears, *Musical Times,* Spring 2003. This is a review of a book by Roger Nichols entitled, *The Harlequin Years: Music in Paris 1917-1929,* London: Thames & Hudson, 2002.

hubbub was the same — the distinctive creak of wheelbarrows on rutted roads; the sing-song cries of coolies bent beneath impossibly heavy loads; the nagging, sibilant wails of hawkers and rickshaw pullers hustling for business; the serpentine sounds of Shanghainese dialect, too full of S's and Z's; the low, throbbing bass of piles being driven into the alluvial soil as supports for yet another new building; the bellow of fog horns, the screeching of automobile breaks, the curses of drivers, the steamy blasts of train whistles. Shanghai's music was constant, an auditory amplification of the city's energy, hubris and hunger for life.

Naturally, there was also music of a more traditional sort, the kind to which the city's 1.5 million Chinese residents preferred to listen. Some of this music was private, like that of the *guqin*, a lute that old-style intellectuals played for their own enlightenment or for the illumination of a handful of close friends. Some was semi-private, like the music that sing-song girls played for the entertainment of their clients in the bordellos of Fuzhou Road. On hot summer nights, their lilting arias, with lyrics of love and lust, could be heard spilling out of second floor balconies. Mingling with peals of laughter and the clinking of glasses, these songs tempted passersby on the streets below to enter, and indulge.

Music of a more public sort was also everywhere in Shanghai. Famine and warfare in other parts of the country had sent untold numbers of refugees fleeing to the city and its streets were overflowing with beggars. Some became street performers and the melancholy notes of the two-stringed *erhu* played by blindmen was as common as the clanging of bicycle bells. Music spilled forth from temples, too, the hypnotic chants of Buddhist monks in prayer and the soulful instrumentals of Taoists engaged in self-cultivation. Tea houses, centers of social life in Chinese areas of the city, were filled with pairs of ping-tan story-tellers who spent weeks, even months, reciting classic stories while accompanying themselves on the *pipa*, a pear-shaped lute with four strings, and the *sanxian*, a three-stringed, plucked instrument. And finally, there was Chinese opera, not just the most popular form of music, but of all entertainment.

The area around Shanghai had been famous for Chinese opera for hundreds of years. Kunju, the preferred operatic form of the literati class from the 16th until the late 19th centuries, had been born just outside Shanghai in the town of Kunshan and grown to maturity in nearby Suzhou. Kunju is elegant and ethereal, its melodic, lyrical music dominated by bamboo flute, rather than the percussive instruments of so many other regional opera forms. Its stories are long, beautifully written love tales, sometimes of 50 acts or more, in which female characters play a major role. Kunju had fallen on hard times by the 20th century when the pace of life became such that few people had three or four days to spend watching the same opera, but it was still performed in excerpts for Shanghai's elites both in tea houses and at private parties.

Percussive-based Peking opera, with its action-packed stories based on great legends or historical military adventures, had gradually eclipsed Kunju in popularity throughout China and was also widely performed in Shanghai. Indeed, despite its northern roots, a whole school of Peking opera performance had evolved in Shanghai, and many of Peking's greatest opera stars regularly journeyed there to perform with their colleagues in the Shanghai school. Some of the most liberal members of Shanghai's Peking opera world even got together in 1908 to found a theater known as the New Shanghai Stage. Heavily influenced by Western drama, they modeled their performance space after a Western-style proscenium theater, used lighting and simple props, and performed "new dramas with contemporary costumes," often with socially liberal themes such as the evils of prostitution.

And, just three years before Paci's arrival, a new form of opera had been introduced to the city from Shaoxing, in neighboring Zhejiang Province. Shaoxing opera was considered by intellectuals to be light entertainment, dependent on beautiful costumes, elaborate props and tear-jerker plot lines, but it became immensely popular and many troupes moved to Shanghai. In 1923, an all-women troupe arrived and caused such a sensation that Shaoxing opera soon came to be performed almost entirely by women, who played both male and female roles.

But of course this vibrant and diverse musical life enjoyed by Shanghai's Chinese residents would not have figured into the calculations of most foreigners eager to make the city into a musical Paris of the East. To them, Chinese music was irrelevant, Paris being a city that possessed and produced great composers and performers of symphonic music and Western opera. To have some right to be called a musical Paris of the East, Shanghai needed Western classical music. More to the point, this music had to be both formal and permanent, not solely dependent on café musicians, church choirs, and traveling artists who gave recitals and then moved on to greener pastures. In short, what Shanghai needed was an orchestra.

The desire for an orchestra was not a new one. On the contrary, in the years before the Great War broke out, valiant efforts had been made to reinvent the city band as an orchestra.[16] Itself an important civic institution, the Shanghai Municipal Band dated all the way back to 1879 and its bills were footed by the Municipal Council, the governing body of the International Settlement, with contributions also made by the government of the French Concession. A Town Band Committee was formed to oversee it in 1881, comprised of two members of each municipal council and two or three Ratepayers who were interested in music. For years, the Band was dominated by Filipino musicians who were recruited from Manila, and thus known as "Manilamen." However, most of these "Manilamen" were not professionally trained and their level of musicianship was routinely criticized by the Band's supporters and detractors alike.

---

16. For an account of the band's early years and the orchestra's history up until 1942, see Harris, E.F. (1942). The story of the Municipal Orchestra. *Souvenir Programme of Farewell Concert*. Shanghai Municipal Orchestra. May 31: 5.

For the band's early history and the orchestra's history up until 1946, see Bickers, R. (2001). "The Greatest Cultural Asset East of Suez: The History and Politics of the Shanghai Municipal Orchestra and Public Band, 1881-1946." In Chi-hsiung Chang (chief ed.), *Ershi shiji de Zhongguo yu shijie* [China and the world in the twentieth century] Taibei: Institute of History, Academia Sinica, Vo.1 2: 835-875. Also, Han Guohuang (1995). Shanghai gongbuju yuedui yenjiu [The Shanghai Municipal Orchestra]. *Yishuxue* 14: 143-205.

In 1906, it was decided that the only means of improving the Band was to recruit professionals from Europe. A scouting trip was made and a conductor named Herr Rudolf Buck was hired in Berlin, together with six musicians whose ranks included several string players. The caliber of concerts given by the Band improved and enough orchestral pieces were added to its repertoire that some people began to refer to it as the Municipal Orchestra, though its formal title did not change. Standard works of the symphonic repertoire by such composers as Beethoven, Haydn, Elgar, Wagner and Tchaikovsky were played for the first time and printed programs "containing historical and analytical notes" accompanied the Band's performances.[17] In the summertime, the concerts it gave in Hongkou Park and the Public Gardens became major social activities, those in the latter venue enjoyed by the wealthiest foreigners from the comfort of houseboats anchored out on the river. Of course, Shanghai's Chinese residents could not attend Municipal Band concerts since they were not allowed in the parks where it played in summer and were even barred from entering the Town Hall, where the band performed in its regular season.

When World War I broke out, five of the band's German musicians were drafted into military service, with one killed in the defense of Qingdao and four shipped off to Japan as prisoners of war.[18] Shanghai's German population was ostracized and finally all German citizens were expelled from China. These were more blows than the Band could absorb and by the time of Paci's arrival in Shanghai, only its remnants survived: 22 men without a regular conductor. *The China Press* described the general attitude toward the Band in this way:

> ...when the few straggling individuals of the Shanghai public attended the Sunday afternoon concert by the Municipal orchestra, they had a reason. In the winter time they went to escape the cold of the streets; in the spring they went to break the monotony of walking in the rain.[19]

But, with the war over and an economic boom in full swing, the time was ripe to once again attempt the creation of a full-fledged orchestra comprised of professional musicians. Shanghai had the money, the ambition, the theaters, and the audiences necessary to support such an orchestra. It even had hundreds of musicians who played Western classical music already on its soil. All that it needed to complete the picture was a talented and charismatic conductor who possessed as much drive and determination as the city itself.

MAESTRO PACI GETS SHANGHAIED

Paci's orchestral concert at the Lyceum was such a smashing success that Mr. Strok hurriedly booked the Olympic Theater for the following Tuesday, April 8, and

---

17. Bickers: 849.
18. Bickers: 851.
19. Municipal orchestra leader leaves today. *The China Press*, May, 1921.

scheduled a second performance for the Italian maestro and his pick-up orchestra. This concert was greeted with as much acclaim as the first and quickly labeled "epoch-making."[20] The events that followed were explained 20 years later, in rather purple prose, by a writer for *The China Press Sunday Magazine*:

> In those days Shanghai was a boom town with a *boom-boom* band that drummed and tromboned with cheerful energy through weddings, funerals and official dances. It was a lusty band to be proud of, and from their heaven of prosperity, the Council said: "Let there be a real Maestro!" They might have shaped one from one of the ribs of the existing orchestral body, but that would not be strictly "Class," and "Class" was the only thing the band needed. Just then an Italian Maestro named Mario Paci was giving concerts in Shanghai — and what could be more classy than an Italian, especially with a name like that?...
>
> So Maestro Paci was invited to hear the band play, which it did with the usual vim, vigor and vitality, and was then asked, "How would you like to conduct Shanghai's orchestra?" — or words to that effect. His answer was to the effect that he would very much like to conduct Shanghai's orchestra, but he had not heard an orchestra in Shanghai yet.[21]

Paci may not have heard an orchestra that he deemed worthy of the name, but Shanghai had heard him. And, once it had, the city's press, music lovers, and international community leaders quickly recognized that the peripatetic pianist who had been carried to their shores unconscious was just the person they needed to build up their long-desired symphony orchestra. The only question was, could they convince him to stay?

Anyone who knew Paci at the time would likely have answered that question in the negative, for the brilliant musician had been a wanderer for most of his life.

Born in Florence in 1878, he was a musically gifted child who started serious study of the piano at the age of 8.[22] He entered the Conservatory of Naples when he was ten and made an acclaimed public debut at the Naples Del Fondo Theater when he was only eleven. Though his mother, Augusta, was a lover of the arts who held a salon on Sundays, his father, Telemaco, was a strict disciplinarian who dreaded the idea of his son growing up to be nothing more than "a mediocre musician."[23] Telemaco refused to let the young Paci pursue music full-time and insisted that he continue his regular studies, with the aim of becoming a doctor.

---

20. Another memorable concert. *Shanghai Times*, April 8, 1919.

21. Austin, A. (1939). Under the baton of Maestro Paci, director of Shanghai's symphony orchestra reviews his career as a music "dictator," *The China Press Sunday Magazine*, May 7: 5.

22. For details of Paci's early life, see Paci, M. (1942). Maestro Mario Paci. *Souvenir Programme of Farewell Concert*, Shanghai Municipal Orchestra. May 31: 13-16. Also, Ho Chia-shui (1946). Paci gives highlights of life in last interview. *The China Press*, October 20. Information also comes from the authors' interviews with Paci's daughter, Floria Paci Zaharoff.

23. See Paci, M. (1942). Maestro Mario Paci. *Souvenir Programme of Farewell Concert*, Shanghai Municipal Orchestra. May 31: 13.

Paci, however, was equally stubborn and he quickly became as determined to dedicate his life to music as Telemaco was to stopping him. At the age of 14, the young Mario sold his books and his only possession of value — "an enormous old pocketwatch"[24] — bought a train ticket, and ran away to Rome. He arrived in the capital with only a few lire in his pocket and went straight to the Via della Croce to the home of Giovanni Sgambati, the close friend, pupil, and protégé of Liszt and the pianist of Paci's dreams.

Sgambati was internationally famous as a pianist, though he was also a respected composer and conductor. He played a key role in reviving the popularity of non-operatic music in late 19th century Italy and was naturally a great promoter of Liszt's works. But, as far as Paci was concerned, his greatest asset was his devotion to teaching talented students, be they rich or poor. Indeed, Sgambati even founded a school called the Liceo Musicale di S Cecilia, which was attached to Rome's Accademia di S Cecilia and specialized in teaching piano students who could not afford to pay tuition. However, when Paci arrived at Sgambati's imposing residence, the door was opened by a frightening valet who told him, "The Professor does not receive anybody without letters of introduction." [25]

That was the valet's final word. With nowhere else to turn, the exhausted, hungry and disappointed young boy used his last two lire to send a cable to his parents, in which he informed them of his predicament, begged forgiveness, and pleaded for help in getting the letter he needed. It is not hard to imagine the scene that must have rocked the Paci household when the cable was received, but in the end Paci's bold move was to serve him well. Augusta took the next train to Rome, found a room for herself and her son, rented a grand piano, and got the letter of introduction to Sgambati.

"And so," Paci recounted in an autobiographical essay written years later, "my happy life of studying six or seven hours per day the Piano as 'pupil of Sgambati' began."[26]

The lessons were a financial strain on the Paci family and when Sgambati realized this, he refused to accept payment and taught his talented young student for free for the next three years. Paci's talent — and Sgambati's discernment — was publicly acknowledged when he turned 17 and won the Liszt Prize, awarded every five years to the best pianist in a field that in 1895 included 63 competitors from across Europe.

With the Liszt Prize under his belt and the continuing support of Sgambati, the young pianist toured Europe for a year, giving recitals in Italy, France, and Austria. This experience in the capitals of Europe proved to be a turning point. As he wrote, "There I heard for the first time marvelous Symphony Concerts and great Conductors.

24. *Ibid.*
25. *Ibid.*
26. Paci, M. (1942). Maestro Mario Paci. *Souvenir Programme of Farewell Concert*, Shanghai Municipal Orchestra. May 31: 13-15.

My piano suddenly seemed to me a poor means of musical expression." The impressionable and passionate young musician wanted to learn a new musical language — that of the orchestra.

With this in mind, Paci returned to Milan the following year, hoping to study composition and orchestration at the city's famous Conservatory. Though more than confident in his own talent as a musician, Paci had little knowledge of music theory and was afraid to sit for the Conservatory's highly competitive exams. But, luck again blessed his talent and determination when he was invited one evening to a salon at the home of the Viscount of Modrone, a gathering place for musical luminaries from the grand opera house La Scala. Asked to perform for the guests, Paci sat down at the piano and played Beethoven's *Appassionata*. When he finished, none other than the great composer Giacomo Puccini himself came forward to compliment him.

On hearing of Paci's desire to enter the Conservatory, Puccini at once offered his assistance. "That gave me courage," Paci wrote.

> I forwarded my application and at the appointed date I presented myself to the "Examining Commission," handing to the Chairman a "closed" envelope containing Maestro Puccini's recommendation, of the nature of which I had not the least idea.
>
> The Chairman read the card and, smiling, passed it to all the other examiners, then said to me: "I think that we may follow the advice of Maestro Puccini. Won't you play for us the *Appassionata*?"
>
> You may imagine how thunderstruck was I at such an apostrophe! Open-mouthed and speechless, I was standing there looking around expecting some explanation. The Chairman then addressed me again: "Perhaps you don't know what Maestro Puccini writes of you? Read his card!"
>
> Mo. Puccini had written:
>
> "Il giovane Paci si presenta agli esami ma non è preparato. Non perdete il tempo con delle domande sulle '*quinte proibite*.' Fategli suonare l'Appassionata di Beethoven e son sicuro che non vorrete perdere un bravo allievo futuro."
>
> [English translation: "Young Paci presents himself at the examination but is not prepared. Do not waste time with questions on the 'prohibited Fifths.' Have him play Beethoven's *Appassionata* and I am sure you will not want to lose a fine future pupil."]
>
> I felt relieved, and I think I played the *Appassionata* for those few but very difficult master-critics as I never played (so well, I mean) during all the long years of my Pianistic career.[27]

Thanks to Puccini's intervention, Paci was accepted at the Conservatory and enrolled. During the three years he was there, he worked at La Scala, assisting some of the best maestros of the day, among them the fabled Toscanini. However, after graduating and spending a year conducting orchestras across Italy, Paci again reversed

---

27. *Ibid.*

course and decided to return to the "pure music" of his piano. This decision caused him to embark on 16 years of "pianistic wanderings" which found him performing throughout Europe and Asia. He finally settled, as it were, in cosmopolitan Batavia, using it as a base for continued concertizing across Asia.

Paci conducted his love life much as he did his career, passionately, determinedly, and with an insatiable desire for change and variety. Though not classically handsome, he was charming, talented, headstrong, intelligent, charismatic, confident, passionate, needy, temperamental, and flawed. In other words, he was the sort of man for whom women fell hard. His attractiveness to the opposite sex was a point of pride and, later in life, he even bragged to his own daughter that he had left Milan because he had three mistresses there with whom he simply couldn't keep up! But, after he settled in Batavia, Paci fell violently in love with a married woman ten years his senior, who was the mother of two children. The woman's name was Elizabeth MacKenzie, but Paci always called her Floria, after the heroine in Puccini's opera *Tosca*.

"Floria" was strikingly beautiful, with blonde curly hair and what foreigners in Java referred to as "a touch of the tarbrush," meaning she had some Javanese blood in her. She was a singer — just like her operatic namesake — and she left her husband and children to be with Paci. Together, the lovers travelled around the world, to India, Ceylon, and Europe, she singing and he accompanying her on the piano. *Tosca* ends tragically when Floria's artist lover — Mario — is shot before a firing squad and she leaps to her death from the ramparts of Rome's Castel Sant'Angelo. Sadly, Paci's romance with his Floria ended with near equal tragedy when she was thrown from a horse and killed, their unborn child dying together with her.

When Paci recovered from his loss, he fell in love with another musician, this one a Dutch pianist named Sara Hillen, whom he met in Surabaya. Sara was beautiful, young, flirtatious and bold, the kind of woman who wiped her piano keys down with cologne prior to playing her graduation recital for a panel of male judges. She had travelled to Java from Holland almost on a whim, when an elderly, wheelchair-bound aunt showed her an ad in the paper for a temporary piano teaching job. On the boat over, Sara met and was courted by a wealthy tea plantation owner who proposed before the ship had even reached its destination. Sara accepted, but then developed a crush on Paci soon after she reached Java. Her crush was at first unreciprocated and when in Batavia she used to ride her bike past Paci's house in the hope of catching a glimpse of the much-admired musician. When Paci finally returned her love, she broke off her engagement to the plantation owner and the two carried on a passionate, tempestuous, four-year romance.

Back home in Holland, Sara's parents were singularly upset. "How could you break off your engagement with that nice man?" they wrote her plaintively. "Be careful of that Paci!" [28]

---

28. This quote was related to us in our interview with Floria Paci Zaharoff, together with the details of Paci's pre-marital love life and his ultimate marriage.

When he was away concertizing, Paci wrote to Sara every day — his daughter still has the letters, penned in Italian, Dutch and French — but everybody said he would never marry her. Sara must have finally reached the same conclusion, because one day when Paci had left on a concert tour, she sold her house without telling him and vanished. On his return, Paci tracked her down and pleaded with her through an interlocutor, an elderly male friend who was protecting her. The friend refused to let Paci see Sara until he finally broke down and proposed marriage. The two were married in February of 1917 and by the time Paci sailed to Shanghai, Sara was pregnant with their first, and only, child.

The life of the wandering pianist with the self-described "restless nature and temperament" had thus changed considerably in the two years before he reached Shanghai, and was about to change more with the birth of his child. Paci weighed these personal considerations together with his professional and artistic concerns as he debated whether or not to take the position offered him. Much later, in the last interview he ever gave, he explained his thinking at this time:

> The Shanghai of 1919 was a most attractive place. It was full of money, life and hope. People thought it would become one of the greatest cities of the world....
>
> Then I received the news of the birth of my first child and I thought that this gypsy life of making music tours ought to stop now that I had become a father. So I decided to stay. I began to build the Shanghai Municipal Orchestra.[29]

Paci had effectively been shanghaied, not in the dictionary definition of the word — which refers to the practice, once common in Shanghai, of dragging a drunken or otherwise insensible man aboard a ship and forcing him into service — but in the opposite sense. He had been carried *off* the boat unconscious and made to stay *in* Shanghai. He had quickly fallen in love with the city — as many foreigners do to this day, a feeling that is sometimes described as being shanghaied — and was pressed into service, not by force, but by the presentation of an offer he couldn't refuse. Shanghai would give him the glamour and adventure he had always craved, as well as the steady employment he needed now that he had a family. More importantly, it would provide a community in which he could prosper artistically both as pianist and conductor, and where it seemed his prodigious talents and energy would be appreciated and make an impact.

His mind made up, Paci wrote to Sara. "Enough of this gypsy life," he said simply. "We are moving to Shanghai." [30]

THE BIRTH OF THE SHANGHAI MUNICIPAL ORCHESTRA

Eager to begin his life as a conductor, Paci bid a temporary farewell to Avray Strok and all his Shanghai friends and then sailed for Java where his wife and baby

---

29. See Ho Chia-shui (1946). Paci gives highlights of life in last interview. *The China Press*, October 20.
30. Quote is as related by Floria Paci Zaharoff.

daughter — whom he named Floria — awaited him. The homecoming must have been a warm one, since he and Sara had been separated for more than four months and each had been through much in the interim. But, as soon as the reunion was over, Paci set out on a final concert tour in the land he had called home for twenty years. He and Sara then made the rounds at numerous farewell parties, wrapped up their affairs, packed up their two Steinway baby grands and Nana (the family collie), and set sail with their infant daughter.

Given that he was traveling in his capacity as husband and new father, this journey to Shanghai presumably involved far less drinking and card-playing for Paci, who stayed healthy and walked off the boat of his own volition. However, little Fofi — the nickname by which his daughter was to be known into adulthood — became sick soon after their arrival and required emergency medical care. This was provided as a *pro bono* courtesy to the eagerly-awaited new maestro by Dr. Anna Strong, an American woman with a practice in Shanghai. The Paci family settled temporarily in the elegant Palace Hotel, which stands to this day at the bustling intersection of Nanjing Road and the Bund, and on Dr. Strong's advice Fofi was taken for regular walks along the river. As soon as Paci was certain that her health was out of danger, he set to work.

The reality of his new life as the leader of an orchestra in a small foreign enclave in an enormous Chinese city must have hit Paci as he walked to his office that first September Monday morning. To get to the general area, he needed only travel a few blocks, by foot or by rickshaw, from the Palace Hotel to 567 Fuzhou Road. But, to actually reach the rehearsal space, he had to pick his way through a vast wet market that rang with the earsplitting clatter of hawkers and reeked with the smells of such delicacies as "stinky tofu," moldy lumps of bean curd fried in vats of bubbling oil. The market started just after sunrise, so by the time Paci was cutting through it in his polished shoes and elegantly tailored suits, the ground was thick with a glistening scum of smashed fruit, rotten vegetables, cigarette butts, and spittle that left it sticky in some places and treacherously slick in others. Paci considered this space, allotted by the Municipal Council, to be utterly unsuitable for a maestro and a symphony orchestra, as did his musicians; to this day, men who played with the orchestra in those years wrinkle their noses in disgust when they recount the indignity of the location in which they were required to rehearse and the smell of fish that wafted through the windows as they played.

Fortunately, however, Paci possessed both the ability to make do and a flare for decorating and he quickly set about creating an oasis of tranquility in his office above the rehearsal hall. Pride of place went to one of his Steinways, which stood alone in the center of the room. Comfortably arranged in the remaining space were a table and chairs, a chaise lounge, book cases and a big rolltop desk. On the desk stood a shaded green banker's lamp by light of which Paci studied scores, planned programs, and did all the various paperwork required of him in his new role. The walls were eventually hung with photos of important moments in his career, together with framed certificates, diplomas and appreciations he had received over the years.[31]

Having settled into his office, Paci proceeded to inspect the Town Hall, where the orchestra played most of its regularly scheduled concerts. The center of municipal life in the International Settlement, the Town Hall stood nearby on Nanjing Road between Guangxi and Yunnan Roads, on a plot of land that now holds the Nanjing Road Food Products Store. Though it was large and conveniently located in the heart of the Settlement, Paci was little more pleased with it than he was with the rehearsal space. Built of brick and wood, the Town Hall had been designed for meetings, not concerts. Its floor was flat, which made it difficult for the audience to see the orchestra, even on a riser. There was a big window right behind the spot where the orchestra played and in winter the room was heated by large wood-burning stoves that made it something of a fire-trap, especially given that it had only one entranceway and "gentlemen" smoked during concerts. However, its acoustics were not bad, and Paci had no real choice but to accommodate himself to it. He implemented the one change he could — ordering the window blacked out to ensure that the audience wouldn't be distracted by anything seen outside — and then focused on the many obligations confronting him in his new role as maestro.[32]

It is the job of every conductor to juggle competing interests and demands, but Paci's position was particularly delicate. He was a newcomer to Shanghai and he had been hired on a probationary contract. He had nine immediate bosses on the Municipal Council, that peculiar institution which made decisions on behalf of all the residents of the International Settlement, and they would ultimately decide his future as a conductor in Shanghai. Pleasing nine bosses would be difficult enough, but he also had to bear in mind the sensitivities of the Ratepayers who elected the Council and determined its budget each April. The Ratepayers were a demanding group and they voted line-by-line on such budgetary expenditures as the orchestra. Only if Paci kept both the Council and a majority of Ratepayers satisfied would he be able to keep his job and receive sufficient funding to create a first class orchestra.

Then, of course, there was the orchestra's audience. Shanghai had 23,307 foreign residents by 1920.[33] Because Chinese were not allowed into the parks where the orchestra played in summertime or into the Town Hall, these 23,307 "Shanghailanders," as they called themselves, comprised the entire potential audience for the orchestra. This was a small base from which to support a full-time professional orchestra, especially since many of these people likely went to concerts only on occasion, if at all. Audience development was thus a crucial part of Paci's job — he needed to get people into the Town Hall for concerts and keep them coming back.

Perhaps most important of all, aside from pleasing the various constituencies who would determine his own and the orchestra's future, Paci had to remain faithful to his own artistic ideals. This meant building an orchestra that was not just popular,

---

31. Description is based on conversations with Floria Paci Zaharoff, and photographs of Paci's office which she showed to the authors.

32. The rehearsal hall was described to Sheila Melvin by Tan Shuzhen, who played with the orchestra beginning in 1927. Mr. Tan also shared photos of the space and described the changes Paci made to it.

33. For figure, see Pott: 245.

but good; introducing modern music by living composers; sharing his talents and training by teaching young musicians; and spreading as widely as possible his own love and appreciation of classical music. This was a heavy brief for a man who had spent most of his adulthood as a nomadic pianist, but Paci was ready for it and he set right to work.

The first task at hand was to fill out the depleted ranks of the Municipal Band *cum* orchestra. Having listened to many of the musicians in Shanghai during his recuperation the previous spring, Paci would have had a good sense of the available talent. He recruited from among the ranks of the pick-up orchestra he had earlier formed to accompany him on piano, and held auditions for other interested players. In the end, he hired 15 new musicians, enlarging the orchestra from 22 to 37. Of course, the members of the orchestra were as foreign as the audience, rather unfortunately described by Municipal Council reports for the year 1919 as "sixteen musicians and twenty-one Manilamen." [34]

Once he had finished auditions, Paci no doubt retreated to his office sanctuary to plan the 23 weeks of concerts that would comprise his first season. The programs for this, his first year, were heavy on works by the great masters and seem designed to attract as wide an audience as possible, albeit with an occasional bow to a lesser-known contemporary composer. For the very first concert, scheduled for November 23, he decided to open with Beethoven's rousing, eternally popular *Fifth Symphony*. This was followed by a serenade for strings called *In the Far West* by the contemporary British composer Granville Bantock, whose work was influenced by a romanticized view of the Far East. The concert was to conclude with Grieg's *Peer Gynt Suite I*.

For the following week he scheduled a crowd-pleasing "Operatic Programme" featuring overtures and airs from operas by Gluck, Rossini, Donizetti, Massenet, Wagner and Strauss. Next came an evening devoted to dance and ballet music, and for his fourth concert Paci once again conducted and played the piano in a performance of Mozart's *Coronation Concerto*. The remainder of the season was heavy with works by Beethoven, Saint-Saëns, Tchaikovsky, Rimsky-Korsakoff and Liszt, though he also slipped in a piece by his teacher, Sgambati. Special programs were devoted to works of "French Composers," "Russian Composers," and pieces performed by Shanghai-based soloists. For the season finale in May, he even scheduled an entire program of music by composers living in Shanghai, including "Three Songs for Soprano" and "Two Songs for Tenor" which he himself had written.

Once he had settled on the programs for the season's first few concerts, Paci set to work drilling his musicians. No one alive today was present at this first rehearsal, but we know enough of Paci's style to imagine that it was a somewhat tense event. [35] On entering the rehearsal hall, Paci always stepped right up to the podium, from which his diminutive stature was less noticeable. He would then look out at the musicians with the same attitude as "a general surveying his troops" [36] and wait

34. Harris, E.F. (1942). The story of the Municipal Orchestra. *Souvenir Programme of Farewell Concert*, Shanghai Municipal Orchestra. May 31: 5.

silently until they had ceased shifting in their chairs and rustling through their parts. Then, dispensing with any pleasantries, he would raise his baton to lead a complete run-through of the piece at hand, in this case Beethoven's *Fifth*. When he had finished running the entire symphony, he would proceed to review the areas that needed more work.

The second part of the rehearsal naturally required Paci to talk, and he would start out in English that oftentimes morphed into Italian, French, or German, with an occasional dash of Russian thrown in for good measure. When he spoke, the musicians paid absolute attention. If his words nonetheless failed to elicit the musical response he was looking for, Paci would begin to lose patience. Sometimes he would shout and sometimes he would simply throw his baton in the direction of the unfortunate soul who missed a note, came in too late or too early, or committed any other of a number of errors that Paci considered egregious. After a time, this habit became so well established that it was deemed wise to keep a full bucket of batons — made of comparatively safe rattan — by the podium to ensure that replacements were at hand for those that doubled as projectiles. If both words and missiles failed to elicit the response he was looking for, Paci unilaterally extended the allotted rehearsal time until he got from the orchestra what he wanted to hear; he was soon as notorious for exceeding the scheduled time as he was for venting his temper.

Given all this, we can guess that when the new maestro finally lowered his arm, closed his score and stepped down from the podium at that first rehearsal, the musicians must have set down their instruments and drooped their shoulders with deep sighs — they, too, had their work cut out for them.

Paci's behavior may sound disrespectful, even cruel, and in today's world would never be tolerated by musicians or management. But, back then there were no unions — the conductor was king and the musicians his pawns — and Paci was by nature a temperamental perfectionist. He had spent three years working under Toscanini, the

---

35. This description of Paci's rehearsal style is based on several detailed conversations with Tan Shuzhen, who attended rehearsals beginning in 1925 and played with the orchestra on and off for many years beginning in 1927. For more on Paci's rehearsals and conducting style, see Austin, A. (1939). Under the baton of Maestro Paci, director of Shanghai's symphony orchestra reviews his career as a music 'dictator. *The China Press Sunday Magazine*, May 7: 5. Mr. Austin describes Paci throwing his baton and storming out of a rehearsal in a rage and writes that "in his professional life Maestro Paci is a musical dictator who brooks no interference in his art. A number of musicians have been liquidated from the ranks for clashing with him, and now the airing of dangerous thoughts is not popular among the orchestra's members." Also see Ullstein, A. (1942). Meet the Maestro, Folks; he fights for city's orchestra" *Shanghai Evening Post & Mercury*, April 4. Ullstein writes, "Far more serious, as far as musicians are concerned, is his opposition to time limits. Paci the conductor makes the musicians repeat portions over and over until they are slumped in exhaustion while his own head is perspiring but unbowed. In the realm of music he is a dictator. Many a time he has swept out of the rehearsal room in fury and many a musician has been purged for airing dangerous thoughts. He brooks no interference with his art. His impatience to opposition even spreads to inanimate objects: at one time he even broke the woodwork of his dais and when it resisted his force, stamped his foot and sank through the stand clean up to his knees."

36. This description comes from Tan Shuzhen.

great conductor whose temper is almost as legendary as his talent, and violent tantrums no doubt seemed to him a normal part of the role of maestro. Moreover, however harsh Paci's approach may have been, it worked — the orchestra improved with each rehearsal. Paci's talent and charisma were such that the vast majority of musicians who would play under him simply accepted the temper as part of the talent. They ducked the batons when they were thrown their way, and practiced harder for the next rehearsal.

With his first concert behind him — and hailed as a great success — Paci soon settled into a routine. Monday was his day for finding and studying the scores to be performed at the following Sunday's concert; any musician wishing to speak to him knew that he could be found rummaging for scores in his office on Monday morning. Tuesday through Saturday mornings were set aside for drilling the orchestra, and Sunday evenings for performances. Then, in his spare time, Paci worked on building the orchestral audience by getting to know as many people as he could in Shanghai.

"My parents went out every night," remembered his daughter Fofi, who now lives in New York near Lincoln Center. "Shanghai was very social. My father had to go out so all the people would come to his concerts."

Always impeccably dressed in the latest style suits, Paci became a dashing figure about town, careering through Shanghai's congested streets in a convertible Austin which he acquired not long after his arrival. He became known for his mercurial temperament, multi-lingual fluency, quick wit, animated gestures, and love of fine food. By February of 1920, he was already enough of a celebrity to be caricatured in the papers with his wire spectacles and slicked-back, receding hair as "the man who with his magic wand can bring the spirits of Beethoven, Schumann and Wagner to the Town Hall every Sunday evening."[37]

Paci's efforts in the rehearsal hall and on the social scene soon bore fruit — the orchestra grew to 45 people, his contract was extended for another year, and by 1921 the Sunday evening concerts at Town Hall were so popular that people were being turned away at the door; one concert had 1500 listeners.[38] Beginning in 1920, he oversaw the development of a string quartet and a jazz band. The Municipal Council decided to commit itself once and for all to the Maestro who had so serendipitously landed on its shores by giving him a long-term contract and granting him leave — and funds — to return to Europe.

A journalist from *The China Press* who interviewed Paci right after this announcement was made in April found him virtually gleeful:

> "I am happy today," he said. "I have just received confirmation of my appointment as conductor. It gives me a free hand in the development of the orchestra. Now I can go to Europe and conduct the business of building up our organisation, of procuring new instruments, of replenishing our depleted music

---

37. Paci, M. (1920). *The Pearl of the Orient*, February 12: 17.
38. Bickers: 853.

library, with a feeling of freedom and confidence. I shall make the Shanghai orchestra second to none."[39]

The same article recorded that a grand send-off was given Paci at the last concert of the 1920-21 season:

> Last Sunday over 1700 music lovers attended the concert, and many more hundreds were turned away. The stage was banked with floral offerings of the admiring public. A gift of a shield was made to the Conductor, Maestro Mario Paci, in appreciation of his efforts at building up a real symphony orchestra.[40]

Paci set sail on the steamer *Trieste*, traveling first to Holland — where Sara and Fofi had gone earlier to stay with Sara's family — and then to France and Italy. For three delightful months he immersed himself in new music, purchased instruments and visited major conservatories in search of musicians who were talented — and adventurous — enough to lead nine of his orchestra's sections. In the end, he found just six who met his qualifications, four from Italy and two from Holland, all of them young graduates of good conservatories with some orchestral experience. Key among them was the concertmaster, a twenty-three year old graduate of the Milan Conservatory named Arrigo Foa who had been awarded the school's gold medal for his violin playing.

Upon returning to Shanghai in the autumn, Paci awaited the arrival of his new sectional leaders and then set to work reshuffling and rehearsing the newly invigorated orchestra. At the first concert of the 1921-22 season, music lovers turned out in full force to hear the results of Paci's efforts. *The Shanghai Times* recorded the warm welcome given Paci even before he lifted his baton:

> If Sir Henry Wood, England's famous musician and conductor, had stepped on to the platform at the Town Hall yesterday afternoon, he could not have received a more spontaneous reception than did Maestro Paci, conductor of Shanghai's Municipal Orchestra. The audience rose to their feet and gave the popular conductor-musician a rousing welcome on his return from home leave. This speaks volumes for the esteem in which the organiser of our excellent concerts and dispenser of real music is held by Shanghai music-lovers. We need scarcely add that it was well deserved, for Maestro Paci is indeed first and foremost in the sphere of music in the community.[41]

Paci intended the concert to mark a new era for the orchestra and he underlined this point by opening it with Dvorak's *New World Symphony*. This was followed, after the interval, by Max Bruch's *First Concerto*, in which Foa took center stage as soloist and "at once ingratiated himself into the hearts of his audience," bringing to mind comparisons with "a young Mischa Elman."[42] The evening was rounded out with

---

39. Municipal orchestra leader leaves today. *The China Press*, May, 1921.
40. *Ibid.*
41. Maestro Paci back again — town hall audience rises to greet his return. *Shanghai Sunday Times*, November 7, 1921.

Liszt's *Souvenirs of Naples*, a fitting close to the first concert led by Paci — who had debuted in Naples, studied under Liszt's last student, and just returned from Italy — in his capacity as official maestro of the Shanghai orchestra. Significantly, the concert also established a programming pattern which would become Paci's signature: a major symphonic work in the first half followed by more relaxing and entertaining pieces after the interval.

With the first concert of the season over, Paci accelerated his push to make "the Shanghai orchestra second to none." Beginning in January of 1922, the orchestra performed each week's program twice, first during the regular Sunday afternoon slot at 5:15 and a second time on Tuesday evening at 9:15. One concert in the summer of that year drew 3500 people to hear the orchestra in Hongkou Park.[43] Paci expanded the number of regular subscription concerts to 32 in the 1921-22 season and to 41 in the 1922-23 season. And he ensured that the new sectional leaders from Europe would be heard in solo performances at least twice a month by starting a series of Thursday night "Chamber Music and Soloist Concerts."

Ever mindful of the need for building his audience, Paci announced that he would invite Shanghai's best resident vocalists and instrumentalists to appear with the orchestra from time to time. He started a series of youth concerts and also a spectacular Christmas gala, the hall decorated with a Christmas tree glowing with candles and the entire audience invited to join in and sing *Silent Night*. To compete with the lower-brow social activities of which Shanghailanders were so enamored, he instituted a series of weekly tea dances where, in his words, "people of Shanghai may drop in after business, for a good cup of tea, and good hour of the best music."[44]

Paci also steadily expanded the orchestra's repertoire, keeping in mind the desires of his diverse and sensitive audience as he made his programs. As he later explained to a journalist, "If I play Debussy, the French will be pleased but the Russians will implore me by the shades of Rachmaninoff to play the *Pathetique*, while if I play Rachmaninoff, the Germans will ask for Wagner and the Italians will demand Respighi, and so on!" [45] In a consummate public relations move, he held a plebiscite at the end of the season through which he allowed the audience to choose the program for the final concert of the season. So many people participated in it that he ultimately devoted not just the last, but also the penultimate concert to the audience's selections.[46]

---

42. Both quotes on Foa, from: Maestro Paci back again — Town Hall audience rises to greet his return. *Shanghai Sunday Times*. November 7, 1921.

43. Bickers: 853.

44. Municipal orchestra leader leaves today. *The China Press*, May, 1921.

45. As quoted in Austin, A. (1939). Under the baton of Maestro Paci.... *The China Press Sunday Magazine*, May 7: 5-6. To keep these various constituent groups happy, Paci built more concerts around national themes such as "Russian Composers," with works by Tchaikovsky, Scriabin, Stravinsky and Borodin; "French Composers," with pieces by Massenet, Berlioz, d'Indy, Chabrier, and Monsigny; "Italian Operatic Composers," with excerpts from *Barber of Seville*, *Cavalleria Rusticana*, *Aida*, and *Tosca*; and an entire night devoted to works by Wagner.

And finally, now that Paci was more secure in his position, he began to concentrate not just on pleasing his bosses and his audience but on the achievement of his own artistic ideals. Building a better orchestra, of course, was a personal ideal that also gratified the nine Municipal Council members and a majority of Ratepayers, and in this he was making tremendous progress. Indeed, in April of 1923 a Japanese musicologist who had heard of Shanghai's up and coming orchestra visited the city to attend several concerts. He was so impressed by what he heard that he declared the Shanghai Municipal Orchestra to be better than any orchestra in Japan or anywhere else in Asia — "the best orchestra in the Far East."[47] This accolade was gratefully acknowledged and echoes in Shanghai to this day, where it is frequently reprinted in the Shanghai Symphony's publicity materials. As if to underline the musicologist's verdict, Paci officially changed the orchestra's name from "Shanghai Municipal Council Public Band" to "Shanghai Municipal Orchestra" that same year.

It was also right around this time that Shanghai's image as an exotic destination — together with the rise of global ocean-going tourism and the dredging of the Huangpu River right up to the Bund — began to draw visitors not just from neighboring Japan, but from all over the world. Starting in the early 1920s and continuing for the next decade and a half, the rich and famous voyaged to Shanghai for business, pleasure, or both, among them the Rockefellers, Albert Einstein, Noel Coward, Mary Pickford, Bertrand Russell, Bernard Shaw, Christopher Isherwood, W.H. Auden, André Malraux, Somerset Maugham, Eugene O'Neill, John Dewey, Charlie Chaplin and Paulette Godard. These luminaries were joined by a galaxy of the world's top musicians, affording Paci the opportunity to work or spend time with talents he would have been very unlikely to encounter anywhere else and further burnishing the reputation of both maestro and orchestra.

Fritz Kreisler, one of the world's most famous violinists, visited the city and played with the orchestra in 1923. The pianist Efrem Zimbalist followed suit in 1924 and the American violinist Jascha Heifetz in 1925. Fofi still keeps a photo of her father and Heifetz together on which Heifetz penned, "In remembrance of a jolly good time spent together." Other famous soloists who would perform in Shanghai, often in collaboration with Paci and the orchestra, included the great Russian bass Fyodor Chaliapin, the Polish-American pianist Artur Rubinstein, and the Irish tenor John McCormack, who travelled to Shanghai at the recommendation of Kreisler, his long-time friend and collaborator.

With his own standing and that of his orchestra increasingly well-established, Paci decided to further broaden the repertoire beyond traditional crowd pleasers and classics by increasing the number of contemporary pieces. A program called "Russian

---

46. The runner-up program consisted of Rossini's *William Tell* overture; Saint-Saëns' *Danse Macabre*; and Rimsky-Korsakoff's *Scheherazade*, while the winning program included two works by Tchaikovsky, *Symphony No. 5 in E minor* and *Capriccio Italiano*; Brahms' *Hungarian Dances*; and Wagner's *Tannhauser* overture.

47. See Han: 157. The Japanese musicologist also noted that no orchestra in Japan was as complete as the SMO, which even had a harp player. He was particularly impressed by the woodwinds section, especially the flute, oboe, and clarinet players who had recently arrived from Italy.

and French Modern Composers" showcased works by Mussorgsky, Scriabin, Liadov, Glazounov, d'Indy, Dukas, Fauré and Chabrier. Another entitled "Modernisme-Impressionisme" consisted of music by Stravinsky, Debussy, and Ravel. Aside from devoting entire concerts to contemporary composers, he also mixed their works into regular programs. Thus were Shanghai audiences exposed to the works of such little known living composers as the Norwegian Johan Halvorsen, the Swede Hugo Alfven, and Gian Francesco Malipiero, who was considered by many to be the most original Italian composer of his generation.

As the Shanghai Municipal Orchestra thrived, so did Mario Paci. He moved his family to a big house in the French Concession, in the neighborhood near the two-steepled red brick cathedral in which Shanghai's Catholics still worship. His talent for decorating came in as handy at home as it did at the office and Fofi remembers that their house bespoke her father's Florentine taste. It was kept up by several servants and the garden was filled with Sara's beloved dogs, Nana the collie and a succession of dachshunds. The family cook was trained to make Florentine food and Paci also developed a great love of Chinese cuisine.

"Food was very important to him," Fofi remembered. "When the food wasn't good he was in a bad mood and when the food was good, he was rhapsodizing. Of course, we didn't go into the kitchen. I didn't cook anything till I was about 30. My mother never cooked — she was a pianist! She couldn't even cut bread!"

When Paci returned home from rehearsals each evening, Sara would play for him on the Steinway baby grand while he drank his Marsala. On those nights when they stayed at home, he himself would play for his daughter at bedtime — Fofi remembers drifting off to sleep to the sound of her father's Debussy and Ravel. Paci loved to swim, and the family went to the seaside every summer, one year to Qingdao and the next year to Weihaiwei. Every few years there would also be a trip back to Europe, usually by boat but once on the Trans-Siberian railway.

Of course, Paci had spent much of his life as a roaming bachelor and not all of his leisure time activities were so domestic. On the contrary, he was well known for extra-curricular activities involving Chinese women. He was also an avid card player and spent many long nights out smoking, drinking, and betting with friends. Eventually, he moved beyond cards to the sport gambling that became increasingly popular in Shanghai. He was a great fan of jai alai — a Basque game derived from handball, played in Shanghai by men with names like Urguidi, Rafael, Jaunito, Olalde, and Urbieta — and spent many hours at the jai alai auditorium on Avenue Joffre. When a massive Canidrome opened — with seating for 50,000, and enough adjacent land for kennels, training grounds, ballrooms and restaurants — Paci became a regular, loudly urging on such poetically-named greyhounds as Zanzibar, Conundrum, Coeur de Lion, and Mandolin as they chased a mechanical hare around the track. Paci's fondness for dog racing became so well known that his musicians joked that he knew the exact number of minutes required to get from the Canidrome to the concert hall, and wasted not one.

But if Paci wasted little time in either his personal or professional life, there was one area in which he continued to procrastinate, and that was in the broader propagation of the classical music he so loved. However much effort he might put into audience development, he was essentially preaching to the choir in drawing concert goers from an elite and privileged group of foreigners who had grown up with the music of European classical composers. To truly make an impact on the city and country he now called home, Paci had to spread his musical gospel more widely among members of Shanghai's Chinese community. But — as Paci well knew — this could happen only when the racist, segregationist policies that prevented Chinese from even attending orchestra concerts were finally done away with.

REACHING OUT TO THE CHINESE

Paci wasn't the only musician to chafe at the absurdity of the implicit "no Chinese at concerts" policy. Indeed, when Artur Rubinstein came to Shanghai, he complained about the absence of Chinese at his performances, writing, "My three recitals took place in a theater and the public was made up entirely of Europeans and Americans. I really had no pleasure in playing for them."[48] To many long-time Shanghailanders, this was the natural order of things, but by the 1920s such blatant and institutionalized discrimination was in fact becoming increasingly untenable.

One reason for this was simple demographics. Although the International Settlement and the French Concession had originally been intended for foreigners only — in large part because the Chinese government had feared that these areas would become tax havens for its citizens — the reality was that Chinese had begun flocking to them from the 1850s onward. Chinese saw the Settlement and Concession as oases of stability in a nation racked by internal uprisings and foreigners welcomed them — not out of altruism, but because they could make money by renting them land. As a result, Chinese had long outnumbered foreigners in both areas, not to mention in the so-called Chinese City, which was still ruled by China.

In 1911, the Qing Dynasty collapsed and the Nationalist Party founded the Republic of China on its wreckage. Corrupt to its very core, the new government was never able to consolidate its hold on power; instead, the nation's instability worsened, causing more Chinese from outlying provinces to seek refuge in Shanghai. By 1930, Shanghai's population reached nearly three million — making it the fifth largest city in the world — with the International Settlement home to 971,397 Chinese and 36,471 foreigners; the French Concession held 434,885 Chinese and 12,335 foreigners; and the Chinese City 1,516,092 Chinese and 9,470 foreigners.[49]

Many among this growing Chinese population were poor and desperate refugees. Indeed, throughout the 1920s, Shanghai police annually collected 20,000 corpses a year from city streets. By 1930, the number of dead collected had surpassed 36,000 and

48. See Rubinstein: 372. Rubinstein notes that there were no Chinese present at his performances in Beijing, either.
49. Wakeman, F. Jr. (1995). *Policing Shanghai 1927-1937*. Berkeley, Los Angeles, London: University of California Press: 9.

the concept of death in the street was so chillingly normal that it barely merited mention in the city's papers. *The North China Daily News* of March 27, 1931, noted the figure for 1930 in a tiny article on page 12, entitled "Unclaimed Bodies":

> Each day collectors are sent out in search of bodies which are placed in coffins and buried before they become a menace to the public health. The necessity for this work is evidenced by the fact that 36,130 bodies were collected and buried during the year 1930; of the total 34, 818 were infants. 246 sets of bones were also collected and buried in jars.

But if many in this burgeoning population were poor and disenfranchised, others were prosperous business people, famous artists, and influential intellectuals. For these people, Shanghai provided a refuge and an asylum not only for the body, but for the mind. Indeed, though the International Settlement and the French Concession had both been created on the basis of an unequal treaty signed after a morally inexcusable war, they had grown into comparatively well-governed municipalities which were islands of security and peace in China's turmoil. Free speech for the most part prevailed and dozens of Chinese language newspapers were in circulation. Even such revolutionaries as Sun Yat-sen, Mao Zedong and Zhou Enlai found refuge in the French Concession at one point or another, and it was there that the Chinese Communist Party was founded in July of 1921 in a house on Rue Wantz, now Xingye Road.[50]

Such educated people were increasingly unwilling to be treated as second class citizens by the industrial nations, especially in their own country. Paci's arrival in China happened to coincide with the moment when these nationalist sentiments came to a head and then exploded in what is known to history as the May 4th Movement of 1919. The movement started out as a simple demonstration by students in Beijing who marched to Tiananmen Square to protest their government's agreeing to sign the Treaty of Versailles. The treaty transferred to Japan the colonial holdings in northeast China that defeated Germany was forced to give up, even though China had fought on the winning side in World War I. But, in a larger sense, the May 4th Movement refers to an era of social awakening and growing nationalism which would resonate for many, many years.

Although the May 4th protesters were bitter at the West's hypocrisy, they were at the same time admiring of its democratic institutions and intellectual and scientific core. Eager to learn from it, Chinese students poured overseas, enrolling in university and graduate programs throughout Europe, the United States and Japan, or simply going off to travel and learn on their own. Missionary schools, of which there were untold numbers in China, also became a valued source of Western learning. On their return from overseas or graduation from missionary college, many students flocked to

---

50. When French Concession police raided the meeting site, the Communists finished their discussions on a boat.

Shanghai, full of new ideas, eager to continue developing, and hoping to make an impact on their country's future.

Paci knew from the piano lessons he gave that it was from among these young Chinese with some exposure to the West that further recruits to classical music could be found. With his firm conviction that great music transcends race and politics, it must have seemed to him mere common sense that such people should be able to attend orchestra concerts if they so desired. So, once he received his permanent appointment as conductor and felt more "free and confident,"[51] he finally started lobbying the Municipal Council to change this policy.

Paci was no freedom fighter, but such a move would nonetheless have required some courage on his part since, beginning in 1923 when Shanghai fell into a mini-recession, many Ratepayers had begun objecting to the cost of the orchestra. This was an old International Settlement battle — a segment of Ratepayers had been opposed to Municipal Council financial support for the Band ever since its founding in 1879 — that grew more vocal along with the size, profile, and budget of the orchestra. However, despite this opposition, which grew loudest every April when the Ratepayers met, Paci finally gave the Municipal Council an ultimatum in 1925 — either Chinese were to be allowed to attend concerts of the Shanghai Municipal Orchestra or he would resign as its conductor.

As Paci told a Chinese reporter for *Wen Wei Pao* many years later,

> ...I wholly believed in the future of music in China; the Chinese have talents in music, they are a musical people. I am also proud of having been able to teach some very talented pupils. I always hope for a great future.
>
> Before 1925, the Chinese were not allowed to enter the Town Hall and so they could not enjoy the concerts. In that year I fought with the Municipal Council, and I won when I would offer resignation if I could not have my wish.[52]

Paci's insistence that Chinese be allowed to attend his concerts soon saw results. As he told the *Wen Wei Pao* reporter, "The Chinese audience grew, till they became 24% of the total audience. I was very happy about it."

One member of the orchestra's expanding Chinese audience — who would go on to play a key role in the development of classical music in China — was an 18-year-old architecture student named Tan Shuzhen. Mr. Tan was the second-generation product of missionary education, the son of a man who came from a desperately poor family of carpenters. His father's older brothers had escaped their poverty by moving to Qingdao after its colonization by Germany, when massive construction projects were undertaken and work for carpenters was plentiful. As the youngest child, Mr. Tan's father was spared from a childhood of labor and instead sent to a German missionary school. He eventually became a doctor and a pharmacist, and even learned to play the violin.

---

51. Municipal orchestra leader leaves today. *The China Press*, May, 1921.
52. See Ho Chia-shui (1946). Paci gives highlights of life in last interview. *The China Press*, October 20.

"Missionaries did a lot of good for people here," Mr. Tan recalled. "They educated, they cured sickness. My father was so poor, and yet he went to German school and learned German, drafting, and violin!"

Thanks to his father's playing, Mr. Tan developed an early interest in the violin, although he was not able to pursue this right away.

"Father's violin broke in a flood, and he threw it away," he remembered. "But I always had a mind to make a violin."

Since his father's violin was gone and he did not yet know how to make one, Mr. Tan studied other instruments, including the piano and such Chinese instruments as the *yueqin, yangqin, dizi*, and *huer*. When he finished his own missionary education at a middle school in Henan, he went to Beijing to study at the American-run Peking Academy. There, he voiced aloud to a close friend named Tian Cong his dream of studying violin. Violins were not easy for a student to come by in the Beijing of 1922, but Tian Cong immediately volunteered to find one, and followed through on his promise. Mr. Tan found a teacher — his first instructor taught him for free — and began his lessons.

It was the desire to find a better violin teacher that propelled Mr. Tan to leave Beijing for Shanghai when he graduated from the Peking Academy. He chose Shanghai because, as he and all his classmates knew, it had an excellent orchestra and a growing community of musicians from around the world. Upon arrival in Shanghai, Mr. Tan found a Russian violin teacher and began regularly attending the concerts of the Shanghai Municipal Orchestra. Much like Paci during his recuperation from pneumonia, Mr. Tan was not only listening to the music, but being inspired by it to dream of a future in Shanghai's classical music world.

As yet, there was no clear path for Mr. Tan and others like him to realize their dreams — the Shanghai Municipal Orchestra remained an all-foreign ensemble. But, the mere fact that he could sit through concerts and contemplate a future in Western classical music were signs that Paci was on his way both to fulfilling his own artistic ambitions and to giving the city an even better version of the "real symphony orchestra" of which its foreign elders had long dreamed.

Shanghai was still no musical "Paris of the East," but it was the most musical city in China and was fast becoming a magnet for young Chinese who were as mesmerized by the "power of a great orchestra" as the young Paci had been. Just as an awareness of the transformative powers of orchestral music had changed Paci's life, so would it change the lives of many young Chinese — and the course of China's own millennia-old musical culture.

Chapter 2. Musical Voyages

A Musical Gift for the Emperor

Mario Paci was the first Westerner to bring the music of the great European composers to China and to devote his life to ensuring that it would take root. But, he was not the first Westerner to bring the European music tradition to China.

Indeed, a full three hundred and nineteen years before Maestro Paci steamed into Shanghai with his Steinway, a fellow Italian named Matteo Ricci was sailing up the Grand Canal from Nanjing to Beijing with a clavichord, an early keyboard instrument. [1] But, where Maestro Paci was a musical missionary, Matteo Ricci was

---

1. The musical instrument presented to the emperor by Ricci and the other Jesuits is variously referred to as a clavichord, a harpsichord, and a spinet by Western scholars writing in English. This is due to a vagueness of terms used in the published versions of Ricci's journals, where it is called both a "clavicembalo" and a "manicordio," with the former meaning harpsichord and the latter clavichord. Both are stringed keyboard instruments, the primary difference being that the strings of a clavichord are struck — like a piano — whereas the strings of the harpsichord are plucked. "Spinet" is itself a problematic term used to describe an instrument that is a smaller version of the harpsichord. Ricci certainly knew what instrument he was presenting to the emperor and this vagueness in terminology may be due to translation errors made in the process of compiling and publishing his journals, which took place after his death. Chinese sources are even more vague, with the earliest extant references calling it a "Western qin" or a "big Western qin." Chinese scholars writing today often simply call it an "ancient piano." The authors believe that the instrument was, in fact, a clavichord, for reasons discussed in the text and because this is the term Ricci used when he wrote out a list of the gifts he intended to present to the emperor and in titling a collection of songs which he wrote for the instrument.

For discussion of this issue by Chinese musicologists, see Feng Wenci (1998). *Zhong-Wai Yinyue Jiaoliushi* [A Chinese Foreign-Exchange History of Music]. Hunan: Hunan Jiaoyu Chubanshe: 232-4; and Tao Yabing (1994). *Zhong-Xi Yinyue Jiaoliu Shigao* [The History of Musical Exchange Between China and the Western World]. Beijing: Zhongguo Dabaikequanshu Chubanshe: 40-2 and 60-1.

a real missionary — a bearded Jesuit priest who spoke and wrote fluent Chinese and dressed in the flowing silk robes of the Confucian literati.

Father Ricci was in China as the pioneer of a new approach to that seemingly impenetrable nation which even the great Francis Xavier had found "closed and protected by vigilant guards." [2] St. Francis had died in 1552 on an island off China's coast and the Macao-based Jesuit missionaries who followed him had failed to get much closer, in part because of their insensitivity to Chinese culture. So, beginning in the late 1570s, the Jesuit Visitor General of Missions Alessandro Valignano had insisted on a new approach to missionary work — instead of "portugalizing" the Chinese by making converts assimilate to Portuguese customs and language, the Jesuits should "sinicize" themselves.[3] It was by thoroughly sinicizing himself that Ricci had gained permission to live in several different areas of southern China, but his sights were always set on Beijing, where no European priest had ever been granted permission to stay.

Ricci's goals for his journey to Beijing were lofty: to meet the Emperor, to gain permission to establish a permanent Jesuit mission in the Imperial Capital and perhaps — in a dream still with him on his deathbed — to convert the Son of Heaven to the Catholic faith. The clavichord was a tool of these goals, one of a trove of gifts to be presented to the Emperor in an effort to spark his curiosity and prompt him to grant Father Ricci an audience and allow the Jesuits to remain in Beijing.

A musical instrument must have seemed the perfect gift to win the favor of the Son of Heaven because in a sense it was two gifts — the instrument itself and the entryway to a whole new world of European music that could be played upon it. And, since no one in the Emperor's palace would know how to perform on it, he would have to grant the Jesuits some kind of access to his court if he wished to hear this European music played.

Because the clavichord is little known today, it is not immediately obvious why the Jesuits chose it from among all European instruments, but they had good reasons. "Musical instruments are quite common and of many varieties," Father Ricci explained in his journals, "but the use of the organ and the clavichord is unknown, and the Chinese possess no instrument of the keyboard type." [4] Given their absence in China, a keyboard instrument would be the most likely to excite the Emperor's curiosity. In fact, St. Francis had employed the same strategy in Japan when he presented a keyboard instrument — quite possibly a clavichord — to the feudal lord of Yamaguchi in 1551.

Of course, any other keyboard instrument — like a spinet or a harpsichord — could have filled the same purpose, but the clavichord has several other qualities which likely recommended it to the Jesuits. It was affordable, a key consideration for a

2. Trigault, N. (1615). *China in the Sixteenth Century: The Journals of Matthew Ricci: 1583-1610.* (Trans. Gallagher, L.J.) New York: Random House, 1953:123.

3. Dunne, G.H. (1962). *Generation of Giants: The Story of the Jesuits in China in the Last Decades of the Ming Dynasty.* Notre Dame: University of Notre Dame Press: 19.

4. Trigault: 22.

mission constantly short of funds. It was compact and light, an equally important quality since it would have to be lugged across China. And, finally, it had close associations with the church since it was widely used as a practice instrument by organists back in Europe. In fact, the cache of imperial gifts was also supposed to include several small, made-in-Macao organs but they were not ready before Father Ricci's departure for Beijing and ended up being used by the Jesuits at their Nanjing mission.

Father Ricci and his fellow Jesuits felt confident that the Emperor would be impressed by the clavichord, not to mention the clocks, paintings, books, maps, statues, prisms, tapestries and other gifts they intended to present him. The obstacle they faced was that having gifts for the Emperor and being permitted to present them were not the same thing. The Son of Heaven could be approached only through intermediaries, and it was difficult to find a person of the right status who was willing to take on the responsibility of petitioning on behalf of foreign priests. Father Ricci had already tried twice, in 1595 and 1598; on the first trip he failed even to reach Beijing and on the second he made it, but was unable to find anyone willing to petition the Emperor on his behalf.

Fortunately, this third try seemed destined to succeed. The political climate in Beijing was better, Ricci had obtained letters of introduction and promises of support from key mandarins, and word of the wondrous gifts he intended to present the Emperor had spread far and wide — maybe too far and too wide.

Indeed, while Ricci and the gifts were still at the Nanjing mission, so many friends and officials had asked to see them that it became something of a problem for the Jesuits. It was always the clocks that attracted the most interest — European timepieces were considered great marvels in China, especially those that chimed. But the clavichord also elicited extreme admiration that, in Father Ricci's words, "was not only exaggerated, it was almost ridiculous."[5] In the interest of courtesy and efficiency, the Jesuits were forced to hold a gift-viewing open-house for several days, but even this was not enough to accommodate all who wished to see the royal presents and finally "the visiting became unbearable and the Fathers had to close their doors."[6]

The excitement caused by the gifts was so great that word of them had even spread along the Grand Canal as Father Ricci sailed northward in a fast sailing ship called a cavalier. Accompanying him on this third attempt to present the gifts were the newly-arrived Spanish priest Diego Pantoia — whose job was to play the clavichord — and two Chinese brothers, Sebastian and Emmanuele. Their ship was part of a convoy bringing silk to the Emperor and their passage on it had been arranged through the good offices of an imperial advisor who lived in Nanjing. The eunuch in charge of the convoy seemed pleased with their presence. He had provided them with commodious quarters and sufficient space to transport furniture for a new house and a fully-equipped chapel, not to mention the gifts. And, at every stopping place along the

---

5. *Ibid.*, 320.
6. Trigault: 348.

way, he invited friends and acquaintances aboard to view the imperial gifts, turning the ship into something of a floating museum.

At first this all worked to the Jesuits' advantage. They made no secret of their hope to win the favor of the Emperor so they could open a residence in Beijing and freely took advantage of the chance to discuss the Christian faith with all who came aboard. In addition to providing them with impromptu opportunities for both politicking and proselytizing, the gifts also helped speed their passage through the crowded waterway on which boats sometimes had to queue for days just to get through a single lock; once the eunuch invited the officials in charge of each lock to view the gifts, their convoy immediately moved to the front of the line.

However, when they reached the port of Linjin, they ran into trouble when a eunuch named Ma Tang asked to see the gifts. Power had been devolving to eunuchs throughout the waning years of the Ming Dynasty and under the reign of the current emperor — Wan Li — it was they who virtually ruled the land. Ma Tang was among the most powerful of them all, a tax collector who was so hated by the people that a mob set flame to his home, killed dozens of his servants and would have killed him, had he not managed to flee in disguise. The extent of Ma Tang's corruption was evidenced by his sumptuous boat, which had so many salons, rooms and cabins so exquisitely decorated with carved, varnished and gold-trimmed wood that Ricci deemed it fit for the Emperor himself.

Ricci had little time for eunuchs, whom he generally looked upon as "unlettered and barbarous, lacking shame and piety, utterly arrogant and very monsters of vice."[7] He sensed at once that Ma Tang would be trouble, but there was nothing he could do to avoid the eunuch who was feared by even the nation's most powerful officials. At first, Ma Tang treated the fathers with the utmost respect, even falling to his knees before the statue of the Virgin Mary that they intended to present to the Emperor. He invited them to his house in the city to attend a feast at which "tight-rope walkers, sleight of hand artists, jugglers of goblets, and other such parasites" put on a spectacle the likes of which Ricci wrote would awe "the greatest potentate that one could imagine."[8] He promised to send a petition concerning the gifts onward to the Emperor and insisted that the Jesuits continue their journey on one of his luxurious boats — and then he sprang his nicely laid trap.

Before Ricci knew it, they had sailed into Tianjin — the gateway to Beijing for anyone traveling by boat — and docked near the big stone citadel that loomed over the city. Forced to don the plain cotton robes of the criminal and the round hat of the commoner, Father Ricci was brought into a courtroom filled with an impressive assortment of mandarins and eunuchs, all arrayed in their official finery. The mandarins wore black hats with ovate wings that jutted out from above each ear and leggings of polished black leather. Their long gowns were belted loosely with a wide, ornamented girdle and adorned at front and back with "Mandarin squares"

7. *Ibid.*, 343.
8. *Ibid.*, 362.

embroidered with one of the nine mythical beasts used to indicate a military official's rank in the same way as stars and bars. The higher ranking eunuchs, like Ma Tang, were attired as elaborately as the officials, mincing about like peacocks in full feather. But eunuchs of the lower ranks were dressed far more simply, in the traditional eunuch uniform of black trousers, covered by a long gray gown and a short, dark-blue coat.

While Father Ricci was waiting, perhaps scanning the assembled crowd, Ma Tang rose and called the meeting to order. As his eviscerated treble filtered through the room, the steady buzz of voices gave way to a rustle of purple damask and silk. Adjusting their gowns, the magistrates settled in their chairs and turned to stare at the short, elaborately coifed eunuch whose puffy features must have betrayed both cunning and cupidity.

Ma Tang explained that he had called them to this assembly so they could hear the reply the Emperor had sent to his petition regarding Father Ricci. To ensure that the officials understood the situation, he ordered his own missive read first: While on the Grand Canal at the port of Linjin, Ma Tang had met a foreigner named Li Madou who was reported to be bringing certain gifts to the emperor. Since this European seemed to be well disposed, he, Ma Tang, wanted to help him, and for fear that the boat he was traveling in might meet with some misfortune, he was transferring the stranger to one of his own boats and sending him to the fort at Tianjin to await a reply which, it was hoped, would not be long delayed. [9]

The Emperor's reply was read from an elaborate gold and dragon embossed scroll, but the gist of its contents was simple: Send a list of the presents.

When the reading of the letters was finished, magistrates and eunuchs alike turned their attention to the tall man with a long beard and piercing blue eyes — clearly he was Li Madou, the foreigner in question. Ricci was commanded to step forward and kneel, as was customary when receiving a command from the Emperor. Thus positioned, he was ordered to write out a complete list of all the gifts he intended to present to the Son of Heaven. Paper, inkstone, ink and writing brush were procured and he was permitted to rise so he could carry out the order.

Dipping the brush into the ink, he began to write in precise, flowing Chinese:

> Three paintings, two small, one large
> Two clocks, a large one with weights, a small one which sounds the hour by itself
> Two prisms
> One statue....[10]

When Ricci completed the list, it was handed to Ma Tang who dismissed the assembly of mandarins and then ordered that the gifts be at once transported to his

---

9. *Ibid.*, 363.

10. For gifts, see Trigault: 361 and 364 and Cronin, V. (1955). *The Wise Man from the West*. New York: E.P. Dutton & Co. Inc.: 159.

own residence. The flabbergasted Ricci understandably assumed that Ma Tang's intent was to steal the gifts, though it also seems possible that he was actually trying to steal credit for presenting them to the Emperor. In any case, as his order was being carried out, Ma Tang turned to Ricci and demanded to know if there were any other gifts that the priest had neglected to write down. There were — a nicely bound Roman breviary; a copy of the atlas *The World Theater*, by Ortelius; and the clavichord.

Father Ricci's reasons for not including these items in the list can only be guessed at. But, whatever they were, the ploy failed and he watched in dismay as the three remaining gifts were carted away. Then he was sent back to his quarters to wait until the list was forwarded to the Emperor and a reply received.

The weeks passed by and a frosty chill crept into the autumn air, a harbinger of the bitter winter that would soon descend. Anxious to head back south before the rivers iced over, Ma Tang moved Ricci and his companions into a temple and sent four soldiers to guard them. They heard little from him until one day he stormed into the temple unannounced, accompanied by a prominent military official and a retinue of 200.

Addressing himself to the startled Father Ricci, Ma Tang demanded that he hand over the cache of precious stones he was hiding. When Ricci flatly denied possessing any such stones, the eunuch ordered his lackeys to search through all the priest's luggage and that of his companions. Traveling trunks and cases were brought forth and Ma Tang examined everything with great care, "adding injury to insult by the fury with which he tossed things about."[11] It had become apparent that there were no precious stones to be found, when a crucifix was pulled from a trunk.

Staring at the image of the lifeless body of Christ nailed to a cross, Ma Tang's anger turned to rage.

"This thing was made, as anyone can see, for no other purpose than to bewitch one with poisonous sorcery," he cried, a prelude to accusations that Father Ricci was plotting to kill the Emperor.[12]

Ricci denied the charges vehemently. He realized it was a waste of time to discuss a divine mystery with a man in a rage, but he explained evenly that Christians believed the man on the cross had died to save men's souls. He was portrayed as he had died, in painting and in sculpture, as a means of remembering him. Predictably, the explanation had no effect; indeed, even the seemingly sympathetic magistrate interjected that he thought it quite unbecoming to honor the memory of any man by representing him in such a death. Ma Tang continued to search the luggage, taking for himself two ebony reliquaries and a silver chalice.

Matteo Ricci's approach to China was one of cultural accommodation and respect. He had decided early on that the only way to succeed in gaining Christian

---

11. Trigault: 365. It seems likely that Trigault supplemented with his imagination portions of the published version of Ricci's *Journals*. So, while the dialogue quoted here is excerpted directly from Trigault, it should probably be taken with a grain of salt.

12. *Ibid.*, 365-6.

converts in this country with its ancient and glorious culture and highly educated elite was to essentially become Chinese. Where other missionaries did not even bother to learn the language, Ricci had become so fluent that he wrote books in Chinese and debated the Confucian classics with Chinese scholars. He urged a policy of tolerance for Chinese cultural traditions, like the ceremonies to honor Confucius and ancestors. He wore Chinese clothes, he ate Chinese food, he drank Chinese wine, and he practiced Chinese etiquette. Acculturated as he was, he knew that as Ma Tang's prisoner he was required to act meek and humble, and he had patiently borne confinement and humiliation for months.

But even Ricci had his limits and he was not about to stand by and let the eunuch steal his chalice. Calmly, he explained that the chalice was an object so sacred that only those specially consecrated to use it in ceremonies offering sacrifices to the God of Heaven and earth were even allowed to touch it.

Ma Tang grabbed the chalice and turned it around in his hands.

"What do you mean by saying that no one can touch it," he asked maliciously. "Don't you see me touching it now?" [13]

The sight of Ma Tang's effeminate hands with their long, pointy fingernails rolling across his chalice was more than Father Ricci could bear. In a voice choked with tears, he cast his money purse at the eunuch's feet and cried, "Take out the weight of the cup in gold, please, or take all you want of it, but give me back the chalice."

A deadly silence fell upon the room, with all eyes on the priest and the eunuch. Nobody ever confronted the powerful Ma Tang in this manner! Finally, the silence was broken by the military magistrate, who had evidently been moved by the foreign priest's brave outburst.

"You see," he told Ma Tang, "He is interested in the cup, not because of its value, but because he considers it to be something sacred. He is offering you double the price for it. I would advise you to give it back to him." [14]

Ma Tang looked long and hard at the magistrate and then turned to Father Ricci and handed the chalice back, together with the purse. Money was something of which he had plenty and he certainly had better drinking cups, too. He gathered together the forty odd items he had decided to keep — cotton cloth from India, several glass vases, some sundials and hour-glasses — and ordered them transported to his own house for safekeeping. Then, with the magistrate and lackeys in tow, he left.

Father Ricci was once again left alone with his colleagues in the temple which had become their prison. Prayer seemed their only resort. Ma Tang had not taken the life-like statue of the Blessed Virgin so they placed it on the temple altar and said Mass. The days passed, each one marked by a Mass, by continual bodily mortification in the cold, damp temple, and by penance. They prayed that God would free them from

---

13. *Ibid.*, 366.
14. *Ibid.*

this trap so they could continue with their endeavors and help the many souls in China who were possibly dependent on their labor.

Towards the end of the year, Father Ricci wrote two letters, one to Ma Tang and one to the military magistrate. The servant who delivered the letter to Ma Tang was beaten and abused, and sent back without an answer. The magistrate dared not send a written reply, but passed word through the servant that their situation was "about as hopeless as could be imagined" — Ma Tang was raving mad at Father Ricci, and their best course was to abandon their project, "annihilate every sample they had in their possession of the man who was nailed to the cross," and flee for their lives in the direction of Canton.[15] Barring this, the next best course of action was to ask magistrate friends in Peking to send a request to the Emperor that they be permitted to return to their native lands.

Acting on this advice, Brother Sebastian snuck out of the temple with letters and gifts for magistrates in Peking, but no one was willing to risk Ma Tang's anger. With no help forthcoming, they abandoned any plan of contacting the Emperor and decided that further human efforts were of no avail. Instead, "Confidently placing their last hope in divine assistance, they turned their thoughts toward God and prepared themselves resolutely and joyfully to meet any difficulty, even death itself, in the cause they had undertaken."[16]

Such was their state when suddenly — with no forewarning whatsoever — "Divine Providence"[17] came to their aid in the form of a reply from the Emperor: He wanted the presents, and he wanted them at once.

As the story was later told to Father Ricci, one day out of the blue, the Son of Heaven had remembered their petition and asked, "Where is that clock, I say, where is that clock that rings of itself; the one the foreigners were bringing to me, as they said, in their petition?"[18]

The Emperor had been informed that he had never answered the petition regarding the foreigners, so the gifts had never been forwarded. A reply was then immediately sent to Ma Tang, who was back south in Linjin; unwillingly, but promptly, he made arrangements for the gifts he had taken to be returned and transported to Beijing together with the Jesuits. As was customary for people bringing gifts to the Emperor, transportation was to be furnished by the government. Since the rivers were frozen, eight horses and thirty porters were provided and an official from the High Court of Ceremonies was sent to ensure their safety en route — the end of Father Ricci's long journey to Beijing was finally in sight.

---

15. *Ibid.,* 368.
16. *Ibid.,* 368-9.
17. *Ibid.,* 369.
18. *Ibid.,* 361.

THE CLAVICHORD IN THE IMPERIAL PALACE

On January 24, 1601, Father Ricci arrived in Beijing for the third time. The gifts he had been trying so long to present were sent on to the palace the next day and word of the Emperor's response to them was filtered back to him through palace eunuchs. Naturally, the Fathers listened to this "with only as much credence as one usually places in what the eunuchs say."[19] But, even discounting for exaggeration, it was clear that the gifts had made the impact of which Ricci and his fellow Jesuits had long dreamed — the Emperor loved them.

Indeed, within just a few days, the Fathers were ordered to report to the palace posthaste — the larger of the two clocks had stopped ticking and the Emperor wanted it repaired. Four eunuchs from the College of Mathematicians were assigned to study clock maintenance with the Fathers, who moved into the eunuchs' quarters to teach the "dull and intellectually sluggish beings."[20] During the lessons, a stream of messengers came from the Emperor to ask questions about Europe — he wanted to know about the customs, land, architecture, kings, marriage and funeral rites, and precious stones, and even ordered servants to report what the foreign priests ate and drank. Taking advantage of this opportunity, Father Ricci asked the messengers to tell the Emperor that the priests' one great desire was to live and die in Beijing, and that they wanted nothing else of him.

When the clock-regulating lessons were completed, the newly-trained eunuchs brought the timepieces to the Emperor, who was so delighted that he promptly gave them promotions and pay raises. Indeed, he was so thrilled with all the presents that he decided he wanted to see the strangers who had presented them. The problem, however, was that Emperor Wan Li almost never met with anybody from outside his immediate circle of family, eunuchs, and concubines. Indeed, it had been years since he had even met with his own officials, with whom he was in near constant conflict and currently involved in the end-game of a long-running battle over his choice of an heir.[21]

Unwilling or unable to reform his court — or himself — the Emperor had gradually just given up. He stopped participating in the public study sessions which all emperors were supposed to hold. He let his in-box pile up for decades, disdaining to answer the petitions sent him from all parts of the land — like Ma Tang's letter regarding Father Ricci and his gifts. When an official died or resigned, he declined to appoint a new one to fill the empty position. He even refused to attend his own imperial audiences. Since his officials insisted on holding the audiences anyway, an unusual practice developed in which all visitors to the Emperor — Ricci included — were forced to rise before sun-up, process into the palace, and kowtow to an empty throne.

---

19. *Ibid.*, p. 372.
20. *Ibid.*, p. 373.
21. For a fascinating account of a year in the reign of Wan Li, see Huang, R. (1981). *1587, A Year of No Significance. The Ming Dynasty in Decline.* New Haven and London: Yale University Press.

Thus, having essentially been on strike for a number of years, the troubled Emperor was faced with a dilemma when Ricci and Pantoia arrived. He wanted to meet the men who had come from across the world to bring him these remarkable gifts, but to grant them an audience would require that he break his own strike and would certainly upset the chemistry of his dysfunctional reign. Seeking another means to satisfy his curiosity, he ordered two of the best court artists to paint full length portraits of Ricci and Pantoia. Upon seeing the painting of the bearded Europeans in Chinese dress, the Emperor announced — assurances to the contrary notwithstanding — that the Jesuits were obviously Muslims. This half-measure solution marked the end of Father Ricci's long-cherished dream of meeting the Emperor of China. It could also have meant the end of his intercourse with the palace, but did not, in part thanks to one gift — the clavichord.

Once the novelty of the clocks had worn off, the Emperor turned his attention to the strange musical instrument. The fathers had rented a little house to live in while they awaited Wan Li's answer to their request that they be allowed to stay in Beijing, and were at home when four palace eunuchs appeared at their door. It was obvious from their colorful dress that they ranked much higher than the sluggish mathematicians, and their superior status was confirmed when they introduced themselves as court musicians — string players, to be exact. They came from the Emperor's inner court, where eunuch musicians were divided into two groups, those who played "elegant music" and those who played "banquet music."

Elegant music was the genre which had been favored by Confucius. Like his fellow sages Laozi and Mozi, Confucius had considered music to be a force of great power. However, where Laozi and Mozi saw this power as primarily negative, Confucius believed that if music was properly controlled by the leaders, it could be of great benefit in regulating the common people, promoting affairs of state, and even achieving universal harmony. Music was therefore an important part of state ceremonies in imperial China, including those intended to honor Confucius himself.

While living in Nanjing, Father Ricci had attended a rehearsal for a Confucian ceremony at which elegant music was played, albeit by priests rather than eunuchs. It was held in a magnificent temple built in the middle of a pine forest and surrounded by a wall twelve Italian miles around. The entire temple was made of wood, much of it ornately carved and gilded with gold. It had five naves, and the orchestral rehearsal was held in one of these. Father Ricci described it:

> The priests who composed the orchestra were vested in sumptuous garments, as if they were to attend a sacrifice, and after paying their respects to the Magistrate, they set to playing their various instruments; bronze bells, basin shaped vessels, some made of stone, with skins over them like drums, stringed instruments like a lute, bone flutes and organs played by blowing into them with the mouth rather than with bellows. They had other instruments also shaped like animals, holding reeds in their teeth, through which air was forced from the empty interior. At this rehearsal these curious affairs were all sounded at once, with a result that can be readily imagined, as it was nothing other than a lack of concord, a discord of discords.[22]

So strongly did Father Ricci dislike the music he heard that he concluded his description by implying that it was so bad, even the Chinese didn't like it. "The Chinese themselves are aware of this," he wrote. "One of their sages said on a certain occasion that the art of music known to their ancestors had evaporated with the centuries, and left only the instruments."[23] While it is doubtful that all emperors and mandarins shared Father Ricci's evaluation of "elegant music," it is true that as early as 350 BC a leader known as the Duke of Wei confessed to his adviser that, "I adjust my diadem and listen respectfully to ancient ritual music, but cannot help falling asleep. Why is it that I am never tired of listening to the music of Cheng and Wei?" [24] If leaders born just a few centuries after Confucius found elegant music to be boring, by the Ming Dynasty it was most definitely not what emperors listened to when they wanted to relax or be entertained — for this, there was Chinese opera and banquet music.

Chinese opera was quickly becoming the dominant form of popular musical entertainment throughout the country and Father Ricci hated it, like a true Confucian conservative. "Without question this is a curse in the empire," he wrote, "and so much so that it would be difficult to discover any other activity which is more prone to vice."[25] Father Ricci's main objection was to the practice of purchasing young children to perform in opera troupes, but he saw nothing worthwhile in the performances, either:

> These groups of actors are employed at all imposing banquets and when they are called they come prepared to enact any of the ordinary plays. The host at the banquet is usually presented with a volume of plays and he selects the one or several he may like. The guests, between eating and drinking, follow the plays with so much satisfaction that the banquet at times may last for ten hours, and as one play leads to another the dramatic performance may last as long again as did the banquet. The text of these plays is generally sung, and it rarely happens that anything is enunciated in an ordinary tone of voice.[26]

But while Chinese opera was growing in importance in the late Ming Dynasty, "banquet music" remained the more common form of imperial entertainment. Each dynasty had its own particular form of banquet music, which in the Ming was of an especially large scale.[27] The ensembles that played this music used many foreign instruments — from Mongolia, Central Asia, Indo-China and even Nepal. Indeed, the

22. Trigault: 336.

23. *Ibid.* See also page 22, where Ricci comments that, "The whole art of Chinese music seems to consist in producing a monotonous rhythmic beat as they know nothing of the variations and harmony that can be produced by combining different musical notes. However, they themselves are highly flattered by their own music which to the ear of a stranger represents nothing but a discordant jangle."

24. For anecdote and quote, see Lai, T.C. and Mok, R. (1981). *Jade Flute: The Story of Chinese Music.* New York: Schocken Books: 42.

25. Trigault: 23.

26. *Ibid.,* 23-4.

27. Kishibe, Shigeo (1980). Court traditions — Banquet music (China, II, 3). In, Stanley Sadie (ed). *The New Grove Dictionary of Music and Musicians,* Vol. 4. London: Macmillan Publishers Limited: 252.

use of foreign instruments at court was already a very old custom, as was the playing of foreign music. In the cosmopolitan Tang Dynasty, the Emperor had actually maintained entire orchestras from Indo-China, Korea, Kucha, Bokhara, Kashgar, Samarkand and Turfan. Given this ample precedent for the playing of both foreign music and instruments at court, Emperor Wan Li clearly felt comfortable in asking to hear a clavichord recital and he had therefore sent the eunuchs to request that the Fathers teach them how to play it.

If this was not the outcome of which Ricci had dreamed, it was better than nothing. He and Father Pantoia readily agreed to the plan and a schedule of daily lessons was arranged, to be held in the Imperial Palace. Though Pantoia's reaction to the arrangement is not recorded, we can guess that he was both excited and anxious.

The Castilian Jesuit's introduction to China had been something of a baptism by fire, especially considering that he had never intended to go there in the first place. His original destination had been Japan, but he was stranded in Macao when the ship he should have sailed on was lost at sea. It so happened that news of the ship's loss reached the Jesuits at the same time that Ricci's colleague Lazzaro Cattaneo was in Macao, visiting from the Nanjing mission. The stranded Pantoia was assigned to go to China with Father Cattaneo, where he could either remain at the Nanjing mission or journey to Beijing with Ricci.

Given the choice between Cattaneo and the new recruit, Ricci would presumably have preferred his old colleague as travel companion on the all-important trip north. Language and experience aside, Father Cattaneo was an accomplished musician — which Ricci was not — and the only one who could play the clavichord. But, Ricci had to put the needs of the mission first, which meant that he assigned Father Cattaneo to stay in Nanjing and run it and Father Pantoia to travel with him to Beijing. There was just one caveat — before departing for Beijing, Father Pantoia had to learn to play the clavichord. Fortunately, he learned quickly and was able to both play and tune the instrument by the time their ship was set to sail. And now, with this request direct from the Son of Heaven, he was transformed from a beginning clavichord student to the first teacher of European music in the Imperial Palace of China.

On the first day of lessons, a palanquin was sent to carry the Jesuits to the heart of Beijing where the Imperial Palace stood, surrounded by four vermilion walls above which rose a shimmering sea of golden rooftops. Etiquette dictated that all visitors descend from their horses or chairs and proceed on foot when they reached the palace, a tradition followed so scrupulously that higher level officials made it a point to walk from even farther away than necessary. Already familiar with the ritual from their first visit, the priests disembarked from the palanquin and walked through one of the side entrances of the Gate of Heavenly Peace, the central door being reserved for the Emperor's exclusive use.

Though they had already spent several days and nights within the palace walls, it must still have been overwhelming to enter it and to know that somewhere, in the back precincts that they would never see, was the misguided sovereign whom they so wished to enlighten with their faith. They passed beneath the Meridian Gate and saw before them the five shimmering white marble bridges that crossed the Golden Stream. Large bronze cranes and tortoises were sprinkled around the courtyard, symbols of longevity, and Ricci no doubt looked about him for signs of the five-clawed dragons which he had already noted were everywhere in the palace — on the roof tiles, on gold and silver vases, on the furniture, and on the draperies. They crossed over the Golden Stream by way of a side bridge, passed through the Gate of Supreme Harmony and entered an immense stone-flagged courtyard.

This was as far as they would go in the Palace, but had they looked up and shaded their eyes from the sun that glanced off the golden roofs, they would have seen the Hall of Supreme Harmony towering at the back of the courtyard. This majestic building was the Emperor's main audience hall — the place where they would likely have been received had Emperor Wan Li's reign not been so dysfunctional. It soared 92 feet into the air and had a massive double-eaved roof supported by 24 hardwood pillars and adorned with intricate interlocking balustrades. A procession of ten porcelain animals paraded down each upturned corner of the roof, tasked with the all-important assignment of guarding the building from fire.

If the fathers were indeed mesmerized by the sight of the Hall of Supreme Harmony, it was left to the eunuchs escorting them to pull their gazes away and point the way into a side courtyard where the College of Musicians was located. The priests entered the room set aside for their lessons and saw that it was full of musical instruments, none of which looked anything like the clavichord. There were "chimes of stones, bells and gongs, flutes like twigs on which a bird was perched, brass clappers, horns and trumpets convoluted to resemble beasts, monstrous freaks of musical nature, a kind of organ without bellows, drums of every dimension, wooden tigers with a row of teeth on their backs, gourds and ocarinas."[28] With great respect, they were ushered to the back of the room and given seats facing south. When they had made themselves comfortable, the four string players came forward, kowtowing deeply. Addressing Father Pantoja as "master," the eunuchs humbly asked him to "teach them with patience but with diligence, and not become impatient if he found them slow to learn this art, hitherto unknown to them."[29] They then turned and kowtowed to the clavichord — over the objections of the Fathers — and asked that it, too, be patient with them.

The clavichord stood silent during these protracted greetings, a rectangular wooden box that was roughly three feet long and five feet wide.[30] Though Father Ricci does not describe it and palace records give only a simple description, the Jesuits took great care to make sure that the presents for the Emperor were aesthetically pleasing as well as functional, and it is likely that the instrument was made from high quality wood and perhaps even embellished with carving. Sound was produced on the

28. Cronin: 178.
29. Trigault: 376-7.
30. Feng: 232.

keyboard which projected from left and center on one of the long sides of the instrument. The sound lasted as long as a key was depressed, and changed accordingly if pressure was either intensified or relaxed; if the key was released, the sound stopped instantly. The clavichord's sensitivity made it an exciting instrument to play, but also a challenging one — Father Pantoia and the eunuchs had their work cut out for them.

Perhaps sensing this, the eunuchs had set modest goals for themselves, each wishing to learn only one song. Of course, they may also have anticipated that the Emperor's interest in the clavichord would not last long. Though foreign instruments, music and even musicians had been readily accepted into the court in earlier dynasties, the Ming was an insular era and the nativist sentiments that dominated intellectual and political life also affected the arts. Various Ming emperors had even made efforts to purge the court repertoire of the foreign music that had already entered it and to discourage the playing of any music outside China's own traditions. Emperor Wan Li wasn't a particular activist where this — or anything else — was concerned, but it was probably safe for the eunuchs to assume that the clavichord would have little lasting impact on their jobs.

Despite their kowtows and pleas for patience, the two older eunuchs did in fact find it hard to learn how to play the strange foreign instrument and the lessons stretched out over a month. However, this was a blessing in disguise so far as Ricci and Pantoia were concerned, since the lessons inside the palace afforded them excellent entrée to the court. Before they knew it, they were being wined and dined by some of the highest ranking palace eunuchs, further securing their position in Beijing and enabling them, on occasion, to explain their religion.

But if the eunuchs were pleased by the clavichord music they learned — possibly the madrigals of Animuccia and Nanino[31] — they were also unsettled by its purely instrumental nature; music in China was virtually always accompanied by lyrics and they feared the Emperor would be displeased if they had no words to accompany their performance. Mid-way through the lessons, they expressed their apprehension and Father Ricci happily obliged them by writing eight sets of lyrics that discussed basic ethics, morals and virtues in simple terms, often using Chinese philosophy and imagery.

One of the songs went like this:

> A shepherd boy fell sad one day,
> Hating the hillside on which he stood;
> He thought a distant hill he saw
> More beautiful by far,
> And that going there would wipe away his sorrows.
> So he set off to that distant hill
> But as he drew near to it
> It looked less good than it had from afar.

---

31. Cronin: 179.

O shepherd boy, shepherd boy,
How can you expect to transform yourself
By changing your dwelling place?
If you move away can you leave yourself behind?
Sorrow and joy sprout in the heart.
If the heart is peaceful, you'll be happy everywhere,
If the heart is in turmoil, every place brings sorrow.
A grain of dust in your eye
Brings discomfort speedily;
How can you then ignore this sharp awl
That pierces your heart?
If you yearn for things outside yourself
You will never obtain what you are seeking.
Why not put your own heart in order
And find peace on your own hillside?
Old and new writers alike give this advice;
There's no advantage to roaming outside,
Keep the heart inside, for
That brings the profit.[32]

When the lessons were complete, the eunuchs presumably gave a recital for Emperor Wan Li. It is pleasant to imagine the Emperor seated on one of his smaller thrones, surrounded by attendants and a few favored concubines and children, giving the order for the musicians to enter his presence. The Emperor was not known for his patience — Ricci wrote that "For a eunuch to make a mistake in the presence of the King is equivalent to placing his life in danger"[33]— and the eunuchs must have been extremely nervous as they crossed the threshold into his presence. After kowtowing to the Son of Heaven, they may have once again executed a quick prostration before the clavichord, silently pleading with it not to fail them on this occasion.

Then, one of the eunuchs — probably the 72-year-old who had the greatest difficulty learning — would have sat down and begun to play from memory, his fingers moving across the keys with increasing confidence as he caught the murmur of pleasure that rippled through the imperial party. The gentle tones of the clavichord — compared by writers of old to the sound of moonlight or the breathing of the heart — rose up to the painted rafters where they were joined by the voices of each eunuch, singing the lyrics penned by Father Ricci. For the first time ever, the sounds of a European instrument playing European music in a formal recital filled a chamber of the Imperial Palace of China.

Each eunuch was certainly given a chance to play the tune he had mastered, and perhaps even played twice so that all eight songs could be sung. But when the recital was over, no further lessons were requested of Father Pantoia, making it safe to

---

32. Spence, J. (1984). *The Memory Palace of Matteo Ricci*. New York: Viking Penguin: 198-9.
33. Trigault: 373.

assume that once the novelty wore off, the clavichord was set aside like so many other gifts.

But if the music that Father Pereira taught the eunuchs was ephemeral, Father Ricci's songs proved longer lasting. Indeed, they became so popular that a number of literati began asking for copies of them, many apparently believing that the Emperor would do well to emulate the virtues they expressed. To meet the demand, the Jesuits put the songs together with several other pieces and printed them as a musical booklet called *Songs for the Clavichord*. Though the original, bilingual edition from 1603 has been lost, a second edition edited by the Catholic convert Li Zhizao and published in 1608 is still extant. It contains a foreword in which Father Ricci tells the tale of how a clavichord — never before seen in China and never before heard — intrigued the Emperor.[34] *Songs for the Clavichord* stayed in circulation for many years, and was even included in a list of China's best literary creations that was compiled in the late 18th century.

True to form, Emperor Wan Li never formally answered any of the petitions that his officials sent asking what they should do about the foreign priests and their request to live in Beijing. Indeed, when Father Ricci died nine years later, they were still waiting for the Emperor's response to their petition. Father Pantoja, who had learned Chinese fluently and become a highly-regarded member of the mission, referred to this long wait in a beautiful, Chinese-style letter that he wrote to the Emperor asking for a plot of land in which to bury his beloved colleague:

> In the nineteenth year of Wan Li, the first moon, we petitioned your Exalted Majesty to assign us a place to live, so that the splendor of your royal clemency and kindness might illumine the lives of newly arrived strangers. We waited for years to learn the expression of your will, and yet in all that time, through no merit of our own, but due rather to your kingly generosity, we never lacked provision for our sustenance.

> On the eighteenth of the third moon, of the thirty-eighth year of Wan Li, the aging Father Ricci died of a malady, leaving me, as it were, an orphan, the subject of a distant realm, in such a state as to elicit universal compassion and pity in my many trials. To return to my native land with his body would mean to undertake a very long voyage, and sailors fear to take a corpse aboard their ships. Hence it is impossible for me to bring his body back to his native soil... As in life we were nourished by your royal bounty, so in death we trust that you will grant us a clod of earth for a shroud.[35]

As Father Pantoja was careful to note, Emperor Wan Li had never answered the Jesuits' petition, but he had effectively given them permission to stay by granting them a small subsidy of gold and a regular allowance of rice, meat, salt, wine, vegetables and firewood. He came through again with a plot of land for Ricci's grave which — almost miraculously — has survived to this day. Matteo Ricci's name is still mentioned with

---

34. Tao: 46.
35. Trigault: 568.

respect in China and his grave is well-maintained, marked by an imposing stone carved with dragons and roses, surrounded by a protective wall, and sheltered by pine and bamboo. The land in which he was buried now belongs to the Communist Party School, but the guards at the gates freely grant entry to visitors who wish to pay their respects to the great Jesuit.

While lying on his deathbed, Father Ricci told the sorrowing priests and brothers who surrounded him, "I am leaving you on the threshold of an open door that leads to a great reward, but only after labors endured and dangers encountered."

Although the door to which he referred was that which would lead to the conversion of souls, the doors that he opened were many. During his 27 years in China, Matteo Ricci laid the foundations of a mission that would see hundreds of Jesuits working in China over the next two centuries. He introduced Chinese intellectuals to European learning on astronomy, surveying, optics, geometry, pneumonics and horology. He made a world map in Chinese which was printed scores of times and even reproduced in a giant version that Emperor Wan Li kept in his chambers. He wrote books on a variety of religious, scientific and philosophical subjects including a treatise on friendship which was so widely admired that it was still being reprinted as late as 1914. He set a standard for cultural adaptation and understanding which would provide a model for Jesuits for the next two centuries. Through the letters he sent back home and the posthumous publication of his journals, he did much to introduce China to Europe. And last — but not least — he cracked open the door to the study of European music in China.

Unfortunately, the door that Ricci had opened nearly swung shut in the tumultuous times that followed his passing. Indeed, it was not until three decades after his death, in the 13th year of the reign of Emperor Chongzhen, that a rectangular wooden box was found in a treasure room of the Imperial Palace. At first it was thought to be a container holding some other forgotten gift, but when it was opened and discovered to be a musical instrument — the clavichord — the Emperor's curiosity was piqued. Like his grandfather before him, Emperor Chongzhen decided that he wanted to hear the strange instrument.

The box-like contraption was covered in dust and sorely in need of repair and it was soon discovered that nobody in the palace had any idea what to do with it. The eunuchs who Father Pantoia had taught to play it were long gone, as was Father Pantoia himself, since he had been expelled from China in an anti-Christian edict issued by the aged and bitter Emperor Wan Li in 1617. The quest for someone who understood the clavichord had to be extended outside the vermilion walls, where it led straight to one man: the German Jesuit Johann Adam Schall von Bell, or Tang Ruowang.

Father Schall had been in China for 16 years, with most of that time devoted to astronomical work and reform of the Chinese calendar. In keeping with the hermetic Ming tradition, Emperor Chongzhen had never received the German Jesuit, but he was grateful to him and his colleagues for their work and their gifts, which included a telescope, a celestial globe, an armillary sphere and a beautiful sundial made from white marble. The Emperor even trusted Schall enough to have allowed him to enter his residential quarters in order to set up the astronomical instruments and construct a small observatory from which Chongzhen himself could watch eclipses.

Since Father Schall's talents were so well known at the palace, it must have seemed natural to call on him when the Emperor wanted to hear the clavichord — a man who could build an observatory and predict eclipses could certainly fix a musical instrument from his native Europe. We do not know if Schall had any formal musical training, but we do know that he came from a wealthy and noble Cologne family and was educated at Jesuit schools from the age of twelve. Although choral music had been expressly prohibited by the founder of the Society of Jesus, Ignatius of Loyola, the prohibition was routinely ignored and music was an important part of life in Jesuit institutions. It therefore seems safe to assume that Schall had some sort of musical background, which could well have included the clavichord since it was an important instrument in 17th-century Germany. In any case, believing as he did that service rendered the Emperor was service rendered the Faith, Father Schall readily agreed to attempt the repairs on the instrument.

On opening up the clavichord to begin work, Father Schall would have seen two psalms written inside the instrument — quite possibly by Ricci himself — which read:

> Let them praise his name in festive dance, make music with tambourine and lyre. (Psalm 149, Vs. 3)[36]

> Give him praise with crashing cymbals, praise him with sounding cymbals. (Psalm 150, Vs. 5)[37]

Father Schall had never met Father Ricci, but he had been drawn to join the China mission after reading the great priest's journals, which were published in Europe to great acclaim in 1615. He must have been inspired by the likely connection to the man who had been so instrumental in his life, and buoyed by the psalms themselves — if praise could be given with dance, tambourine, lyre and cymbals, so could it be given on a clavichord.

Inspiration aside, however, the task of repairing the clavichord was complicated enough that Father Schall called for help from the other missions and finally a lay brother from Henan named Xu Fuyuan who knew how to make metal string was sent to the capital to help with the repairs. Working with Brother Xu — who unfortunately died not long after his arrival — Father Schall finally managed to complete repairs on the clavichord. Aware that there was nobody in the palace who would know how to play it, he also wrote a manual explaining its construction and how it was meant to be played. In the manual, he included Chinese translations of the psalms and added the plainsong music for a hymn (psalmenmelodie) that could be

---

36. For psalm numbers, see Tao: 60-1. The original source of this information is Phillipe Couplet, SJ. *Histoire d'une dame Chretienne de la Chine.* Translation of the psalms used here comes from the *New American Bible,* usccb.org/nab.

37. *Ibid.*

used for practice. He then sent the newly repaired instrument back to the palace together with the manual and several gifts from the Duke of Bavaria which the mission had been trying to present — unsuccessfully — for more than twenty years.

With the clavichord repaired, Emperor Chongzhen now had at least three European keyboard instruments at his disposal, since the Jesuit Francisco Sambiaso (Bi Fangji) had presented him with an organ and another keyboard instrument that may have been a clavichord just a year earlier. But, as it turned out, he did not have much time to enjoy any of the instruments since his hold on power was growing increasingly precarious, in part because of the dynastic scourge of corrupt eunuchs.

Although Emperor Chongzhen once again turned to Father Schall for help — this time ordering him to make hundreds of cannons — he was soon overwhelmed by rebels and invaders. Inexplicably, he put the defense of Beijing under the command of his eunuchs, and in the spring of 1644 one of them opened the gates to the army of bandits outside. As the bandits swarmed into the city, the beleaguered Emperor jumped on a horse and fled, only to have the cannons manufactured under Father Schall's direction turned upon him by another bunch of traitorous eunuchs. He was forced to turn back to the palace and Father Schall saw him — for the first and last time — as he galloped past the Jesuit residence.

When he got back home, Emperor Chongzhen ordered his wife to hang herself and his sons to hide. He tried to kill his 15-year-old-daughter but she defended herself, losing a hand to his saber in the process. Having thus dispatched of his family, the Emperor went out the back gate of the palace, climbed Coal Hill and hanged himself. The 276-year old Ming Dynasty was over.

The close relationship of the Jesuits — and especially Father Schall — with the defeated dynasty could have proved dangerous. Instead, however, the remarkable priest became a tutor and grandfather-like confidant of the Qing Dynasty's first emperor, the youthful Shunzhi. Emperor Shunzhi made Father Schall director of the Bureau of Astronomy, visited him at his home on numerous occasions, and gave him land to build a church.[38] The church was completed in 1652 and once an organ was installed, it became a vehicle for spreading European liturgical music, as well as a center of Christian worship. Father Schall's friendship with the Emperor and his position in the bureaucracy were seen as tacit endorsement of the Christian faith and brought great benefits to missionaries — both Jesuit and non-Jesuit — for the remainder of his reign.

But, when Emperor Shunzhi died at age 25 — grief-stricken after the death of his favorite consort — enemies of Father Schall and Christianity came out of the woodwork. The German Jesuit suddenly found himself disgraced, jailed and sentenced to death by strangulation. His colleagues were locked up with him, the churches were closed, and Jesuits, Franciscans and Dominicans around the nation were imprisoned

---

38. Although the building burned down several times in the following centuries, the "Southern Cathedral" still exists today, one of the major Catholic churches of Beijing.

or expelled. Disabled by a stroke, Schall could not defend himself so the Belgian Jesuit Ferdinand Verbiest (Nan Huairen) served as his lawyer.

In a series of sham trials, Father Schall was accused of having picked an unlucky burial day for the Emperor's infant son and the overall accuracy of the Jesuits' astronomical predictions was debated. Though Verbiest mounted an excellent defense and the Jesuits' science was never disproved, Schall's death sentence was upheld and even changed to the worst of all — the lingering death, in which the body is cut into thousands of small pieces with a sword, each wound cauterized with a red hot iron so as to minimize blood loss and keep the condemned man alive as long as possible.

However, on the very day the 73-year-old Jesuit was condemned to die this cruel death, an earthquake struck Beijing. Days later, a fire broke out in the imperial palace. Both were quickly interpreted by Father Schall's friends and enemies alike as signs that Heaven was displeased with the harsh sentence meted out to him. Four days after the earthquake, his death sentence was commuted. He remained in chains for another month, and was then freed and allowed to return to the Jesuit residence, where he died a year later, in August of 1666.

This interregnum marked a low point for the Jesuits — and for the progress of Western music in China — but it ended as suddenly as it had begun. In 1668, Emperor Shunzhi's 13-year-old heir Emperor Kangxi dismissed the regents who had been ruling in his name and took power for himself. After ordering an investigation, he exonerated Father Schall, posthumously restored all his titles, and punished those who had accused him. He allowed missionaries to resume their activities and went on to retain Jesuit priests as court astronomers, mathematicians, cartographers, armaments supervisors, artists, doctors — and music teachers.

EMPEROR KANGXI'S MUSIC LESSONS

Emperor Kangxi's first music teacher was Father Verbiest, the man who had so eloquently defended Father Schall at his sham trial. The two started out studying philosophy and mathematics and soon bonded over Euclid's geometry, the first six books of which had been translated into Chinese by Matteo Ricci and the renowned Catholic convert Xu Guangqi.[39] For one five-month period early in his reign, Emperor Kangxi had Father Verbiest come to his apartments every day to tutor him. As Verbiest wrote:

---

39. Xu Guangqi, who is also known as Paul Hsu, came from an illustrious Shanghai family. The Xujiahui area of the city where the Jesuits later established their mission was his family's land. He and Matteo Ricci became good friends and Xu is generally given credit for providing much help to the cause of Christianity as he rose up through the imperial bureaucracy. He became vice president of the Board of Rites in 1629 and the period following his appointment to this position was one of tremendous growth for Christianity. Several Chinese musicologists, including Feng Wenci, also point out that he deserves indirect credit for the spread of Western music in China, since he did so much to ease the way for the Jesuits both at court and in the provinces.

At break of day I went to the palace and was immediately admitted to the Emperor's apartments, and often did not leave until three or four after mid-day. Alone with the Emperor I read and expounded. Often he kept me to lunch and served exquisite meats on a plate of gold.[40]

When the Emperor expressed an interest in Western music, Father Verbiest taught him what he could, but he himself was not a musician. When he could teach no more, he recommended the talented Macao-based Jesuit musician Tomas Pereira, known in China as Xu Risheng.

Father Pereira arrived in Beijing in 1673 and was received by Emperor Kangxi together with Father Grimaldi, who became director of the Board of Mathematics. The pair presented the Emperor with a small organ and a harpsichord, which he accepted. Emperor Kangxi then became busy with other matters, but six years later he called them back in order to hear the instruments played. The Jesuit Jean-Baptiste du Halde described the scene:

> ... he [Kangxi] liked our European Airs, and seemed to take great pleasure in them. Then he ordered his musicians to play a Chinese Air upon one of their Instruments, and play'd himself in a very graceful Manner. In the meantime, P. Pereira took his Pocket Book, and pricked down all the Tune, while the Musicians were playing; and when they had made an End, repeated it as perfectly as if he had practised it long before, without missing one Note: This so surprized the Emperor, that he could scarcely believe it. He bestowed great Commendations on the Justness, Harmony and Facility of the European Music; But above all he admired the Missionary had in so short a time learned an Air which had given him and his Musicians no small Trouble; and that by help of certain Characters he was become so thoroughly Master of it, that it was not possible for him to forget it.[41]

Emperor Kangxi was so amazed by Father Pereira's feat because China at the time had no standard notation; most music was passed down by ear and learned by rote. The little music that was notated used different systems, perhaps the most common being a word-based system known as *gongchipu* that did not indicate rhythm and provided no visual clues as to pitch. Still unable to believe Father Pereira's skill, Emperor Kangxi continued to test him:

> To be the more sure of this, he made several farther Trials, and sung many different Airs, which the Jesuit pricked, and repeated immediately with the greatest Exactness: *It must be owned*, cry'd the Emperor, *the European Music is incomparable, and this Father,* (speaking of P. Pereira) *has not his equal in all the Empire.*[42]

---

40. Allan, C.W. *Jesuits at the Court of Peking.* Shanghai: Kelly and Walsh, Limited (reprint edition by University Publications of America, Inc., 1975): 187.

41. Du Halde, J.B. (1738, 1741). "A description of the Empire of China and Chinese Tartary, together with the Kingdoms of Korea, and Tibet: from the French of P.J.B. Du Halde, Jesuit" (trans. R. Brookes), 2 vols., London, 1738, 1741. In Harrison, F. (ed.) (1973). *Time, Place and Music. An anthology of ethnomusicological observation c. 1550 to c. 1800.* Amsterdam: Frist Knuf: 124.

Du Halde was secretary to the Jesuit confessor of Louis XIV and compiled his description from letters and reports sent back to Europe by Jesuits in China.

Convinced of the worth of European music, Emperor Kangxi decided to learn how to play some tunes on the harpsichord; one of the first songs he mastered was the Daoist prayer song *Pu Yen Zhou*, which had originally been written for the *pipa* back in the Song Dynasty but was adapted for the *qin* in 1592. He also asked Father Pereira to give a series of lectures on Western music theory, which were attended by several of the Emperor's 56 children. Emperor Kangxi's third son, Prince Yinzhi, became an especially attentive student and later worked with Father Pereira to produce a book based on these lectures. The book — called *The Elements of Music* — discussed Western notation, theory, scale, mode, harmony, and more and was edited with vermilion ink by Prince Yinzhi himself.

When Father Pereira died on Christmas Eve of 1708, the Emperor and his sons were left without a music teacher for three years. This hiatus was unplanned and undesired; in fact, Emperor Kangxi had requested the Pope to send another music teacher from Rome many years earlier and the Pope had willingly complied, commissioning an Italian Lazarist musician named Teodorico Pedrini (De Lige). Father Pedrini was supposed to accompany the papal legate Carol Tommaso Maillard de Tournan, who was being sent to meet with Emperor Kangxi and the China-based missionaries to resolve some festering disagreements over whether a Chinese Christian could participate in ceremonies to honor familial ancestors and Confucius.

However, Pedrini was late reaching the Canary Islands — the starting point for ships sailing to Asia — and the papal legate's ship left without him. The legate's ship followed the normal path, around the coast of Africa to Goa in India, and then to Manila and finally to Macao. But the ship which Pedrini caught ran into strong winds and was forced to turn west into the Atlantic, ending up in South America. Upon reaching Peru, the ship's captain gave up and decided to go back to Europe, leaving Father Pedrini stranded.

Undeterred, Pedrini made his way by land and sea to Guatemala and then to Acapulco, Mexico, where he caught a ship bound for Manila. When he arrived in Manila, he discovered that the King of Spain had interdicted all intercourse between his subjects and China, so there were no ships available to take him to his final destination. Demonstrating the chutzpah that evidently characterized him, Father Pedrini disguised himself as a ship's captain and chartered a boat to take himself and several other stranded missionaries from Manila to Macao. One of his passengers was a secular priest from Naples, named Matteo Ripa (Ma Guoxian), who later wrote that Father Pedrini's "inexperience in nautical matters nearly cost us our lives two or three times."[43] Nevertheless, after three harrowing months at sea, the intrepid Father Pedrini managed to anchor safely in Macao. He finally reached Beijing a year later, at noon on January 5, 1711 — ten years after he had left Portugal.

---

42. Du Halde, in *Time, Place and Music*: 124.
43. Ripa, M. (1844). *Memoirs of Father Ripa during Thirteen Years Residence at the Court of Peking in the Service of the Emperor of China.* Trans. Fortunato Prandi. London: John Murray: 31-2.

Having already waited for his new music teacher for a number of years, Emperor Kangxi did not care to wait any longer. Father Pedrini was brought straight to the Imperial Palace that same afternoon, together with the four other missionaries who had accompanied him northward on the Grand Canal, among them Father Ripa. Arriving at the Palace, the missionaries were escorted into a spacious open hall and offered cushions to sit upon, in the Manchu custom.[44] It is easy to imagine Father Pedrini sinking into a silken pillow and thinking with relief that his ten years of travel had finally come to an end and his new calling as music teacher to the Emperor of China was about to begin. Whatever that future held, it could not possibly be as difficult as getting to China in the first place — or so it must have seemed then.

Since it was dinnertime, the missionaries were obliged to wait until the Emperor had finished his meal, but Kangxi graciously sent out two large golden bowls full of meat and fish from his own table. To receive this great honor, Father Pedrini and the others were instructed to get down on their knees, raise the bowls high above their heads, and kowtow in thanks. This done, they were invited to sit down again and eat. Since the day happened to be a Friday, they did not partake of the meat, but hungrily ate the many other foods presented them. When the meal was finished, they were asked solemnly if they had come prepared to serve the Emperor, even unto death — only after replying affirmatively were they ushered in to see the Son of Heaven in his private apartments.

Emperor Kangxi was seated cross-legged on a velvet-covered divan in front of which stood a low table covered with books and writing materials. Eunuchs and European missionaries stood to his right and left, their feet close together, their shoulders bent forward, and their arms hanging down in front of them in a sign of respect. At a signal from the mandarins, Father Pedrini and the others quickly stepped forward and stood before Kangxi in the same submissive posture. When a suitable amount of time had passed, the master of ceremonies lowered his hand in a pre-arranged sign and they dropped to their knees as a group. After a pause, they lowered themselves forward and touched their heads to the ground three times. Another order was given and they stood back up and then repeated the entire process of prostration and head-knocking two more times — the three full cycles done, their first formal kowtow to the Emperor was complete.

With the formalities over, the atmosphere lightened. Using the missionaries at his side as interpreters, Emperor Kangxi asked the new arrivals to state their names, countries, professions and whether they had brought any new mathematical works with them. He asked Father Pedrini to perform on the harpsichord and was immediately impressed by his talent. When the audience ended, he gave his new music teacher a few months to rest from his epic voyage and to accustom himself to China. Then he summoned him to a second audience and ordered Pedrini to lodge in a house within the Imperial Palace so that he might take charge of tuning "the cymbals and spinets, which his Majesty had in great numbers in all his palaces." [45] Told that Father

---

44. This account of Father Pedrini's first audience with Kangxi is taken from Ripa: 47-9.

Pedrini did not understand Chinese, Emperor Kangxi replied pragmatically that this was of no consequence, since cymbals were tuned with the hands and not with the tongue. However, he nonetheless assigned the learned French Jesuit Dominique Parennin — who was fluent in Chinese, Manchu, Spanish and Italian, as well as French — to act as Father Pedrini's interpreter.

Emperor Kangxi's interest in music had been growing deeper over the years and the arrival of the talented Italian priest seems to have further energized it. He soon sent other members of the Imperial Household to study with Father Pedrini, including Prince Yinzhi and his fifteenth and sixteenth sons. He also asked Pedrini to set up a workshop to maintain the growing number of Western instruments in the palace collection and to build new ones, including an organ. Because he was fascinated by mechanical things, he followed the process of making and maintaining these instruments closely and came to understand more of the differences between Chinese and European music, including the fact that Chinese music does not have a half step. Suddenly dissatisfied with certain of the Chinese instruments built "after the ancient Manner," Emperor Kangxi had some of these "corrected by the more modern rules."[46]

After a time, he decided that his sons and the other students of Father Pedrini were not learning enough. On the 22nd day of the sixth month of the 53rd year of his reign (1714), the evidently frustrated Emperor gave the official Zhang Qilin this order:

> The students of the Westerner Pedrini are not just supposed to learn how to play; the purpose is to study the roots of music theory. If I want to find someone who can play, I can find anyone! Up till now these children cannot even understand do re mi fa so la xi, so what are they being taught? You can tell Pedrini clearly to make great effort to teach them the most important roots of music.[47]

To further deepen their understanding of these roots, Kangxi asked Father Pedrini to write a treatise about Western music theory and instruments. And finally, in what is historically the most important manifestation of his deepening interest in music, he commissioned a major encyclopedia of music theory known as the *Luluzhengyi*, or *The True Meaning of Pitch Temperament*.

The True Meaning of Pitch Temperament as it existed in Emperor Kangxi's time was divided into three parts, known as *shang*, *xia* and *xu bian*. The first two parts are a record of Chinese music theory and instruments that begins with an explanation of the dominant Yellow Note which was made by the Yellow Emperor long, long ago. The Yellow Note was then divided into three so as to make more notes, and so on.

The third part, or *xu bian*, is a systematic and thorough overview of Western music theory that is based on Father Pereira's *The Elements of Music* and Father Pedrini's subsequent treatise. It starts simply with an explanation of staff notation and then moves on to such topics as the relationship between tonality and mode; half tone, whole tone and scale; the relationship of rhythm to music; harmony; and intervals. The

45. Ripa: 63.
46. Du Halde, in *Time, Place and Music*: 163-4.
47. Tao: 97.

approach taken by the authors reflects both the era and the intended audience. For instance, the length of notes is discussed, but without time measurements — a double whole note is explained as being so long that a person's voice cannot hold it. Diagrams are provided that explain how to physically write a note; if you are under the third line, the stem goes up, if you are over the third line, the stem goes down.

Like the rest of *The True Meaning of Pitch Temperament*, the portion devoted to Western music is written in classical Chinese with no punctuation other than periods at the end of sentences. It is block printed, diagrams and all, on thin folded paper and the text is written in columns that are read vertically from right to left, as was standard back then. However, examples of staff notation that are sprinkled throughout are printed horizontally and read from left to right. The two volumes of the *xu bian* — like the rest of the book — are covered in celestial blue paper flecked with silver and stitched together. They are held in the rare book collection of the National Library of China.

In addition to being the co-author of the Western music portion of *The True Meaning of Pitch Temperament*, Father Pedrini is the only one of all the missionary musicians in the Imperial Palace who was himself a composer. An undated copy of his compositions that originally came from the library of the Northern Cathedral, or Beitang,[48] is now in the collection of the National Library under the pseudonym Nepridi, an anagram of Pedrini's surname. They are hand-written in an oblong, hide-covered book of 76 pages entitled *Sonate a Violino Solo col Basso del Nepridi Opera terza*, or *Sonatas for solo violin with bass by Nepridi, opus 3*.[49] Because the sonatas are opus three, it seems there must have been an opus one and two that have been lost somewhere along the way, and some scholars also suspect that Father Pedrini wrote vocal music which has similarly been lost or mis-catalogued.[50]

In any case, the twelve sonatas are written in a style similar to Corelli, who was active in Rome at the same time Father Pedrini lived there. They are scored for violin solo with accompaniment by basso continuo, probably a harpsichord or similar keyboard instrument. The musician Jean-Christophe Frisch, who was involved in making a recording of Pedrini's music in the 1990s, explained that:

> It is no use looking for Chinese influences in Pedrini's sonatas. But it nevertheless becomes obvious when we play them that — either because of his isolation or because of his venturesome nature — Pedrini experimented with musical forms that were never heard in Europe. Some of the linking of chords, for example, would be considered as errors, and our first reaction was to correct them. On listening, however, they proved to be of interest, rather than in any way being disturbing. The tonal structure of some of the movements is also very unusual.[51]

---

48. The churches were Nantang and Dongtang, run by Portuguese Jesuits; Beitang, run by French Jesuits; and Xitang, run by the Missionaries of the Propaganda, or the Lazarists.

49. Father Pedrini's sonatas were recorded in the Forbidden City in 1997, and are available on a compact disc entitled *Baroque Concert at the Forbidden City*, released by Astree Records.

50. Frisch, J.C. (trans. Mary Pardoe). European Music in China, 17th and 18th centuries. In *Baroque Concert at the Forbidden City* (compact disc liner notes). Astree Records: 17.

Although there are no records of a performance of the sonatas either in the palace or the churches, it is nonetheless easy to picture Emperor Kangxi lounging on a velvet cushion as he enjoyed one or all of his favorite musician's compositions. Indeed, the Emperor's reputation for appreciating Western music was already such that the French Jesuit Joachim Bouvet (Bai Ji) had written to Louis XIV about it back in 1697. Emperor Kangxi liked Western instruments and theory so much, Father Bouvet wrote, that whenever he was not engaged in affairs of state, he studied and practiced.[52] Eighteen years later, in 1715, Fathers Pedrini and Ripa sent a similar letter back to Rome. Their missive — which was edited by Emperor Kangxi himself — reported that the Emperor thoroughly understood the roots of music theory and asked the Pope to send more missionaries who understood music theory, astronomy, painting, math and medicine.[53] When these new musical missionaries began to arrive in 1717, Emperor Kangxi was delighted. After hearing the Bohemian Father Charles Slaviczek (Yen Jiale) play on several instruments, he said that "for a long time he had been waiting for someone of such merit, who was at the same time a good mathematician and excellent musician." [54]

While it is certain that Emperor Kangxi had a long-held appreciation for both Chinese and Western music, it is somewhat harder to determine the actual extent of his musical accomplishments. In his memoirs — written after he left China for good — Father Ripa had this to say:

> The Emperor supposed himself to be an excellent musician, and a still better mathematician; but though he had a taste for the sciences and other acquirements in general, he knew nothing of music, and scarcely understood the first elements of mathematics. There was a cymbal or spinet in almost every apartment, but neither he nor his ladies could play upon them; sometimes indeed with one of his fingers he touched a note, which was enough, according to the extravagant flattery practised at the court of China, to throw the by-standers into ecstasies of admiration, as I myself have often witnessed.[55]

For good measure, Father Ripa added that he "was not a little surprised to find that Kangxi, who was really a man of enlarged understanding, believed all the exaggerated praises of his courtiers, and was childishly vain."[56]

Like his predecessor Father Pereira, Father Pedrini was obliged by circumstance to focus most of his energy on musical work inside the palace. But, music was an important element in attracting Chinese to Catholic churches and both priests made time to share their talents outside the palace. As Father Verbiest wrote:

---

51. Frisch: 17.

52. Feng: 236.

53. Tao: 98.

54. Pfister, L. (1932). *Notices Biographiques et Bibliographiques sur Les Jesuites de L'Ancienne Mission de Chine 1552-1773.* Shanghai: Imprimerie de la Mission Catholique: 655.

55. Ripa: 63.

56. *Ibid.*, 63-4. Ripa wrote his memoirs after becoming disillusioned with missionary efforts in China and returning to Naples, where he started a school for training Chinese priests.

We have built a carillon in one of the church towers and in the other we have had an organ set up, built with tin pipes, according to the rules of music. All may visit it, and I do not think it has its equal for grandeur in the whole of the Orient. These two works of art, which we owe to the skill and ingenuity of Father Pereira, a very able musician, are quite perfect. It is unbelievable how these two instruments draw the crowds to our church.[57]

Father Pedrini later built a new organ for the church, which he described in a letter home:

The organ has four registers, which is sufficient for any church in Peking, but it is much more beautiful than those of Europe, because all the pipes at the front are decorated with gold flowers; it is coated with black lacquer and it is portative... It is eight feet high."[58]

The chance to build more churches with more organs that would help entice Chinese to worship the Christian God seemed assured when Emperor Kangxi issued the Edict of Tolerance of Christianity in 1692. The edict expressly ordered tolerance of the foreign religion and apparently vindicated the Jesuits' unorthodox strategy of serving the Emperor in order to gain a solid foothold for their faith in China. Instead, however, the status of missionaries — and Chinese converts — was slowly undermined by the nagging debate over whether Chinese Christians could participate in the traditional rites to honor their ancestors and Confucius.

The controversy over the Chinese rites had started in the years following Father Ricci's death, when Dominican and Franciscan missionaries took exception to the policy of cultural accommodation that the great Jesuit and his superior Father Valignano had pioneered and ultimately complained to Rome about it. Their main argument was with the Jesuit decision to view Confucianism as a purely civil and political cult — they believed that the rites carried out by Chinese to honor their ancestors and Confucius were idolatrous. They also objected to two of the Chinese terms that Father Ricci had used to translate the word "God," an issue that sounds obscure nowadays but was of burning importance back then. Other Jesuit accommodations that upset them were the decision to exempt Chinese Catholics from fasting on holy days and even the fact that the Jesuits didn't preach that Confucius was in hell.

The Jesuits understandably found these criticisms hard to swallow. Most Dominicans and Franciscans could not even speak Chinese, let alone read it well enough to analyze the writings of Confucius as Ricci and other Jesuits had done. Their missionaries wore European dress and preached in the streets through interpreters of doubtful skill. To the Jesuits, it was obvious that fasting should not be forced upon Chinese converts — many of them lived on a subsistence diet and even those who ate well would be singled out if they fasted, making their lives unnecessarily difficult. As

---

57. Frisch: 16.
58. *Ibid.,* 17.

to Confucius being in hell, they simply replied that he had been a moral man and probably was not in hell!

The discussion of the Chinese rites issue started out as a private and civil discourse, but gradually devolved into an ugly, public disagreement. By 1700, it was the subject of such great debate in Paris that it precipitated a wave of popular interest in China. After much back and forthing, Pope Clement XI finally sided with the Dominicans against the Jesuits' liberal interpretation of the rites. He sent his legate De Tournon — with whom Father Pedrini was supposed to have travelled — to inform the missionaries and Emperor Kangxi that henceforward Chinese Christians would not be permitted to participate in ceremonies honoring Confucius or their ancestors.

The task of delivering this unwelcome message to Beijing was not an easy one and De Tournon was woefully unprepared for it. Rather than resolving the matter, he succeeded only in alienating most of the Jesuits and infuriating Emperor Kangxi, who ultimately had him deported to Macao and handed over to the Portuguese. Since Portugal viewed itself as father of the Catholic Church in the East, the Portuguese at Macao were also unhappy with the Pope's interference and they kept De Tournon under house arrest until he died of illness in 1710.

The Holy See tried again to impose its position in 1715 by issuing a decree reiterating its anti-accommodation stance and five years later sent a second legate to China to meet with the Emperor. Although Emperor Kangxi received the legate politely, he was growing increasingly weary of the bickering, which he correctly suspected had as much to do with national and even individual rivalries as it did with religion.

Determined that all missionaries in China should abide by his will, rather than the foreign Pope's, Emperor Kangxi declared that only missionaries who accepted Matteo Ricci's interpretation of the rites would be permitted in his country — to prove their loyalty, they were also required to sign a guarantee promising to stay in China for the rest of their lives. He did not see the Pope's 1715 decree until 1721, but when it was translated for him, his response was unequivocal:

> Reading this proclamation, I have concluded that Westerners are petty indeed. It is impossible to reason with them because they do not understand the larger issues as we understand them in China... To judge from this proclamation, their religion is no different from other small, bigoted sects of Buddhism or Taoism. I have never seen a document which contains so much nonsense. From now on, Westerners should not be allowed to preach in China, to avoid further trouble.[59]

Emperor Kangxi did not follow through on his threat to bar Westerners from preaching, but his displeasure was eagerly noted by anti-Christian officials throughout China, and the position of missionaries and Chinese converts in the provinces became increasingly insecure. The issue also frayed his relationship with Father Pedrini, who as a Lazarist took the Pope's side against the Jesuits.

59. Li, J.D., trans. (1969). *China in Transition, 1517-1911*. New York: Van Nostrand Reinhold Company: 22.

Pedrini's musical ability had made him something of a favorite with the Emperor, who sometimes sent him food from his own table and on one occasion presented him with a superb silk and ermine coat. Such favoritism naturally aroused jealousy in others, but seems to have inspired enough confidence in Father Pedrini that he openly made known his belief that missionaries in China were obligated to obey the Pope on the matter of the Chinese rites. The Jesuits who disagreed with the Pope and valued Emperor Kangxi's support of their position were naturally unhappy with Pedrini's stance, resulting in arguments and intrigue.

During the Chinese new year celebrations in February of 1720, Father Pedrini was seized in his apartments by bailiffs who tied his hands with a handkerchief and led him away. They took him straight to the palace where they forced him to kowtow in homage to the Emperor — the reason given was that all the Europeans had kowtowed that morning, except for Pedrini. Emperor Kangxi warmed to Father Pedrini again later, explaining that although he had punished him, he had done so in the manner that a father treats his son, without any publicity. However, when Father Pedrini maintained his stance on the rites by refusing to sign a report regarding the second papal envoy's visit, Emperor Kangxi again lost patience.[60] This time, Pedrini was beaten in the Emperor's presence and again imprisoned.

We do not know if Emperor Kangxi's love of music and admiration of Father Pedrini's talent would have once again triumphed over his need to be obeyed, because he caught cold while hunting in December of 1722 and died soon thereafter. The son he named to succeed him, known as Emperor Yongzheng, had been tutored by missionaries — including Father Pedrini — but had come of age during the rites controversy. Although he continued to employ a handful of missionaries at court, he did nothing to stop the persecution of Christians which had begun in the later years of his father's reign. Instead, in 1724 he signed an edict forbidding Chinese to become Christian and expelling all missionaries except those in his service. There were no Western music lessons during Emperor Yongzheng's reign, although he did release Father Pedrini from jail. However, Emperor Yongzheng died after only 13 years on the throne and was succeeded by his fourth son, who is known to history as Emperor Qianlong, a true heir to Emperor Kangxi in terms of intellect, curiosity, and competence.

EMPEROR QIANLONG'S MUSICAL PURSUITS

Emperor Qianlong, like his grandfather Kangxi, had an insatiable appetite for learning and seemingly limitless energy. He arose every day before dawn to begin his studies and kept numerous Jesuit and other Catholic missionaries in his service. His

---

60. The Chinese rites controversy was finally laid to rest in 1742, when the Papal Bull *Ex quo singulari* put an end to the policy of cultural adaptation which had enabled the Jesuits to so rapidly expand their mission in China. To prevent any efforts to controvert its spirit, all China-based Catholic missionaries were required to take an oath swearing to abide by it.

great fascination with mechanical devices and curiosities meant that every missionary at court had to learn to make things that would please him — chiming clocks, mechanical fountains, hydraulic machines, spun glass. One brother wrote that "they looked forward with dread to the day when the emperor would demand a 'robot' who should be able to talk."[61] But if Emperor Qianlong was intense in his passions, he also had a reputation for being mercurial. As the Bohemian Jesuit Jean Walter (Lu Zhongxian) complained, "The emperor's hobbies always change. Sometimes he likes music, sometimes he likes water fountains, sometimes he likes big building projects, and sometimes he likes to collect curiosities. We have to be there waiting for his call."[62]

In any case, Emperor Qianlong's interest in Western music seems to have begun on the 30th day of the tenth month of his sixth year on the throne (1741), when he sent an official out to learn if there were any foreigners in Beijing who knew about music, particularly about the differences between Chinese and Western music.[63] Three days later, the official reported back that there were three who understood music — Father Pedrini, Father Walter and Father Florian Bahr (Wei Jijin). Father Pedrini was already 71 years old and had been involved in the making of Emperor Kangxi's *The True Meaning of Pitch Temperament*, so he understood the most; he was also himself a composer and could play Chinese music on Western instruments. Regarding the basic difference between Chinese and Western music, the official explained, in rather simplified terms,

> The [Western] system is to use do re mi fa so la xi — the seven notes make a scale. The first three, the fifth, and the sixth are full tones; fa and xi are half tones. There are seven keys. So, it is similar to our ancient system of five tones [gong, shang, jiao, zhi, yu] plus two changing tones [bianzhi and biangong]. To be more precise, do is gong, fa is bianzhi, xi is biangong, and so on. So from this we know that the theory of music has no differences between China and the West.[64]

Judging from Emperor Qianlong's questions, he had not read *The True Meaning of Pitch Temperament* that his grandfather had commissioned and to which Father Pedrini had contributed the overview of Western music. Nonetheless, he decided to supplement the work with a fourth part — known as *hou bian* — devoted to music of the Qing Dynasty. When his supplement was finally printed in 1746, it proved to be as grand as all his other projects, filling 120 volumes and including descriptions and illustrations of all Chinese instruments, of the instruments used by Chinese minority peoples and even extensive discussions of Mongolian, Hui (Chinese Muslim), and Korean music.

---

61. Rowbotham, A.H. (1942). *Missionary and Mandarin: The Jesuits at the Court of China*. Berkeley and Los Angeles: University of California Press: 228-9.

62. Tao: 136. The original is Du Halde and Gobein. (1819). *Lettres edifiantes et curieuses, ecrites des missions etrangeres.* [Letters from the missions].

63. See introduction to *Luluzhengyi houbian*. [The True Meaning of Pitch Temperament]. The book is in the rare book collection of the National Library of China.

64. Tao: 135.

To his credit, Emperor Qianlong also built on his initial basic inquiries and seems to have developed a genuine appreciation for Western music. He employed Bahr and Walter as palace music teachers and ordered them to teach 18 palace eunuchs to sing in a chorus and play in a European music ensemble. Members of the ensemble played upon instruments that had been presented to the court by missionaries and diplomats; in Emperor Qianlong's reign alone, the palace had received 10 violins, 2 cellos, 1 bass, and 8 woodwind instruments, as well as a mandolin, guitar, xylophone and harpsichord.[65] The Fathers wrote a songbook for the ensemble to use and palace procurement records from the autumn of the 14th year of Qianlong's reign — 1750 on our calendar, the year Bach died — show that Western-style suits, shoes and even wigs were ordered for its members to wear when they performed![66] Presumably because this was a rather unusual request, the eunuch who placed the order — Hu Shijie — asked that a sketch of the entire outfit be provided for approval before the tailoring commenced.

The same year that the ensemble got underway, Emperor Qianlong requested that the French Jesuit Joseph-Marie Amiot (Qian Deming) be sent to join his staff of Western music teachers. Father Amiot was a talented flutist and harpsichord player who was passionate about both performance and teaching. He was also a scholar and his interest in Chinese music led him to write a "Dissertation on the Music of the Chinese both ancient and modern" which was published in Paris in 1779. The palace music staff was further augmented in 1768 when the French priest and violinist Jean-Joseph de Grammont joined as both music and math teacher.

With Western music soloists, chorus, and instrumental ensemble at court, Emperor Qianlong had potentially been exposed to much in the mainstream of Western music — except for opera. This omission was corrected — or so the story goes — in 1778 when a light comic opera called *La Cecchina*, or *The Good Daughter*, was performed in the palace.

La Cecchina, which premiered in Rome in 1760, is the work of the Italian composer Nicola Piccini. Piccini is largely forgotten today, except by music historians who tell the story of the time in the late 1770s when he unwittingly became the center of a feud in Paris as to whether Gluck or he was the better composer. The feud became so furious that intellectuals meeting for the first time would demand of one another, "Sir, are you a Gluckist or a Piccinist?"[67] But if history soon decided that Gluck was the superior composer, some of Piccini's operas, including *La Cecchina*, remained popular in Italy and the European capitals well into the 1800s.

Since the image of Emperor Qianlong being entertained by an Italian comic opera performed by eunuchs — China's own castrati — is a compelling one, this story is repeated in a variety of Chinese and Western sources.[68] The problem, however, is that

65. *Ibid.*, 139. The names given to these instruments by palace record keepers are inexact translations, so some educated guesswork is involved in determining what they were.
66. *Ibid.*, 138.
67. Blom, Eric (1958). *Stepchildren of Music*. London: G.T. Foulis & Company, Ltd: 65.

all these sources seem to trace back to an early biography of Piccini which tells the story of the opera performance without offering any details. One Western writer[69] states that the opera was directed by Father Walter and Father Bahr, but this is not possible since Father Bahr died before *La Cecchina* even premiered in Rome and Father Walter died in 1771, seven years before the alleged palace performance date.

However, true or not, this tale shows that Western music study and performance had become so much a part of court life that it is at least conceivable that the Emperor of China had sat down on a throne of cushions and listened to his eunuchs sing an opera that was all the rage in Rome.

The study and appreciation of Western music was also deepening outside the palace, in the churches run by Jesuits and other missionaries. Emperor Qianlong's reign was not an expansionary period for the Catholic Church in China; despite his respect for individual priests, he had inherited many of his father's anti-Catholic prejudices and did little to curtail the often violent anti-missionary activities of local officials. However, Beijing's churches were allowed to remain open and several Jesuits wrote letters home in which they described the musical activity that went on in them during Emperor Qianlong's reign.[70]

Father François Bourgeois, for example, explained that Chinese people enjoyed the Mass very much and that they sang and danced "to our beloved European instruments." [71] He described a Christmas Eve service at which 20 musicians played in a church that was "lit up like a white night for midnight mass." In another letter written to a woman in France in 1773, Father Cibot explained that his church had an all-Chinese "Congregation de la Musicque," or choir, that sang motets and cantiques. Only the most talented applicants were admitted into the group, which included three sons of officials but was mainly comprised of regular people who "have given up their free time to use music to worship God." The church also had a "petits chantres" made up of 10- to 12-year-old boys. A third letter from Father Michel Benoist — the Jesuit cartographer who created a magnificent map of the Chinese Empire for Emperor Qianlong — described the progress made by the choir at his church, particularly by an official's son named André, who had been a parishioner for 25 years and was so talented that he had been made a "préfet de la musique" responsible for rehearsing the choir before mass each week.

European music had come a long way in China since that first clavichord recital, back in 1601. It was performed in the palace and in the churches. It was studied by emperors, princes, and poor Christians alike. It was explained in the great music encyclopedia, *The True Meaning of Pitch Temperament*, more than fifty years before any similar analysis of Chinese music appeared in Europe. And yet, despite this

---

68. See, for example, Cramner-Byng, J.L., Ed. (1962). *An Embassy to China, Being the journal kept by Lord Macartney during his embassy to the Emperor Ch'ien-lung, 1793-1794*. London: Longmans: 365, note 23. Also, Tao: 140-1.

69. See Cramner-Byng: 365, note 23.

70. Tao: 145-8.

71. For stories and quotes in this paragraph, see Tao: 145-7. Original source is Gobien and du Halde.

considerable progress, it still remained largely an amusement for the princely classes and a religious accoutrement for China's 200,000 Catholic converts.[72] As the refined Father Amiot wrote of the Chinese, in an apparent fit of pique:

> Their organs of hearing are dead or dulled: I am judging by the small impression our finest Musical melodies make on them, and even our most tender and most poignant pieces, such as certain Adagios and certain movements by the greatest composers, both Italian and French, played by skilful musicians such as some of the German Jesuits who are at this court...[73]

"Dull" ears aside, there are several reasons for the apparently "small impression" made by European melodies up to this point. China's own music, as Father Amiot noted in his book on the subject, was an ancient art intimately connected with politics, morals, religion, social life, and even science — only considerable social and political change could lessen its role in society, thereby creating room for a more open consideration of the alien system of European music.

A change in missionary methods would also be needed. The Jesuit decision to focus so much effort on converting the top levels of the imperial bureaucracy meant that many of their musical resources were also concentrated in the palace. However, the gifts and the learning that went into the palace never came out of it. Clavichords and telescopes, European music theory and astronomical instruction — all were used to entertain the Emperor or strengthen his power, not to benefit the Chinese people. Even *The True Meaning of Pitch Temperament* never circulated outside a closed circle of palace familiars.

While European music did reach far more people through the churches, its spread was still limited by the strong anti-foreign and anti-Christian current that was never far below the surface in this era. A broader acceptance of the foreign religion — and of all things foreign — would be required for European music to spread beyond the handful of Christian converts.

Finally, there is the simple issue of musical taste, which would also have to evolve and expand in order for European music to grow deeper roots. For, as Father Amiot noted, Chinese composition and performance seemed:

> ...to follow a course that is exactly the opposite to the one followed in Europe. In our countries, for Example, a Composer applies himself first of all to the fundamental bass, and it is from this fundamental bass that he draws all the chords which are to serve to fill the other parts. Here, there is neither bass, nor tenor, nor treble, everything is unison, but that unison is varied according to the nature and capacity of each instrument, and the composer's skill, the beauty of a piece and the whole art of music lies in that variation. It would be useless to try and fight against national prejudice in this. It would be of no avail to endeavour to prove to the

---

72. Latourette, K.S. (1967). *A History of Christian Missions in China.* New York: Russell & Russell: 182. This figure is an estimate.

73. Amiot, J.M. (1754). On the Modern Music of the Chinese. In Picard, François (trans. Mary Pardoe). Chinese music and the missionaries. *Baroque Concert at the Forbidden City.* Astree Records: 25.

Chinese that they must find pleasure in something in which they really find none at all. As disciples of what is natural (so they claim), they would consider they were moving away from the rules of nature, if, in order to pleasantly titillate the ear, they presented it with a multiplicity of sounds that it finds wearisome. 'Why play several different things at the same time?' they ask. 'Why play them so fast? Is it to show off the lightness of your Mood and the nimbleness of your fingers? Or is it simply as a means of recreation for yourselves and, at the same time, to please those who listen to you? If it is the former that leads you to play in this manner, then you have achieved your aim, and we readily admit that you surpass us. But if it is simply as recreation for yourselves and to please us, we think you are taking the wrong course. Your concerts, especially if they are rather long, are violent Exercises for those who perform them and small tortures for those who listen. After all, it is inevitable that European ears are built differently to ours. You like things that are complicated; we are fond of things that are simple. In your Music, you often run until you are out of breath; in ours, we always walk at a serious and measured pace. Nothing tells one more about the genius of a nation than the music it appreciates."[74]

In fact, however, by the final years of Emperor Qianlong's reign and the end of the 18th century, the socio-political circumstances that inhibited the spread of Western music were on the cusp of change. The old era of musical transmission through missionary music teachers at court was also reaching its conclusion. Indeed, no new music teachers had arrived in years, partly because squabbling in Europe had led the Pope to abolish the Society of Jesus in 1773 and partly because the aging Qianlong was no longer studying Western music. China's view of itself and the world beyond was also about to be radically altered, in a long and painful process that can reasonably be traced to the summer of 1793, when yet another European sailed into Chinese waters bearing musical instruments and high ambitions.

But, though his ships carried two violins, a viola, a violincello, an oboe, a bassoon, two basset horns, a clarinet, a flute, and a fife,[75] Lord George Macartney was neither musician nor missionary, but diplomat. His trip had been funded by the British East India Company, which was running a trade deficit with China and wanted to expand its exports, and his goals were straightforward, if not simple: to sign a treaty of friendship and commerce between Britain and China, to establish formal diplomatic relations, and to improve the highly restrictive conditions under which British merchants were permitted to trade.

In keeping with protocol, Lord Macartney had brought plenty of gifts for Emperor Qianlong, including a planetarium, globes, clocks, and a pair of beautiful enamel watches set with diamonds. The musical instruments, however, were not intended for the Emperor but for the band of five German musicians and its leader, John Zapfal, who were included in Macartney's 95-man entourage. For, unlike the

---

74. *Ibid.*, 25.

75. Cramner-Byng: 364. The instruments were provided by Charles Burney, the first major English historian of music and author of a book called *History of Music*. In return for providing the instruments, Burney asked Macartney to learn what he could about Chinese music.

European missionaries who preceded him to China, Macartney's goal was not to entertain, enlighten or arouse the curiosity of the Son of Heaven with European instruments and music — it was to impress Emperor Qianlong and his officials with the dignity and power of Great Britain.

In support of this goal, Lord Macartney's little band played aboard ship when he hosted high-ranking mandarins at Western-style dinners, perhaps performing the music of such composers as Haydn and Mozart, who were then popular in Europe. It played in the procession of "gentlemen of the embassy," servants, and guards that accompanied him when he went ashore on Chinese soil. And it performed in the vast palace with eleven courtyards that was provided to him in Beijing. In the purpose of impressing, both band and instruments seem to have succeeded. Indeed, Macartney recorded in his journal that, while in Beijing.

> ... we were every day visited by numbers of Mandarins of the higher ranks, some engaged to it by the duty of their stations and employments, others allured by curiosity, and not a few by my band of music, which performed a very good concert in one of my apartments every evening. Among these visitors was the chief Mandarin of the Emperor's orchestra, who attended constantly and listened to the performance with all the airs of a virtuoso.[76]

The leader of the Emperor's orchestra was so intrigued by the band's wind instruments that Macartney offered to give them to him, but he politely declined. Instead,

> [he] sent for a couple of painters, who spread the floor with a few sheets of large paper, placed the clarinets, flutes, bassoons and French horns upon them, and then traced with their pencils the figures of the instruments, measuring all the apertures and noting the minutest particulars, and when this operation was completed they wrote down their remarks, and delivered them to their master. I was told that his intention is to have similar instruments made here by Chinese workmen, and to fit them to a scale of his own.[77]

The band's presence apparently created many similar opportunities for musical exchange and when the delegation returned to Europe, several of its members wrote about their impressions of Chinese music — which were generally unfavorable — and European music in China.

John Barrow, the delegation comptroller, noted that Chinese ensembles "have not the least notion of counterpoint, or playing in parts"[78] and commented that "the merit of a performance should seem to consist in the intenseness of the noise brought out of the different instruments."[79] But, despite his criticisms, Barrow also included the music for several popular Chinese tunes in his book. Johann Huttner, who served

76. *Ibid.*, 104.

77. *Ibid.*

78. Barrow, J. (1806). Travels in China. In, Harrison, F. (ed.) (1973). *Time, Place and Music. An anthology of ethnomusicological observation c. 1550 to c. 1800.* Amsterdam: Frist Knuf: 192.

79. *Ibid.*, 192-3.

as Greek tutor to the son of Lord Macartney's secretary, noted that "the Chinese almost always sing in falsetto which makes their vocal music more like bagpiping than singing, and cannot be pleasing to our ears. Many people compare Chinese singing to mewing of cats, and their numerous trills often remind the foreign listener of the bleating of a goat."[80]

However, Huttner — whom Macartney describes as "a good judge of music"[81] — was open-minded enough to distinguish among different styles of music and song, and spoke highly of an opera the delegation attended in Canton and of the "ravishing sounds" they heard when they were finally received by Emperor Qianlong. Like seemingly all the members of the embassy, he was also enthralled with the songs sung by northern Chinese boatmen as they synchronized the strokes of their oars. "I remember with the liveliest pleasure," he wrote,

> the evening when, sent by Lord Macartney, we entered for the first time in a small boat the estuary of the River Peiho, in the province of Chihli, and met hundreds of large and small boats, each one passing by us with the song *Highodee highau* as they put out from the harbour with the falling tide. The crowd on the boats, the measured movement of the many oarsmen and the repetition of this song by many hundreds of voices striking up on all sides — how full of liveliness, what a tumult! London, Liverpool, Venice and other ports seemed to me to have nothing like it.[82]

Naturally, members of the delegation were also sensitive to the impression that their German band made upon Chinese listeners. While all concur that the band aroused curiosity, there is disagreement as to whether the Chinese who heard it actually liked the music it played. It seems that Huttner, for one, very much wanted the Chinese to appreciate European music, but was too honest to claim that they did:

> What judgment the Chinese formed about the music that the embassy brought with it I could not determine with any certainty, since I have never made express enquiries about this. I certainly heard that the mandarins, when others asked them about it, gave as an answer: Chau, that is, good. But since our interpreter told me that they found no pleasure in our music, I am very much afraid that it was only through politeness that they declared their approval of a thing which is so strange to them. When we had music, I observed the expressions of high-ranking and of ordinary Chinese and Tartars, but I could never detect any sign of their having unmistakable pleasure in any of it. However, the particularly clever handling of our instruments, learnt by long practice, could not of course but excite their attention.[83]

---

80. Huttner, in *Time, Place and Music*: 186.

81. Staunton, in *Time, Place and Music*: 178.

82. Huttner, in *Time, Place and Music*: 191. Huttner transcribed the boatmen's song into staff notation and the delegation's surgeon, Dr. William Scott, wrote a song-poem for it in English. The London-based German composer Karl Kambra then incorporated both into a piece called "The Peyho Boatmen," which was published in the German magazine *Journal des Luxus und der Moden* in 1796, with an introduction by Huttner.

83. Huttner, in *Time, Place and Music*: 187.

In a meeting with Father Grammont, Huttner sought to better understand the general opinion of European music in China and the retired palace music teacher told him:

> Our slow songs please them most... they are enchanted with the silvery sounds of our pianofortes, harpsichord and flutes; but a third or a fifth, pleasant as they are to our ears, is to them a discord.[84]

While Huttner genuinely wanted to know how Chinese listeners felt about European music, Barrow managed to convince himself that the evident lack of appreciation for the band's music was all a massive subterfuge. In his words, the Chinese "affected to dislike the Embassador's [*sic*] band, which they pretended to say produced no music, but a confusion of noises."[85] However, the only evidence he could offer for the falseness of this "affected dislike" was the Chief Mandarin's demonstrated interest in the band's instruments.

If the band proved a vehicle for some interesting cultural exchanges, its main purpose was to support the delegation's diplomatic and commercial goals. So, when Lord Macartney and his entourage travelled to Emperor Qianlong's mountain palace in Chengde, where the formal audience was to be held, the musicians stopped just outside the town and changed into sumptuous green and gold livery. Thus impressively attired, they marched ahead of the rest of the delegation and played "God Save the King" to announce Lord Macartney's arrival in Chengde. And finally, on September 14, the band once again led the way on the three mile, pre-dawn walk to the Imperial Audience tent.

The audience went well, or so it seemed at the time to Lord Macartney. Emperor Qianlong accepted his gifts and reciprocated with some lanterns, silks, porcelains and tea for King George. He acted graciously toward the delegation, treating its members to a banquet at which the service was so exacting that Lord Macartney compared it to the "celebration of a religious mystery."[86]

However, gracious as he was, Emperor Qianlong acquiesced to none of Lord Macartney's proposals. Instead he sent him home with a letter for King George in which he praised the British monarch for his sincerity and earnestness in inclining himself "towards civilization," but informed him that:

> ...we have never valued ingenious articles, nor do we have slightest need of your country's manufactures. Therefore, O King, as regards your request to send someone to remain at the capital, while it is not in harmony with the regulations of the Celestial Empire we also feel very much that it is of no advantage to your country. Hence we have issued these detailed instructions and have commanded your tribute envoys to return safely home. You, O King, should simply act in conformity with our wishes by strengthening your loyalty and swearing perpetual obedience so as to ensure that your country may share the blessings of peace.[87]

---

84. *Ibid.*, 185.
85. Barrow, in *Time, Place and Music*: 194.
86. Cramner-Byng: 123.

This is not the response for which the British monarchy had expended its prestige and the East India Company the considerable sum of 78,000 pounds,[88] and this rebuff would not soon be forgotten. Since Emperor Qianlong could not fathom a world in which his Celestial Empire operated as an equal among other nations and Britain could not accept a world in which its right to "free" trade on advantageous terms was not recognized, the world view of one nation or the other would have to give —— and thus the failure of the Macartney embassy did much to set the scene for the Opium War that would occur less than half a century later, beginning in 1839. The Opium War is considered by many scholars to mark China's entry into the modern era, and it is also presages the start of a new era in the transmission of Western music in China.

BEYOND THE PALACE: WESTERN MUSIC AFTER THE OPIUM WARS

Missionaries remained the major conduit for bringing Western music to China in the years that followed China's Opium War defeat, but the ways in which they spread it changed dramatically. Emperor Qianlong's successors did not share his or his grandfather's passion for music or for learning from missionaries, so there were no more opportunities to teach music in the palace. Indeed, by the 19th century emperors, mandarins and literati widely viewed Christianity as a subversive religion bent on undermining the entire Confucian basis of Chinese society, a point of view that had much to do with the final resolution of the Chinese rites controversy. As a group, missionaries were increasingly viewed with suspicion and the periodic persecutions against them increased.

But if the missionaries were unwelcome by China's elite, this did not stop them from coming. The first Protestant missionaries arrived in 1805 and the Jesuits returned to China after their re-establishment as a Society in 1814. In this new era, Catholics and Protestants alike largely ignored the Confucian elite and concentrated their efforts at the grassroots, often working among the poor and disenfranchised; even the Jesuits based their new headquarters in Shanghai, rather than Beijing. As missionaries spread across the country, the number of Chinese exposed to European music — rich and poor, Christian and non-Christian — grew rapidly.

At first, the churches were the primary source of musical dissemination. Organ music and choral singing remained important parts of Catholic services and congregational singing became a key part of Protestant services. Hymns were translated into Chinese so rapidly that by 1877 there were 63 different hymn books in circulation.[89] These hymnals sometimes spread in ways that the missionaries who brought them could hardly have imagined. Indeed, in a fascinating — but tragic —

87. *Ibid.*, 340.
88. This figure comes from Cramner-Byng: 35.
89. Jones, A.F. (2001). *Yellow Music: Media Culture and Colonial Modernity in the Chinese Jazz Age.* Durham and London: Duke University Press: 31.

historical footnote, the tune to the Protestant hymn *Old Hundred* was borrowed for the state song of the Kingdom of Heavenly Peace, which was based in Nanjing from 1853-64. The kingdom's founder was a rebel, named Hong Xiuquan, who learned about Christianity through a missionary tract, studied the Bible with an American Baptist for several months, and then became convinced that he was the younger brother of Jesus Christ. The anti-Manchu, pseudo-Christian, utopian rebellion that Hong launched left millions dead and carved a huge swathe of devastation across southern China

After 1860, when China lost a second Opium War — this one to Britain and France — the rights of foreigners in China were vastly expanded. Granted greater freedom of movement and given assurances regarding the legality of Christianity, missionaries came in ever larger numbers. Increasingly, education became an important component of their work, and a key vehicle for the spread of Western music.

Missionary schools were at first widely considered to provide an education of last resort; as the missionary-educated violinist Tan Shuzhen explained it, "poor people were Christians" and it was poor people who went to missionary schools. Families with financial means would send their children to schools that would prepare them for the Confucian civil service exams which were the all-important entrée to a career as an official. But as recognition of the importance of Western learning began to spread, this attitude changed. After the Confucian exams were first radically altered, and then abolished outright in 1905, missionary schools became even more popular.

So, while there were roughly 17,000 students at all Protestant mission schools in 1899, by 1915 this number had grown to 169,707.[90] The curriculum and quality of these schools varied greatly, but for the most part they offered a standard Western education in English. Singing was widely used for devotional and educational purposes in primary schools, often accompanied by piano or harmonium. Every missionary-run university — and many secondary schools — had a choir and a glee club. The choirs at Yenching University in Beijing and at the all-women Jinling University in Nanjing were particularly good, and became famous among Christian schools.

Music was also taught as a subject in many secondary schools and colleges. Chinese students studied the lives of the great classical European composers and, when possible, listened to their music. Many also learned how to play Western musical instruments, especially piano and violin. As early as 1849, a Chinese priest conducted the student orchestra at Shanghai's Xuhui School in a performance of a Haydn symphony. Although the goal of missionary schools was to produce good Christians, not good musicians, the musical education that they provided was so

---

90. Varg, P.A. (1958) *Missionaries, Chinese and Diplomats: The American Protestant Missionary Movement in China, 1890-1952*. Princeton: Princeton University Press: 90.

thorough that an overwhelming majority of China's early generations of classical musicians would be the product of missionary education.

The post-Opium War era also marks the true start of the spread of Western music through secular channels, primarily bands. The first band founded in China was, of course, the all-foreign Shanghai Municipal Band. But, an all-Chinese band was formed up north just a few years later by Robert Hart, the legendary Briton who served as Inspector-General of the Imperial Chinese Customs from 1863 until 1908.

Mr. Hart, who was himself an amateur violinist, was so devoted to his band that in September of 1889, he wrote to a friend that "My Peking Band (all Pekingese, 16 to 19 years old, and fourteen of them) is doing very well, and it is about the only thing I am interested in apart from work."[91] Shortly after writing this letter, he added string players to the ensemble and in 1895 he hired a Portuguese bandmaster named E.E. Encarnacao to teach and conduct.

If the band lent dignity to Mr. Hart's office by playing military-style marches at official Customs functions, it also provided entertainment at the many lavish soirees he hosted at his downtown home, which was shaped like an "H" after his own initial. There, in the beautiful Chinese garden, crowds would dance to such Hart favorites as *Nuit d'Amour, When the Lights Are Low, Gnomes Polka,* and *American Barn Dance.*[92] The band was evidently a major draw for Chinese officials who were invited to these parties, since Mr. Hart wrote that the mandarins attended just "to get a sight of the two curios of Peking, the I.G. and his queer musicians."[93]

The example of the two bands in Shanghai and Beijing and a growing understanding of the role that music played in motivating, disciplining and coordinating troupes in Western armies led several Chinese to call for a reform of China's own military music. The great reform-minded intellectual Liang Qichao, for example, argued that Chinese music had a "lethargic"[94] quality and that this was partly to blame for China's weak military spirit. Believing that Western music was more powerful than Chinese and would help to motivate and stimulate Chinese soldiers, he called for military reforms that would include Western music. Two of China's most powerful generals, Zhang Zhidong and Yuan Shikai, were of the same opinion and they proceeded to put their beliefs into practice.

Zhang Zhidong was the governor-general of Hunan and Hubei provinces who coined the highly influential formulation, "Chinese learning for the essence, Western

---

91. Fairbank, J.K., Bruner, K.F., Matheson, E.M. (eds.) (1975). *The I.G. in Peking, Letters of Robert Hart, Chinese Maritime Customs 1868-1907.* Cambridge: Harvard University Press: 761.

92. Seagrave, S. (1992). *Dragon Lady: the life and legend of the last empress of China.* New York: Knopf: 4.

93. Seagrave: 4.

94. Witke, R. (1977). *Comrade Chiang Ch'ing* [Jiang Qing]. Boston, Toronto: Little, Brown and Company: 387.

Liang's view was shared by Huttner of the Macartney embassy, who wrote that "the military music of the Chinese is extremely poor, without beat, without tune and without the slightest expressiveness. Shawms and horns go back and forth over the same five or six notes, without the smallest variation, even when they are blown for an hour at a time; occasionally they add to these instruments a kind of cornett, which truly makes a sound like the howling of a wolf."

learning for the application," to express the idea that modernization did not have to exclude Confucianism, and vice versa. In 1897, he formed a band for his army and hired a German to train its fifteen members in music and marching. When General Zhang's troops staged a military parade in Shanghai on May Day of 1897, the band gave a public performance.[95]

Yuan Shikai was a career military man who was given the job of training officers for the modernized military that the Qing Dynasty set out to establish after its 1895 defeat in a war with Japan. He was a loyal follower of Empress Dowager Cixi, and was probably involved in her overthrow of Emperor Guangxu in 1898, after the young sovereign attempted to implement far-reaching reforms in government and education. However, General Yuan was by no means a reactionary and he himself implemented those reforms useful for his work, including the Western military band. His band was established in 1898 and, like Zhang Zhidong's, was trained by a German advisor. In 1903, when he was governor-general of Hebei province, General Yuan organized three military band training camps in Tianjin, each of which graduated 80 people. A Chinese officer who had studied military music in Germany also ran a special session for 50 Manchu Bannermen from the Imperial Guard.

By the turn of the century, Western-style bands were already an accepted enough part of China's changing political-military culture that they sometimes played for Empress Dowager Cixi. Indeed, an American artist named Catherine Carl, who had been commissioned to paint the Empress Dowager's portrait, saw both Robert Hart and Yuan Shikai's ensembles perform in a sort of friendly battle-of-the-bands at the Summer Palace. The occasion was a performance by a European circus, in a turnip field that had been harvested just for the occasion, with the Empress Dowager herself pulling up the first turnip. Ms. Carl described the scene:

> About two hundred officials had been invited to see the circus, and, contrary to the usual custom, there was no screen between them and the Imperial party. On the right were two bands of foreign music, or rather of Chinese musicians who played foreign music on European instruments. These were the bands of Yuan-Shih-Kai, Viceroy of Tientsin, and of Sir Robert Hart, the Inspector-General of Imperial Customs. Sir Robert's band was formed about eighteen years since, when, as music is his hobby, he decided to try to have some Chinese taught European music on European instruments. He has now a well-equipped band of twenty trained Chinese musicians under a competent European conductor. They play on both brass and stringed instruments. His efforts have been so successful that his example has lately been followed by several high Chinese Officials, first among whom was Yuan-Shih-Kai. The latter's band is military, with fifty musicians, who play only on brass instruments. The two bands played alternately during the intervals of the performance.[96]

---

95. For a brief overview of Chinese military bands, see Feng: 265-6.
96. Carl, K. A. (1986). *With the Dowager Empress of China*. London and New York: KPI: 182.

The Empress Dowager invited musicians into the palace to play Western instruments on several other occasions, including one related by Guan Yin, a bassoon player who joined the Shanghai Symphony in 1948. Mr. Guan tells the story of his father's friend, a cellist named Li Bianchen, who performed at the palace. When the Empress Dowager saw the cello for the first time she exclaimed, "What's that?! It looks like a bedbug! Its body is so big and its head so small."

Mr. Li knelt down respectfully, held the cello above his head with both hands and answered simply, "This is chai-lou."

In 1909, a 20-person military band was formed from among the ranks of the palace guard that protected the Forbidden City, although it was limited in both repertoire and technique.[97] Since there were no Chinese songs for Western-style bands, it played mainly European tunes, like *Auld Lang Syne*, *Home Sweet Home*, and *Old Black Joe*, as well as some pieces imported from Japan. The band had little chance to improve since the dynasty was overthrown just two years later, but military bands continued to thrive and by the end of the decade there were fifteen of them around the country, with six of these based in Shanghai.[98]

By the early 20th century, the Western-style band was an institution with enough recognition and prestige to become highly sought after as a part of funeral corteges in Shanghai and other cities. Music was a traditional part of a Chinese funeral procession and the deceased was given extra status if his send-off included one — or two, or three — marching brass bands. Even the Shanghai Public Band was hired out for such occasions, a fact which upset the foreign musicians who considered it "detrimental to the prestige" of their band to march in a cortege.[99] In the spring of 1919, the pre-Paci Conductor-in-Charge asked that the band be relieved of this obligation but the Municipal Council's Town Band Committee rejected his request on financial grounds, since "the relatives of influential Chinese will pay almost anything to get the municipal Band for such occasions."[100]

If the adoption of the Western-style brass band by Chinese for their own purposes is an important milestone in the indigenization of Western music in China, a second turning point is the start of the "school song" movement. This aptly-named movement began in the early 20th century, when large numbers of Chinese students began going to Japan to study. Perverse though it may sound, Japan's easy victory over China in the 1895 war had impressed many in China, who rightly figured that there was much to be learned from the Asian neighbor to whom their nation had long

---

97. Feng: 266.

98. See Zhuang Yongping (2002). Yinyuede Bainian Huixiang [Looking Back at a Century of Music]. In *Shanghai Bainian Wenhuashi* [Shanghai Cultural History of the 20th Century]. Shanghai: Shanghai Kexuejishu Wenxian Chubanshe: 745.

99. See Bickers, Robert. (2001). The Greatest Cultural Asset East of Suez: The History and Politics of the Shanghai Municipal Orchestra and Public Band, 1881-1946. In, Chi-hsiung Chang (chief ed.), *Ershi shiji de Zhongguo yu shijie* [China and the world in the twentieth century] Taibei: Institute of History, Academia Sinica, Vol. 2: 850-1.

100. Bickers: 851.

condescended. One of the many things these students observed in Japan was the important role that song played in its schools.

School song in Japan dated back to the 1870s, when the Ministry of Education opened a committee for the study of Western music under the direction of Isawa Shuji. Isawa was an educator with an interest in music who had been sent to the US by the Meiji government to study teacher training in Boston. While there, he had met Luther Whiting Mason, the renowned music educator and author of the National Music Course, a graded music textbook series which was then in use throughout the US. So, when the Ministry of Education decided to undertake a reform of music in Japan's schools, Isawa invited Mason to come to Japan and serve as a special advisor. Together, they helped to develop the first Japanese music textbook series, which included dozens of 19th-century European and American hymns and folk songs that were stripped of their lyrics and set to Japanese texts.

These school songs became a regular part of elementary education throughout Japan, and many Chinese students and intellectuals were impressed by the sight of Japanese children singing Japanese poetry and morality lessons to Western melodies. Struck by the usefulness of song as a tool for imparting such things as proper moral behavior and nationalistic ideals, Liang Qichao and several reform-minded students founded a Music Research Society in Tokyo. Upon returning to China, several of its members informally launched a school song movement of their own. This was done largely by borrowing Japanese school songs — most of which were themselves borrowed from the West — and setting them to new lyrics. To make the songs easier to learn, the school-songers also adopted a simple system of musical notation that they had seen used in Japan. Known in China as *jianpu* — or simple notation — the system uses numbers 1-7 instead of notes and is actually European in origin. It was created back in the 16th century as a means of popularizing music and later was improved upon by the 18th century French philosopher and musician, Jean-Jacques Rousseau. European missionaries introduced simple notation to both China and Japan, but it was the school-songers who popularized its use.

Three of the earliest school-songers were Zeng Zhimin, Shen Xingong and Li Shutong, all of whom studied in Japan and returned to China to publish collections of school songs in the first years of the 20th century.[101] Zeng is particularly interesting, since he published the first serious article about school songs in 1903 and was the first person to introduce Western music terminology to China in a systematic manner. He also started a summer music lecture series about Western music and instruments in 1907, and in 1908 founded a Poor Children's School in Shanghai. The school had a music department and an orchestra of 40 children, with Zeng as conductor.[102]

---

101. See Tao: 224. Zeng's collection was published in 1903, Shen's in 1904 and Li's in 1906. For an English language discussion of the school song movement that includes mention of its early proponents, see Gild, G. (1998). Early 20th-century "reforms" in Chinese music. *Chime*, Spring/Autumn: 116-123. Also see Jones: 33-35.

102. See Tao: 228 and Zhuang: 745. Some call this the first orchestra organized by Chinese, although this is something of a stretch since it was not professional and was never performed in public.

With their new songs, lyrics and musical notation system in hand, the school-songers began their push to have school songs integrated into the primary education curriculum. As it happened, the timing for their initiative was perfect since the Qing Dynasty government — in one of its many belated attempts at reform — had introduced a series of education reforms in 1904 and happily adopted the concept of school song. As a part of the reform effort, many Japanese educators were invited to come to China to manage schools or to work as advisers to large school districts and they helped to further spread the practice of school song. So, with the government on board and reform-minded intellectuals equally enamored of the idea, it was not long before Chinese school children were singing Chinese lyrics to Western tunes, in imitation of their Japanese counterparts.

Through school songs, untold millions of children — and their parents, and friends, and neighbors — gained a basic familiarity with Western music. Although ordinary Chinese had already had access to Western music by way of churches, military parades and funeral processions, the size and influence of the school song movement had no precedent. While most students just sang their songs and went on with their lives, some were motivated to form choral groups, to learn instruments, or to study more about Western music. This trend accelerated when the May 4th era started in 1919 and ever greater numbers of youth who were eager to learn from the West also became motivated to listen to Western music, play Western instruments, and even to explore ways that both could be adopted to China's own culture.

Had the dispirited Father Amiot seen the changes — in society and government, in missionary methods, in attitudes towards thing foreign — and the impact this had on the general appreciation of European music, he would have marveled. If, as his Chinese friends had told him, nothing tells one more about the genius of a nation than the music it appreciates, then one thing was certain: the genius of the Chinese nation was changing.

CHAPTER 3. SOWING AND REAPING

A CHINESE VIOLINIST JOINS THE ALL-FOREIGN ORCHESTRA

One Monday morning in March of 1927, Maestro Paci was in his office as usual, collecting the scores for the music he would be conducting that week. The concert for which he was preparing was a special one, an all-Beethoven performance to mark the 100th anniversary of the great composer's death. The program included the Shanghai Municipal Orchestra's first performance of Beethoven's *Ninth Symphony* and Paci had just sat down and begun to study it when there was a knock at the door.

"Come in," he called, without looking up from his score.

The door creaked open.

"Maestro?" the visitor queried politely.

Hearing himself so addressed, Paci looked up and saw a slim, bespectacled young Chinese man dressed neatly in a Western suit and tie standing in the doorway. He was undoubtedly surprised — Chinese people did not normally come to his office at this time of day, except for the cleaning staff and Old Jiang, the man responsible for setting out and collecting the parts for each rehearsal and concert. However, since the young man was so well attired and knew enough to address him by his proper title, Paci put down his pencil and waited to hear what he had to say.

Speaking in quiet but confident English (that was better than Paci's own), the young man introduced himself as Tan Shuzhen — the same Tan Shuzhen who had studied violin in Beijing, moved to Shanghai to find a teacher, and quickly become a regular in the audience at SMO concerts.[1]

Mr. Tan got straight to the point: he knew that the SMO was short a violin player. He himself was a violinist, and he wanted to play in the orchestra.

Maestro Paci was silent for a moment as he digested the request — perhaps he was thinking that he had only managed to get the Municipal Council to allow Chinese to attend SMO concerts two years ago and now here was a Chinese musician wanting to play in the all-foreign orchestra. Certainly there would be people who would object — there were always some Ratepayers who objected to anything he did, and letting a young Chinese musician play on stage with the Europeans and Filipinos would be sure to raise some hackles. But, it was true that the orchestra was missing a violinist — the Dutchman Franz Hirst had gone home on the furlough granted European musicians every five years, and would be gone for the rest of the season. And, what did it really matter if the musician was Dutch or Chinese — a violinist was a violinist. The SMO was his orchestra and it was his responsibility to hire musicians, not that of the Ratepayers or the Municipal Council.

Without betraying the least surprise, Paci asked Mr. Tan a few questions about how long he had been playing and who had taught him. Then he looked at him and said simply:

"Come tomorrow."

That was all Mr. Tan needed to hear.

He thanked Maestro Paci and then left the office and walked back downstairs and outside. His steps were light, even as he picked his way through the detritus of the market that surrounded the Fuzhou Road rehearsal hall. He had vowed to dedicate his life to the violin and in the past two years he had done everything he could to this end. He had moved to Shanghai in search of a teacher, become a faithful regular at SMO concerts and rehearsals, and started teaching violin at two schools, the New China Arts University and the attached preparatory school at Jiaotong University. While all this was well and good, the problem was his own lessons — he simply was not making as much progress as he had hoped. Indeed, his first instructor had quickly told him there was nothing more he could teach him and his most recent teacher had just left Shanghai.

Time that could be spent learning violin was too precious too waste, so when he had learned that the SMO was short a violinist, he had decided at once upon his rather daring plan. Playing in the orchestra would not be the same as studying to be a soloist, but Maestro Paci was a great musician and performing under him would give Mr. Tan important — and unique — experience. Of course, he'd had no idea how the temperamental maestro would respond to his request, but now — with those two words, "Come tomorrow" — the pieces of his plan seemed to be falling into place.

The next morning, Mr. Tan left his room and headed over to the rehearsal hall.

---

1. Mr. Tan's description of joining the orchestra is based on many conversations held with him in his home in Shanghai between October 1999 and July 2002. Most of the conversations were with Sheila Melvin, although Jindong Cai joined in several times in 2001 and 2002. All quotes and anecdotes from Tan Shuzhen in this book are drawn from Sheila Melvin's notes of these conversations, except where otherwise stated.

"I knew when rehearsal started and got there early," he remembered. "I didn't know where to sit, so I waited for Paci to get up on the stage. Then he saw me and said: 'Second violin, inside seat.'"

With some apprehension, Mr. Tan took the seat indicated.

"There was a man from the Philippines sitting next to me — Mr. Sato. He played very beautifully. I told him I was new, and he said, 'Not important. Don't worry about it.'"

Then the rehearsal started.

"The music was Beethoven's *Fifth* — the sound was so big! Da da da DA! I'd never heard it so loud! It was just like a concert — we played all through without stops. Mr. Sato was very good and when it was over, Paci pointed at me and asked him, 'How is he?' Mr. Sato said, 'He's alright.' And Paci said, 'Come tomorrow.'"

The rehearsal had been an audition, and Mr. Tan had passed it. Mr. Sato told him to take home the next day's music to study and the next morning Mr. Tan was at rehearsal again, struggling to get through Beethoven's *Ninth* — which he had never even heard. Though Mr. Tan had not been nervous about asking Paci if he could play, or about joining the rehearsals, he was less sanguine about the concert itself.

"The first performance, I was nervous. I didn't want to look at anyone."

However, he not only made it through his first orchestra concert, but acquitted himself well enough that, with little ado, he unofficially became the first ever Chinese member of the Shanghai Municipal Orchestra. The city's major Chinese-language newspaper, *Shen Bao*, reported on it, and word of his ground-breaking appearance quickly spread. Soon, more Chinese faces appeared in the audience, most of them young men and women like Mr. Tan himself.

"Nobody had ever seen a Chinese in the orchestra, so many people came to see me."

Life as a member of the orchestra — even an unofficial member — was challenging and exciting.

"It was very exciting during Paci's rehearsals, never boring. And, he lost his temper every time. He threw so many batons in one rehearsal!"

Mr. Tan smiled as he recalled Paci's outbursts.

"Once the trombone played a wrong note — Paci threw his baton at him. He was a big Russian and he just put his trombone down slowly, got up, picked his chair up over his head and walked over to Paci. The concertmaster stopped him, and Paci said, 'Be careful next time.'"

Another time, the subject of Paci's fury was a concertmaster filling in for the regular concertmaster, Mr. Foa.

"Concertmasters don't like to be criticized — it's a face thing. One time Paci criticized the concertmaster and he slapped him. After that, the concertmaster never played again. Paci wouldn't dare hit back — he was too short, and the Russians were all big. He used to stand on his platform whenever he yelled at anybody!"

Mr. Tan's smile turned to seriousness.

"But, nobody hated Paci. He had such great ability — he brought the orchestra together. And, he only ridiculed you when you played wrong. Paci understood."

To release some of the tension that came with playing for Maestro Paci, the musicians sometimes played ping-pong together before rehearsal and now and then would go out to eat together at an Italian restaurant called Bianchi's. A group of them also liked to hang out on the street outside a White Russian restaurant and coffee bar not far from the Canidrome called Kafka's — they didn't often go inside Kafka's, however, because then they would have had to spend money.

"It was very interesting — there were musicians from all over the world. Philippines, Germany, Italy, England, Holland, Russia. Relations among the musicians were all good — I never saw any problems."

Mr. Tan became friendly with Arrigo Foa, the concertmaster whom Paci had brought back from Milan. He used to visit Foa at his garden home, often stopping to chat and trade novels with Foa's wife. Mr. Foa would also stop by Mr. Tan's room to have dinner, or to see if he could go out. A 1929 photograph shows them together, two young violinists in formal dress and pomaded hair, staring intently into the camera.

Mr. Foa had plenty of time for going out, because he never seemed to practice — a fact which amazed the diligent Mr. Tan.

"One day I went to him and he was looking at the music. He was going to play solo, St. Saëns. I said, 'Don't you ever practice?' He said, 'No, that's a bad habit.' He played beautifully and he never practiced! But, he wasn't a good conductor — he was too lazy."

Outside of rehearsal time, Mr. Tan continued his busy schedule of lessons and life. When he wasn't practicing, playing, or teaching, he strolled in Hongkou Park, prowled used bookstores for old copies of *The New Yorker*, *Harper's* and *Punch* and devoured any books he could find about music and art.

"I ran around everywhere."

When the season drew to a close in May, Mr. Tan still hadn't received any payment for his playing. He wasn't worried about this, but he was the only Chinese in the orchestra and Old Jiang — the Chinese worker who took care of the music — was concerned on his behalf.

"Old Jiang told me to ask Paci for my salary. I was embarrassed, but he said, 'Ask, or he'll gamble it all away!' So, I asked if I was to be paid and Paci said, 'Of course not! This is a chance for you to study.'"

Mr. Tan laughed at the memory.

"My goal was to study, so I didn't care. My family gave me money, so it didn't matter!"

XIAO YOUMEI AND HIS MUSICAL MISSION

Tan Shuzhen had first found it necessary to move to Shanghai in search of a violin teacher and then to join the SMO as a means of studying because China as yet had no real system of formal music education. Students of Chinese instruments generally found an old master willing to take them on as disciples and students of Western instruments were largely obliged to do the same. Naturally, this was a far more difficult undertaking for students of Western instruments, since there were few teachers — especially at an advanced level — and even the instruments themselves were hard to come by.

While there were many musicians, aspiring musicians, and modern-minded intellectuals who regretted the lack of a formal system of music education, there was only one who planned to dedicate his life to creating one: the German-educated intellectual Xiao Youmei.

A native of the southern province of Guangdong, Xiao had spent much of his childhood in the Portuguese colony of Macao, where he grew up in a stimulating and international environment. His father was a respected Confucian scholar and through him the young Xiao met an assortment of interesting and important people. One family friend and neighbor was a Portuguese minister who introduced Xiao to Western classical music and another was the revolutionary leader Sun Yat-sen, who introduced him to nationalism and politics.

Xiao Youmei was drawn to both music and nationalist politics, but his love of music proved the greater and when it came time for university, he chose to study piano and education in Tokyo. As it happened, however, politics caught up with him in the person of Sun Yat-sen himself. Mr. Sun had gone to Japan to escape the secret police sent after him by the Qing government and Mr. Xiao offered shelter to the great revolutionary, who lived with him for more than a month.

Xiao returned to China in 1909 and just two years later Sun Yat-sen's revolution succeeded in overthrowing the Qing Dynasty and permanently ending the imperial system that had held China together for more than two thousand years. When the Republic of China was founded on October 10, 1911, Sun was made provisional president. He offered the young friend who had sheltered him in Japan a position as a secretary in his presidential office and Mr. Xiao accepted, but did not forget his desire to continue with his music studies. The chance to pursue his dream came sooner than he expected, because the self-effacing President Sun relinquished his position to Yuan Shikai after little more than a month. When the outgoing president learned that Mr. Xiao's goal was to study music in Europe, he helped him to get a government scholarship.

Thus, in 1912, Mr. Xiao left for Germany and enrolled in the Leipzig Music Academy, where he studied piano and composition, and wrote a dissertation on pre-17th-century traditional Chinese music ensembles. He graduated with a doctorate and returned to China in 1921, greatly influenced by his experience in Europe. Although the May 4th Movement had begun while he was away, he was very much a member of the May 4th generation of intellectuals who wanted to re-evaluate Chinese traditions and introduce Western ideas and practices in order to create a new China. Where other intellectuals concentrated on such things as reforming literature by replacing classical Chinese with the vernacular, introducing equal rights for women, or studying the philosophy of thinkers like Bertrand Russell, John Dewey and Rabindranath Tagore, Mr. Xiao focused on music education.

Looking around him with a critical eye, he made three major observations about music and music education in China.[2] First, he determined that there was no viable system of national music education because music teaching had for so long been based on a master-student relationship. Since the masters themselves often had no formal training and each had his own philosophy of teaching and playing, this presented a barrier to the widespread propagation and standardization of music education. Second, he complained that Chinese music was backward because it did not have keyboard instruments or staff notation. Failing to invent either keyboard instruments or standard notation was bad enough, but China's past music masters were so conservative that they had even neglected to adopt these superior technologies and systems when they were introduced from the West. Finally, he bewailed the disappearance of much old music and blamed its loss on both the lack of standard notation and the system of teaching; since musicians learned by listening to music rather than reading it, much music died with its performers. Music that did survive was played differently by different performers, so it was impossible to know which version — if any — was authentic.

Mr. Xiao considered it vitally important to China's future that its music should be reformed — and for reasons that went well beyond the musical.

"Music is a true international language," he wrote. "When we hear a foreign language that we have never studied, it is necessary to ask someone to interpret, but when we play music from another country, we can understand its quality without any interpretation. So music belongs to the world and is the best way to connect human feelings."[3]

In addition to linking China with the world, he believed that music could help to improve the Chinese people themselves.

"Nowadays, many of our citizens are drowning in bad habits. If we could have at least one public concert every week, we could help to change some of these bad habits. If a few people in a family love music, you don't have to worry about finding gamblers in that family — if a society has more groups of people who love music, then these bad habits will naturally be reduced."[4]

Mr. Xiao's gold standard of music was Western music, which he considered to be almost like an absolute truth. But this did not mean that he wanted to abandon Chinese music, the way some intellectuals wanted to abandon their nation's literature, philosophy and even its system of writing. Instead, he wished to reform and revitalize it by creating a new form of "national music." National music would combine Chinese

---

2. For an account of Xiao Youmei's thinking, see Ming Yan (2002). *Ershishiji Zhongguo Yinyue Piping Daolun* [A Guide to 20th-Century Music Criticism in China]. Beijing: Renmin Yinyue Chubanshe: 59.

3. Xiao Youmei (1990). Guanyu guomin yinyuehuide tanhua. In Chen Lingqun, Qi Shuyi, Dai Penghai (eds). *Xiao Youmei Wenji* [Collection of the Writings of Xiao Youmei]. Shanghai: Shanghai Yinyue Chubanshe: 230.

4. Xiao: 231

melodies with Western harmony and musical forms in order to represent the modern Chinese spirit, thinking and emotions. Spirit and emotion were its most important aspects — with this, there could be many different kinds of "national music." To this end, he advocated the collecting of old folk songs which could be improved by removing the lewd parts and adding some harmony. The best of the old operas could also be revised so as to make them appropriate for a modern civilization.

But the most important aspect of Mr. Xiao's plans for music reform was the establishment of a formal music education system based on European methods. Such a system could teach both a standardized and improved version of Chinese music and Western music. And, as the methodologies of Western music became more widespread, Mr. Xiao argued, it would soon be inaccurate to call it "Western" since new Chinese music would become a part of this tradition and national musical boundaries would be rendered obsolete.

While some of Mr. Xiao's views may sound iconoclastic, they were largely in line with the thinking of other May 4th intellectuals. This widespread tendency to criticize Chinese tradition and admire Western ways represented a sea-change in attitude — for much of recorded history, China had been a nation that valued the past more than the present and disdained most things foreign. It was this attitude that helped prevent China's past music masters from adopting the clavichord that Father Ricci brought or the staff notation that Father Pereira taught, leaving them to remain imperial curiosities for three hundred years — a fate to which most of the scientific instruments and learning brought by the Jesuits were also doomed. Intellectuals of the May 4th era were determined to change this attitude and, if they sometimes went to extremes in condemning their own culture and admiring that of the West, they ultimately succeeded in their goal of breaking the hold of antiquity and opening their nation to new ideas from outside.

Two other German-educated intellectuals largely shared Mr. Xiao's views on music and did much to push for the spread of Western music and the reform of Chinese music: Wang Guangqi and Cai Yuanpei. Wang Guangqi had gone to Berlin to study law and politics in 1920 but been so impressed by German musical life that he switched to the study of music in 1923. Between 1923 and his untimely death in 1934, Wang wrote 17 books about Western music, including *Musical Life of the Germans*, which argued that Germany's prosperity and power were in part attributable to its flourishing musical culture.[5] While Wang's works did not have a wide circulation in China, they influenced many scholars and intellectuals, as did his calls upon the Nationalist government to support a "musical renaissance" for China.

Cai Yuanpei was a widely renowned scholar who had been Minister of Education under Sun Yat-sen and was president of Peking University during the May 4th Movement. He was passionate about education, believing that it should include morality, knowledge, physical exercise and aesthetics, the combined study of which

---

5. Jones, A.F. (2001). *Yellow Music: Media Culture and Colonial Modernity in the Chinese Jazz Age.* Durham and London: Duke University Press: 38.

would create well-rounded people. He was particularly interested in aesthetics as a potential substitute for religion, and in music as a crucial part of aesthetics.

Cai was an early supporter of the school song movement and his time in Germany made him a convert to both the pleasures and supposed virtues of Western classical music. Indeed, he came to believe that the popularity of classical music in Germany contributed to the nation's strength and to what he considered the orderly and civic-minded nature of its people. Upon taking the helm at Peking University, he organized a series of "music reform groups" that aimed to introduce Western classical music and reform Chinese music by eliminating its deficiencies and making it more "scientific."[6] These groups were merged into the Peking University Music Research Group in 1919 and this in turn was given the status of a university department in 1921 and renamed the Institute for the Promotion and Practice of Music at Peking University.[7] Cai then invited Xiao Youmei, who had established or expanded small music faculties at the University for Women Teachers and the Academy of Fine Arts after his return from Germany, to move to Peking University and take over the management of this new music institute.

Tan Shuzhen studied at the Institute for the Promotion and Practice of Music for a time, in 1923, and recalled it as a small, dark facility in an old Ming Dynasty building that was below street level. Tuition was only one yuan per semester, as compared to five silver dollars for a single lesson with a foreign teacher in Beijing, and payment was submitted directly to Xiao Youmei. The teachers were of varying quality — Mr. Tan's violin teacher was primarily a clarinetist who taught Mr. Tan by singing, since Mr. Tan played the violin better than he did. However, other professors were more distinguished, among them the renowned musician Liu Tianhua.

Mr. Liu was a *pipa* player, the brother of a Peking University professor named Liu Fu who had begun an important project to collect the lyrics to folk songs in 1918. Liu Tianhua had little exposure to Western music prior to joining the Institute for the Promotion and Practice of Music and did not have much interest in it; in his view, there was no music purer than China's own and it would only be a matter of time before Westerners came flocking to China to study it.[8] But during his time at the Institute, he exchanged ideas with professors of Western music and gradually came to have enough respect for the foreign art that he began to study harmony and violin with a Russian violinist. He practiced day and night and became such an accomplished player that he apparently astounded many of his colleagues.

But Liu Tianhua didn't stop there. With the fervor of a convert, he decided that Western music was in many ways more advanced than Chinese and began to reform Chinese music for *pipa* and *erhu*. His reforms were particularly important with the two-

---

6. Jones: 36.

7. In Chinese, the name is Beijing Daxue Yinyue Chuanxi Suo.

8. This discussion of Mr. Liu is drawn from Xiao Youmei (1990). *Wen guoyue daoshi Liu Tianhua Xiansheng qushi yougan* [A few thoughts heard at the death of Chinese music master Liu Tianhua]. In Chen Lingqun, Qi Shuyi, Dai Penghai (eds). *Xiao Youmei Wenji* [Collection of the Writings of Xiao Youmei]. Shanghai: Shanghai Yinyue Chubanshe: 324-5.

stringed *erhu*, which was widely looked down upon as a street instrument played by blind men and beggars. By applying violin technique to *erhu* playing, Liu helped to revolutionize the general view of the instrument — which, largely thanks to him, is nowadays as likely to be heard in a concert hall as on a street corner and is often referred to as "the Chinese violin."

Because the Institute for the Promotion and Practice of Music did not have enough advanced students to form an orchestra, Xiao Youmei founded one by recruiting musicians from around Beijing. Most of its 17 members were Manchus who had played in the Empress Dowager Cixi's short-lived ensemble, and a few came from the band *cum* orchestras of Robert Hart and Yuan Shikai. A Russian was concertmaster and Xiao himself conducted the orchestra in playing the works of Haydn, Mozart, Beethoven, and Schubert.

However, despite his success in attracting students like Tan Shuzhen and in forming an orchestra, Mr. Xiao was growing increasingly frustrated with the results of his efforts. That many Chinese in Beijing had a strong interest in Western music, he had no doubt. Indeed, the strength of this interest is underlined by the experiences of the great violinist Fritz Kreisler, who travelled to Beijing in 1923 on a tour that included performances in Shanghai and Tokyo.

Kreisler's trip to China and Japan — like that of Paci and so many other musicians — had been arranged by Avray Strok.[9] His performances in Japan were attended primarily by Japanese, including 8 sold-out recitals at the 2500 seat Imperial Theater, and he was wined and dined by the cream of Japan's intellectual and political elite. However his Shanghai and Beijing concerts were attended almost exclusively by foreigners, a situation which Kreisler apparently did not think about much until just before his departure from Beijing when a Chinese intellectual visited to ask if he would consider giving a concert for the city's Chinese music lovers.

Taken aback, Kreisler responded, "But I thought my concerts were for Chinese as well as Europeans; neither my manager nor anybody else has told me that Chinese could not come to the concerts at which I have so far played."[10]

His visitor replied — perhaps more out of pride than truth — that the Chinese did not wish to attend any function unless they themselves had organized it. He added that no European artists had yet performed for the Chinese themselves. Kreisler seems to have been an accommodating man and he was not averse to adding a concert at the last minute, but he was booked in the European compound the following night and due to depart the day after that. When the man suggested that the concert take place the following afternoon, Kreisler expressed surprise that it could be arranged at such short notice but nonetheless agreed to do it.

Kreisler's interlocutor did an exemplary job of spreading word about the concert. Tan Shuzhen heard about it from his violin teacher, who told him that it was an

---

9. For an account of Kreisler's trip to China, see Lochner, L.P. (1950). *Fritz Kreisler*. New York: The Macmillan Company: 209-220.
10. Lochner: 28.

opportunity he could not miss.[11] Ecstatic at the chance to hear the world's greatest violinist, Tan Shuzhen went early to the movie theater that was to serve as concert hall — so early that he was the only person there for more than an hour and was able to select a seat in the middle of the very first row. From this vantage point, Mr. Tan watched the house fill up and even saw the Chinese president Li Yuanhong enter the theater and sit in a reserved box followed close behind by the great Peking opera star Mei Lanfang and his family.

If Mr. Tan was impressed by the sight of the president and Mei Lanfang, Kreisler and his wife were impressed by the entire scene.

"Never in all my life have I seen a stage more beautifully and artistically decorated," Mrs. Kreisler told her husband's biographer. "It looked like a huge altar. And the gowns of the ladies! One seemed to look out upon an ocean of silk. There were most gorgeous colorings of silk costumes, and the ladies' jewels were too lovely for words — not set in elaborate Western style, but simply and thereby most effectively. The stools on which the audience sat were in variegated silks. It was an unforgettable experience."[12]

Prior to the start of the concert, a niece of Sun Yat-sen took the stage to explain proper concert etiquette to the audience. She was followed by Kreisler, his accompanist, and a foreigner who introduced the great violinist in Shandong-accented Chinese; Tan Shuzhen guessed that he was the Austrian ambassador to China. When Kreisler was finally alone on stage, he reclined his head slightly in the direction of the presidential box and the rest of the audience, and then began to play an unaccompanied Bach suite. His playing was so enthusiastically received that for the first time ever in his career he found it necessary to repeat the piece then and there. The Bach piece was followed by a Beethoven sonata and a group of small pieces, one of which — Cyril Scott's *Lotus Land* — also had to be repeated. Tan Shuzhen — who was certain that Kreisler had looked right at him several times and sensed that he was an aspiring violinist — wrote that the end of the concert was like awaking from a dream. He would remember it for the rest of his life, though he could never adequately describe the height of Kreisler's artistry or the depth of the emotions it inspired in him.

The president and other government officials in attendance were also impressed by the performance, so much so that when it ended they asked Kreisler if he would be willing to tour through the Gobi Desert on a private train that would stop each evening so he could give a concert wherever he happened to be. The government would pay Kreisler whatever fees he requested and provide soldiers to protect him from bandits. Kreisler's wife was thrilled with the idea of traveling through the Gobi on a private train, but Kreisler himself had already promised to return to Shanghai to give two more recitals and, according to his biographer, "felt that he could not let down the music lovers of Shanghai." [13]

11. See Tan Shuzhen (1997). Chishi nianqian ting kelaisile yinyue hui [Seventy Years Ago: Listening to Kreisler's Concert]. *Audio-Visual World* No. 51: 68-9.
12. Lochner: 219.

However, if government officials in Beijing were willing to write a blank check to a famous foreign violinist, they were less willing to support the efforts of their own musicians and music educators. By the mid-1920s, Xiao Youmei sensed a general and growing resistance to formal music education on the part of the bureaucracy. Although most officials could see the utility of adding Western science to the education curriculum, music — with the exception of didactic school songs — was not perceived as a subject that belonged in school and few people wanted to waste money on it. The difficulty of convincing the relevant authorities of the importance of music education was compounded by the precarious political situation, in which China was increasingly divided into fiefdoms ruled by feuding warlords. Mr. Xiao had tried hard in Beijing, but most members of his own little orchestra could not even read music; there were few professionally trained musicians to hire as teachers; and the level of his students was not as high as he would have liked. These factors, together with the lack of government support, gradually led him to believe that the environment in Beijing was simply not conducive to teaching Western music or reforming Chinese music.

It became increasingly clear to him that the best place to locate a music school was not Beijing, but Shanghai. Students of music needed to be nurtured by a musical environment and Shanghai was the only place in China where they could get such nurturing. Equally important, the many foreign musicians there could presumably be hired for much less than professors who had to be brought from abroad. [14]

Xiao hesitated to act on his growing conviction that Shanghai was the best place for a music school, only because he did not like the commercial southern city with its foreign-dominated concessions where "the majority of people believe that profit is the greatest joy." [15] In fact, his opinion of Shanghai was so low that when he first heard from friends about the Shanghai Municipal Orchestra, he could scarcely believe that in the "practical, vulgar Shanghai concessions one could find this God-given medicine that comforts the soul" and that this "treasure" was supported by the government of the International Settlement.[16] However, when the warlord government of Beijing declared that music was harmful to moral decency and ordered the Institute for the Promotion and Practice of Music shut down in 1927, Mr. Xiao finally swallowed his prejudices and decided to move to Shanghai.

"I strongly believe that the best teachers produce the best students," he wrote. "So, we will borrow a chicken to produce eggs."

---

13. *Ibid.*, 220.

14. See Xiao Youmei (1990). Tingguo Shanghai shizhengting dayue yinyue hui houde danxiang [On first hearing the Shanghai Symphony]. In: Chen Lingqun, Qi Shuyi, Dai Penghai (eds.), *Xiao Youmei Wenji* [Collection of the Writings of Xiao Youmei]. Shanghai: Shanghai Yinyue Chubanshe: 238-242. Also, see Tan Shuzhen. Xiao Youmei yu Beida Yinyue Chuanxisuo, in: Dai Penghai, Huang Xudong (eds.) (1993). *Xiao Youmei Jinian Wenji*. Shanghai: Shanghai Yinyue Chubanshe: 53.

15. See Xiao Youmei: 238

16. See Xiao Youmei: 238 and 241.

Having made up his mind, Mr. Xiao presented his plan to establish a National Conservatory of Music in Shanghai to Cai Yuanpei, who by this time was minister of higher education for the Nationalist government in Nanjing.[17] Cai approved the plan and also agreed to be the new school's first president. Although the position would be largely ceremonial on his part, it would do much for the reputation and credibility of the new institution. So, with funding assured and a prestigious president signed on, Xiao Youmei moved to Shanghai, found a place for the school on Rue Dollfuss in the French Concession, and prepared to begin his mission of founding the nation's first conservatory.

REFUGEE MUSICAL LIFE IN SHANGHAI

The rich Shanghai musical life that Xiao Youmei so admired was, of course, a function of all the foreigners who had settled there over the years. But just about the time that Mr. Xiao was planning to move down to the semi-colonial, southern metropolis, the composition of this foreign population was starting to change dramatically.

Shanghai's population of Russian exiles was already significant in 1927 and it continued to grow throughout the 1930s. Most of these exiles were White Russians, men and women who remained loyal to the Czar even after the Bolsheviks came to power in the Russian Revolution of 1917. Because of this loyalty, they were forced to flee their country in order to save their lives. While some of the earlier immigrants came directly to Shanghai by sea, others came overland, oftentimes after settling first in China's northeastern city of Harbin. Those Russians who came to Shanghai via Harbin brought with them experience living in exile and in creating a quasi-European cultural environment that included much music.

For, strangely enough, Harbin was in many respects a Russian city, sometimes referred to as the "St. Petersburg of the East." Its Russification had begun back in 1896 when the Qing Dynasty government granted Russia a concession to build and operate a railway in northeast China in exchange for a 15-year defensive alliance. The agreement also included the rights to exploit a thousand-mile tract of land alongside the railway, which was Russia's true goal. Since economic prospects were not bright

---

17. The conservatory that Xiao Youmei founded in 1927 has been known by ten different names over the course of its history, with the first name change coming in 1929 when it was effectively demoted to a vocational school. For a complete list of these names with the dates they were used, see Editorial Committee (1987). *Shanghai Yinyue Xueyuan Jianshi, 1927-1987* [Shanghai Conservatory of Music]. Shanghai: Shanghai Yinyue Xueyuan: 59.

To avoid confusion, the authors have chosen to use just two names. For the years before 1949, we call it the National Conservatory of Music. This is a reasonable translation of its first Chinese name (Guoli Yinyue Yuan) and reflects the fact that it was intended to be a national music school. It is also the English name used for the conservatory throughout the 1930s and 1940s. After 1949, we call it the Shanghai Conservatory of Music, which became the school's official name beginning in 1956. The change from "national" to "Shanghai" reflects the fact that after 1949, the Central Conservatory in Beijing effectively became China's national music school.

back home, many of the Russians brought in to help with construction opted to settle in cities along the railroad, with the majority choosing Harbin.

These turn-of-the-century economic migrants were soon joined by Russian Jews fleeing the Czarist government's increasingly harsh anti-Semitic policies. Recognizing that Jewish businesses could help to supply their operation, the management of the China Eastern Railroad made it clear that Jews were welcome to move to Manchuria and set up shop. By the mid-1920s, there were 15,000 Russian Jews living in Harbin, many of them owners or employees of successful trading firms, furriers, sugar refineries, flour mills, and banks. After the Bolshevik Revolution in 1917 and the fall of Vladivostok in 1920, White Russians joined the mixture and by 1922, some 120,000 of Harbin's 485,000 residents were Russian.[18]

With so many Russians and Russian Jews living in one city, a diverse Russian-style cultural life soon sprang up. Harbin supported numerous newspapers, schools, sports teams, religious organizations, youth organizations, theatrical performances, churches, and synagogues. Naturally, there was also plenty of music. Young Russian and Jewish musicians were trained at the First Harbin Music Academy, which one enthusiastic graduate described as "the premier music conservatory in Manchuria, and probably in all of China." [19] The Academy's dean of faculty was Vladimir Davydovich Trachtenberg, a graduate of the Saint Petersburg Conservatory who had studied under the famous violin teacher Leopold Auer, whose other pupils included Jascha Heifetz, Mischa Elman, and Efrem Zimbalist.

In addition to its Music Academy, Harbin had a symphony orchestra that consisted of 60 Russian musicians, a large number of whom had been principals and soloists in orchestras throughout Russia. It performed in the Railway Assembly Hall and, like many of the city's cultural organizations, was sponsored by the China Eastern Railway. The symphony was led by a Russian named Geschkowitsch, who became acquainted with Xiao Youmei on a trip to Beijing to guest conduct for a visiting Russian opera in the early 1920s. In fact, the two hatched a plan whereby Maestro Geschkowitsch would send 20 members of his orchestra to Beijing to join up with Mr. Xiao's orchestra, and occasionally come to conduct it himself. Although both were committed to the idea — which would have created the first integrated orchestra in China — a lack of funding prevented them from following through on it.

In addition to its orchestra, Harbin had a string quartet, led by Trachtenberg, and numerous informal musical performances in such places as the Hotel Moderne. Indeed, the city had such a plethora of musicians that its movie theaters even had orchestras that provided live accompaniment to films well into the 1930s.[20]

---

18. See Schickman-Bowman, Z. (1999). The Construction of the Chinese Eastern Railway and the Origin of the Harbin Jewish Community, 1898-1931. In Goldstein, J. (ed.), *The Jews of China, Volume One: Historical and Comparative Perspectives.* Armonk: M.E. Sharpe: 190-1. Of the remaining population, 300,000 were Chinese, 34,000 Korean and 5,000 Japanese.

19. Menquez, A. (pseudonym) (2000). "Growing Up Jewish in Manchuria in the 1930s." In Goldstein, J. (ed.), *The Jews of China, Volume Two: A Sourcebook and Research Guide.* Armonk: M.E. Sharpe: 78.

Life in Harbin was good for many Russians and Jews, who dominated the city to such an extent that it must have seemed like a more secure version of home. However, in the early 1930s, that security vanished when the Japanese began their invasion of Manchuria. Once again looking for a place to call home, thousands of Russian exiles turned their sights on Shanghai.

Most of these new refugees settled in the French Concession, with Avenue Joffre (today's Huaihai Road) attracting so many that it soon became known as "Little Russia." The better educated and more enterprising among them opened clubs and restaurants (like Kafka's, the hang-out for SMO musicians) held literary discussions, and ran Russian-language newspapers. They raised funds to build orthodox churches, with their distinctive domes; two of these churches still stand as magical monuments to the White Russian presence in Shanghai, although they now house restaurants and a securities brokerage. Like all the foreigners in Shanghai, the Russians also formed organizations — the Russian Benevolent Society, the Russian Emigrants Committee, the Union of Russian Army and Navy Men. Russians had their own detachment in the respected Shanghai Volunteer Corps and in 1932 Shanghai's Jews, who were then primarily Russian, formed their own unit as well.

Some White Russians became well-established members of Shanghai's international community, like the former Imperial Army officer Georgi Sapojnikou — better known by his pen name of Sapajou — the caricaturist for the *North China Daily News*. Maestro Paci was a favorite subject of Sapajou's witty sketches, especially around the time of the annual Ratepayer's meeting when the Maestro was called upon to defend his orchestra and its budget. One Sapajou sketch, captioned, "The Municipal Orchestra begins to perform its annual 'Danse Macabre,'" shows Maestro Paci dodging torpedoes as he frantically conducts. Another, called "A narrow escape," shows a firefighter putting out the burning embers of the "orchestra abolition campaign" while Maestro Paci and the orchestra once again strike up the music. Paci's daughter still has many of Sapajou's sketches, framed and autographed, hanging on the walls of her home.

Another successful White Russian immigrant was Mme. Eleanora Stahl Holstein von Lilienthal Garnett, the city's most sought-after dressmaker and something of a legend in her own time. A stunning blonde married to an Italian count, Madame Garnett lived in a house with a turret and went to the Cathay Hotel (now the Peace Hotel) every Saturday night, sitting at the same table and taking to the dance floor with such exquisite grace that all the other dancers stopped to watch her. Her shop was as stylish as she, decorated completely in gray, and though all the foreign women in Shanghai clamored after her fashions — including Maestro Paci's wife and daughter — she was highly selective about her clientele.

---

20. Information about orchestras in Harbin movie theaters comes from Li Delun, who spent nearly a year there in the 1930s. He also said, "Harbin was strange — people were running everywhere. It was the St. Petersburg of the East. I was there nearly a year — there were so many Russians, the lifestyle was Russian. Half the city was Russian, half was Chinese."

Fortunately for the Paci women, Madame Garnett was also a devoted amateur pianist. Her long-held ambition was to study piano with Maestro Paci, but he refused to teach her because she did not have enough talent. So, for years she took lessons with Sara Paci, who was thus assured of a steady stream of Madame Garnett creations to wear when she hit the town with her husband. But Madame Garnett never let up in her quest to study with the Maestro himself, and finally, when Fofi Paci was of an age to desire beautiful clothes, Maestro Paci grudgingly agreed to teach the determined dressmaker so that his daughter could be assured of the same supply of couture.

"But he really couldn't stand it," Fofi remembered. "He kept saying, 'Have you got enough dresses yet?'"

However, if a few White Russians rose to the top of Shanghai's intellectual and social elite, many more struggled to eke out a living as bodyguards, taxi dancers, prostitutes, rickshaw pullers, even beggars. Because so many of them were poverty-stricken — and perhaps because they had nowhere else to go — White Russians as a group were looked down upon by many in Shanghai, both foreign and Chinese alike.

Caught somewhere in the middle, between respect and disdain, were the many White Russian and Russian Jewish musicians who immigrated to Shanghai. These musical refugees could be heard everywhere — in hotel orchestras, in dance halls, even serenading diners in candle-lit cafes. Many gave lessons and the classified section of the newspapers was filled with announcements like this one:

> Pianoforte school, with full course, by Mrs. N. V. Marinitch, graduate of Petrograd Conservatoire. For particulars apply 634 Rue de l'Observatoire, off Avenue Dubail.[21]

These emigrant musicians formed a Russian Musical Society that staged concerts and operatic productions, including a 1932 production of *Boris Godunov* that had a 30-member orchestra and a 35-person chorus; it was so popular that its run at the Embassy Theater was extended. The Ballets Russes performed with the SMO, putting on such ballets as *The Tzar Maiden* by Caesar Pugni, and the Russian Light Opera staged light operas that became a highlight of the Shanghai stage under its leader Alexander Slobodoskoy. Following the example of Britons, French, Americans and other nationalities, the Russian Jews founded a Jewish Club in 1932. The Jewish Club — which was located on the spot where the Shanghai Conservatory now stands — hosted numerous cultural activities, including ballet, opera, theater and music; and many of the artists who performed there were White Russians. The June 8 birthday of the great Russian writer Alexander Pushkin was known as Russian Culture Day and was marked by concerts featuring music of Russian composers like Glinka, Dargomygsky, Rimsky Korsakoff, Tchaikovsky and Mussorgsky.

Beginning in 1938, Shanghai's Russian Jews were joined by a group of refugees even more desperate for sanctuary than they or the White Russians had been — European Jews fleeing the Nazis. Shanghai was not a first-choice destination for

---

21. *North China Daily News*, October 3, 1921: 16.

European refugees; some Jews had emigrated there as early as 1933 and sent back word of an alien, disease-ridden city overflowing with refugees of all kinds. But since neither visa nor passport was required to enter it, the city was the best — often only — option for Jews who could not get visas to anywhere else. Indeed, up until 1939, some Jews were even able to free themselves from concentration camps by proving that they had passage to Shanghai. By the time the immigration ended in 1941, approximately 18,000 Jewish refugees managed to find haven in Shanghai.[22]

Arriving with little more than the clothes on their backs, the majority of refugees lived in squalor in tenement housing, struggling just to survive. Relief efforts were poorly managed, resources and charitable organizations were already severely strained, and thousands were forced to subsist on hand-outs. They lived in miserable refugee centers known as *heime*. Since Shanghai was already inundated with Chinese and Russian refugees, even the most humble work was hard to find. While many of the refugees were highly educated professionals, few spoke English (the lingua franca of the International Settlement), which made integration into the larger foreign community doubly difficult. Malnourished and unaccustomed to the heat and humidity of Shanghai, many became ill or died.

Most refugees ended up living in an area of the International Settlement called Hongkou, which by the late 1930s was essentially controlled by the Japanese military and was widely known as "Little Tokyo." However, as the Jewish refugees settled in and transformed it with small cafes, bakeries, restaurants and other businesses, this nickname changed to "Little Vienna." Although living conditions in "Little Vienna" were terrible, a vibrant cultural life soon sprang up there.

Relief organizations counted 267 professional artists among the refugees — including an astonishing 15 conductors[23]— and together with amateur artists they mounted variety shows, art shows, theatrical productions in both German and Yiddish, and many musical activities. Operettas like *The Merry Widow*, *Die Fledermaus* and *The Count of Luxemburg* were big crowd-pleasers, as was a women's choir founded by a singer named Margit Klemann.[24] There were trios and quartets, albeit short-lived, and even a chamber music ensemble. A young refugee named Horst Levin, who had been in the Sachsenhausen concentration camp before coming to Shanghai, started a Jewish radio hour on the American-owned radio station XMHA, an NBC affiliate that had a near complete set of RCA Victor recordings.[25] Levin introduced his show each

22. For possible reasons as to why this Jewish immigration was permitted, see Kranzler, D. (1988). *Japanese, Nazis and Jews: The Jewish Refugee Community of Shanghai, 1938-45.* Hoboken, NJ: KTAV Publishing House, Inc. Kranzler argues that the Japanese allowed Jewish immigration to Shanghai largely because they believed that Jews controlled much of the financial, political and media worlds of the United States and Great Britain and hoped that their benign policy toward Jews would improve public opinion of Japan in the West and encourage Jews to invest in Japanese-controlled Manchuria. Kranzler believes that the Japanese decision to restrict Jewish immigration from Europe was made under pressure from the Municipal Councils of the International Settlement and French Concession and from prominent Shanghai Jews, who were fearful that the city could not absorb any more refugees.
23. Kranzler: 282.
24. For musical life of Jewish refugees, see Kranzler: 373-4.

day with the "Soldiers' Chorus" from *Faust*, played classical music recordings, and frequently invited refugees to perform live on the show.

As a refugee named Ernest Heppner wrote,

> We attended countless lectures, literary and musical recitals, and chamber concerts and could listen to German-language radio programs. Over the years we had our choice among the more than sixty plays produced. We especially enjoyed the operettas that were performed by actors who had once been well known on the stages of Vienna and Berlin.[26]

Naturally, music was a livelihood as well as an entertainment. Amateur musicians found work playing in cafes, dance halls, cabarets and even on the street, while professionals tried to establish themselves in Shanghai's serious music world. This latter group included men of great talent, several of whom had been well-established — even famous — before they were forced to flee Europe.

Alfred Wittenberg was in the twilight years of an illustrious professional career in Berlin when he was forced to flee to Shanghai. He had been one of the best pupils of the Hungarian violinist Joseph Joachim and became first violinist at the Koenigsliches Operahaus at the age of 20. Two years into his tenure at the Operahaus, his "ravishingly beautiful tone"[27] was noticed by the renowned Austrian pianist Artur Schnabel and the Dutch cellist Anton Hekking, who invited him to join a trio they planned to form. Now known in music history as "the first Schnabel trio," the threesome was tremendously successful on the Berlin night scene and its performances sold out for years.

Wolfgang Fraenkel was also a Berliner, a brilliant, multi-talented lawyer and judge who composed and played piano and violin in his free time. He was interred in the Sachsenhausen concentration camp, but managed to get to Shanghai in 1939. There were no professional opportunities for German lawyers in Shanghai, but Fraenkel's musical talents were soon recognized and he was recruited by the SMO to play both violin and viola, as needed. Fraenkel had a photographic memory and the story is still told in Shanghai of a violinist who wanted to play Mozart's *Violin Concerto No. 3 in G Major*, but had only the piano score. Unable to find the full score that he needed to perform, he turned to Fraenkel for help — Fraenkel complied by writing out the entire piece from memory.

Otto and Walter Joachim were brothers from Düsseldorf, the sons of the opera singer Emil Joachimsthal. Walter, a cellist, was forced to play in a dancehall to make a living when he first arrived in Shanghai. But, serendipitously, the hall happened to be a favorite haunt of Arrigo Foa, who soon recommended the cellist to Maestro Paci, enabling him to join the SMO. Otto, a violinist and composer, organized the Jewish

25. Ross, J.R. (1994). *Escape to Shanghai: A Jewish Community in China*. New York: The Free Press: 81.

26. Heppner, E. G. (1993). *Shanghai Refuge: A Memoir of the World War II Jewish Ghetto*. Lincoln: University of Nebraska Press: 86.

27. Saerchinger, C. (1957). *Artur Schnabel: A Biography*. New York: Dodd, Mead & Company: 76.

chamber orchestra, which specialized in playing Jewish music, synagogue music and new music. He also opened a music store in the French Concession, right across the street from the Lyceum Theater, where the SMO performed. This store became a gathering place for musicians, who came to purchase scores, have their instruments repaired, or just chat. Tan Shuzhen was a frequent visitor and remained forever grateful to Otto for managing to find him the complete scores of Mozart, Schubert and Brahms string quartets, not an easy achievement in wartime Shanghai.

For so many stellar musical talents from Europe and Russia to be forced by desperate circumstance to gather in a single area of one country as distant and unfamiliar as China was unprecedented. Indeed, it is likely that while Xiao Youmei had sensed correctly that Shanghai would provide a more promising environment for his conservatory, even he had no idea just how fertile this environment would ultimately prove to be.

CHINA'S FIRST CONSERVATORY

Once Xiao Youmei had chosen a location for the Conservatory, he set to work on his most crucial task, that of recruiting the city's best musicians to be professors. This entailed contacting anyone who would be able to help him gain entrée to the city's musical circles — including the young man who had briefly studied violin at the Institute for the Promotion and Practice of Music and was now the only Chinese musician in the Shanghai Municipal Orchestra, Tan Shuzhen.

When Mr. Tan received Mr. Xiao's note in the morning post, he slit open the envelope at once — it was not every day that a young violinist received a personal correspondence from a man as important as Xiao Youmei. Inside, he found a thin piece of traditional letter paper, its vertical red columns filled with brush-written calligraphy. The contents of the note were simple, an invitation to stop by and visit Mr. Xiao at the site of the new school whenever he had the time. As it happened, Mr. Tan was not busy that day and he went at once to the Rue Dollfuss.

Over tea, Mr. Xiao explained his plans for the Conservatory and then got to the point — he wanted to hire Shanghai's best musicians as teachers and he needed introductions to them. Mr. Tan replied that the best brass and strings teachers would be the sectional leaders of the SMO. To meet them, and to find teachers for piano, voice, and composition he suggested that Mr. Xiao call on Maestro Paci, who would know all the reputable musicians in Shanghai. Much facilitated by Paci's introductions, Mr. Xiao set to work implementing his plan to borrow foreign chickens to produce Chinese eggs.

Hiring the best musicians for a start-up conservatory was not as easy as it may sound; in its first year, Xiao himself had to teach harmony, composition and music appreciation because he could not find enough teachers. Arrigo Foa, for instance, was the most logical candidate to head the violin department, but he was on home leave in

1927. Many of the foreign musicians had their own private students, and not all were eager to work at a Chinese music school.

The attitude of some of the best foreign musicians seems reflected in that of Boris Zaharoff, a Russian pianist who had been touring the world with his wife, the famous British violinist Cecilia Hansen. The couple was showing signs of stress when they got to Japan and their marriage came to an end by the time they arrived in Shanghai. Mr. Zaharoff stayed in Shanghai on his own and soon made a big splash with his talent and personality. However, when Mr. Xiao approached Mr. Zaharoff with an offer, the pianist reportedly replied coldly, "Chinese music students are like newborn infants. Is it worthwhile for me to go and teach them?"[28] Undeterred, Mr. Xiao called upon him again — and again — until in 1929 Zaharoff was finally won over by his determination — and, no doubt, by the increasingly sweet offer which in the end gave him the same salary as Xiao himself.

Of course, not all foreign chickens were as demanding as Zaharoff. Indeed, for most, the opportunity to teach talented Chinese students at a genuine music school was a welcome opportunity — Foa, for instance, happily accepted a position as head of the violin department when he returned from Europe. And for those foreign musicians who came to Shanghai because they were fleeing persecution, rather than seeking opportunity, the Conservatory was something of a godsend. Xiao Youmei happily availed himself of this refugee talent and a remarkable — and mutually beneficial — relationship developed between the National Conservatory and Shanghai's refugee musicians.

Since White Russians had gotten to Shanghai first, they were naturally the earliest refugee teachers to be hired. Igor Shertzoff, a graduate of the St. Petersburg Conservatory, joined the faculty in 1928 and eventually became head of the cello department. Like many of the best refugee musicians, he also played in the Shanghai Municipal Orchestra. He eventually rose to the position of principle cellist but when Paci replaced him with a German named Winkler, he quit the orchestra in a huff, returning to play only when he was invited as soloist.

Vladimir Shushlin was a well-known bass who joined the faculty in 1930. A versatile musician, he had studied piano and violin before switching to voice and going on to join the Mariinsky Theater in St. Petersburg. Before leaving his homeland in 1924, he performed in such operas as *Boris Godunov* and even shared the stage with the world famous bass Fyodor Chaliapin. On arriving in China, Shushlin settled first in Harbin, where he taught in the conservatory and gave solo performances. After three years, he left for a performance tour of Japan and the Philippines and then returned to China, where he settled in Shanghai and joined the Conservatory.

Boris Lazareff was a pianist who had been quite well known in his homeland until he was overcome with severe stage fright. Once he could no longer perform in public, he dedicated himself to teaching and in 1916 became head of the Ekaterinburg

---

28. Dai Penghai (1993). *Ding Shande Yinyue Nianpu* [A Musical Chronicle of Ding Shande]. Beijing: Zhongyang Yinyue Xueyuan Xuebaoshe: 9

Conservatory. He moved to Siberia in 1919, where he taught at two conservatories, and finally moved to China in 1928. He also settled first in Harbin, teaching at its conservatory for several years before coming to Shanghai and joining the Conservatory faculty in 1934.

In later years, Xiao and his successors also hired European Jewish refugees. Walter Joachim taught cello and Wolfgang Fraenkel joined the composition department in 1941, introducing his students to such contemporary theories as Arnold Schoenberg's "Treatise on Harmony" and Ernst Kurth's "Theory of Linear Counterpoint."[29] Fraenkel was eventually succeeded by his friend and fellow refugee Julius Schloss, who had been the student and the secretary of the avant-garde composer Alban Berg.[30] Wittenberg joined the faculty to teach both violin and piano. Since gramophone records were in short supply, he personally demonstrated the interpretative styles of such famous violinists as Fritz Kreisler, Mischa Elman, Efrem Zimbalist and Jascha Heifetz, greatly impressing his students.[31]

Of course, Xiao Youmei did not only hire foreigners to teach at the Conservatory. Such courses as Chinese literature, English, French, musicology, and Chinese music history were taught by Chinese professors with well-established reputations, as were lessons in Chinese instruments. Although most Chinese faculty members were Chinese-educated, several had studied abroad for long periods like Xiao himself. Zhou Shuan, for instance, had been one of the first Chinese women to study in the US, enrolling at Radcliffe College in 1915. While at Radcliffe, she had also studied voice, piano, and ear training at the New England Conservatory and she continued this double-tracking after graduation when she went to New York and attended both Columbia University and the New York College of Music. She then returned to China to teach at various universities and in 1927 went back to the US to study at the Peabody Conservatory for a year, before returning to Shanghai and being recruited by Xiao to teach voice.

But the most prominent of all the Chinese professors was the promising young composer Huang Zi, who became head of the composition department in 1930. Mr. Huang was a native of nearby Jiangsu who had fallen in love with Western music early in life. Indeed, he dated this interest back to the lullabies he heard while a child in his mother's arms, though his formal music education did not begin until he was a teenager at the Tsinghua School in Beijing.

The Tsinghua School was a unique institution in China, founded in the wake of the anti-foreign and anti-Christian Boxer Rebellion of 1900. The Empress Dowager Cixi had initially opposed the rebellion, but as the rebels gained force, she switched her support to them. This proved to be something of a tactical error, since her support of the rebels who were killing foreigners and Chinese Christians led eight foreign

---

29. Xu Bozeng (2000). Jews and the musical life of Shanghai. In Goldstein, J. (ed.) *The Jews of China*, *Volume Two*: 234.

30. Rosenson, H. (2000). Jewish musicians in Shanghai: bridging two cultures. In Goldstein, J. (ed.) *The Jews of China, Volume Two*: 245-6.

31. Xu Bozeng. (2000): 235.

powers — including the United States — to form a coalition and invade Beijing. The coalition forces crushed the rebels, soundly routed the Qing Dynasty troops, and then exacted a humiliating financial settlement to pay for their troubles. But, in a calculated gesture that generated longstanding goodwill, the United States used its portion of the reparations to establish the Tsinghua School — now Tsinghua University — which was intended to prepare Chinese students for higher education in the United States. Several of Huang Zi's older brothers had attended the school and he happily followed in their footsteps.

Western music was a part of Tsinghua's curriculum and Mr. Huang played clarinet in the school orchestra and sang in its choir. He soon decided that he wanted to pursue music as a profession, but his father did not consider it to be a real career and did not want to see his son sidetracked by it. Mr. Huang bowed to his father's wishes by pursuing a degree in psychology at Oberlin College in Ohio, but continued to study music on his own. Among his teachers was Tan Shuzhen's older sister, who was also at Oberlin and taught him piano. But, when it came time to graduate, Mr. Huang could no longer repress his desire to be a musician. He enrolled in the Oberlin Conservatory to study music theory and composition and then went to Yale to continue his studies with the renowned composer Paul Hindemith.

Mr. Huang graduated from Yale in 1929 with a BA in composition. His graduation composition was called *In Memoriam*, written in the mid-nineteenth century style of romanticism and dedicated to the memory of a former girlfriend who died at the age of 27. It was performed at Yale's Woodsey Hall by a combined orchestra of the New Haven Symphony and the Yale Symphony on May 31, 1929 — the first symphonic work by a Chinese composer ever performed by an orchestra. The piece was written up in the local newspaper and the reviewer said that he "thoroughly enjoyed" it.[32]

Upon returning to China in August of 1929, Mr. Huang taught music at a middle school before Xiao Youmei discovered him and brought him over to the Conservatory. Although Huang was the head of the composition department, he taught virtually everything related to music theory — harmony, advanced harmony, keyboard harmony, counterpoint, fugue, form, orchestration, free composition and even history and music appreciation. Despite this heavy course load, he made time to edit music text books for elementary and middle school students, to write reviews and articles for such publications as *Music Magazine*, and to introduce Western classical music on Chinese-language radio stations. He also continued to compose, adapting folk songs for orchestra, writing songs and even some movie scores. In short, he quickly became a major force in the propagation of Western classical music.

Having hired such outstanding faculty on a tight budget and in a relatively short period of time, Mr. Xiao could rest assured that he was right to establish the nation's first conservatory in Shanghai. It certainly had the best potential teachers. But, if he

---

32. As quoted in Qian, Renkang (1997). *Huang Zide Shenghuo yu Chuangzuo* [The Life and Music of Huang Zi]. Beijing: Renmin Yinyue Chubanshe: 6.

had solved the faculty problem, he still had plenty of other hurdles to surmount. Cai Yuanpei, the Conservatory's prestigious president, resigned from his position after only one year in order to pursue other education-related activities for the Nationalist government. This blow was compounded by the school's perpetual financial problems, which grew worse as China's political stability continued to erode.

In 1927 — the same year the Conservatory opened — the Nationalist government launched a campaign to re-take the Chinese-controlled areas of Shanghai, which for some years had been under the command of a warlord. The Nationalist campaign succeeded, in large part because Communist operatives helped to organize wide scale strikes that eroded the warlord's power. However, soon after assuming control, the Nationalists turned on the Communists who had helped them. This campaign to purge Communists and their sympathizers from the ranks of the Nationalist Party — known as the "White Terror" — left up to 4000 Communists, leftists, and labor organizers dead and severely damaged the "united front" under which Nationalists and Communists had been cooperating in an effort to unify their nation.

It also set off a chain of events that affected the Conservatory. Pressed for funds to wage its broadening war, the Nationalist government moved to cut many non-military expenditures. In 1929, it considerably reduced its financial support to the Conservatory and effectively lowered its status to that of a vocational school. The only way to make up for the reduced subsidy was a tuition hike, which forced many students from less wealthy families to drop out and also led to student protests. The true impact of the school's diminished status hit home in 1930 when Mr. Xiao applied to the government for a 50,000 yuan grant to buy books and instruments, but was given only 10,000, just enough for a few books and a gramophone.

Even so, Mr. Xiao managed not only to hold the school together, but to improve its quality and reputation. In 1934, his success received some welcome external validation when the faculty was temporarily joined by the internationally renowned pianist and composer Alexander Tcherepnin.

Tcherepnin was born into a family for whom music was a "religion."[33] His father was the well-known Russian conductor and composer Nikolai Tcherepnin and his mother was a shy mezzo-soprano named Marie Benois, who would not perform in public, but sang often for her only son. Musical gatherings at the family home in St. Petersburg were frequent, and included such musical luminaries as Rimsky-Korsakoff, Stravinsky, Prokofiev and Chaliapin. The young Alexander was allowed to join these gatherings and to accompany his parents to the many ballets, concerts and operas that they attended. Perhaps unsurprisingly, given this background, he could write musical notes before he learned the alphabet and knew from his earliest days that music would be "my goal, my religion, my life — in fact, the very reason for my existence."[34]

Tcherepnin entered the St. Petersburg Conservatory at the age of 19, but his studies were soon interrupted by the Russian Revolution, which caused his family to

---

33. Tcherepnin, A. (1964). A short autobiography. *Tempo*, Issue 130 (1979): 12.
34. *Ibid.*, 12

flee first to Tbilisi, Georgia and then to Paris. The young musician took to Paris at once, quickly establishing himself as both pianist and composer. The great dancer Anna Pavlova commissioned him to write her a ballet inspired by the Buddhist frescoes on a temple in India. Called *Ajanta's Frescoes*, the ballet was premiered at Covent Garden in 1923 and Pavlova danced it on her American tour the following year. Tcherepnin himself made his musical debut in the US in 1926 and his first symphony was performed at the Theatre du Chatelet in Paris in 1927. Parts of it — particularly the scherzo for percussion and violin "sul ponticello" — so upset members of the audience that they stamped and hissed until the police had to be called to the scene.[35]

The notoriety generated by the response to his first symphony served to help, rather than hinder, his career. But in the late 1920s, Tcherepnin suddenly began to explore a latent interest in Eastern music and folk music. He came to the conclusion that folklore and folk music are as important to the composer as a knowledge of human anatomy is to the painter:

> The lines of folk music are the lines of musical survival, for the folklore of all nations shares the quality of having lasted through the centuries; it represents in music what the human body represents in painting. Thus, in operating with material from folklore, the composer uses the eternal lines in whichever way he feels is appropriate.[36]

A 1934 concert tour to China and Japan, arranged by Avray Strok, served to whet Tcherepnin's appetite for the traditional music of both countries and caused him to return for "another year of concerts, of teaching, and of learning"[37] that included his sojourn in Shanghai.

Curious and enthusiastic by nature, Tcherepnin was smitten by Shanghai from the moment he arrived on its shores. He was seduced by the sounds of its streets and loved to wander around, just listening. "To see some of the real China, go out and take a walk," he wrote in an article for *The Musical Quarterly* in 1935:

> As soon as you leave the main street, or Nanking Road, you find yourself in one of the animated business streets, decorated with all sorts of flags. Here is a popular eating place. In the interior, you see a nimble cook preparing chops from a peculiar grayish stuff. Even from afar you hear the penetrating rhythm of his handiwork, as he beats the chops with his wooden utensils. The rhythm is a definite one. It constitutes his individual "trade mark."

> Then you will notice that, wherever work is going on, it is done in a distinct rhythm: the shoemaker will hammer nails into a shoe-sole at a regular beat; the carpenter will work according to a certain "pulse"; likewise the mason, the dish-washer, and everyone else. When a job offers no opportunity to produce rhythmic sound, the worker will mutter a sort of song, or rather of rhythmic recitation, reminding you of your first acquaintances, the coolies who carried your trunk.

---

35. Arias, E.A. (1989). *Alexander Tcherepnin: A Bio-Bibliography*. New York: Greenwood Press: 9.
36. Tcherepnin A. (1964): 17.
37. *Ibid*.

In attracting your attention by sound, the ingenuity of the Chinese knows no limit: each motor-man of the street cars proudly clings to his own rhythm for the sounding of his gong, to warn you of coming danger; there are hardly two Chinese chauffeurs who would use the same rhythmic phrase for the blowing of their horns; the street vendors tax your imagination by the variety of their rhythms and by the percussion instruments they use in order to produce those rhythms. You soon discover that rhythm is fundamentally related to the life and work of the Chinese people.[38]

Having agreed to teach at the National Conservatory, Mr. Tcherepnin joined forces with Mr. Xiao, Mr. Huang, Mr. Foa, Mr. Zaharoff and the rest of the faculty in working to ensure that symphonic music, too, would become fundamentally related to the life and work of the Chinese people.

DISCOVERING MUSICAL TALENT

The National Conservatory of Music officially opened its doors at No. 56 Rue Dollfuss on November 27, 1927. A formal opening ceremony was held to mark the occasion, presided over by Cai Yuanpei and Xiao Youmei and attended by the 23 students who had been accepted into the very first class of the very first conservatory in China.

A photograph taken at the opening shows the students clustered together with Mr. Xiao and Mr. Cai in the doorway of the school. Mr. Cai is wearing a traditional Chinese *changpao* while Mr. Xiao is dressed in a Western suit and tie; the students sport the same combination of old and new fashion. No one is smiling and the serious expressions on their faces call to mind the sensitive Tcherepnin's description of Chinese music students:

> The Chinese student who decides to take up music as his profession does so, on the whole, not because his parents or relatives know anything about western art or western musical instruments, but perhaps because he found pleasure in playing one of the native instruments, or because he somehow had a chance to hear pieces of western or native music that impressed him, or because he tried to play a harmonium or half-broken piano during his free hours at a missionary school or church. Whatever the external reasons, it is an inner love for music and respect for art that are urging him, often against the will of his family, to devote himself to the study of music. Everything is foreign to him: the notation, the musical idiom, the instruments. An enormous will-power is required to overcome all these obstacles.[39]

If it was an inner love of music that drew this first class of students to the Conservatory, it was the rather more pragmatic criteria of musical experience and

---

38. Tcherepnin, A. (1935). Music in Modern China. *The Musical Quarterly*, Vol. XXI, No. 4, October: 392.

39. *Ibid.*, 397.

ability to pay that decided whether most were admitted. This meant that the majority of students were of middle-class background with some form of Western education. A young woman named Li Cuizhen, for example, had attended missionary schools in Shanghai and learned piano as a child. When she was accepted into the Conservatory in 1930, she could already play all 32 Beethoven piano sonatas from memory. A favorite of Professor Zaharoff, she completed the entire curriculum — which would take most students four to six years — in just one year. Similarly talented was a young woman named Li Xianmin, who also became Zaharoff's student. Zaharoff introduced her to Tcherepnin, who was so overwhelmed by both her talent and her person that he composed a piano piece for her.

Had Xiao Youmei accepted students based on experience and financial means alone, the Conservatory would have filled up with talented musicians from comfortable families like these. While there is nothing wrong with this, he wanted to do more than run a finishing school for pianists — his aim was to spread musical education far and wide in China. To achieve this goal, he needed a more diverse student body; and to get it he added a third criterion for admission: potential. It was most likely potential that led him to admit three early students who would go on to become crucial players in the development of symphonic music in China: Ding Shande, Xian Xinghai and He Luting.

Ding Shande was from a rural background and had none of the benefits of early piano lessons and exclusive missionary education. His introduction to music came through a gong and drum set that his mother bought him as a young child and from there progressed to *erhu, pipa* and Chinese flute. He was particularly drawn to the *pipa* and would spend long hours watching a local *ping-tan* storytelling master perform on the instrument, rushing back home to try to play what he had just heard. After a time, the master noticed the young boy and offered to give him a few pointers. This included such advice as plunging his hands into ice water before practicing, playing until they warmed up, and then repeating the process — this, the master told him, makes your fingers strong and gives you discipline.

When Ding Shande was only four years old, his mother was left a widow with seven children; but she still managed to send him to the local public elementary and middle schools. This was the era in which music education was being introduced into the education system and Ding became the leader of his school's Chinese instrument ensemble. Later, when the school bought some trumpets and Western-style drums, he learned staff notation and played a bit of trumpet in the school's small band. As he was preparing to graduate from middle school, the principal told him that a conservatory was starting up in Shanghai and urged him to apply. With Cai Yuanpei and Xiao Youmei involved, the principal said, it was certain to be a school worth attending.

Mr. Ding took this friendly advice and travelled to Shanghai for the auditions. The Conservatory was housed in an imposing foreign-style building and the people he saw there all seemed extraordinarily fashionable and modern; to the end of his life, he remembered the shock he felt when he first entered campus and saw a student couple walking arm-in-arm — in public! But, he swallowed his apprehensions and went to sit for the auditions. Mr. Xiao greeted him politely and then asked, "Can you play piano?"

"No."

"Can you play violin?"

"No."

With the two main Western instruments ruled out, Xiao quizzed Ding about his experience with Chinese instruments, asked him to play a few pieces on the *pipa* and then excused him. Mr. Ding went back to his village and soon received a letter telling him he had been wait-listed. When he heard nothing more, he took it upon himself to venture back to the big city and find out whether or not he was to be admitted. Mr. Xiao met with him again, reviewed his academic records and then asked,

"Do you have enough money?"

Mr. Ding replied in the affirmative and this, together with his *pipa* playing — and his persistence — got him admitted as a *pipa* major and a piano minor.

Delighted to be accepted to this seeming citadel of music and modernity, Ding Shande plunged himself into his studies. He became so obsessed by the piano that he completed a year's worth of lessons in two months and soon made it his major, rather than *pipa*. He spent so much time in the practice room that he gained a reputation as the campus nerd, seen outdoors in his French beret and black wool Sun Yat-sen jacket only when he was en route to class or practice. When he was once spotted at a concert with his girlfriend — and future wife — it became the talk of the school, because no one could imagine how the country boy who never stopped practicing had ever managed to find a girlfriend.

When Zaharoff joined the National Conervatory in 1929, all the piano students wanted to study with him. However, part of the deal he had made in accepting the job was that he need only teach seven students. Since Ding Shande was such a novice to the instrument, he did not bother to apply to study with the famed Russian; when the list of accepted students was posted and his name was on it, he was stunned. It was only at his first lesson that he learned that Xiao Youmei had recommended him to Zaharoff.

Studying with Zaharoff was something of a life-changing experience for the young man who had grown up learning Chinese instruments from relatives and old-style masters in the countryside. At his first lesson, he played Mozart's *C Major Sonata*, and thought he had carried it off quite well until Mr. Zaharoff pointed out the problems: tempo, dynamic, rhythm, fingering, and expression. So demanding was his new professor that Mr. Ding could not sleep or eat before his lessons and his heart would race and hands shake when he heard Mr. Zaharoff's footsteps in the hall.

Like many piano teachers back then, Zaharoff was strict. Indeed, Ding soon became accustomed to his professor's habit of twisting his neck and shoulders, striking his head, and even shouting "I KILL YOU!"[40] However, if Zaharoff made no

---

40. Quote comes from Dai Penghai (1993). *Ding Shande Yinyue Nianpu* [A Musical Chronicle of Ding Shande]. Beijing: Zhongyang Yinyue Xueyuan Xuebaoshe: 20.

effort to restrain his anger when his student failed to meet expectations, he was similarly effusive when he played well, patting him on the shoulder, giving him bear hugs, and praising him with the words, "Dink, good boy." He was also so devoted to his student's progress that he would attend every performance Mr. Ding gave and then offer him a detailed critique.

Xian Xinghai, who was also accepted into one of the Conservatory's first classes, was from a background far more disenfranchised then that of his classmate. Mr. Xian — whose given name, Xinghai, means "Stars and Sea" — came from a family of boat people who made their living off the waters in the southern province of Guangdong. Back then, boat people were social outcasts who lived lives of often desperate poverty, and the Xian family was no exception. His father died before Xinghai was born and his widowed mother took him first to Macao and then to Singapore, where some of her husband's relatives had emigrated. Determined that her son should get a proper education, she worked as a servant in order to put him through school. Xian reciprocated his mother's love and sacrifices through hard work, and eventually ended up returning to Guangdong to enroll in the prestigious Lingnan University, which was run by American missionaries.

Xian flourished at Lingnan. He studied clarinet and violin with an American teacher and spent hours after class listening to an American philosophy professor talk about Beethoven, Bach, Picasso and Matisse. He joined the university's brass band and orchestra, and was even elected a leader of the school's YMCA chapter. Since he was still poor, he supported himself with odd jobs, including so many gigs playing the clarinet that he was nicknamed the "Clarinet King of South China."[41] In 1925, Xian moved north to study at the Institute for the Promotion and Practice of Music that Xiao Youmei had founded at Beijing University.

"Beethoven's mother worked for rich people in the kitchen — my mother did the same," Xian Xinghai told Xiao Youmei. "My goal is to contribute to music just like Beethoven did." [42]

Mr. Xiao was impressed with the penniless young man's intensity and helped him find a job in the Beijing Library, as well as extra employment copying scores. When the Institute for the Promotion and Practice of Music was shut down the following year, Mr. Xian returned to Lingnan to graduate and then followed Mr. Xiao to Shanghai to study violin and piano at the National Conservatory.

Immersed in music though he was, Xian Xinghai was not the sort to spend his life in an ivory tower, oblivious of the world around him. Unsurprisingly, given his background, his political sympathies lay with the leftists and he soon became involved with a leftist literary and art group called the Southern Society that had been started by the writer Tian Han. Through the Society, he became increasingly caught up in the

41. Kraus, R.C. (1989). *Pianos & Politics in China: Middle-Class Ambitions and the Struggle over Western Music.* New York: Oxford University Press: 42.

42. Xiao Shuxian. Huiyi wode Shufu, Xiao Youmei [Remembering my uncle Xiao Youmei]. In Dai Penghai, Huang Xudong (eds.) (1993). *Xiao Youmei Jinian Wenji* [Collected Articles on Xiao Youmei]. Shanghai: Shanghai Yinyue Chubanshe: 83-99.

politics of the moment and it was he, in fact, who organized the protests against the tuition hike at the National Conservatory — a leadership role which got him dropped from its roster. Barred from attending the only conservatory in China, but determined to keep studying Western classical music, Xian got a job stoking coal on a British ship sailing to Singapore and from there made his way to Paris.

The third student admitted largely on the basis of potential, He Luting, was born into a peasant family in a remote village in the mountains of south central Hunan, Mao Zedong's home province. Mr. He's father was a member of an amateur local opera troupe that performed at weddings and funerals, so music was a part of the family's life. His introduction to Western music came indirectly via his third brother, who went off to France in the early 1920s and left behind a music text book. The curious Mr. He started reading the book and soon became so fascinated by Western music that he taught himself staff notation, and dreamed of becoming a music teacher. In pursuit of this dream, he applied to the Yueyun School in Changsha — a prestigious, new-style school that was also attended by Mao Zedong's first wife, Yang Kaihui, and the feminist writer Ding Ling — and was accepted.

Soon after his arrival at his new school, Mr. He saw a piano and, rather like Ding Shande, became obsessed with learning how to play it. He sneaked into the practice room whenever he could and, according to his roommate, once fell out of bed in the middle of the night with his hands moving, as though over a keyboard. He worked almost as hard at drawing as at music and gained a reputation for qualities that would one day make him famous — diligence, talent, stubbornness and outspokenness.

On one occasion when a new drawing teacher was hired, Mr. He evaluated his work and, finding it lacking, announced to his fellow students, "He's not very good — I am better." [43] Asked how he dared say such a thing of a teacher, he replied, "I am telling the truth." The other students told him to drop it, since there was nothing he could do; but Mr. He replied that there was something he could do — and went straight to the school principal to inform him that the new teacher was not qualified. In a short time, the new teacher was gone and, upon graduating, Mr. He was hired to teach music to the whole school.

While teaching at the Yueyun School, Mr. He read Karl Marx's *Das Kapital* and then shocked his friends once again by quitting his highly desirable job after only one year, in order to go back to his hometown of Xiangyang to participate in the peasant movement. Back in Xiangyang, he taught art and music at the local middle school, joined the Communist Party and also met his future wife, Jiang Ruizhi. Then, in 1930, he heard about the National Conservatory and left his job and travelled to Shanghai in the hopes of attending. Since he did not have enough money to pay the tuition, he taught at an elementary school for a year and then enrolled in the Conservatory, where he studied harmony with Huang Zi and piano with Zaharoff. Under Huang Zi's tutelage, he translated into Chinese a book on harmony by the British music theorist

43. For anecdote and related quotes, see Shi Zhongxin (2000). *He Luting Zhuan* [A Biography of He Luting]. Shanghai: Shanghai Yinyue Chubanshe: 15.

Ebenezer Prout. As the first Chinese-language work on the subject, Mr. He's translation of Mr. Prout's work was used by musicians for decades to come.

And so, with this sprinkling of poor, rural — but extremely determined — students added to the pool of privileged, urban musicians that comprised most of the student body, the National Conservatory of Music got off to a dynamic, if sometimes bumpy, start. Before long, it stood alongside the Shanghai Municipal Orchestra as a second pillar of Shanghai's burgeoning European music world.

PACI'S "MISSIONARY WORK"

At the end of May in 1932, a Shanghailander named Geraldine T. Fitch penned a letter to the *North China Daily News,* praising the final concert of the SMO's regular season. Having just heard the orchestra in a program that included Maestro Paci's rendition of Mozart's *Coronation Concerto,* Ms. Fitch wrote that she wondered "if Vienna or Paris or New York City has anything better to offer."[44]

Such enthusiasm might have been considered excessive by residents of the cities Ms. Fitch named, but it does indicate the progress that Shanghai's music lovers felt had been made in achieving for their city that longed-for designation, "musical Paris of the East."

Indeed, in the month Ms. Fitch was writing, music lovers could attend performances almost every night of the week. On May 4, for instance, the Russian Musical Society staged *Boris Godunov* at the Embassy Theater. On May 5, the Farren troupe of ballet dancers — just back from touring in Manila — performed at Astor House. On May 7, the "leading mezzo-soprano Lisa Jouravel" of the "Royal Theater" of Turin sang at the Carlton Theater, accompanied by the SMO under Maestro Paci. On May 8, the Music Section of the Shanghai Art Club gave its 13th Chamber Music Concert in the Hall of the American Women's Club on Bubbling Well Road. On May 9, the "brilliant young Russian prodigy virtuoso, Miss Lalia Fuchs," held a piano recital at the Embassy Theater. On May 12, Messrs. Foa, Zaharoff, Lifshitz, Gerzovsky, and Shertzoff performed Erno von Dohnanyi's *Piano Quintette in C minor Op. 1* "by general request" — and the list goes on.[45]

Though Shanghai's many concerts, ballets, operas and recitals were performed by diverse groups of musicians, it was Maestro Paci and the Shanghai Municipal Orchestra that stood at the center of its flourishing professional music world.

By the early 1930s, Maestro Paci had been at the helm of the SMO for more than a decade, exerting himself so whole-heartedly that Tcherepnin wrote of him as the "enlightened musician and conductor, Mario Paci" who "looked upon his job as missionary work." [46] He had inarguably completed his self-given task of "building up a real symphony orchestra" and gone far in making the SMO "second to none," at least in

44. Fitch, G. (1932). Letters, a tribute. *North China Daily News.* May 4: 4.
45. All information taken from pages of *North China Daily News,* May 1-7, 1932.
46. Tcherepnin: 395.

Asia. He had also done much to further such of his secondary missions as promoting contemporary classical music, broadening the SMO's audience base, and nurturing China's first generation of professional classical musicians.

Although Maestro Paci's commitment to music written by the composers of his day was not shared by many in Shanghai, he insisted on performing such works — whether his audiences and employers liked it or not. Again, in Tcherepnin's words:

> In his independent mind [Maestro Paci] conceived a plan to educate his public by introducing it not only to the usual symphonic repertory, but also to the latest compositions of the moderns. He played, sometimes in advance of his Western colleagues, works of Respighi, Rieti, Malipiero, de Falla, Ravel, Kodaly, Bartok, Graener, Hindemith. Although his choice did not always meet with the approval of the Municipal Council, the high standard of his performances, together with his great authority, left no valid ground for an effective attack on his venturesome programs.[47]

Paci had more support for his outreach efforts which, by the late 1920s, were increasingly directed at Shanghai's Chinese community. Radio broadcasts were started in 1926, concert announcements were placed in the Chinese-language press from 1928, and gramophone recordings were made beginning in 1929.[48] Around this time Paci also started a sophisticated series of "young people's" concerts, in which Chinese children were active participants. The program for a young people's concert devoted to the music of Schubert in November of 1928, for example, featured a Chinese girl named Lao Ming How, while a program from May of 1929 featured five Chinese children on various instruments, including a young violinist who studied with Arrigo Foa. The Shanghai Municipal Council began allowing Chinese to enter International Settlement parks in 1928 and many Chinese took advantage of this opening to hear the SMO's summer concerts — indeed, in the summer of 1928, three-quarters of the audience at these outdoor concerts was Chinese.[49]

To reach Chinese adults interested in music, Paci took on the job of conducting a group of all-Chinese singers, called the "Shanghai Songsters," in 1929. Though the men

---

47. *Ibid.* For similar comments, see Austin, A. (1939) Under the baton of Maestro Paci.... *The China Press Sunday Magazine*, May 7. Austin writes, "He is a conductor who closely follows modern music and often gives it to the public in spite of ultra-conservative listeners for whom the last composer died with Bach, Mozart and Beethoven. He is intensely interested in Japanese and especially Chinese music...."

48. See Bickers, R. (2001). The Greatest Cultural Asset East of Suez: The History and Politics of the Shanghai Municipal Orchestra and Public Band, 1881-1946. Chi-hsiung Chang (chief ed.), *Ershi shiji de Zhongguo yu shijie* [China and the world in the twentieth century]. Taibei: Institute of History, Academia Sinica: Vol 2: 854 and 856.

49. Attendance figure comes from Bickers: 856. The subject of the ban on Chinese entering the parks has been much discussed and written about; virtually every tourist to Shanghai knows the story of the "No Chinese or Dogs" sign which was said to have hung on the gate of the Public Gardens. (The sign actually listed many different regulations regarding the park; among them, but cited separately, were that neither dogs nor Chinese could enter, unless the Chinese was in the employ of a Westerner.) It is worth noting that Tan Shuzhen laughed about this story and told Sheila Melvin that he often went into all the parks, including the Public Gardens, before the ban was lifted and that he never had any problem. He stated that the guards may have kept poor Chinese out, but that they did nothing to prevent well-dressed Chinese from entering the parks. Of course, this does not make the ban right.

and women were all amateurs, he made it a requirement that they "religiously" attend the weekly rehearsal each Friday.[50] He thought highly enough of the group to invite them to perform with the orchestra and the last SMO concert of the 1929 season featured the Songsters in a program that included sacred music, gypsy music, and English music.

Paci was also interested in Chinese music and supportive of the efforts of Chinese composers. In 1930, he gave Huang Zi's *In Memoriam* its Chinese premiere and in May of 1933 he involved the orchestra in an eclectic event known as a "Grand Chinese Evening." This unusual program was held in place of the orchestra's 29th symphony concert and drew the biggest audience of the year, 1800 people.[51] It was produced by the International Arts Theater group and sponsored by Mei Lanfang, the great Peking opera star who was then at the peak of his career. It was divided into two parts, the first consisting of Chinese musicians performing on Chinese instruments and the second devoted to the Chinese-inspired works of a Russian émigré composer named Aaron Avshalomov.

Avshalomov came from a wealthy family of Caucasian Jews who lived in Eastern Siberia. As a young child, he had been cared for by a Chinese "all-around man" who introduced him to Chinese song and theatrics and evidently instilled in him a life-long fascination with Chinese music. Intrigued by China since childhood, he moved there as a young man, living first in Harbin and then in Tianjin where he worked at various jobs — including abattoir employee, cattle dealer, and grocery store owner — to support himself and his family while he composed music based on Chinese melodies, often using tales or legends from Chinese history as the theme. His devotion to China's music and culture made him many Chinese friends and, after moving to Shanghai in 1931, he managed to integrate himself in both the foreign and Chinese artistic communities.

For the "Grand Chinese Evening," the SMO played three Avshalomov pieces, including *The Hutongs of Peking*, which had actually been performed in the US two years earlier by the Philadelphia Orchestra under Leopold Stokowski. *Hutongs* was scored for a full western orchestra supplemented with Chinese percussion instruments and — since it was intended to evoke the sounds of Beijing's alleys — a metal tool that itinerant Chinese barbers used to alert potential customers to their presence.

"The Grand Chinese Evening" was a big event, but of all Paci's outreach efforts, perhaps the most ambitious was a concert tour to Nanjing in the spring of 1937. The SMO had been invited by the Ministry of Education to celebrate the opening of the new National Assembly Hall and Paci saw it as an excellent opportunity both to showcase the orchestra he had built and to spread Western music. Shanghai's papers gave the tour considerable press and the *North China Daily News* — in an article subtitled, "Arousing Interest in Western Music" — even called it, with some exaggeration, "the first time that a symphony orchestra has ever visited the capital, or

---

50. *The North China Daily News*, March 15, 1931.
51. For attendance figure, see Bickers: 857.

for that matter, anywhere else in China outside Shanghai."[52] Two thousand four hundred people attended the concert, which included performances of Beethoven's *Fifth Symphony*, Wagner's *Tannhauser Overture* and a short cantata sung by a Chinese chorus for which Chiang Kai-shek himself had written the lyrics.[53] The day after the concert, the SMO played for a performance of Haydn's *Creation* that was sung by students of Nanjing's Central University.

Maestro Paci's work with Chinese musicians took place on two fronts, in the teaching studio and the concert hall. Unsurprisingly, studying with Paci was a very serious undertaking, requiring not just talent but absolute dedication and commitment. The Steinway in his office was placed on a riser and as the student played, Paci circled it as a lion might his prey. As with the orchestra, his hand was apt to slip and rap the student's knuckles or head if he played too many notes in error. In his teaching, Paci practiced a policy of zero tolerance for amateurs — when his daughter Fofi grew old enough to play he would not even allow her, his own flesh and blood, to take lessons because he did not consider her talented enough.

"He hated amateurs," Fofi recalled. "If a student wasn't good enough, he would say to the parents, 'Buy him a gramophone!' Once when he was being operated on and the anesthesia didn't take, he shouted 'Amateurs!' That was the worst thing he could say."

If Paci had no sympathy for untalented pianists, he was color-blind when it came to teaching those who did have ability and he accepted Chinese students on the same terms as Westerners.

"My father admired the Chinese very much," remembered Fofi. "He thought they had the greatest culture and history. He had so many Chinese students — he said they were very, very talented."

Dong Guangguang, who studied with Paci as a child and now lives in New York, recalled that she was accepted as Paci's student after playing Beethoven at her audition — and then agreeing to "start from scratch" by spending the first three months of her lessons doing fingering.

"Maestro Paci was so strict with me I couldn't even think," she laughed. "The piano was on a riser, and it was so loud. It was very frightening — he would bang on the riser if the tempo wasn't right, and the echo! And when we had visitors during a lesson, he'd pick the most difficult thing and say 'Guangguang, play that.' Oh, he was very, very strict. He'd pinch and pull hair... But, Paci made me — he really made me."

Paci organized recitals for his best students, and Ms. Dong remembered the evening of her first one.

"After my first recital, my cousin came backstage to see me and I was very happy. But Maestro Paci was very displeased. He said, 'I want to see your parents tonight.' So,

---

52. Orchestra's visit to the capital. *North China Daily News*, April 1937.

53. Attendance figures come from Bickers: 863. Repertoire comes from (1937) Orchestra's visit to the capital. First symphony concert ever to be given in Nanking. Arousing interest in Western music. *North China Daily News*. Article is missing publication date, but is from first half of April.

he took a rickshaw and came to my house and my parents were very scared. He sat down and said, 'Who was that boy?' I said, 'He's my cousin, Samuel.' Paci said, 'Oh! Well, this is a good opportunity. I want you all to know that you are not an ordinary pianist — you are special, you have a future. You cannot be friends with just anyone.'"

When Ms. Dong was older, Paci again approached her on a semi-personal matter, telling her, "Do you know that Ma Sihong? He's good enough to be your friend. You can play chamber music with him.'"

Ma Sihong was a talented violinist and Dong Guangguang took Maestro Paci's advice, perhaps more so than he could have imagined — years later, in America, she married him.

Paci was also serious enough about the training of Chinese musicians that he became involved in plans to establish a conservatory in neighboring Zhejiang Province. Although he was supportive of the National Conservatory — even to the point of personally issuing special cards to its students so that they could attend all SMO rehearsals and buy reduced-price concert tickets — he did not consider it to be in the same class as a true conservatory, because it required students to pay tuition. The conservatory he intended to help found would be funded by the Zhejiang government, so that students could attend without charge. In this way, he explained, "really talented pupils [can] be discovered and given an opportunity to apply themselves wholeheartedly to the study of music. Then a selection is made once a year, and only the most capable ones are to remain. After having gone through such sifting several times, when a student finally graduates from the conservatory, he really amounts to something."[54]

As a conductor, the most obvious step Paci could have taken to further the development of Chinese musicians was to integrate the orchestra, but his progress in this was somewhat slow. Tan Shuzhen had left the SMO after only one season in order to continue his studies more formally, so the orchestra again became all-foreign in 1928 and stayed that way for another decade. In the meantime, however, Maestro Paci lent his support to Chinese musicians by inviting them to perform with the orchestra as soloists. [55]

The very first Chinese soloist to play with the SMO was a 17-year-old Cantonese violinist named Ma Sicong — the older brother of Ma Sihong — who later became known outside China as Sitson Ma. Mr. Ma came from a prosperous, intellectual family that was also politically active; his father supported Sun Yat-sen's revolution and afterwards became treasurer of the Guangdong government. Although Ma received a basic musical education at the prestigious missionary school he attended from the age of six, his musical turning point came when his older brother returned on holiday from his studies in France and brought him a French violin.

---

54. Ho Chia-shui (1946). Paci tells of orchestra's growth, treatment by the Japs. *The China Press*, October 21: 12.

55. For a complete list, see Han, *Shanghai gongbuju yuedui yenjiu*: 83.

Mr. Ma fell instantly in love with the instrument and begged so persuasively to be allowed to study it in France that in 1923 — when he was still only 11 — he found himself living in Fontainebleau under his brother's supervision and studying violin with a private teacher. When his brother decided that his young charge needed more systematic lessons and language study, the two moved to Nancy, where Mr. Ma attended music school and learned French, music theory, solfege (or sight-singing), violin, piano and clarinet. He was able to play a Paganini violin concerto after only a year, causing his brother to announce that it was time to go to Paris. Mr. Ma applied to the Paris Conservatory and in 1928 became the first Chinese accepted to that august institution. At home on holiday from the Conservatory in December of 1929, he was invited to play Mozart's *Violin Concerto in E Flat Major* with the SMO. Ma Sicong's premiere performance with the SMO was a success, one which reflected well on him, the orchestra, and Maestro Paci.

But, Paci had his limitations both as a person and as a musical missionary, and another of his attempts to provide a platform to Chinese musician — who, like Ma, would go on to be famous — ended acrimoniously when he changed his mind at the last minute. The musician was none other than Xian Xinghai, who returned to Shanghai from Paris in 1935.

Mr. Xian's time in what was then the classical music capital of the world had been difficult. He had crossed paths with Ma Sicong soon after his arrival and Ma had introduced him to his violin teacher, Paul Oberdorfer. This introduction was of great help to Xian, since Oberdorfer not only agreed to teach him, but refused to take payment when he learned of his poverty. Unfortunately, Mr. Ma was unable to offer Mr. Xian any further help or friendship since his own family's finances soon took a turn for the worse, forcing him to drop out of the Paris Conservatory and return to China.

Xian seems to have been left friendless in Paris, so short of money that he found it a struggle just to fill his stomach. He finally found a job as a waiter, but it proved to be a mixed blessing — he was able to eat, but it was only after working a ten hour day that he could go back to his garret to practice the violin and study music theory. This schedule left him so exhausted that one day he fainted from dizziness, smashed a tray of dishes, and was promptly fired. After that, he spent two more years living from hand-to-mouth, growing increasingly frustrated because he had not yet found a way to study music formally.

It was in this unhappy condition that he went to the Overseas Chinese Trade Union office to watch a documentary about the sufferings his fellow countrymen had been forced to endure since the Japanese takeover of Manchuria. Devastated by what he saw, he returned to his bleak lodgings and tried to capture his emotions in music. As he described the experience,

> Paris is always colder than South China, and on that winter night there was also a raging wind. I had no blanket and could not get to sleep. The only thing to do was to light the lamp and start writing. The wind blew fiercely into the room and the kerosene

lantern (I could not turn on the electric light) blew out again and again. I became very depressed, and as I listened, shivering, to the freezing wind shake the walls and roar through the windows, my heart beat fiercely along with the wind. All of the bitterness, cruelty, pain, and misfortune of life in our homeland surged forth. I could not control my own feelings, but took advantage of the wind to write out my emotions and complete this composition.[56]

The composition that came from Mr. Xian's emotions on this bleak night was an orchestral piece with a solo female voice, called *Wind*. He submitted it with his application for admission to the Paris Conservatory of Music and the composition professor, Paul Dukas, accepted Xian into his senior composition class. Dukas was a renowned composer as was another of Xian's professors, Vincent D'Indy, and through their support he found his entrée into the Parisian musical world greatly eased. His compositions were played publicly and on one occasion a piece he wrote was broadcast on the radio, with an introduction by the great composer Sergei Prokofiev.

However, despite these successes, poverty continued to dog Xian. Dukas gave him clothes and money and Oberdorfer continued to teach him for free, but he apparently got little sympathy from other Chinese students who were studying in Paris, most of whom came from wealthy families and found it embarrassing that one of their fellow countrymen played his violin on the street for money. Resentment and unhappiness seemed to weigh heavily on him, even as he struggled onward with his studies and compositions.

When Dukas died in 1935, Xian left the Paris Conservatory without graduating and returned to China. Settling back into Shanghai, he began to make contacts with members of its professional music world and, somewhere along the way, Paci evidently agreed to let the him conduct the SMO in a performance of Beethoven's *Eighth Symphony*. However, as Xian Xinghai recounted it, after the start of rehearsals, "Foa created opposition to me in the orchestra because seven years ago I opposed the corruption of the National Conservatory and was the leader of the protests." [57] Nonplussed by this opposition from Mr. Foa and other musicians who were connected to the Conservatory, Paci rescinded his invitation, "humiliating [Xian] in front of everyone."[58]

Looking for help to remedy the situation, Xian Xinghai turned to the composer Aaron Avshalomov, who willingly interceded with Paci, but to no avail. When Paci refused to change his mind, Avshalomov invited the unhappy Xian home for dinner. He comforted him with words which Mr. Xian would always remember: "Don't get discouraged. A musician's life and career do not depend on one performance. You work

56. Kraus: 47.
57. Xian Xinghai (1989). Minzu Jiefang Jiaoxiangyue [People's Liberation Symphony]. *Xian Xinghai* [The Complete Works of Xian Xinghai]. Guangdong: Guangdong Gaojiao Chubanshe: Vol. I, 148.
58. Xian: 148.

hard and two years from now when you know the Chinese situation better, you will become China's first composer." [59]

MUSIC AS A WEAPON

Avshalomov's words of comfort to Xian Xinghai were motivated by more than compassion. Indeed, the foreign composer sincerely hoped that Xian Xinghai would become China's "first composer" because he was genuinely worried about the increasing "Westernization" of China's musical life.

To vent his concern, he began to write articles and give talks on the subject. In one such article dating to the mid-1930s, he described the "invasion" of "Western-European music" that had begun in the early 20th century. It accelerated with the founding of the National Conservatory, he wrote, and the influence of Western music had then begun to spread so rapidly — through brass bands, the gramophone, jazz-bands, cinema and radio — that there was a danger it would entirely eclipse Chinese music.

> The present generation in China is so much influenced by all this that within a decade or two it may "Europeanize" Chinese musical activity entirely. If this happens we should regret that classical Chinese music would no longer exist to serve as a basis for building a truly Chinese modern music. [60]

Alexander Tcherepnin shared Avshalomov's concerns. Over the course of the 1930s, Chinese musicians were becoming increasingly visible in Shanghai's classical music world and the Conservatory's success in training them was apparent. However, the music that these students played was almost always Western in origin; there were 110 advanced students at the Conservatory in 1937, but only two of them studied traditional Chinese instrumental music. [61] Similarly, the music written by young Chinese in the composition department was often so derivative that it may as well have been written by a Westerner.

With his strong opinions on the value of folk music, Tcherepnin thought it a shame that Chinese composers did not dig deeper into their own culture for inspiration. In his words,

> Great musical activity is going on in China. The Chinese composer has under his hands one of the richest sources of native music. He has the world's most populous country to support him. The more national his product, the greater will be its international value. [62]

Tcherepnin tried to encourage Chinese composers to create more "national products" in several ways, including by example. One of his earliest efforts at

---

59. *Ibid.*
60. Avshalomov, J. and A. (2001). *Avshalomov's Winding Way.* Xlibris Corporation: 75.
61. Jones: 42.
62. Tcherepnin: 399.

composing "Chinese" music was a piano method based on China's pentatonic scale. This was followed, in 1936, by *Technical Studies on the Pentatonic Scale Op. 53*, which was soon adopted by the government as the official piano method and used in lessons throughout the country.[63] More ambitiously, he set out to compose an opera based on the great Qing Dynasty novel *Dream of the Red Chamber*, and even got the much revered writer Lu Xun to agree to write the libretto. Unfortunately, Lu Xun was ill at the time and died soon after, so all that remains of the project is the tantalizing possibility of what could have been.[64]

To further motivate his Conservatory students to compose, Tcherepnin sponsored a competition for which they were invited to submit compositions with "Chinese flavor." The judges were an all-star panel of French composers — Arthur Honegger, Jacques Ibert and Albert Roussel — and the results were announced on November 26, 1934. First prize was awarded to He Luting for a piece called *Buffalo Boy's Flute*, which Tcherepnin said showed originality, clarity, and a sure hand at counterpoint and form. The competition was reported on in the local Chinese press and one newspaper, *Xinyebao*, even asked Mr. He to write a short article about himself. He submitted the following poignant piece:

> My father passed away in June of this year and at home there is a big hunger. My third brother is ill and has to stop his profession to recover. In order to live, I may have to temporarily stop my studies. My journey of life will always be circuitous. Most of my knowledge of music I learned from Huang Zi. The harmony book I translated he also read many times to correct and point out mistakes. So, I must say that Huang Zi is my most compassionate teacher and the director of my future journey. I will never forget this.[65]

Because he recognized that the works of Chinese composers would have little impact if they were not disseminated, Tcherepnin also founded his own publishing company, called "Collection Tcherepnin," which specialized in printing and promoting the works of young Chinese and Japanese composers. The prize-winning composition by He Luting was published in "Collection Tcherepnin" and the image of a buffalo boy playing a flute was chosen as the logo for the firm.[66]

---

63. Arias: 13.

64. For Tcherepnin's plans to compose the opera and Lu Xun's consent to collaborate, see Shi Zhongxin (2000). *He Luting Zhuan* [A Biography of He Luting]. Shanghai: Shanghai Yinyue Chubanshe: 90-1. Mr. He told his biographer that he went to visit Tcherepnin one day and saw *The Dream of the Red Chamber* lying open on a table. Tcherepnin explained his plans to compose the opera, and added that he hoped Lu Xun would write the libretto but feared that since he was the greatest author in China, he might not have the time or interest. Mr. He suggested that Tcherepnin write to Lu Xun and then delivered the letter to a bookstore that the famous writer frequented. When he returned to visit Tcherepnin again a few days later, the composer excitedly showed him Lu Xun's letter agreeing to the project. Mr. He was amazed not only by Lu Xun's positive response, but at the speed with which he had delivered it.

65. He Luting (1999). *He Luting Quanji* [The Complete Works of He Luting]. Shanghai: Shanghai Yinyue Chubanshe: Vol. 4: 16.

66. Interestingly enough, *Buffalo Boy's Flute* was one of the few pieces of Paci's music that his daughter still possessed decades after she left Shanghai, when the authors met her in New York.

The concern and support of foreigners like Avshalomov and Tcherepnin was welcomed by young Chinese composers such as Xian Xinghai and He Luting. But the creation of national music products would only be meaningful and sustainable if initiated by Chinese themselves. And, in fact, an indigenous movement to develop and promote China's own modern music began in Shanghai around 1930, although it took a different path than Avshalomov and Tcherepnin might have envisioned. It was closely tied to China's political situation and accelerated after the Japanese bombed the city's Zhabei district in 1932.

The movement was known by several different names over the course of the decade — the National Salvation Song Movement, the National Defense Song Movement, the New Music Movement — but all were essentially one revolutionary music movement that originated in Shanghai. Although many of its proponents had connections with the Conservatory, their primary inspiration came from outside the ivory tower of academia in the real world of poverty, imperialism, and impending war. They linked up with each other, not in classes on harmony and counterpoint but through Communist Party-affiliated associations like the League of Left-Wing Writers, the Soviet Union Friendship Society, and the Chinese New Music Research Society. Music, to them, was more than the beautiful art and sometime tool of social change and nation-building promoted by men like Xiao Youmei; instead, it was "a weapon for liberating the masses" which it was their obligation to wield.[67]

Because this music was meant to awaken the masses to action, much of it was unaccompanied song intended to be sung in the streets by thousands of people. The songs used Western tonality and were usually written in major keys. They had short and simple melodies, lyrics that intended to motivate resistance to Japan or sympathy with the plight of common Chinese people, and they often sounded like battle marches. Of course, using song to incite revolutionary change was not a new idea; the French Revolution was a deliberate model and songs had been used by Marxist organizers in China for some years. However, most of the songs used previously were imported, like *The Internationale* and a host of Soviet pieces, and thus did not have the same impact as songs written by native composers with lyrics reflective of China's own situation.

The most representative member of this movement is perhaps Nie Er, the composer of *The March of the Volunteers*, which became the national anthem of the People's Republic of China in 1949. Like Xian Xinghai, Nie Er was an outsider in Shanghai society, a member of the Dai minority from distant Yunnan Province. As an impressionable and romantic young man, he came under the tutelage of a cultured European who taught English at the YMCA in the provincial capital. Under this teacher's guidance, Nie Er studied everything from classical music to Nordic mythology and even adopted the English name George Njal in homage to the hero of

---

67. The quote is from the composer Lu Ji, writing in the magazine *Guangming*, in August of 1936. See Ming Yan (2002). *Ershishiji Zhongguo Yinyue Piping Daolun*. [A Guide to 20th-Century Music Criticism in China]. Beijing: Renmin Yinyue Chubanshe: 161.

the 13th-century Icelandic folk epic, *Njal's Saga*. In his late teens, he enrolled in a teacher's college and began to teach himself violin. He was so devoted to learning the instrument that he carried it with him everywhere and practiced whenever he had a free moment. When he was not playing the violin, Nie Er studied Marxism and became so involved in Communist Party activities against the warlords who ran Yunnan that in 1930 he was forced to make plans to flee for his safety.

He decided to go to Shanghai, and shortly before leaving went for a walk with his older brother. They had just sat down in a pavilion to chat when the sky darkened, the wind began to blow, and torrents of rain came down. Thrilled by the sudden cloudburst, Nie Er pulled out his violin, telling his brother that the sound of the wind and the rain would be a nice combination with the color of his instrument. He played Schumann, a Chinese piece, and the French national anthem, the *Marseillaise*. When he finished, his brother told him that he hoped someone in China would one day compose a piece like the *Marseillaise* and Nie Er replied that he need not worry — China would definitely produce such a composer.[68]

Once in Shanghai, Nie Er began to play violin in the extraordinarily popular Bright Moon Song and Dance Troupe led by Li Jinhui, a pioneer in the composition and performance of a kind of Sinified jazz that was pejoratively known as "yellow music."[69] He also pursued his interest in classical music by attending SMO concerts, playing with an amateur orchestra in the French Concession, and taking violin lessons with the renowned Czech teacher, Josef Padushka.[70] As was the case with so many students from the provinces, these lessons were like a bucket of cold water for the young violinist, who soon discovered that everything about his playing technique was wrong. So determined was he to improve that he spent 12 yuan per month of his 25 yuan salary on lessons, borrowing money from his boss and then resorting to pawnbrokers as he fell ever deeper into debt.

The January 1932 bombing of Shanghai's Zhabei district, which left untold numbers of civilians dead, affected Nie Er deeply; it seems to have caused him to have a crisis of conscience. "How to create revolutionary music?" he wrote in a March 7 journal entry that was sprinkled with English words (in italics),

> That's the question I've been thinking about all day, but I haven't come up with any concrete plans yet. Isn't so-called *classic* music just a plaything of the leisure class? I spend a few hours every day slaving over my basic exercises. After a few years, even a decade, I become a *violinist*. So what? Can you excite the laboring masses by playing a Beethoven *Sonata*? Will that really be an inspiration to them? No! This is a dead end. Wake up before it's too late."[71]

---

68. For this anecdote, see Qi Teng Xiao Zhi (translated from the Japanese by Zhuang Li) (2003). *Nie Er. Shanguangde Shengya* [Nie Er: a shining life]. Shanghai: Shanghai Yinyue Chubanshe: 8. The anecdote comes from Nie Er's brother, whom the author of this biography interviewed.

69. For a thorough discussion of Li Jinhui's career, influence and subsequent vilification, see Jones, *Yellow Music*.

70. For an account of Nie Er's studies with Padushka drawn from Nie Er's journals, see Qi Teng Xiao Zhi: 108.

Nie Er did not completely forsake classical music; he even applied to the National Conservatory in 1933, but was not accepted, apparently for reasons that had more to do with politics than music.[72] However, he completely rejected the "soft tofu"[73] music of his one-time boss, Li Jinhui, and from 1932 onward began to actively integrate his revolutionary ideals with his musical talents. The influential Communist dramatist Tian Han encouraged him to found the Soviet Union Friendship Society, which became a vehicle for the study of socialist realism and contemporary Soviet music aimed at the masses. Tian Han also urged Nie Er to compose, and the young musician quickly began to churn out songs, many of them composed to lyrics by Tian Han himself.

Nie Er's songs reflect the lives of China's most unsung people — dockworkers, newspaper sellers, miners, coolies, bricklayers, pile-drivers, child laborers, sing-song girls. Before composing, he often spent time with the people about whom he intended to write so he could better mirror their world in his music. Once the song was finished, he would go back and teach it to the men and women about whom he had written, and they would then teach it to others of their class or profession. His songs could soon be heard all over Shanghai, and many places beyond. Nie Er's talent was noticed and he was hired to write music for the French-owned Pathe Record Company and the Chinese-owned Lianhua movie studio, whose orchestra he also conducted.

Movies were a primary vehicle for the spread of music in 1930s China. Through films, Chinese audiences became familiar with such works as Schubert's *Ave Maria*, Stravinsky's *Firebird*, and Kreisler's *Gypsy Song*, all of which were frequently chosen by arrangers to provide background music.[74] Although music was rarely commissioned in the early years of film, by the 1930s China's domestic film industry was well-enough developed that it began requiring original compositions. With war looming on the horizon, many films had a patriotic "Resist Japan" theme and were thus the perfect vehicle for songs by Nie Er and like-minded composers of revolutionary songs.

The March of the Volunteers was commissioned from Nie Er for a patriotic movie called *Children of the Storm*, the scenario of which was written by Tian Han. However, Tian Han's leftist activism had made him a target of the Nationalist government and, just as he was completing the script, he was forced to go into hiding to avoid arrest. It was thus in great haste that he penned the lyrics to *The March of the Volunteers*, writing them on tea-stained liner paper from cigarette boxes:[75]

Arise, all you who refuse to be slaves!

---

71. As quoted in Jones: 106.

72. See Qi Teng Xiao Zhi: 184. The author states that Nie Er passed all the musical tests but was not accepted because of his work playing "yellow music" with Li Jinhui; his political activities; and because he was fired by Lianhua.

73. Ming: 166.

74. Tuohy, S. (1999). Metropolitan sounds: music in Chinese films of the 1930s. In, Yingjin Zhang (ed.), *Cinema and Urban Culture in Shanghai, 1922-1943*. Stanford: Stanford University Press: 210.

75. See Qi Teng Xiao Zhi: 201-3.

With our flesh and blood, let us build our new Great Wall!
The Chinese nation faces its greatest peril,
The thundering roar of our peoples will be heard!
Arise! Arise! Arise!
We are many, but our hearts beat as one!
Selflessly braving the enemy's gunfire, march on!
Selflessly braving the enemy's gunfire, march on!
March on! March on! March on! On!

Tian Han was arrested shortly after he finished these lyrics. But when the movie was released in 1935, it was an instant sensation, as was *The March of the Volunteers*. The song was also released on gramophone record to help promote the film and became so wildly popular that the musicologist Feng Zikai reported he heard it being sung by crowds of people in rural villages from Zhejiang to Hunan, just months after it was written.[76] Within a few years, it was also known outside China. The legendary African-American singer Paul Robeson recorded it in 1941 under the title *Arise*, donating all proceeds to help China in its war against Japan. [77]

Nie Er had increased his political activism around the same time as he composed *The March of the Volunteers*, organizing amateur choruses with the leftist composer Lu Ji and helping to organize mass song rallies. This activism, his increasing success as a revolutionary song composer, and his close association with Tian Han brought him to the attention of the Nationalist authorities. In the spring of 1935, he was warned by friends that he was on the government black list. Fearing for his safety, he decided to go to Japan.

Nie Er's plan was to stay in Japan for a year to learn the language, translate Japanese songs, operas and articles into Chinese, and organize his own compositions. He also intended to learn Russian, so he could move to the Soviet Union for further study. [78] One windy July day just a few months into this plan, he and his friends decided to go to Tokyo Bay. The beach was crowded and they soon lost track of each other, although one noticed that Nie Er had swum out well beyond the shore. When it came time to leave, he was nowhere to be found. Nie Er's friends searched fruitlessly for several hours, reported him missing, and then continued to scour the beach until near midnight. They had resumed their search the next morning when the police came to stop them: Nie Er's swollen corpse had already been found.

Nie Er's life had ended tragically at an age when most people are just beginning to pursue their professional vocations. But, if he died young, he also bloomed early. Although he would never know it, in writing *The March of the Volunteers*, he had composed the song that would be for China what the *Marseillaise* is to France, thus himself becoming the composer he promised his brother that China would produce.

76. See Ming: 167.
77. Yu Hedeng (1986). Commemorating Top Two Composers. *Beijing Review*, Volume 29, No. 9, March 3: 30.
78. See Qi Teng Xiao Zhi: 210.

When word of Nie Er's tragic death reached Shanghai, his loss was widely mourned and the process of his beatification as a great revolutionary composer begun. But revolutionary songs were still needed and a new wave of composers stepped in to fill the gap. After his rebuff by Paci, Xian Xinghai became one of the most important of these and by 1938 he had written nearly 400 revolutionary songs, some of which were sung that summer by a chorus of almost 100,000 singers stationed on 200 boats in the Yangzi River.[79] He Luting also became well known for his efforts, especially *Song of the Guerillas*, a piece that became so popular that many Chinese can still sing it to this day. Lu Ji, who played a leading role in the League of Left Wing Writers music group, wrote two widely sung compositions, *The Chinese Nation Will Not Perish* and *Defend Madrid*. As the movement picked up steam, even composers who did not belong to the inner circles of leftist associations began to compose these songs. The Yale-educated Huang Zi wrote more than a dozen revolutionary songs — *Fight the Enemy* was his most famous — and also arranged for Conservatory students to participate in fundraising drives for anti-war efforts. Even the venerable Xiao Youmei tried his hand at the genre.

With so many musicians involved in writing these songs, it is perhaps not surprising that a debate on the future of music in China eventually developed.[80] It was largely spurred by several articles that the composer Lu Ji wrote in 1936, in which he expanded on some precepts outlined by Zhou Yang, the Marxist culture critic who edited the League of Left-Wing Writers' literary magazine.

Zhou Yang had translated an article on music in the Soviet Union and published it together with an essay in which he argued against music for music's sake. Lu Ji accepted Zhou Yang's argument and then established several principles for revolutionary songs, namely that they should use the vernacular language and lean towards the style of folk music. He also suggested that everything associated with them — lyrics, notation, teaching methods, and conducting — should be easy for the broad masses of people to understand. By way of example, he lavished great praise on Nie Er's work, arguing that the songs he composed for films heralded a new era for Chinese music. Most controversially, he referred to the revolutionary songs as "Chinese new music."[81]

In He Luting's judgment, revolutionary songs had to be evaluated as music, rather than mere propaganda. He supported the national salvation song movement, but disagreed with Lu Ji on specific issues. Many of the songs sounded alike, demonstrated poor mastery of technique, and were disorganized in structure. Put bluntly, a good many songs were just "revolutionary poetry or slogans with some Arabic numerals added [for simplified notation]."[82] To call these a new wave for Chinese music or a "new music" movement was an outright exaggeration. Any

---

79. See Kraus: 52.

80. For a discussion of this debate, see Ming Yan (2002). *Ershishiji Zhongguo Yinyue Piping Daolun* [A Guide to 20th-Century Music Criticism in China]. Beijing: Renmin Yinyue Chubanshe: 159-189.

81. See Ming: 173. Also, Wang Yuhe (2002). *Zhongguo Jinxiandai Yinyueshi* [A history of modern Chinese music] (3rd edition) Beijing: Renmin yinyue chubanshe, Huale Chubanshe: 231.

82. For quote, see Ming: 177.

discussion of new music required a broader vision, since music is far more than just songs. China needed to have symphony, orchestra, opera and more, and to have these it needed technique. Technique was often criticized by people who supported revolutionary songs, but the truth was that every art requires technique which does not just fall from the sky — it has to be learned.

Xian Xinghai joined in the debate, essentially taking the same view as He Luting when he wrote, "Of course the songs have their strong points, but they have far too many weak points." [83] Others also contributed their ideas, with several critics taking exception to Lu Ji's use of the phrase "new music." How could these songs be called "new music," they asked, when there was nothing new about them? Such songs were old hat to the rest of the world — in Europe, new music had already completely rejected the tonal system and these songs had done nothing of the kind!

Lu Ji was not bothered by the criticism. In his mind, there was no problem with revolutionary songs; the problem was with people who had for so long been poisoned by other musical forms such as local opera. It would take time, but in due course everyone would come to understand this "new music."

As the discussion over "new music" heated up, war loomed ever closer. Feeling anxious and threatened, Nationalist government officials banned the public singing of national salvation songs, so the debate over their merits and the validity of such terms as "new music" was laid aside. It would be restarted with a vengeance in later years, but the exigencies of wartime required unity among patriotic composers, or at least its appearance.

Looking back on the debate, it seems apparent that both Lu Ji and He Luting were right. Political circumstance had caused Chinese music to change course. Young musicians who were drawn to Western music and would likely have been content to compose etudes under the tutelage of foreign-trained professors or play Beethoven sonatas on their violins were forced, in Nie Er's words, to "wake up before it's too late!"

Their initial reaction upon waking up was to write songs to inspire the masses to save their country. But many of the revolutionary composers were Conservatory graduates and most had at least some formal conservatory training. If they could not ignore the needs of their country in time of war, neither would they be able to ignore the demands of their art when time and space permitted. A new era for Chinese music was at hand, but it would involve more artistic and political struggle than anyone could have envisioned at the time.

---

83. For quote, see Ming: 178. Also see Xian Xinghai (1989). Jiuwang geyong yundong he xin yinyue de qiantu [The national salvation song movement and the future of new music]. In *Xian Xinghai Quanji* [The Complete Works of Xian Xinghai]. Guangdong: Guangdong Gaojiao Chubanshe: Vol. 1: 27.

CHAPTER 4. THE ORPHANED ISLAND

THE OUTBREAK OF WAR

The clouds of war that had been gathering over China throughout the 1930s finally burst in the summer of 1937 when fighting broke out between Chinese and Japanese troops stationed in the outskirts of Beijing, near Marco Polo Bridge. Although the skirmish was occasioned by a misunderstanding, it came on top of years of persistent Japanese aggression aimed at making China a raw material supplier and junior partner in the "Greater East Asian Co-Prosperity Sphere." Weak and divided, China had so often submitted to Japanese ultimatums that the Japanese government must have expected humble acquiescence when it angrily demanded an apology for the incident at the bridge.

This time, however, the Japanese demand came as something like the straw that broke the camel's back. General Chiang Kai-shek bluntly refused to apologize, saying, "If we allow one more inch of our territory to be lost, we shall be guilty of an unpardonable crime against our race."[1] This defiant response infuriated the prince who led the Japanese government and ultimately caused him to retaliate — and thus did all-out war come to China, a defining moment which some historians view as the true start of World War II.

Shanghai was initially unaffected by the outbreak of hostilities, but General Chiang soon decided to attack Japan's positions there as a means of distracting it from its military campaign in the north. By mid-August, the entire city was in a frenzy. Five Japanese warships sailed into the harbor and anchored offshore from the Bund. A barricade of ferryboats and junks was stretched across the Huangpu River, intended to keep the Japanese warships at bay. Rumors flew, one of the

---

1. Spence, J. (1990). *The Search for Modern China*. New York: W.W. Norton & Company: 445.

main ones being that the gates to the International Settlement would soon be closed. Desperate to seek safety, Chinese who lived outside the Settlement and the Concession began pouring into the foreign-controlled areas. As the August 13 *North China Daily News* described it:

> Hordes poured out of streets and alleyways with belongings piled high on every conceivable form of conveyance and converged on all roads leading into the Settlement. Wide thoroughfares and bridges were literally jammed tight with suffering, sweating humanity as the exodus to the foreign-controlled areas continued during the day and well into the night.[2]

The next day, Saturday the 14th, foreign forces were mobilized to protect the Settlement and Concession from what seemed near-certain war. The papers ran announcements asking that "Owner drivers willing to offer their services and the use of their cars, kindly communicate with the Deputy Commissioner, Specials, Headquarters, Central Market, 567 Foochow [Fuzhou] Road."[3] Mario Paci was one of the many volunteers who responded to the request.[4] Other volunteers were requested to join a special police force mustered to help defend the foreign concessions, and most of the SMO musicians responded to this by putting down their instruments and picking up truncheons.[5]

Since there was no truth to the rumor that the gates to the Settlement would be locked, refugees continued to flood into the Settlement and the Concession, swelling the weekend sea of people on major streets. Many thousands of shoppers and strollers were congregated around the intersection of Nanjing Road and the Bund, some just hanging about and others trying to push their way onward to other destinations. A few minutes shy of 4:30, ten Chinese airplanes appeared in the sky above the crowd, flying downriver in the direction of the Japanese cruiser *Idzomo* and other Japanese positions.

This was the first time the Chinese had used planes to bomb the Japanese positions off Shanghai's shore, so a number of people turned their faces skyward to see the Northrop fighters. Those who did watched the first six planes vanish into the clouds and then — uncomprehendingly — saw four torpedoes fall from one of the four planes lagging in the rear. Two of the torpedoes plummeted into the Huangpu River

---

2. *North China Daily News*, August 13, 1937: 1.
3. *North China Daily News*, August 14, 1937: 1.
4. Paci also accepted a position as adviser to the Nationalist government's Ministry of War, tasked with the organization of a special musical academy for military bands to be founded at Nanjing. The job initially gave him a salary of $1000 a month but after only one month he was informed that he would retain the position, but not the salary. If there was no money to pay Maestro Paci's salary, there was even less to organize the academy and it never got off the ground. For information on this, see Ho Chia-shui (1946). Paci gives highlights of life in "Last interview." *The China Press*, October 20. Also, Paci made adviser to Ministry of War, April 1939 (newspaper clipping provided to authors by Floria Paci Zaharoff from an unnamed English-language Shanghai paper).
5. See, Municipal concerts resumed. *Shanghai Times*, October 16, 1937.

with such force that they caused a tidal wave. The other two fell on Nanjing Road at the intersection of the Bund. The *North China Daily News* described the scene:

> A bomb curved through the air, struck the Palace Hotel a glancing blow and dealt carnage indescribable. A scene of dreadful death was uncovered as the high explosive fumes slowly lifted. Flames from a blazing car played over distorted bodies. In shapeless heaps where they had been huddling in shelter bodies in coolie cloth turning scarlet lay piled up in the entrances to the main doorways and arcades of the Palace and Cathay Hotels. Heads, legs, arms lay far from smashed masses of flesh. For the full long stretch of both buildings, pavements and roadways were littered with objects of hideous death. Across the tramline was the body of a tall European, his suit of white flannel unmarked so cleanly had head been separated from body. Dead in his tracks as he had been directing the corner traffic lay the corpse of a Chinese policemen with shrapnel through his head. A disemboweled child was nearby.[6]

The clock on the Cathay Hotel, the center of social life for so many Shanghailanders, was stopped by the bomb at 4:27.

Incredibly, this horrible tragedy was not the only one to strike the city that afternoon. Only a short time later, a damaged fighter was returning to Hongqiao Aerodrome when it accidentally dropped two shrapnel bombs over the French Concession. These landed near the Sincere Department Store and the Great World Amusement Center — an area that was being used as a refugee food distribution center — killing and mutilating thousands more civilians.

On August 15, the *North China Daily News* reported 600 dead and 1000 injured. The next day, the death toll was up to almost 1200, with several thousand more injured — and the Nationalist bombers had managed to miss the Japanese battleships entirely.

Shanghailanders and Shanghainese alike were in shock — the safe havens they had carved out from the sea of war and suffering that surrounded them suddenly were safe no more.

"In August 1937, everything was closed," Fofi remembered. "You couldn't even get money from the banks — of course, my father never had any money anyway. So, he volunteered to drive. He got a special armband and drove everywhere. His office was on Fuzhou Road and there was a bomb dropped right next to it. There were all these dead people, everyone was scared. And this was his whole career — he said this could be the end, the only place I can go where someone will give me a piece of bread is Java."

Despite his army's initial blunders, General Chiang was determined to overcome the Japanese forces at Shanghai. However, the tide never turned in China's favor and by late October the Japanese had broken the Chinese lines and were attacking them from both front and rear. When the Chinese-controlled areas of Shanghai fell, the Japanese soldiers started their march toward Nanjing. They reached it in December — just half a year after the SMO's jubilant performance in the new assembly hall — and the Nationalist capital was plunged into an orgy of rape, torture and killing that left up

---

6. *North China Daily News*, August 15, 1937:1.

to a quarter million people dead in what is now known as the Nanjing Massacre, or the Rape of Nanjing.

In the face of this onslaught, the Chinese armies retreated up the Yangzi River to the west, where they planned to regroup in the important industrial city of Wuhan. When Japanese soldiers threatened to attack there, General Chiang ordered that the dykes on the Yellow River be blown up. The ploy worked — temporarily — but only by causing a flood that destroyed more than 4000 northern villages, killing untold numbers of peasants and altering the course of the Yellow River. Wuhan finally fell to the Japanese in the autumn of 1938, and the Nationalists retreated to the far southwestern city of Chongqing. China was effectively divided into ten separately governed regions, with various parts ruled by the Nationalists, the Communists, Japanese puppet governments, an assortment of warlords and even minority groups seeking autonomy or independence.

Because they were ruled by nations with whom Japan was not at war, Shanghai's International Settlement and French Concession together escaped the scourge of the invasion but were largely cut off from the rest of China and the world, an "orphaned island" afloat in a sea of suffering and devastation.

THE CONSERVATORY BATTLES TO SURVIVE

The Conservatory's adjustment to wartime conditions was difficult. After having to move the school several times in the first years of its existence, Xiao Youmei had finally managed to purchase permanent quarters in 1935. But when his newly hired dean, the French-educated Chen Hong, arrived in August to start his job, he walked through the gates of the tree-filled campus and was instantly struck by the eerie silence — not a single note of music could be heard.[7]

Finding no one at the school, Dean Chen went to look for his new boss in the small, foreign-style house that he rented nearby. He found Mr. Xiao at home, looking thin and coughing frequently, but busily at work. The campus was deserted, Xiao explained, because the school was moving again — it was simply too close to the Japanese positions for him to feel comfortable about the safety of his students or teachers. When Chen Hong expressed consternation at the bother of moving and the shame of leaving such a beautiful campus, Xiao Youmei brushed it aside, telling him that this was "everyday fare" for the Conservatory.

So, on August 2, Mr. Xiao abandoned the campus he had struggled so hard to obtain and moved to rented quarters in an old bone hospital in the French Concession's Xujiahui area. The wisdom of his decision was proved just weeks later

---

7. This account of the Conservatory's wartime travails is taken from an account written by Chen Hong. See Chen Hong (1993). Yi Xiao Youmei Xiansheng yu kangzhan chuqide Shanghai guoli yinzhuan [Mr. Xiao Youmei and the Shanghai National Conservatory in the Early Years of the War of Resistance Against Japan]. Dai Penghai, Huang Xudong (eds.), *Xiao Youmei Jinian Wenji* [Collected Articles on Xiao Youmei]. Shanghai: Shanghai Yinyue Chubanshe: 60-74.

when hostilities broke out and three bombs fell on the campus, hitting the empty women's dorm and the athletic field. Unfortunately, the new location proved little safer than the old one. Xujiahui was on the edge of the Concession and the fighting was visible from the school windows. Every now and then, the Japanese shot into the Concession, as though for fun, and when a White Russian bystander was killed, Mr. Xiao decided that it was once again time to seek safer quarters. This time he chose a location on Masinan Road, in the Chinese city.

Moving the school every few months to avoid bombs and bullets — while at the same time making sure that classes were held and battling against ill health — would be enough to make most people despair. Instead, Xiao Youmei channeled all his energy into encouraging his faculty and students.

At the opening ceremony of the 1937 academic year — the school's 10th anniversary — he told his students, "Don't feel pessimistic. When I looked back on the past ten years and all the difficulties we have experienced, I originally thought to have a big event. Of course, it's not possible now. But, although our campus is under fire, we have saved most of the equipment and all of the books and instruments .... We need to keep going and not be pessimistic — we want to build an even greater school."[8]

Unwilling to let the war interfere with his dreams and his goals, Mr. Xiao further announced several ambitious plans for the coming year. A journal would be started, called *Music Monthly*, with Chen Hong as editor. A 25-person orchestra would be founded with himself as manager, Professor Shertzoff as conductor, and Dean Chen as associate conductor. Mr. Xiao had three goals for the ensemble: to play more Chinese compositions; to systematically and purposefully build up a repertoire; and to prepare all program notes in Chinese. The orchestra's first concert would be held in November, to mark the 10th anniversary of the founding of the school and to raise money for refugees in Shanghai.

As it turned out, the plan for *Music Monthly* was overly ambitious and after four issues the "monthly" was dropped from its name, to reflect a less frequent publication schedule. Neither was the orchestra ready to perform in public, though it did rehearse regularly. The promised concert was delayed until 1939 but when it was held — on May 4th, in the American Church — it drew a large crowd and raised a good amount of money for the refugees. A celebration for the school's 10th anniversary was held in November of 1937 as planned, after which Mr. Xiao got back to work on achieving his most important goal, making the Conservatory even greater.

Despite his unflagging optimism, it was a constant battle just to maintain the status quo. The most pressing problem continued to be the deteriorating security situation in Shanghai. Just a few months after the school had settled into its new location in the Chinese city, Mr. Xiao decided that it was too dangerous to keep all the students in one building and orchestrated yet another move back to the French Concession. His own personal security was also increasingly a concern.

---

8. See Chen, in *Xiao Youmei Jinian Wenji*: 64.

Since the outbreak of war, the administrators of Shanghai's national-level universities and schools had been meeting together once a week to discuss how they were managing to keep their respective institutions viable. Xiao was a member of this group and was understandably taken aback when it came under Japanese observation because of its members' links to the Nationalist government. As he well knew, the Japanese could be ruthless with those they considered to be anti-Japanese or pro-Nationalist — a fact that was confirmed when one of the administrators in the group was assassinated.

In response to the murder, Mr. Xiao hastily added the word "private" to the Conservatory's name, in the hope of cloaking its affiliation with the Nationalist government. For good measure, he also changed his own name to Chen Sihe. Then, in the spring of 1938, he went to the Nationalist government's wartime capital of Hankou and asked the Education Ministry to allow him to move the Conservatory inland, to Guilin, where many universities from occupied areas had relocated. His request was turned down — the Ministry said it wasn't practical to move because of the school's many foreign professors. With his health worsening — it was obvious to many that he had tuberculosis — and fears of assassination dogging him, Mr. Xiao went to Hong Kong for a time.

Sadly, the rest and recovery that Mr. Xiao so desperately needed were to elude him even in Hong Kong. Crises at the Conservatory continued to require his intervention via telegram and in May he received shocking news — Huang Zi, the talented, Yale-educated composer and dedicated professor, had been struck down by paratyphoid. Though he was rushed to the hospital as soon as he became ill and many of his students turned out to donate blood for his transfusions, it was to no avail and within 24 hours, he was dead. Only 34 years old, Mr. Huang left behind his wife, three children, many grieving students and colleagues, and an unfinished symphonic work called *The Tragedy of the Imperial Concubine Yang Guifei*.

Coming on top of all the stress and strain of war, Huang Zi's death hit the Conservatory hard. Students and faculty alike became gripped with fear and uncertainty as to how they would go on. Though still sick and anxious, Mr. Xiao returned to Shanghai in the autumn, determined to work with his colleagues to keep the one and only conservatory in China alive. Money moved up high on his list of perpetual problems, since government remittances were increasingly sporadic and many students were unable to come up with their tuition. In response to this, Mr. Xiao added teaching to his list of responsibilities and implemented a wartime austerity program of "one in, one out," whereby no new student could be accepted unless one had graduated or dropped out.

Unsurprisingly, given the circumstances, the "one out" part of this policy was not hard to implement. Some students left to take refuge in places that they or their families deemed safer and some had to drop out for financial reasons. Still others gave up their studies to participate in the anti-war efforts in whatever way they could, among them He Luting.

When war broke out, Mr. He was eager to join Shanghai's Save the Country Performance Troupe, but hesitated because it would mean leaving his family.[9] But when he finally broached the idea, his wife was encouraging, so with her blessing he boarded a plane for Nanjing and from there a boat to the wartime capital of Wuhan. Soon after he arrived, his *Song of the Guerillas* was performed to great acclaim. The audience at one performance included none other than Red Army Commander-in-Chief Zhu De, who personally asked Mr. He and the troupe to go out to the army units and teach them the song.

After Wuhan fell to the Japanese, Mr. He moved to the new Nationalist capital of Chongqing. Students and intellectuals from around the country were clustering in the foggy mountain city and Mr. He was soon in demand as a teacher and a composer. By 1940, the city had so much musical talent that the Soviet Union offered seed money to found an orchestra that could play at diplomatic functions. China's Education Ministry provided additional funding and Sun Ke, the son of former president Sun Yat-sen, agreed to act as honorary chairman while Ma Sicong became conductor and solo violinist.

The orchestra, which eventually became known as the Zhonghua (China) Symphony Orchestra, grew to include roughly 50 musicians. Its ranks included no foreigners; it was the first all-Chinese professional symphony orchestra.[10] Its repertoire included Beethoven's *Third*, *Fifth* and *Sixth Symphonies*, works by Mendelssohn and Mussorgsky, and pieces by Ma Sicong, He Luting and other Chinese composers. By borrowing musicians from student orchestras, it could expand to 80 or 90 musicians and in 1943 it performed Shostakovich's *Seventh Symphony* for the ambassadors from the United States, England, France and the USSR. On another big occasion, Ma Sicong conducted He Luting's works before an audience that included Zhou Enlai and his wife, Deng Yingchao; Guo Morou; and a host of officials from the USSR embassy.[11]

Another student who left the Conservatory in part because she wanted to participate in Save the Country activities was a talented young singer named Zhou Xiaoyan.[12] Madame Zhou, as she is now known, came from a wealthy family in Wuhan where she was educated at St. Maria's, a girls' school run by Italian Catholics. She

---

9. See Shi Zhongxin (2000). *He Luting Zhuan* [A Biography of He Luting]. Shanghai: Shanghai Yinyue Chubanshe: 98-9.

10. Musicians who played with the Zhonghua Symphony included concert master Li Guoguan; orchestra leader Si Dude; and Lin Shengxi and Wu Bozhao, both of whom conducted at different times.

11. Information about the Zhonghua Symphony comes primarily from Sheila Melvin's interview with Guan Yin, bassoon player at the SSO, in Shanghai in July of 2000 and from her interview with Li Ling in April of 2000 in Beijing.

12. Sheila Melvin conducted two formal interviews with Zhou Xiaoyan in Shanghai in August of 1998 and May of 1999 and has met her informally on a number of occasions at Shanghai cultural events. All direct quotes from Madame Zhou are from the formal interviews, unless otherwise noted. Much supplementary information about Madame Zhou's background and life experiences comes from her authorized biography. See Zhu Yongzhen (1997). *Zhou Xiaoyan Zhuan* [A Biography of Zhou Xiaoyan]. Shanghai: Shanghai Yinyue Chubanshe.

enjoyed music and was considered quite talented, since she could sing, dance, and play the piano; her parents decided to send her to the National Conservatory in 1935.

Arriving in Shanghai as a music student was something of a shock for Madame Zhou, who quickly discovered that there are "mountains beyond the mountains and heavens beyond the heavens." [13] Used to thinking of herself as a good piano player, she had planned to major in piano. She was thus rather stunned to discover that other students could play the most difficult sonatas while she herself could only handle little waltzes or sonatinas, like those a Shanghainese child might play. Sensing that piano was not her best option, she decided to develop her voice. However, this decision soon caused her further angst when the sound of a student soprano singing "Vissi D'Arte" from *Tosca* in a Conservatory practice room made her stop in her tracks — it was so beautiful, she could hardly believe it. To make matters worse, the soprano, Lang Yuxiu, was the very same age as Madame Zhou and she had already made a recording! Madame Zhou felt overwhelmed by all the talent that now surrounded her — clearly, she had picked the best place to study, but she feared that she was starting her serious musical education far too late and would never catch up with her classmates.

Despite her apprehensions, Madame Zhou settled into her new life as a student of piano and voice. Professor Shushlin became her primary voice teacher and she made considerable progress under his tutelage, until war broke out. At her father's request, she returned to Wuhan for safety and joined a chorus that specialized in Save the Country songs. The chorus became extremely popular after the Nationalist government made Wuhan its capital, and Madame Zhou often found herself singing solo before crowds that included both cultural celebrities and political dignitaries. When the chorus decided to go to the US to raise money for anti-war efforts, she asked her father's permission to go along, but he told her honestly that she was not ready — she was still a beginner at her art. Rather than go overseas to perform, she should first go overseas to study and improve herself. Thus, in 1938 Madame Zhou boarded a ship with her brother and set out on the long ocean journey that would take her across the world to Paris.

The departure of Conservatory students like He Luting and Zhou Xiaoyan, who left of their own accord, was compounded by the difficulty of recruiting new students from outside the orphaned island of Shanghai. It was even necessary to suspend a program to recruit students from the poor interior provinces of Shaanxi, Guangxi, and Gansu that Mr. Xiao had started in 1935, since the journey from these provinces to Shanghai was so difficult and dangerous.

And yet, despite the difficulty of retaining and recruiting students, the Conservatory's reputation was so strong that Mr. Xiao had no more problem with the "one in" portion of his policy than he did with the "one out." On the contrary, enough young men and women were willing to travel across the war-torn country in order to pursue a dream of becoming a musician that auditions were still full and the student

---

13. See Zhu: 58.

body remained steady at around 100. One such would-be student who arrived in time for the start of school in 1940 was a gregarious young man named Li Delun.[14]

Mr. Li came from a well-to-do family of Beijing Muslims that fell on hard times when an uncle turned traitor to the Japanese in 1931. After the uncle was captured and executed, Mr. Li's father lost his high-level job in the police bureau and turned to opium for solace. Though these were weighty troubles, they did not affect the young Mr. Li's appetite for life, or his love of the Western classical music which had enthralled him since he first began piano lessons in middle school.

Instead, Mr. Li continued to attend every concert he could, and went to see every Hollywood movie that came to town five or six times since the movies always had musical accompaniment. Nothing could move him from his spot beside the radio when classical music was played on the foreigners' radio station, especially during the Saturday opera broadcasts. Mr. Li gradually found himself drawn to the violin, but he could not afford either an instrument or a teacher. Finally, however, he found a friend who agreed to pool funds to buy a used Honda violin for 5 yuan — they traded it off every three days, and each taught himself to play. Luckily for Mr. Li, when the Japanese invaded in 1937, the friend left for a Communist-controlled area and Mr. Li got to keep the violin for good.

Mr. Li's love of music led him to dream of studying it full time and in 1938 — over the strong objections of his family — he enrolled in Catholic Furen University to do just that. He immersed himself in the school's musical life, playing flute in the university band and studying violin with Ma Wensheng, a worker's son who had been taught by a kindly priest and gone on to become an accomplished musician. The priests who ran Furen made a big impression on Mr. Li and he often went to church to hear one of them give organ recitals of works by Bach, Handel and Franck. Another European priest introduced him to *Das Kapital* and urged that he and his classmates sympathize with the proletariat. Mr. Li had been interested in Communism for several years and had joined the Communist Youth League in 1936 and the Communist underground Party shortly thereafter, so this subject was of particular interest to him. Indeed, studying Marxism in a university setting right alongside Western music cemented his growing conviction that there was no contradiction between music and revolution — and helped him decide for certain that music would be his life's work.

After two years at Furen, Mr. Li decided to go to Shanghai to enroll in the Conservatory. Once again his father opposed the plan — war was raging throughout the country and, more significantly, he did not want his son to further pursue as a career something so unreliable as music. Faced with these objections, Mr. Li left without telling his father and took a boat from Tianjin to Shanghai.

---

14. Sheila Melvin and Jindong Cai interviewed Li Delun twice at his home in Beijing in July of 2000. All direct quotes come from these interviews, unless otherwise noted. Much supplemental information comes from his authorized biography. See Luo Junjun (2001). *Li Delun Zhuan* [A Biography of Li Delun]. Beijing: Zuojia Chubanshe.

Upon arriving, he went to hear the SMO at the first opportunity he had. Since it was August, the concert was held outdoors and the program was a light one — "Arab Dance," from *The Nutcracker*, performed with a dancer on stage; the second movement of Dvorak's *New World Symphony*; and Grieg's *Piano Concerto*, with a Chinese pianist. Even so, Mr. Li became tense with excitement from the moment he heard the clarinetist warming up and when the concert began, he felt transformed — it was the first time in his life that he truly understood what a profound experience it was to listen to live music, and how different it was from a recording.

Mr. Li quickly became a regular at SMO concerts.

"I remember everyone from the Shanghai Municipal Orchestra!" he recalled more than fifty years later. "I remember Fortina — he was very handsome. And Wittenberg, Addle, Krause — he went to the Berlin State Opera. Alexander Hinsburg — he came from Russia, and was concertmaster in Shanghai. Padushka — he was Czech. Many people studied with him."

One concert in particular impressed him, a performance of Beethoven's *Triple Concerto* (with Mr. Foa on violin, the principal cellist Mr. Winkler on cello, and a student of Mr. Zaharoff's on piano) that was followed by Brahms' *Fourth Symphony*. Thinking to get as much out of the performance as he could, Mr. Li had searched Shanghai's second-hand book stores beforehand and managed to find copies of the scores for both pieces. He followed the Beethoven all the way through as the orchestra played, but the Brahms was new to him. Within minutes after it started, he had lost his place and quickly became so intent on trying to find it that he forgot to listen to the performance! Years later, this memory would cause Mr. Li great mirth, but in the meantime the experience made him even more determined to study.

When autumn came, Mr. Li set about trying to enter the Conservatory but found himself stumped as to what instrument he should play for the auditions. Violin was the most logical choice, since he had actually studied it, but there were so many violinists that he feared he might not be accepted. He could bypass the instrument audition altogether by testing for music theory, but since he had never taken a class on the subject, this didn't seem very practical either. In the end, he decided to apply as a cello student — even though the full extent of his training was that he had once played a few notes on someone else's instrument. Having selected an instrument, he next confronted the problem of repertoire; since he was particularly fond of Jascha Heifetz's recording of Sarasate's *Hebrew Melody*, he decided to practice the main theme and play that.

On the day of his audition, Li Delun entered a big room filled with other applicants. Xiao Youmei and Chen Hong were presiding and when Mr. Li's turn came, he found that his bow was shaking from nervousness. Fortunately, his musicality — and nerve — won the day and he was accepted into the Conservatory as a cello student, with Shertzoff as his primary teacher.

Mr. Li was delighted with his new life as a student at the Conservatory and particularly impressed by the quality and dedication of the professors. Shertzoff helped him to find an affordable used German cello and would even copy out music by hand for Mr. Li and other students, if they didn't have the piece. He and Mr. Li became friendly and would often jump into Professor Shertzoff's Austin to drive to a French Concession café, where they would sip coffee and talk about music. In addition to his cello lessons and other classes, Mr. Li sang in the school chorus once a week, as was required of all students. The piece they generally sang was Handel's *Messiah*, and Mr. Li eventually grew to know it so well that he could sing every part, and would sometimes do just that to make his friends laugh.

Sadly, however, just as Mr. Li was beginning his joyful life as a student at the Conservatory, the school itself was about to enter one of its darkest hours. Indeed, the prolonged stress of managing under wartime conditions together with fear for his students' safety — and his own — was slowly wearing Mr. Xiao down. His home life, too, was stressful since the woman he had married in 1932 was constantly pushing him to become Christian, a conversion that he could not make. When the security situation again deteriorated, Mr. Xiao mustered his energy to orchestrate one final move, to three separate buildings on Aiwenyi Road. The site was not desirable, since many trolleys passed by outside and the classrooms were noisy, but it was affordable and at least temporarily safe. Unfortunately, the move took a serious toll on Mr. Xiao's already fragile health. He stopped wearing the smart three-piece Western suits that were his regular dress and began appearing at the school in a long Chinese gown, a scarf and a hat. He coughed frequently into a handkerchief and students and colleagues alike struggled to mask their sorrow when they looked at him, none daring to mention the dreaded word *feibing*, or tuberculosis.

By the autumn of 1940, Mr. Xiao appeared at school only sporadically, sending memos from home to communicate about operational issues. When he caught a cold and ran a high fever, he was sent to hospital — he deliberately chose an inexpensive one, since the Conservatory was paying his bills — but his fever continued to rage. Since the doctors forbade him from reading any memos, he had someone from the school come daily to his bedside to give him a report on its activities. At the end of December, Chen Hong visited to report to him for the last time. It was a typically damp and cold winter day and Mr. Xiao expressed concern about the hall where the students held piano recitals. He asked Dean Chen to see that the windows in the hall were repaired so the students would be warm and able to play better. Two days later, at sunrise on December 31, Xiao Youmei died.

Students and teachers contributed the money to pay for Mr. Xiao's funeral, since wartime inflation and his record of sacrifice for the school had left his family with little savings. His body was laid out in the Hongqiao Road Funeral Home, where dozens of sorrowing students and colleagues turned out to pay their last respects. At his wife's insistence, he was given a Christian funeral and then laid to rest in the Hongqiao Road Cemetery. Tcherepnin had once written that Xiao Youmei's "administrative vision is as extraordinary as his musical talent,"[15] and the stone on his tomb could have borne

---

15. Tcherepnin, A. (1935). Music in Modern China. *The Musical Quarterly*, Vol. XXI, No. 4, October: 398.

many other words of praise. But in keeping with Xiao Youmei's modesty and dedication, it held only the simple epitaph, "President of the Shanghai Conservatory."

With heavy hearts, Xiao Youmei's colleagues and students bid him goodbye and returned to their work and study, determined that the Conservatory should survive the war, even if its beloved founder had not.

THE MUSICIANS' STRUGGLE

The notes of violins and cellos are naturally drowned out by the sounds of gunfire and bombs and the demands of orchestras and music schools outweighed by those of armies and refugees. A war-era Sapajou cartoon called "Brass and Strings" shows a diminutive Mario Paci standing on a podium conducting the SMO in a program that includes *Romeo and Juliet*, *Tosca*, Ravel, Respighi and Rachmaninoff. Next to him — while the orchestra audience snoozes — is a hulking general in a military uniform evocative of ancient Rome with the word WAR written on it. He, too, is conducting, but his "orchestra" consists of tanks and guns and his program of the "Capriccio Huangpu-Pudong," the "Anti-Aircraft Symphony" and the "Ouverture Big Push." [16]

If the image of an orchestra giving concerts as war raged and soldiers fought and died was laughable — or even offensive — to some, it was a source of great solace to others. The many professional musicians in Shanghai who had devoted their lives to classical music were not about to lay down their instruments and batons in the face of Japanese aggression.

The Shanghai Municipal Orchestra was silent for two months while Paci and his musicians did their stints as volunteers in the anti-war effort. But, as life in the International Settlement and the French Concession gradually regained a semblance of normality, the orchestra returned to the rehearsal hall. By mid-October, it was able to open its season with a program of works by "the three 'B's" — Bach's *O Man thy grievous sin bemoan*, Brahms' *First Symphony* and Beethoven's *Triple Concerto*. [17] From then on, it carried on with its regular schedule of concerts as planned before the outbreak of war.

The 1938 season opened on time and was marked by a major milestone: the official integration of Chinese players into the ranks of the orchestra. This integration finally came about because Paci persuaded the Italian government to provide funding to pay the salaries of four Chinese musicians, thus skirting the Municipal Council and the Ratepayers altogether. The only *quid pro quo* in the arrangement was that the SMO perform more works by Italian composers, a requirement which he undoubtedly minded little.

---

16. A photocopy of this cartoon was given to the authors by Floria Paci Zaharoff. It was published in the *North China Daily News*, but the copy provided to the authors is undated. Another Sapajou cartoon from 1937, called "Overture Up-To-Date," shows Paci standing on a rooftop conducting while Shanghai burns beneath him. A man in a hat — perhaps a reporter — is asking Paci, "Why 1812? Why not 1937?"

17. Municipal concerts resumed. *Shanghai Times*, October 16, 1937.

Because the number of Chinese musicians qualified to play in the orchestra was still small, the SMO had only hired three — the violinists Chen Youxin and William Shu and the trumpet player Huang Yijun — when it was time for the start of rehearsals. But, it just so happened that the day before rehearsals were scheduled to begin, Tan Shuzhen decided to visit Arrigo Foa, the SMO concertmaster who by now was also assistant conductor.

Mr. Tan had been living outside of Shanghai for much of the decade since he first played with the SMO. His search for a good violin teacher had led him to Japan, where the classical music world was far more developed than in China — Tokyo alone had four symphony orchestras and the musicians were virtually all Japanese. While there, he studied with Josef Koenig, a White Russian from St. Petersburg's Mariinsky Orchestra, and also played in the Tokyo New Symphony Orchestra. Upon returning to Shanghai in 1929, he opened the Metropolitan Music House on Nanjing Road, a small store that soon went bankrupt in spite of its grandiose name. He then went back to his parents' home in Qingdao, where he studied violin making with two enthusiastic amateur violin makers, one British and one American, and married the woman who would be his wife for 71 years.

When war broke out in 1937, Mr. Tan was in Henan attending to some family business while his wife and baby were in Shanghai. Desperate to make sure that his young family was safe, he rushed to Shanghai through a countryside in turmoil and arrived with little more than the clothes on his back. Under these circumstances, he could not afford to dress in a manner that he considered proper and was too embarrassed to visit Mr. Foa, or any of his other former colleagues from the SMO. When he at last got a new suit in 1938, he called on his old friend Foa, who — after berating him for not coming earlier — told him, "The orchestra needs four people — we're waiting for you!"

Since Mr. Tan was very much in need of a job, he jumped at the opportunity to officially join the SMO; but he had one major problem.

"I told Foa, 'I don't have a violin.' He said, 'Buy one.' I said, 'I don't have money.' He said, 'Borrow one.' So, I borrowed one."

And with that, Mr. Tan was once again a member of the Shanghai Municipal Orchestra — this time a paid one.

"It was God watching," he explained. "The rehearsal was the next day! They would have found someone else."

Unfortunately, Mr. Tan soon found out that the salary paid by the orchestra was nowhere near enough to support his family in the fast-deteriorating wartime economy.

"Payment for orchestra members was 100 silver dollars for Chinese, 200 or 300 for foreigners. But the wages got smaller and smaller because of inflation. I met a cellist and he said, 'My monthly salary is worth one shoe — not even a pair of shoes.' The money just devalued and devalued."

To make ends meet, Mr. Tan — like most musicians — was forced to take any job that came his way. He found work in two of the primary venues for classical music outside the concert hall: churches and movie theaters.

Church work was mainly for the Catholics, who had an abundance of holy days. Mr. Tan would arrive at the church early and, together with the organist, play for penitents who came to pray in silence or say the rosary. When the mass began, the organist would stop and Mr. Tan would play solo accompaniment as the priest sang in Latin.

"It was very beautiful," he remembered. "And the sermons were pretty short, too. Afterwards, I always had lunch with the priest. It was great — so much Italian food. And after lunch there was always coffee and brandy in bowls — not cups, big bowls, and each had a whole glass of brandy!"

The movie theaters were an important source of extra income for Shanghai's musicians, but work recording music for films was somewhat harder than playing in a church.

"We would work from 8:00 PM until 5:00 AM and then drink coffee, go home and wash our faces, maybe sleep for a few hours, and then at 9:00 AM we started rehearsal for the orchestra," remembered Mr. Tan.

Li Delun also worked in the theaters, though his main job was providing live accompaniment to dramatic plays. This was a position that demanded extreme flexibility — while his contract stipulated that he was responsible for music, he sometimes jumped on stage to fill in for a missing actor. If there weren't enough musicians to make up an orchestra, he had to play recorded music instead, a job that made him so familiar with phonograph records that he could tell what they were just by looking at the grooves. This skill proved useful several years later when he found himself a new job as a classical music broadcaster at the Voice of the USSR radio station in Shanghai.

Since Mr. Li and Mr. Tan were both musicians working in the theaters, they soon met and became friends. Like all Beijing Muslims, Mr. Li loved to eat mutton so Mr. Tan and he would often go to eat hot pot mutton at a little restaurant near the Temple of the City God. Mr. Tan earned extra money by buying and repairing the used violins that impoverished refugees sold to second-hand stores and whenever he sold a refurbished instrument, the meal would be his treat. As they dipped their chopsticks into the sizzling pot, Mr. Li would cry, "Another mutton violin!"

Despite their struggles to make ends meet, Mr. Li and Mr. Tan both found time for extra-curricular musical activities. Mr. Li even founded an orchestra, which he called the China Youth Orchestra, and Mr. Tan played violin in it. The orchestra was conducted by SMO violist Wolfgang Fraenkel and Ma Sihong served as concertmaster. Most of the rank-and-file musicians were Conservatory students, though various members of the SMO would sometimes come to play with them. The China Youth Orchestra performed Bach's *Brandenberg Concertos* in the Shandong Assembly Hall, played on-the-air for the Soviet radio station, and held several charity concerts. Unfortunately, as its profile increased, the Japanese occupation government moved to take it over. Mr. Li dissolved it, rather than turn it over to the enemy.

Tan Shuzhen was faced with a similar ethical dilemma when the SMO agreed to do a concert for a Japanese general in 1940. Mr. Tan didn't blame Paci — he said the

Italian maestro "couldn't refuse" — but as a Chinese, he himself could not in good conscience participate. So, after discussing the situation with his three Chinese colleagues — who all decided that paychecks had to come before principle in these trying times — he wrote a letter that said, "I resign from my job, today" and asked Foa to pass it on for him. From then on, he had an even harder time making ends meet.

"Once, I used the whole night to play background music for the movies," he remembered. "In the morning I received a bundle of money. I took it and went to a restaurant to eat a bowl of noodles. After I finished, I asked the waiter, 'How much?' He said, '600,000.' I said, 'How much is this?' He said, 'About right.' We didn't count money then, we just looked at it."

But if things were bad in 1940, they only got worse when Japanese planes flew over the Pacific and dropped their bombs on the US Pacific Fleet at Pearl Harbor on December 7, 1941. Within hours of this attack, Japanese soldiers fired on the British gunboat HMS Peterel,[18] which was moored in the Yangzi River near Shanghai. Then, at 10:00 AM on December 8, troops marched into the International Settlement and assumed control.

Japanese soldiers occupied the International Settlement's banks, clubs, and best residential buildings. They accepted the "resignations" of British municipal department heads and replaced them with Japanese. Japanese flags — known locally as "poached eggs" — were hung from the buildings. Chinese and foreign-language newspapers were taken over, journalists were detained, and all citizens were ordered to remove the short-wave bands from their radios. Although the Japanese did not technically occupy the French Concession, they took control of it for all intents and purposes — Maestro Paci and his family watched from their window as troops marched down the Rue Joffre, now Huaihai Road.

The International Settlement and the French Concession were no longer isolated from the war; the temporary calm that had cloaked both enclaves was shattered. The war with Japan had already begun to change the course of musical history and now its impact would become even greater.

THE END OF THE PACI ERA

Once the Japanese consolidated their military and economic hold over the International Settlement, they moved to take control of its cultural life. It was announced that the Shanghai Municipal Orchestra would not be allowed to continue as a municipal enterprise, but instead would be re-organized as the Shanghai Philharmonic Orchestra and placed under the control of a Japanese "art patron" named Mr. T. Tesumi.[19] Members of the SMO would be welcome to join the Philharmonic, but first they had to apply to Mr. Tesumi at the newly-formed Philharmonic Society.

---

18. According to hmsfalcon.com, "The correct spelling should have been HMS Petrel (like the bird), but the mistake was noticed only after she had been launched and no attempt was made to change it." Website is available at http://www.hmsfalcon.com/gannet/gannet.htm.

Unsurprisingly, Maestro Paci — the man who had taken a dissolving Town Band, turned it into a renowned symphony orchestra and served as its maestro for more than two decades — was not about to apply for his own job.

"Paci was an artist," Mr. Tan explained simply. "He couldn't work for the Japanese."

However, it was this very artistry that made Maestro Paci attractive to the Japanese — many of Shanghai's Japanese residents were big fans of the orchestra and the occupation government very much wanted Paci to keep conducting. In their efforts to persuade him, they even held him for 24 hours in Bridge House, the Japanese gendarmerie's notorious headquarters which doubled as a torture and interrogation center. After his detention, Maestro Paci conducted one concert a month for five months, but still refused to take the position. Instead, he announced that the last scheduled concert of the Shanghai Municipal Orchestra would also be his final concert.

"They finally had to find somebody else," he later explained to a reporter. "After this, the Japanese regarded me as an enemy. My name could not appear in printed matters; even when my pupils gave concerts, the fact that they were my pupils could not be made known."[20]

The last scheduled concert of the Shanghai Municipal Orchestra was Sunday, May 31, 1942, entitled simply "Farewell Concert." Although the wartime price of paper was exorbitantly high, a special souvenir program was printed that included a history of the orchestra and an autobiographical sketch written by Maestro Paci, in which he recounted how he had run away from home to study in Rome, performed for Puccini, roamed the world playing piano, and then — "tired of 16 years of Pianistic wandering, dreaming of a great orchestra future"[21] — settled down in Shanghai as conductor of the SMO.

Most audience members were probably still leafing through their programs and absorbing the romantic life story of the conductor who had stood in their midst for a quarter century when Maestro Paci appeared on stage. The applause that greeted him was thunderous and only when the last clap had faded away did he begin his final concert with the very first orchestral piece he had performed on arriving in Shanghai: Mozart's *Coronation Concerto*. Once again, he played and conducted from the piano. He followed with his rendition of the piece that had so delighted Puccini — Beethoven's *Piano Sonata in D Minor*, the *Appassionata*. After the interval, he concluded with Brahms' *Symphony No. 1 in C Minor* — the same Brahms that the orchestra had once happily rehearsed for two weeks — played by the full Municipal Orchestra.

When the last notes of the Brahms had faded away, the Shanghai Municipal Orchestra officially ceased to exist, and Maestro Paci's reign as its conductor came to

---

19. See, Orchestra to continue functioning but not as a municipal enterprise. *Shanghai Times*, May 30, 1942. Also, Maestro Paci to give last performance. Final concert of group under S.M.C. will be given tonight. *Shanghai Sunday Times*, May 31, 1942.

20. *China Press*, October 21, 1946.

21. Paci, M. (1942). Maestro Mario Paci. In *Souvenir Programme of Farewell Concert*, Shanghai Municipal Orchestra. May 31: 16

an end. With the audience still applauding, Arrigo Foa walked off-stage and returned to present Maestro Paci with a conductor's music stand, a gift from the orchestra. As the two men hugged, they began to cry and soon many in the orchestra were crying with them. An era had ended, and everyone knew it.

The orchestra's demise may have brought sorrow to many, but this was not a time for sentimentality. SMO musicians still had to make a living and most applied to the re-organized Shanghai Philharmonic Society, including Foa, who was made principal conductor. The orchestra's re-launch as the Philharmonic was celebrated with a Great East Asia Concert for which one of the Italian violinists wrote a composition called "Great East Asia Symphonic Poem"; Li Delun was in the audience, and considered the piece to be "a joke."[22]

Conducting the reorganized orchestra under the eye of the Japanese occupiers cannot have been easy, and Foa was assisted by a number of guest conductors including long-time Shanghai resident A. Slovtsky; Henry Margolinsky, a German Jewish refugee who taught piano at the Conservatory; and the Japanese musician Takashi Asahina.[23] The orchestra's situation grew even more difficult in 1943 when the city's foreign musicians — and audiences — were hit by two harsh edicts: the creation of a Jewish ghetto in Hongkou and the internment of "enemy" nationals.

The order creating the Hongkou ghetto — the result of Nazi pressure on their Japanese allies — applied to European Jews who had arrived in Shanghai since 1937; Sephardic and Russian (Ashkenazi) Jews who had moved to Shanghai before 1937 were exempt. Once the ghetto-ization was implemented, Jews could no longer leave the ghetto without passes and thus could not attend concerts, even if they could afford tickets. European Jewish refugee musicians in the SMO and at the Conservatory now found it difficult to continue their professional lives, since permission to leave the ghetto even for work was dependent entirely on the whims of a Japanese soldier named Ghoya.

Ghoya — who called himself "King of the Jews"[24] — was detested by ghetto residents for his erratic behavior, which could sometimes be kindly but was more often sadistic. Musicians were obliged to have more contact with him than many ghetto residents, since he happened to be an amateur violinist and a great classical music fan. His love of music was a mixed blessing; most of the professionals were able to keep their jobs, but they were also often invited by Ghoya to play with him, an invitation they could not refuse. On one such occasion he is said to have had a clash of

---

22. See Luo: 113.

23. On returning to Japan, Takashi Asahina went on to become a major conductor, known to some as the "Karajan of Japan." He is widely credited with popularizing the works of such composers as Bruckner, Beethoven and Mahler in Japan and is the most recorded of all Japanese musicians. He was the world's oldest active conductor until his death in 2001 at the age of 93. His role conducting in Shanghai during the Japanese occupation was considered a blot on his record by some, but the Shanghai Symphony did not hold a grudge against him; the orchestra travelled to Osaka in October 1989 and performed under Asahina's baton.

24. Kranzler, D. (1988). *Japanese, Nazis and Jews: The Jewish Refugee Community of Shanghai, 1938-45*. Hoboken, NJ: KTAV Publishing House, Inc.: 499.

harmony with the esteemed violinist Alfred Wittenberg and told him, "You play as I direct, or I kill you."[25] Non-professional musicians were frequently denied passes to leave the ghetto for their work playing in cabarets and cafes and some were reduced to busking on the street in order to survive.

The internment camps, euphemistically called Civil Affairs Centers by the Japanese, were actually the outgrowth of a system of control already in place. Since the autumn of 1942, foreigners deemed "enemy nationals" had been required to wear numbered armbands and were frequently refused entry to public places of amusement, including cinemas and concert halls.[26] When the camps were created, thousands of American, British, Dutch, and other male "enemies" were simply locked up, precluding the possibility of their participation in musical — or any other — activities. Italians were at first considered friendly, but when Mussolini was overthrown in September of 1943, Shanghai's Italians were also declared enemies and were ordered to remain at home until further notice. That evening, bayonet-wielding Japanese soldiers appeared at the door of the Paci home to make sure that the recalcitrant maestro was abiding by the regulations. Paci was out at the Sevilla Restaurant playing cards as usual, but returned home while the soldiers were still standing on his doorstep.[27]

Paci's social status had changed from esteemed maestro to enemy national, the Shanghai Municipal Orchestra that he had built into "the best orchestra in the Far East" had been taken over by the Japanese, and his career as a conductor was over. However, he had devoted the most productive years of his life to his classical music "missionary work" in Shanghai and he made no move to leave. Instead, he channeled all his prodigious musical energy into teaching.

Although the conservatory he had been so eager to build in Hangzhou had been an early victim of the war, Paci had many private students.[28] A photograph taken on the occasion of his 67th birthday in June of 1945 shows him surrounded by 55 students, all but eight of whom are Chinese. Many of these students had trouble affording Paci's tuition — which was the very high sum of 20 US dollars a month — so Paci extended to them the same courtesy that Sgambati had shown him, teaching them for free.

"His pupils brought huge packages of Central Reserve Bank (CRB) dollars which we could not count," his daughter Fofi recalled. "The more affluent pupils paid more while the very talented, and often not affluent, did not pay." [29]

---

25. Kranzler: 499.

26. Collar, H. (1990). *Captive in Shanghai.* Hong Kong: Oxford University Press, 1990: 57.

27. Zaharoff, F.P. Adventures in China in the 1940s. Unpublished speech: 10.

28. In the interview that Paci gave just before his death, he stated that the building for the conservatory had been purchased, 16 professors hired from Europe, and entrance exams held, with 500 students taking them and 150 admitted. But, when war broke out, he had been obliged to cable all the professors — including six who had already sailed as far as Singapore — and inform them that the opening of the conservatory had been postponed indefinitely. See Ho, C.S. (1946). Paci tells of orchestra's growth, treatment by Japs. *The China Press.* October 21.

29. Zaharoff, F.P. Adventures in China in the 1940s. Unpublished speech: 10.

Whether they paid him or not, Maestro Paci continued to watch out for his best students and it was during this time that he learned that the Italian woman to whom he had sold one of the three tropicalized Steinways he had brought with him to Shanghai was preparing to leave the city and sell the instrument. Upon discovering that the asking price was only one gold bar, Maestro Paci immediately informed his student Dong Guangguang and told her that she should buy it. Ms. Dong was thrilled with the idea of owning such a magnificent piano — and one that had belonged to her much-esteemed teacher — but one gold bar translated into 8 million Chinese cash and it was far more than her family could possibly afford.

"I didn't know what to say," she explained. "But, I did have a sponsor so I called him up and told him. He said, 'Why don't you come this afternoon?' Then I got there and he said, 'I have made some inquiries and it is a good deal.' So, he opened up the safe and gave me a gold bar. I said, 'I cannot take it just like this!' So, he wrapped it in a newspaper and I rode off on the back of my brother's bike and bought the piano."

China's eight-year war with Japan finally ended in August of 1945. For a few tense days, both Japanese and American troops patrolled the streets of Shanghai, but no fighting broke out and massive celebrations soon spread across the city. In the following weeks, Maestro Paci received a call from the Nationalist government in Chongqing; since the British and Americans had given up their concessionary rights in 1943, and the French followed suit in 1945, all of Shanghai was now under the control of the Nationalist government. The victory celebrations that Nationalist culture officials were planning for Shanghai included a concert, and they wanted Paci to conduct it.

Paci accepted the invitation and returned to his old orchestra. For a short time in the autumn of 1945, it must have seemed as if his childhood dreams of "marvellous Symphony Concerts and great Conductors" had never been derailed by war. Mr. Tan went back to the orchestra for the occasion and recalled that Maestro Paci gave a hint of his emotions when he entered the Fuzhou Road rehearsal hall, took off his jacket, and reflexively turned around to find his usual place to hang it. Spotting the nail on which he had hung his coat for 25 years, he looked out at the musicians and said, "This is my nail." He then hung up his jacket and for the next week, it was as if he had never laid down his baton.

The victory concert was a gala affair. The internment camps had been liberated and the ghetto abolished, and crowds of Shanghai's music lovers once again dressed up and turned out for a concert conducted by Mario Paci. The program included one composition representing each of the victorious nations — it opened with *Victory of Democracy*, by Zhang Hao, played by the full orchestra together with a 100 voice chorus, and the United States was represented by Dvorak's *New World Symphony*.

Later that autumn, the orchestra was renamed the "Shanghai Municipal Symphony Orchestra," and Maestro Paci was invited to conduct the first two concerts it held under its new name. However, he was not offered his old job back, in part because he was Italian and thus on the losing side of the war. Since Foa was also Italian, he was no longer welcome as the permanent conductor, either, and a series of guest conductors took his place, including three members of the US occupation forces, three Chinese musicians, two local foreign musicians, and the composer Aaron Avshalomov.[30] In 1946, Henry Margolinsky was named conductor, but in 1947 the job was given back to Foa.

The war was over but the political situation in China still far from stable; many of Paci's colleagues and students were preparing to leave for calmer shores. Newspaper entertainment columns that had once been filled with announcements about visiting musicians were now devoted to farewell concerts given by local artists, both foreign and Chinese. However, Paci again made no move to leave. Instead, he kept to his normal schedule of teaching and socializing. Then, one night in the summer of 1946, he went out as usual to play cards with his friends. In the midst of the game, he picked up a cigarette for a smoke and stuck the wrong end into his mouth.

"It was the beginning of a stroke," said his daughter. "They took him to the hospital — he was half paralyzed."

Three days later — on August 3, 1946 — he was dead.

In the days following, tributes to Maestro Paci appeared in Shanghai's English and Chinese press. The "Letters" column of the *North China Daily News* — which, over the years, had published countless diatribes from Ratepayers critical of the SMO and its conductor — ran letters from Chinese students who urged "that something should be done to commemorate the services rendered by the late Maestro toward music in China."[31] The *China Press* seconded this in an editorial that called for a music scholarship for needy Chinese students in honor of Paci and noted — perhaps a touch condescendingly — that:

> There is no doubt that Maestro Paci had served this city well. To the Chinese community in particular, he did more than any other person in bringing western music to the uncultivated ears of the populace. He was the source of inspiration to the many Chinese pupils who received training from him and later became well-known artists. To thousands of Chinese, he opened the doors to the immortal compositions of the greatest masters of all time.[32]

A former student who signed her name Grace T. responded to the editorial the next day, referring to Maestro Paci as "a great tutor from whom I received every encouragement and inspiration," and echoing the calls to commemorate "what he has done for the Chinese." She added,

30. For a list of guest conductors, see Shanghai Symphony Orchestra 1989 informational brochure: 4. The three members of the US occupation forces were Jonathan Sternberg and W. O. Frederick, US Army; and Lt. Italiano, US Navy; the three Chinese musicians were Ma Sicong, Dai Cuilun, and Huang Yongxi; and the two local foreign musicians were Sloutsky and Sarichieff. In his book, Aaron Avshalomov's son Jacob says that Avshalomov was made conductor of the Shanghai orchestra after the war, but the Shanghai Symphony Orchestra lists Avshalomov only as a guest conductor.
31. *North China Daily News*, August 6, 1946: 5.
32. To Honor Paci. *The China Press*, August 7, 1946.

There is little doubt that Western music has come to China to stay, and I think all will agree with me that no other person, foreign or Chinese, has done as much as Maestro Paci. Individually and collectively, we must show him our deep gratitude.[33]

Mario Paci's funeral and burial were held at the Hongqiao Road Cemetery at 4 PM on August 5.[34] Paci's students turned out en masse, helping his distraught wife and daughter with all the details of the funeral and even penning the words that would mark their teacher's tombstone.

Tributes to the deceased maestro continued throughout the autumn. The first concert of the season was dedicated to Paci, "the Builder of the Orchestra." Under the baton of Henry Margolinsky, the orchestra played Beethoven's *Eroica* and Wagner's *Meistersinger* prelude, and also accompanied Dong Guangguang in a performance of Grieg's *Piano Concerto in A Minor*, which she had so often practiced under Paci's sharp eye.

A "Paci Memorial Concert," organized by the Shanghai Municipal Symphony Committee, the Shanghai Music Society and the Paci Memorial Committee, was held on November 2. Dong Guangguang again performed, playing Beethoven's *Sonata in E-Flat Major, Opus 81 a*, known as *Les Adieux*, while another of Paci's best students, Robert Kohner, performed Schumann's *Symphonic Etudes*.

Among the tributes and reminisces that continued to sprinkle the press was an interview that Maestro Paci had given to the Chinese-language newspaper *Wen Wei Pao* shortly before his death. The interviewer, a Miss Ho Chia-shui, thought that the city's foreign community would be interested in the story and therefore translated it into English after Paci's death. She asked questions that a foreign reporter would have been unlikely to broach, including a direct query as to why Paci had left his homeland and stayed so many years in China. His answer — simple, sad, and revealing — was "I...believed that to be a music pioneer in China was better than to work in my own country, because my own country did not need me."[35]

Ms. Ho ended the article with her own musings:

> It was late, the interview came to an end. And now Mr. Paci is here no more. I remember distinctly the expression of the unhappy old man who had sacrificed the brilliant life of concert artist in order to spend the days doing pioneer work in a country. It makes one wonder just what would have happened to the musical life in China if Mr. Paci had not fallen ill that Christmas Eve, or if there had been no war in 1937....[36]

---

33. To Honor Paci. *The China Press*, Letters, August 8, 1946.

34. *North China Daily News*, Sunday, August 4, 1946.

35. Ho Chia-shui (1946). Paci gives highlights of life in last interview. *The China Press*, October 20.

36. *The China Press*, October 21, 1946.

LI DELUN GOES TO YANAN

The initial burst of excitement that followed the end of the war with Japan was short-lived. Indeed, in Shanghai, as around the nation, inflation skyrocketed, the expected post-war rebuilding boon failed to materialize, and people's lives grew even harder. The political situation, too, grew murkier. Unable to agree on a shared vision for the future of their nation, the Nationalists and the Communists teetered on the brink of an all-out civil war.

Far across the Pacific, the United States was anxious that such war be avoided. Naturally, the US government wanted to see its Nationalist allies take power without any further bloodshed. There were, moreover, many American troops still in China helping to disarm and repatriate the defeated Japanese and nobody wanted to see them caught up in a civil war. Looking into the future, the US was also concerned that war in China would leave a power vacuum in Asia into which the increasingly hostile Soviet Union would blithely step.

So, in the hopes of brokering a compromise between the Nationalists and the Communists which would lead to a coalition government under Chiang Kai-shek, President Truman sent just-retired Chairman of the Joint Chiefs of Staff General George C. Marshall to China as his special envoy. In retrospect the assignment was a doomed one — as many people on the ground thought, even then — but no one could fault the prestige and the sincerity of the man sent out to accomplish it. Arriving in Shanghai at the very end of 1945, General Marshall set about brokering talks between the Communist representative Zhou Enlai and the Nationalist representative Zhang Zhizhong and in surprisingly little time negotiated a cease-fire, albeit a short-lived one.

These negotiations required all participants to travel frequently, especially Zhou Enlai. During one such visit to Shanghai in September of 1946, Mr. Zhou hosted an elegant reception for the city's artistic community. Many of China's most famous left-wing writers were among the guests, including the dramatist Tian Han, the feminist novel and short-story writer Ding Ling and the novelist Ba Jin. Also among the invitees — and somewhat in awe to find himself there — was the young cellist from the Conservatory, Li Delun.

While Mr. Li moved among the famous guests at the reception with apparent ease, inwardly his thoughts were churning. Back in Beijing, he had been a leader of a Marxist study group and even a member of the underground Communist Party. However, his underground membership had been single-line — meaning he only had one contact within the Party — and he had lost touch with this person just before coming to Shanghai. Since then, he had been so immersed in music and socializing that he had done little to act upon his political convictions.

Now, however, he could not stop himself from gazing at the urbane and charismatic Zhou Enlai, who radiated integrity and looked especially handsome in his Western suit. Mr. Li listened intently when Mr. Zhou spoke to the gathering about the current state of negotiations between the Nationalists and the Communists. The Nationalists, Mr. Zhou explained, were not sincere participants in the negotiation process — their true goal was simply to get rid of the Communists.

Listening to Mr. Zhou and looking at the famous leftist artists who surrounded him, Mr. Li's Communist sympathies were hotly rekindled and he was soon overwhelmed by a burning ambition to become a revolutionary. Indeed, the reception confirmed what he had felt since he was a teenager, drawn to the works of both Mozart and Marx — that there was no contradiction between art and revolution.

In the days following, Mr. Li set about resuming contact with the Party and was soon visited by a woman composer and Party member named Qu Xixuan. Comrade Qu told him not to worry too much about his membership — the important thing was to be working for the cause. But, she also promised to help him be readmitted and asked that he write a short autobiography that explained his underground Party involvement.

Mr. Li wrote out the autobiography as soon as he got the chance and was just putting the finishing touches to it when a friend dropped by to invite him out to eat. Never one to turn down an invitation, Mr. Li accepted at once, but then hesitated — what should he do with the autobiography? Nationalist spies and operatives lurked everywhere in Shanghai and they still routinely arrested, tortured and even executed Communists — if anyone should suspect him of involvement with the Party and search his room while he was out, they would find the autobiography; and then, who knew what could happen? The safest thing, he decided, was to take the paper with him.

Mr. Li's friend had just been paid and was eager to have some fun. So, after having a meal at a restaurant, the two went to a movie, ate again, and then they went to a local opera performance. By the time the opera was over, it was already late so Mr. Li took a pedicab home. Leaning back in his seat to wind down after the day's entertainment, he put his hand in his pocket and was suddenly overcome by a wave of anxiety — his autobiography was gone! If the document fell into the wrong hands, or if someone turned it into the Nationalist authorities... Mr. Li shuddered even to think of it.

A search of all his pockets turned up nothing and re-hashing the day's activities proved of little use — he was always losing and forgetting things, and the paper could have fallen out anywhere. Mr. Li passed an anxious night and the next day found his Communist Party contact to tell her what had happened. Comrade Qu listened carefully but could offer little reassurance — losing the document was a big mistake, she agreed, but she would try to help.

A few days later Comrade Qu contacted him again to tell him that the underground Party had decided it was too dangerous for him to stay in Shanghai. Handing him an envelope of money, she told him that they wanted him to leave for Hong Kong. Mr. Li demurred at once. He did not want to go to Hong Kong — he wanted to go to Yanan, the base of the Communist Party and incubator of the revolution.

Having given voice to this suddenly overpowering desire, Mr. Li determined to fulfill it as soon as possible. He spoke to his friend Ouyang Shanzun, a drama director who had close connections with the Party, and Mr. Ouyang promised to contact Zhou Enlai directly at his Nanjing headquarters. A few days later he delivered a reply from Mr. Zhou himself — the Communist Party needed people like Li Delun and he was welcome to go to Yanan.

Mr. Li's excitement upon hearing this news was great — his long-suppressed dream of joining the revolution was about to come true! But, secrecy was of the utmost importance and he had to be careful not to betray his churning emotions. The next day he went to his job at the Voice of the USSR as usual and was broadcasting Beethoven's *Ninth Symphony* when a phone call came from Zhou Enlai's Nanjing office. The time had come — Mr. Li was to leave Shanghai for Nanjing that evening and from there journey onward to Yanan.

Mr. Li sat still for a moment to absorb this information, suddenly realizing how hard it would be to leave behind the life he had built in Shanghai. But, this was no time for regrets and he hurriedly called Li Jue, his girlfriend of three years, to tell her the news. Then, after finding a composition student who could take over his job at the radio station, he went to bid his Russian boss goodbye with a big bear hug. Grabbing the score to Beethoven's *Ninth* that he had been following as he played the music, he ran out of the station and hurried back to his room.

Li Jue was there, waiting with a suitcase packed with music — she herself was a violinist, a student of Foa's, and she knew that Li Delun would care more about music than clothes. She had invited a few friends over to say goodbye and Mr. Li told them that he was going to Beijing for the funeral of his father, who had in fact just passed away. That evening, Li Jue and his sister accompanied him to Shanghai Station. With trains hissing on the platform and travelers surging around them, Li Delun and Li Jue gazed at each other for a long moment. Although they were both certain that Mr. Li was doing the right thing in going to Yanan to work for the revolution, they had no clear idea when they would meet again and it was hard to say goodbye. When the Nanjing-bound train's arrival was announced, Li Jue hugged Li Delun sadly and said, "From now on, be a bit more diligent."[37]

The crowded train pulled into the station and Mr. Li scrambled aboard with his cello, a few French horns, some medicine he had decided to bring along at the last minute, and his suitcase full of scores. When the train finally pulled away at midnight, his little sister ran alongside it while Li Jue stood silently gazing into the distance. Mr. Li waved to both of them until the platform ended and the lights of the station vanished. Then he sank down on his suitcase and pondered all that he had left behind, all that lay ahead.

The train to Nanjing took only a few hours, so it was still dark when Mr. Li arrived in the Nationalist capital. With all of his heavy bags, he had no choice but to take a taxi to Zhou Enlai's headquarters. The fare was extortionate and Nationalist

---

37. Luo: 156.

military police stopped him en route, allowing him to pass only when he showed them his instruments and fibbed that he was there for a concert. His heart was fluttering when he finally reached his destination, knocked on the door, and heard a voice cry, "Who is it?"[38]

"I am from Shanghai," he shouted through the closed door. "I am Li.... "

"Oh, Comrade Li Delun?" came the expectant voice.

The door opened and Mr. Li was ushered in. All his anxieties vanished as he was warmly welcomed and given a room in which to rest. Lying down, he noticed with satisfaction that there was a violin tucked under the bed next to him. Two days later a car came and took him to an airfield. An American C-47 military aircraft with a beautiful woman painted on it stood on the tarmac, its engines running.

Mr. Li climbed the stairs to the plane and settled into a window seat near the front. A pang of regret passed over him — he had left Shanghai in such a hurry that he had forgotten the books he planned to read en route to Yanan, Beethoven's *Fifth Symphony* and a collection of Lu Xun's essays. So, instead of reading, he gazed out the window as the plane rose high above the Nanjing countryside. Most everywhere had been flooded by the Yellow River, still off course from Chiang Kai-shek's wartime bombing of its dykes.

As the plane approached Yanan, the American pilot looked back into the cabin and asked Mr. Li if he spoke English. When he replied in the affirmative, the pilot asked him to tell all the other passengers to move to the front of the plane — it was going to be a bumpy landing and he needed the ballast up front. The plane circled, dipping and diving as the pilot searched for a place to land in the bald yellow mountains. Soon, many of the passengers were throwing up. When they finally landed safely on a make-shift dirt runway, Mr. Li walked down the stairs of the plane and saw — nothing. Not a building or a person was in sight, only the bleak, windswept yellow mountains of Shaanxi Province.

Some of the other passengers — including several Americans involved in the Nationalist-Communist negotiations — had been to Yanan before and they knew what to do, so Mr. Li walked along with them to the nearest village. They went into a local peasant's house and sat down on a *kang*, the raised earthen platform heated from within that still serves as bed and furniture in rural areas of northern China. An American truck arrived to pick up the plane passengers; but it could only accommodate a few people, so it took the Americans first.

Mr. Li ate dumplings and tried hard not to appear shocked by the bleakness and poverty that surrounded him. Yanan — the cradle of the revolution, the base of the Communist Party of China — was certain to be much more prosperous and flourishing than this backwater town.

The sound of a motor outside interrupted Mr. Li's thoughts — a second truck had arrived for the remaining passengers. His life as a Communist guerilla musician was about to begin.

---

38. *Ibid.*

Chapter 5. From Classical To Communist

Chairman Mao's Vision for the Arts

Yanan, as Mr. Li soon discovered, was in fact even poorer than the village where his plane had landed. Like most of northern Shaanxi, it was home to peasants who had long lived at the mercy of roaming bandits and rapacious landlords. They survived — barely — by using primitive agricultural methods to eke out a living from the rugged terrain. If a natural disaster struck, it was calamitous — in the Great Northwest Famine of 1928-33, as many as 2,500,000 peasants in Shaanxi are thought to have died, roughly one-third of the province's entire population.[1] Yanan's isolation compounded its poverty. Indeed, the roads in and out were so narrow, rutted and steep that transportation was limited to pack animals and the occasional American airplane. Building materials were so scarce and costly that housing for everyone — from Mao Zedong and Zhou Enlai on down — consisted of caves that had been carved into the loess hillsides.

But, if Yanan was at first glance bleak and poor, it was also the nerve center of the Communist Party that would soon take control of the world's most populous nation. Energetic young idealists from urban areas were drawn to Yanan because they wanted to work for the Communist cause. The Party gave them further enticement by offering an easy path to membership and promising free higher education, together with room and board.

To fulfill this promise, the Party had founded a number of schools, including the Central Party School, the North Shaanxi Public School and the Resist Japan Military and Political University. Left-leaning intellectuals flocked to Yanan to help run these new institutions and the once-barren village quickly sprouted

---

1. Holm, D. (1991). *Art and Ideology in Revolutionary China*. Oxford: Clarendon Press: 6.

newspapers, poetry clubs, theatrical troupes, and associations dedicated to drama, music, fine arts, and culture in general. Indeed, while political and military planning were of paramount concern to the Communist leadership, culture — especially performing and visual arts — also played a vital role in their revolutionary blueprints because of its tremendous value as a propaganda tool.

Since its earliest days, the Communists had supported a number of drama and dance troupes, often managed by artists trained in the Soviet Union.[2] "There was no more powerful weapon of propaganda in the Communist movement than the Reds' dramatic troupes," wrote the American journalist Edgar Snow, "and none more subtly manipulated."[3]

By the mid-1930s, the performing arts were such a regular part of life at Communist bases that many foreign journalists wrote about it in dispatches sent overseas. Snow described a typical production in his book, *Red Star Over China*:

> Cadets, muleteers, women and girl workers from the uniform and shoe factory, clerks from the cooperatives and from the soviet post office, soldiers, carpenters, villagers followed by their infants, all began streaming toward the big grassy plain beside the river, where the players were performing. It would be hard to imagine a more democratic gathering — something like old-time Chautauqua....

> Across the stage was a big pink curtain of silk, with the words "People's Anti-Japanese Dramatic Society" in Chinese characters, as well as the Latinized Chinese, which the Reds were promoting to hasten mass education. The program was to last three hours. It proved to be a combination of playlets, dancing, singing and pantomime — a kind of variety show, or vaudeville, given unity chiefly by two central themes: anti-Nipponism and the revolution. It was full of overt propaganda and the props were primitive....

> What it lacked in subtlety and refinement it partly made up by its robust vitality, its sparkling humor, and a sort of participation between actors and audience. Guests at the Red Theater actually seemed to *listen* to what was said: a really astonishing thing in contrast with the bored opera audience, who often spent their time eating fruit and melon seeds, gossiping, tossing hot towels back and forth, visiting from one box to another, and only occasionally looking at the stage....[4]

During the Yanan years, these cultural activities became more formal and professional, a trend that accelerated after the founding of the Lu Xun Academy for Arts and Literature in the spring of 1938. Headquartered in an old, two-steepled Catholic church, the Lu Xun Academy was designed to introduce Communist cadres to art, literature, music and drama and the ways they could be used for propaganda. It was headed by Zhou Yang, the Marxist literary critic who would become Mao's main

---

2. See Holm: 23-30

3. Snow, L.W. (1972) *China On Stage: An American Actress in the People's Republic.* New York: Random House: 102.

4. Snow: 119-120.

spokesperson on cultural matters. While the first class at Lu Xun Academy had only 300 students,[5] this number was quickly expanded and branches of the school were opened in several of the liberated areas.

In the beginning, the Lu Xun Academy was dominated by intellectuals of the May 4th generation, men and women whose tastes were high-brow, and often internationalist, and whose education and experience was decidedly urban middle or upper class. Students were encouraged to focus on quality by learning from the best of the world's writers and artists. Great works of world literature made up a core course of study and theatrical performances included such dramas as Molière's *Le Bourgeois Gentilhomme*; Gogol's *The Wedding* and *The Inspector-General*; Pogodin's *Man with the Gun*; Ivanov's *Armoured Train 14.69*; several one-act plays by Chekhov; and *Sunrise* and *Thunderstorm* by China's own Cao Yu.[6]

However, the high standards and artistic quality that were of paramount importance to many of the intellectuals who made the trek to Yanan were not foremost in the mind of such key revolutionary leaders as General Zhu De and Mao Zedong himself. In 1940, Zhu De visited the Lu Xun Academy to talk about "Art Work and the Propaganda War in North China over the Last Three Years." In his address, Zhu warned that the Japanese had been appropriating Chinese art forms and using them to spread propaganda, and suggested that Chinese artists needed to do the same thing.[7] That same year, Mao made passing comments on this topic when he called for the creation of a "national, scientific and mass culture" in which foreign cultural elements could be used, albeit selectively.[8] He followed these brief remarks two years later with what turned out to be his seminal statement on literature and the arts.

This historic address, known ever after as "Talks at the Yanan Forum on Literature and Art," was given at a May 1942 meeting of arts and culture workers that Mao had called in part because he was increasingly dissatisfied with some of the work being produced by those artists who had travelled to Yanan to support the revolution. Since conditions at Yanan were rustic and the assembly hall was still under construction, Mao spoke outdoors on a flat stretch of land in front of some cave-dwellings. One of the meeting participants recalled the atmosphere of that night years later, in rather poetic reminisces:

> ...May in Yanan is enchanting. Summer is drawing near but there is still a trace of spring chill in the air. There was no wind at dusk. As the blue sky gradually darkened, the evening star appeared over the far horizon....
>
> In the open space in front of the loess caves, wooden supports had been fixed up for the acetylene lamps to be lit that evening and many of us gathered there well ahead of time. Suddenly clapping burst out from one corner of the meeting-place. The clapping came closer and closer, accompanying a group of new arrivals....

---

5. Holm: 45.
6. Holm: 78.
7. Holm: 77.
8. Holm: 74. The speech is "On New Democracy."

These were Chairman Mao, Commander-in-Chief Zhu De and other members of the Party Central Committee. With a spring in his step, Chairman Mao strode to the small rectangular table in the center of the crowd. There, under the dark blue night sky of Yanan in early summer, in this simple, open-air meeting-place, he delivered the conclusion of his famous "Talks at the Yanan Forum on Literature and Art," now known as an epoch-making Marxist-Leninist classic....

Without any sign of fatigue Chairman Mao spoke on. It was already past midnight. The moon overhead made the night as bright as day. Under the moon and the stars, hills nearby and distant were darkly silhouetted. Not far away, the Yenhe River flowed merrily, its surface shot with silver.... [9]

Mao talked until nearly dawn, explaining to his audience of eager intellectuals that,

"A good number of comrades have come here from the garrets of Shanghai, and in coming from those garrets to the revolutionary base areas, they have passed not only from one kind of place to another but from one historical epoch to another.... Here the people around us and the audience for our propaganda are totally different." [10]

Since some artists and writers did not understand their new audience — and some did not even understand that their purpose was ultimately to create politically useful, rather than pure, art — Mao needed to explain his thinking.

He began by emphasizing the importance of culture in revolution — though an army with guns was the main force, a "cultural army" was also "absolutely indispensable for uniting our own ranks and defeating the enemy." [11] However, for this cultural army to succeed, its members had to be absolutely clear as to their mission and understand the answer to the simple question: Literature and art for whom?

The answer was that literature and art should be created for the masses of the people, meaning the workers, peasants, soldiers and urban petty bourgeoisie who comprised 90% of the population. Art and literature were not to be created for petty-bourgeois intellectuals and other exploiters and oppressors; any such art geared to these classes was feudal art and it had no role in revolution.

Mao then raised a second question concerning the problem of how artists and writers should serve the revolution: "Should we devote ourselves to raising standards, or should we devote ourselves to popularization?" [12] Again, he provided the answer, explaining that the people demanded popularization first, and after that, higher standards. Because the Chinese people had been so long repressed by the feudal and bourgeois classes, many were illiterate and uneducated. So, "for them the prime need is not 'more flowers on the brocade' but 'fuel in snowy weather.'" [13]

9. Huang, K. (1977) An Unforgettable Night in Yanan. *Chinese Literature* 9: 91-5.
10. Mao Zedong (1942). Talks at the Yanan Forum on Literature and Art. In *Mao Tse-Tung on Literature and Art*. Peking: Foreign Languages Press (1977): 38.
11. Mao: 1.
12. Mao: 16.

In order to popularize the arts and literature — and then raise standards — artists and writers had to learn from the masses and strive to reflect the real lives of the people in their art. Under no condition should they confine themselves to an ivory tower or blindly copy from the ancients and the foreigners. Art that pleases only a few, but is useless or even harmful to the majority of people, not only insults the masses but reveals the artist's own ignorance — to be good, art and literature must bring benefit to the masses.

Having raised and answered these two key questions, Mao went on to emphasize what he saw as the political nature of all art:

> In the world today, all literature and art belong to definite classes and are geared to definite political lines. There is in fact no such thing as art for art's sake, art that stands above classes or art that is detached from or independent of politics.[14]

In other words, art and literature would always be subordinate to politics — any artists or writers who hoped to contribute to the Communist cause would have to accept this and disabuse themselves of any notions of art as a form of self-expression or love of humanity. An artist's job was to reflect the real lives of the people in a way that was beneficial to the masses — to do this, he first had to understand the masses and their lives. This would be hard work, Mao warned, and would involve "much pain and friction."[15] But he was confident that those with the determination would fulfill his requirements.

Not even Mao himself could have realized the depth of the "pain" and the extent of the "friction" that would accompany the implementation of Communist Party arts policies in years to come. In the short-term aftermath of his speech, however, the friction was mainly mild as various intellectuals and artists tried to work out ways to follow Mao's suggestions without completely forsaking their own opinions and goals.

Put simply, Yanan was divided into two camps. In one camp were those who felt — as did Mao himself — that the needs of the revolution could best be served by adding new, revolutionary content to traditional or "national" Chinese art forms, like local opera and folk art. In the other were those who felt that the revolution and the new era it presaged required completely new art forms with new, revolutionary content, like spoken drama or symphonic music imported from the West but adapted to China's own particular culture and conditions. Those in the first camp tended to be more concerned with popularization and reaching the broad masses of Chinese people, while those in the second camp tended to emphasize artistic quality and the importance of raising the cultural level of the masses.

Reflecting the desire and the need to show support for Mao's opinions, there was more talk about "national forms" as the 1940s wore on, and the camps would grow increasingly polarized. However, opposing viewpoints were generally permitted to co-

13. Mao: 20.
14. Mao: 25.
15. Mao: 40.

exist at Yanan, so Western music and technique continued to be taught in the Lu Xun Academy's music department right alongside Chinese music. This relative plurality of opinion and education made fertile ground for the creation of music of all kinds.

MUSICAL LIFE AT YANAN

The Music Department at the Lu Xun Academy had a five-fold mission: to teach progressive music theory and technique; to train Resist Japan music cadres; to promote the study and development of Chinese music; to promote the development of Resist Japan music; and to organize and lead music activities. Its curriculum was as broad as its mission, including politics and art theory, conducting, composition, harmony, music appreciation, solfege, voice and instrumental playing.[16]

It was initially headed by the composer Lu Ji, who had gone to Yanan after the Japanese occupation of Shanghai. He first took charge of musical activities at Resist Japan University and then became involved in the founding of the Lu Xun Academy, quickly rising from head of the music department to vice president of the university. Lu Ji built a strong teaching staff with such composers as Li Huanzhi and Zheng Lucheng but was determined to make it even better. Given his strong belief in the value of songs for inspiring the masses to resist the Japanese, one candidate stood out as ideal: Xian Xinghai.

Xian Xinghai had joined a Save the Country Performance Troupe after the outbreak of war and left Shanghai for Wuhan. There he had done as Avshalomov advised — worked hard and gotten to know the Chinese situation more clearly. He had been appointed head of music activities for the Joint Commission for Military Affairs, a position he used to organize a series of mass song rallies and which made him increasingly sympathetic to the Communist cause. He also continued to compose his own songs, which were sung by ever greater numbers of people. He was thus productively engaged in Wuhan when he received a letter asking him to become a professor at the Lu Xun Academy in Yanan.

The letter was personally signed by every member of the Lu Xun Academy music department and the idea of working for the revolution in its cradle held great appeal, but Xian Xinghai hesitated. He was concerned whether Yanan would prove to be an environment in which he could compose freely, and whether he would be able to leave once he got there. Friends who knew more about Yanan than he did assured him that he need have no worries on either count, and as he continued to ponder, two successive — and persuasive — telegrams arrived from the eager faculty. Won over by their enthusiasm, Xian decided that he should at least give the Lu Xun Academy a try.

---

16. For mission and curriculum, see *Zhongguo Yinyue Cidian* [Dictionary of Chinese Music]. (1984) Beijing: Renmin Yinyue Chubanshe: 246.

When he reached Yanan in November of 1938, Xian found that music and especially song played an important role in life at the Communist base. One of his colleagues, the composer Zheng Lucheng, described its more populist side:

> Everyone was singing then, morale was very high. At first we sang Red Army songs, like *The Three Main Rules of Discipline and the Eight Points for Attention*, and we also had local folk songs. Later, the songs by Nie Er, Xian Xinghai and Lu Ji also became popular.... Resist Japan University had nearly ten thousand students, divided into a great many companies, each one of which had a conductor. Whenever major reports were made, from five to six thousand up to ten thousand people were gathered on the field. We learned songs for half an hour or an hour before we began: this group would sing, then that group would sing, all very enthusiastically.... Yanan is a small place, between the mountain and the river. When ten thousand people sang at once, the earth seemed to move and the mountain to shake.... Yanan was not only the sacred place of the revolution, it also became a true city of song.[17]

Xian soon became involved in both the serious and the populist sides of musical life at Yanan. He taught students how to compose for and to conduct choral groups. He personally conducted the Lu Xun Academy's own chorus and also taught music at several other schools in Yanan. He composed or co-composed two operas, part of his first symphony, two cantatas, and hundreds of save-the-country songs. Like most intellectuals and artists who came to Yanan, he also became at least peripherally involved in the debate as to the form that art should take in new China.[18]

In an essay entitled "On National Form in Chinese Music," Xian made a strong argument in favor of developing new art forms, rather than recycling old ones, at least so far as music was concerned.

> A national form for Chinese music can be sought in many places. However: old forms and old content, though they can accompany each other harmoniously, are absolutely not appropriate for today. New content accompanying old form is a little bit incongruous. New content set to new form is not only harmonious but very necessary as well, though often the masses cannot accept it very quickly or very naturally. Thus the problem of how to deal with Chinese musical forms really is not an easy one. Personally, I propose that we let content determine form, and use the modern advanced musical viewpoint to produce new content. We should ensure that the content of music can reflect reality — the thoughts, feelings, and lives of the nation.[19]

He then demonstrated what he meant by doing precisely this in some of his own compositions. Working together with colleagues, he wrote an opera called *March of the Army and People*, which was performed by staff and students of the Lu Xun Academy in January of 1939. The opera — really more of an operetta — had two acts and three scenes

---

17. Kraus: 55. From Zheng, L.C. (1983) Gechang Geming [Singing Revolution], in Ding X.S. *Zuoqujia Zheng Lucheng* [Composer Zheng Lucheng] Shenyang: Liaoning Renmin Chubanshe: 289.

18. For more on this debate, see Holm: 51-66.

19. Holm: 61

which depicted the sorrows and suffering brought about by war. While its musical structure of overtures, arias and recitative were Western, its melodies were taken from Chinese folk songs and its instrumentation included first and second violin; accordion; harmonica; *huqin*; *sanxian*; *dizi* (Chinese bamboo flute); and a Chinese percussion section with drums, gong, temple blocks, and bamboo clappers.

He followed the opera with what has become his signature work, the *Yellow River Cantata*. The Yellow River is known both as the "cradle" of China's civilization and as its "sorrow," since it so frequently floods its banks. Xian's cantata eulogizes the struggles of the people who live on its shores and must battle both the mighty waters and the Japanese in their daily struggle to survive. The cantata has lyrics by the revolutionary poet Guang Weiran and is divided into eight sections with narration to link them together. It includes a chorus, orchestra and soloists, with many of the choral sections based on the style of National Salvation songs and many elements of folk songs integrated in the orchestral parts. As with the *March of the Army and People*, Xian wrote *Yellow River* for both Western and Chinese instruments, a decision he made more for practical than artistic reasons, since there were not enough Western instruments in the Communist base to comprise a full orchestra.[20]

Xian Xinghai wrote the *Yellow River Cantata* in only six days and it was first performed on April 13, 1939 before an audience that Edgar Snow described as "roughly-clad students and soldiers of the Eighth Route Army, and an overflow crowd of peasants."[21] Mao Zedong was among the students, peasants and soldiers, as were Snow and a young chemistry student who recorded his memory of the event, Ma Ke.

Ma, who would be inspired by the performance to become a composer himself, described the premiere of *Yellow River* with lyrical admiration:

> After the curtain went up, young people from the auditorium filed up to the stage. Since there was not room enough there for them all, some of the chorus fanned out on either side down below, making it difficult to distinguish between the performers and the audience.
>
> A man in shirt-sleeves, shorts and straw sandals mounted the stage with a baton in his hand — that was Xian Xinghai. Conditions in the revolutionary base were so hard that even well-known figures dressed like poor peasants. He looked about thirty, bronzed and vigorous. In reply to a great ovation from the audience, he saluted us with a smile and then turned slowly round. An actor launched into an impassioned recital of the prologue to the *Yellow River Cantata*, carrying us with him in imagination into the world conjured up by the composer.
>
> "Friend, have you ever seen the Yellow River? Have you ever crossed the Yellow River? Do you still remember how the boatmen there pit their lives against the angry waves? If you have forgotten, listen!"

---

20. Xian wrote, "I am just now researching the characteristics of Chinese musical instruments, and am thinking of using their strong points to make up for the current lack of Western instruments." See Kraus: 57.

21. Snow, E. (1962). *The Other Side of the River*. New York: Random House: 568-9

That same instant Xian Xinghai's arm swept up and the chorus nearly lifted the roof with their singing:

"Row, row; on we go! Forward now, row on! Row on!..."

The exultant tone and dramatic rhythm of this song so stirred the audience that some of us could not stay in our seats. The music expressing the battle with the rushing torrent made us feel as if we too were struggling against the river. When at last the boatmen won through the storm, the chorus broke into laughter and the audience stood up to cheer.[22]

Snow's description is far more dispassionate, though he also notes that the audience was much moved:

That was a weird orchestra [Xian] put together.... The Catholic church organ for a piano, two or three violins, a home-made cello or two, some Chinese flutes, clarinets, yang-ch'ins, and hu-ch'ins, improvised instruments of some kind made of old Standard Oil tins with gut strung over them, a few pieces of battered brass, cymbals, army drums and trumpets. Did he also use a few cannon? Somehow he got his melody and his fugue out of them. Before he began he told me what the cantata was all about, scene by scene, movement by movement; the whole epic of the historic river down to the enemy invasion, the struggle to hold the banks, and the prophecy of victory, revolution, liberation. He was passionately sincere about it. The audience listened raptly to the mystifying half-Western, half-Asian noises. In that starlit night you could almost feel the Yellow River itself joining in the final roar of the cantata — and the Japanese were not far behind. At the end of it people wept and cheered.[23]

The day after the premiere, Mao Zedong sent Xian Xinghai a gift of a Parker fountain pen and a bottle of ink to signify his enjoyment of the composition and his support of the composer's work.[24]

Xian continued to prosper at Yanan, following the *Yellow River* with more songs, operas and cantatas. In the spring of 1940, the Central Committee of the Communist Party ordered him to go to Moscow to write music for a Soviet documentary about the Communist Eighth Route Army. Chairman Mao and his young wife Jiang Qing invited Xian and his wife for a farewell dinner at their cave, and then the composer who had spent so much of his life abroad once again departed for Europe. Although no one present at this farewell dinner would have guessed it, it was the last time they would see the ambitious composer.

Arriving in Moscow as planned, Xian Xinghai soon found himself completely cut off from China. The Nazi invasion of the USSR caused work on the documentary to be suspended and apparently made Mr. Xian something of a burden on his hosts. He tried to get back to China, but the Nationalist Army would not let him in and he ended up

22. Ma Ke (1965). Hsien Hsing-hai [Xian Xinghai] the Composer. *Chinese Literature* 12: 110-111.
23. Snow: 569. Snow was quoting himself in a conversation held with music workers in Shanghai during a visit to China in the early 1960s. He incorrectly writes Xian Xinghai's name as Hsieh (Xie).
24. See Kraus: 58.

spending a year in Mongolia and a year in Kazakhstan. However hard this exile may have been personally, it gave him ample time to study, attend concerts and compose. He completed his first symphony, entitled *National Liberation Symphony*, and dedicated it to "The Central Committee of the Great Chinese Communist Party and its Glorious Leader Comrade Mao Zedong." He re-orchestrated the *Yellow River Cantata* for a conventional Western orchestra so that it could be performed outside China, and he wrote a second symphony, called *Sacred Battle*, which he dedicated to Stalin and the Soviet Red Army.

Unfortunately, the frequent moves in wartime conditions took a toll on his health and by the spring of 1945 Xian was so ill that his embarrassed hosts sent him to the Kremlin Hospital in Moscow. His body was ravaged by disease but he continued to be productive, using his time in hospital to write a "thirty-five year plan" for his future musical activity.

Sadly, Xian Xinghai's earnest optimism could not overcome his illness and he died on October 30, 1945 at the age of 40. When word of his death was sent back to Yanan, a large memorial service was held and Mao contributed an inscription that read, "Mourn the People's Musician, Comrade Xian Xinghai!" Some months later, the former Communist Party chairman Li Lisan brought two suitcases full of Xian's hand-written documents, compositions, scores, diaries and notes back from Moscow to Yanan. These, together with the composer's early death and Mao's beatification, would ensure that his name, and some of his music, would live on in China in a way that would never have been possible had he himself survived. Although he did not live to see New China, he nonetheless managed to become — as Avshalomov predicted — its "first composer."

Xian Xinghai's example also inspired many other budding composers, including Ma Ke, the young man who was so overwhelmed by the premiere performance of the *Yellow River Cantata*. In the months following the cantata's premiere, Ma Ke had started to study composition with Xian Xinghai. He continued his studies with other professors at the Lu Xun Academy after Xian left for Moscow and was further inspired by a movement to adapt *yangge* — a vaudeville-like combination of dances, songs and variety acts that was popular among the peasants of northern Shaanxi — for revolutionary purposes. [25]

The *yangge* movement followed on Mao's "Talks" at Yanan, which themselves precipitated a big meeting of the Lu Xun Academy music department.[26] The four-day meeting was attended by more than sixty people and involved heated debates over the direction of music education and whether the department was too influenced by formalism. Performance activities were also discussed, with many people faulting the department for organizing such activities as a January 1942 concert that was all foreign symphonic music except for one piece by Lu Ji. Critics also complained that

---

25. For an extensive discussion of the Yangge movement at Yanan, see Holm, D. (1991). *Art and Ideology in Revolutionary China*. Oxford: Clarendon Press.

26. See Ming: 204-5.

the music department emphasized raising standards at the expense of music creation — students were so busy trying to compose artistic songs that they did not want to write songs for the masses. Revolutionary *yangge* was the department's answer to these complaints and the first big production was staged for the 1943 Chinese New Year celebrations, which is when *yangge* was normally performed by peasants.

Ma Ke's response to the dual examples of Xian Xinghai and the *yangge* movement was to collaborate with his colleagues to write an "opera" called *The White-Haired Girl*. [27] In this first of what would be many incarnations, *The White-Haired Girl* tells the story of a poor peasant girl named Xi Er whose father is forced to sell her to a landlord as payment for a debt. Xi Er's father is so stricken by guilt that he soon kills himself, while she herself is constantly abused and then finally raped by the evil landlord. When she becomes pregnant, the landlord decides to sell her to a brothel; she flees to the hills and hides in a mountain cave, where she gives birth. Xi Er keeps herself and her child alive by stealing the offerings from a temple but the poor diet and the darkness of the cave make her long black hair turn white. Her salvation finally comes when her old boyfriend, who is now a member of the Communist Eighth Route Army, returns to fight the Japanese and rescues her from her cave. The landlord is captured and tried before a spontaneous court of farmers, at which Xi Er gives passionate testimony. Originally, this was the end, but after it was staged in public rehearsal, a number of people — including Mao Zedong himself — said that the landlord should be shot, so the ending was changed to an execution scene.

Musically, *The White-Haired Girl* uses a chorus and arias, as in Western opera, but the singing-style is based on the folk songs of north Shaanxi peasants. A Westerner who saw a packed performance of *The White-Haired Girl* in Beijing in 1949 wrote this description:

> The music, which is charming and often poignant, is neither Western nor does it include any of the falsetto singing of the traditional Chinese opera. Much of it is based on Chinese folk music.... The orchestra is a combination of Western string instruments (violin, cello, contrabass) with the native *erhu*, flute, drum, gong and wooden clapper. In some themes the Western instruments predominate; in others, the Chinese. The result is remarkably successful and constitutes a new musical genre. Most reminiscent of the old-time drama is the use of drum, gong, and clapper to punctuate and accentuate the movements of the actors. This technique is highly effective when, for example, the percussion instruments burst into a crescendo of fury during a pursuit or a scene of violence. As a result, this play, despite the realism of its plot, resembles — as does the old-time drama — a stylized ballet. Even when the actors are not singing, they frequently move about the stage with the rhythmic steps and gestures seen on the traditional stage. [28]

---

27. Ma Ke was the principal composer of *The White-Haired Girl* but he had many collaborators from the Lu Xun Academy. Working with him on the music were Zhang Lu, Qu Wei, Huan Zhi, Xiang Ou, Chen Zi, Liu Zhi. The libretto was written by He Jingzhi and Ding Yi. See *Zhongguo Yinyue Cidian:* 11.

28. Bodde, Derek (1950). *Peking Diary, a year of revolution.* New York: Henry Schuman, Inc.: 166-67.

The White-Haired Girl was a smash hit at Yanan when it premiered in 1945 during the Communist Party's seventh congress. It was soon being performed throughout Communist-controlled areas of the country, where it inevitably generated "class hatred" of the peasants for the landlords. For Ma Ke and the others who had worked on it, it was proof that they had absorbed the lessons that Xian Xinghai had taught. As Ma Ke put it, "Xian Xinghai was a revolutionary musician. He used music as a weapon and threw himself whole-heartedly into the struggle for national liberation. His most important lesson to us was: We must not write music for music's sake; the only way to develop music successfully is to make it serve the revolution."[29] That Xian would have agreed with this view of his musical philosophy is far from clear, but since he was dead, his views were now left for others to interpret — or manipulate — as they saw fit.

He Luting's journey to Yanan was less direct than that of Xian Xinghai and his time there less musically fruitful — as Mr. He had already said of himself, his journey in life was destined to be circuitous. Although he had been productively occupied in Chongqing, his situation there had become increasingly dangerous after 1941, when relations between the Nationalists and the Communists took a turn for the worse. Mr. He asked the Party if he could go to Yanan and was told that he would be welcomed, but that it was currently quite difficult for men to travel there because of Nationalist Army blockades.[30] However, since women and children were generally permitted through, Mr. He's pregnant wife and their children could go first, and he could follow later. Mr. He and his wife agreed to this plan, and he stayed in Chongqing to work under Guo Morou organizing musical activities while his family travelled onward. As it turned out, the bus on which Mr. He's family was travelling was stopped by the Nationalist Army and ultimately allowed to continue to Yanan only after Zhou Enlai personally called Chiang Kai-shek to insist that it be let through the blockade.

With relations between the two parties so tense, the atmosphere in Chongqing also worsened and soon Mr. He was asked by the Party to leave first for Hong Kong and then Shanghai, where he visited the widow of his much-loved mentor, Huang Zi. The Party had given him 500 yuan for his travels but he had managed to spend only 200, so he gave the remainder to his professor's bereaved, and financially-strapped, wife. After bidding her goodbye, he boarded a boat out of Shanghai that took him to a liberated area called Liuzhuang that was controlled by the Communist New Fourth Route Army.

The New Fourth Route Army was under the leadership of General Chen Yi, who would later become a marshal, mayor of Shanghai, vice premier and minister of foreign affairs. Like his Party colleagues Zhou Enlai and Deng Xiaoping, Chen Yi had been a worker-student in France for several years following World War I. He had also

---

29. Ma: 116.
30. This discussion is largely drawn from Shi Zhongxin (2000). *He Luting Zhuan* [A Biography of He Luting] Shanghai: Shanghai Yinyue Chubanshe: 123-134.

studied at the Université Franco-Chinoise in Beijing and, like Mao, was considered a talented poet.

Chen Yi came out to greet He Luting when he arrived, saying cheerfully "Comrade He Luting! I've known your name for a long time. Your *Song of the Guerillas* is great!"[31] Liu Shaoqi, the nation's future head-of-state, also came out to meet Mr. He. Offering him a cigarette, which Mr. He declined, Liu Shaoqi mentioned casually that "Enlai" had telegraphed to inform them that He Luting would be arriving en route to Yanan. Unfortunately, he said, the situation was a bit difficult at the moment and it would be better for Mr. He to stay in Liuzhuang for the time being.

This was not welcome news to Mr. He, who had not seen his wife and daughters for months — or even met his third, newborn daughter — but he replied that if he was to stay, he wanted to work and could perhaps train the music workers. His suggestion was welcomed enthusiastically by both Chen Yi and Liu Shaoqi, who confessed that they had already considered this possibility and would like to send him to their branch of the Lu Xun Academy. Mr. He was soon teaching violin, music theory, and composition. When Yanan telegraphed that they needed him, in the spring of 1943, he made his way there by a route so round-about that he did not get there until July. Shortly after his arrival, Mr. He was introduced to Mao Zedong — a fellow Hunanese — and as they chatted, Mr. He discovered that his older brother and Mao had once been classmates, a connection that would one day be more important than Mr. He could ever have imagined. Chairman Mao left Mr. He with a compliment he would long remember: "Your *Song of the Guerillas* is very well written — you have done a great service for the people and they will never forget you." [32]

Cultural activities at Yanan had gradually begun to shift leftward after Mao's "Talks" at the Yanan Forum, even though the discussion as to the relative importance of popularization versus raising standards continued. The Propaganda Troupe at the Lu Xun Academy was largely dedicating itself to the creation and staging of *yangge*, but it also had an 18-member "orchestra" of rather limited talents, which Mr. He joined as a violinist. The main problem with this work was that the musicians were often required to perform on stage, which left them so short in numbers that their ensemble could hardly be called an orchestra — on one occasion, 15 people went on stage, leaving a drummer, a gong player and Mr. He

Mr. He had expected to be more gainfully employed at Yanan, and he naturally had an opinion when it came to the leftward trend and its impact on cultural life. Time spent among the masses was definitely important; he knew from experience that he could never have composed works like *Song of the Guerillas* if he hadn't spent time living with soldiers and peasants. But, neither could he have written these works if he had not had his conservatory education in Shanghai; time among the masses had to be balanced with a sound music education. Moreover, since he was not only a professional musician but also a revolutionary, he felt that he could not just write

---

31. See Shi: 133.
32. See Shi: 150.

music for popularity. Since he had more free time than he anticipated, he used it to compose some short orchestra pieces based on Chinese folk melodies for the Propaganda Troupe ensemble and taught its members some harmony and music theory.

When the war with Japan ended, the Lu Xun Academy was broken up into two troupes and relocated to northeast China. He Luting and his family left Yanan for Suide, where they were to await orders on the move north. The conditions there were harsh — Mr. He's newborn daughter died of illness — and there was no opportunity for any kind of music-making or teaching. Mr. He's chance for making a more significant contribution to the development of music education and the raising of musical standards at Yanan had seemingly slipped away and his chances of furthering these goals in the future must have appeared rather bleak.

A RED ORCHESTRA

In the months following his arrival in China, the American envoy General Marshall had somehow managed to get the Nationalists and the Communists to agree to a cease-fire and to hold serious talks aimed at bridging their differences. He then spent the winter of 1946 pushing them to hammer out agreements on such issues as demobilization and integration of their respective armies. There were, however, so many stumbling blocks that in March he decided to take a quick visit to important northern cities with his Chinese negotiating colleagues, Zhou Enlai and the Nationalist representative Zhang Zhizhong, so he could hear about the issues on the ground. One of the cities on his itinerary was Yanan, where he was scheduled to meet Mao Zedong for the very first time. General Marshall's entourage was to number 30 people — including several journalists — and Zhou Enlai and other Communist officials wanted to make very sure that he would be impressed with the reception he received at their base.[33]

Since a welcome banquet is always customary for greeting a visitor from afar, a big one was planned in honor of General Marshall. Normally, this would consist of performances of Peking opera or the *yangge* that was then the politically-correct fashion. However, many cadres felt that while such entertainment was fine for Chinese visitors, it would be better to include some Western music for General Marshall since he did not speak Chinese and would be unlikely to appreciate songs he couldn't understand.[34] Thus, after much discussion, it was decided that the Lu Xun Academy and the Communist Party School would together organize a concert for the banquet

---

33. For the story of the founding of the Yanan Central Orchestra on which this account is based, see Li Gang (2001). Jiangshu Yanan. [A story of Yanan] *Arts Today. Com.* January: 15-18. The same story was told to the authors by Li Delun, but in less detail.

34. In fact, General Marshall was stationed in Tianjin with the US Army between 1924-27 and did learn to speak some basic Chinese, but had apparently forgotten most of it by the time he returned to China two decades later.

that would include traditional Chinese folk songs, Xian Xinghai's *Yellow River Cantata*, and a cello solo by Zhang Zhenfu, a former member of the Shanghai Municipal Orchestra.

Marshall and his delegation arrived in Yanan on March 4, 1946. The General himself was quite fatigued, since he had been working without rest since his arrival in China and was due to depart for a trip to the US just days later. Nonetheless, it was an important occasion and as a well-mannered diplomat, he apparently mustered all his energy to make it through the banquet and the concert, which an American journalist described in passing as "an elaborate performance of drum dancers and folk singers in an icy auditorium"[35] that left the General with a bad cold the next day.

However, where the Americans saw a cold and tired diplomat trying to be polite, his Chinese hosts saw a man much moved by the performance they staged for him. To those of his hosts who paid attention, he seemed particularly enchanted by Zhang Zhenfu's playing of *Gavotte* from one of Bach's unaccompanied cello suites. How romantic the American general must have found it to hear an 18th-century masterpiece played on the cello in the bitter cold mountains of Yanan!

In any case, when the performance ended both Zhou Enlai and General Ye Jianying — a close friend of Zhou's who had also spent time in Europe — came forward and asked its organizers, including Jin Ziguang and Zhang Zhenfu, to stay. As they gathered round in the empty hall, Zhou told them that so many different kinds of people were now coming to visit Yanan that he hoped cultural activities at the Communist base could develop more. Indeed, Yanan had so much musical talent that it would really be wise to establish a symphony orchestra — and that was precisely what he wanted them to do.

Moving quickly from idea to implementation, Zhou asked Jin Ziguang to make a list of all the instruments that would be needed to start an orchestra. The instruments would be bought in Beijing, he promised, and General Ye would pay for them.

"Symphonic music is, naturally, an expensive undertaking," he added, perhaps for General Ye's benefit.[36]

And so, just when the prospects for such non-revolutionary arts as classical music had perhaps seemed dimmest at Yanan, General Marshall's visit and the cultured Zhou Enlai's response to it suddenly opened a whole new path.

Jin Ziguang delegated the task of creating an instrument shopping list to the cellist Zhang Zhenfu, and it was then passed on to General Ye. He, in turn, delegated his subordinates with the task of searching the second-hand stores of Beijing to fulfill the unusual purchase order. When they had come up with as many of the required instruments as possible — primarily used Yamahas left behind by the Japanese — the

---

35. See Pogue, F.C. (1987). *George C. Marshall: Statesman*. New York: Viking: 102. The quote is from the March 18, 1946 edition of *Time Magazine*.

36. As quoted in Li: 16. In explaining Zhou's role in founding the symphony, Li Delun told the authors, "Zhou Enlai was a renaissance man — he liked music. And Yanan was an important place for the CCP. They often received foreign guests there and they needed the orchestra to greet the guests."

instruments were flown into Yanan on American planes. More instruments were donated from Shanghai, with many coming from a shipping magnate named Cao Shijun who was secretly supporting the Communists; his wife was a cellist who had studied with the great Spanish cellist Pablo Casals. Finally, it was determined that on-going financial support for the orchestra would be jointly provided by the Central Committee of the Communist Party, the border region government, and the Communist Party School.

With the instruments secured and financial backing in place, it was suddenly realized that the orchestra would need a leader. A hurried message was sent to He Luting, who was still in Suide: he was to return to Yanan at once in order to became president of the newly established Yanan Central Orchestra. Mr. He's chance to make a real contribution had reappeared, almost as if by magic.

On May 16, the Yanan newspaper *Liberation Daily* carried news of the imminent establishment of the Yanan Symphony Orchestra and on the following day it published a recruitment announcement. Anyone between the ages of 15 and 25 was invited to bring a letter of recommendation and attend the auditions for the listed instruments on May 26 in the music room of the Communist Party School. Those who passed would then be asked to take a physical exam. If accepted as a member of the orchestra, they would be provided with food, housing, clothing, instruments, and expenses. To ensure that Yanan's most talented people would actually attend the auditions, the announcement noted that the orchestra would belong to the Central Committee and that all work units would be ordered to allow all who were accepted into its ranks to leave their current jobs, unconditionally.

Despite the important support of the Central Committee, recruitment for the orchestra was not easy — Zhou Enlai's estimation of the abundance of talent at Yanan was perhaps over-generous, at least when it came to players of symphonic music. The few professionally-trained musicians, like Li Gang, were accepted at once. Li Gang's wife was asked to join too; although she had been trained as a singer, she seemed to have a strong build, so she was asked to play clarinet. Since the original recruitment did not produce enough people to complete an orchestra, He Luting travelled around to numerous nearby villages hoping to find some young people with both interest and potential. Many of the teenagers he attempted to audition were too shy even to open their mouths; in one instance, when a young peasant boy named Wang Xiang actually agreed to sing a song, Mr. He accepted him at once.

In the end, the orchestra consisted of forty people, a few of whom were trained musicians and many of whom had never even heard of a symphony orchestra before they were asked to join it. Though they had little time to rehearse — or even to begin learning their instruments — the official ceremony for the start of the orchestra was scheduled for July 17, the anniversary of the composer Nie Er's untimely death. As it happened, the river that bisected Yanan swelled so high that day that no one could cross it, leading to a two-day delay. But, ready or not, the ceremony was rescheduled for July 19 with dignitaries including General Zhu De and Jiang Qing in the audience.[37]

Among the pieces the orchestra played were a Bach minuet and three works by He Luting.

It is hard to imagine that the musical level of this first concert was very high, but it nonetheless marked the official establishment of the Yanan Central Orchestra. Soon the orchestra was performing regularly, with a standing gig every Saturday night when the high level cadres held their ballroom dances. For if *yangge* song-and-dance was the officially sanctioned entertainment for the masses at Yanan and beyond, it was ballroom dancing that the high-level leaders themselves enjoyed most. These Saturday night soirées were described by the leftist American journalist Anna Louise Strong, who lived in Yanan for six months in 1946-47:

> The chief social event of the week was the Saturday-night dances, attended by many of the party leaders. Zhu De came almost every week, Mao Zedong about twice a month. Chinese musical instruments mingled with Western, making dance rhythms of such ancient favorites as "Old Black Joe." There were waltzes and two-steps and one-steps and a four-step to *Yangge* music, which is like fox trot music but with more swing. People expressed themselves with easy freedom. Those who wanted to stamp, stamped; those who wanted to glide, glided. Some professional dancers of the theater brought the agility of acrobats to the floor....[38]

Strong also described the dancing styles of the highest ranking attendees, who presumably danced better now that they had an orchestra instead of the single drum and harmonica which had previously provided music for these occasions.

> Meet, then, the four leading Communists as they appeared at the Yanan dances. Zhou Enlai...danced with the grace of a diplomat. He was perfection in the waltz — sometimes too restrained perfection. After a dance with him one might like to take on one of the *yangge* acrobats, or the Russian doctor, Orloff, who liked to stamp it, Cossack style. But always one returned to Zhou Enlai as number-one dancer....

> Liu Shaoqi, who next to Mao is the leading Marxist theoretician, danced with a scientific precision in which two plus two inevitably made four. But about once in three dances, when he had begun to seem too arithmetically exact, he would go in for higher mathematics with a few exciting flings....

> Zhu De, commander-in-chief of the armies, danced as if doing his famous Long March. He kept a steady one-step, no matter what the band played. If you were caught with Zhu De when they gave an enticing waltz, you might look longingly at that perfect dancer, Zhou Enlai, stepping it with the equally perfect Mrs. Mao Zedong....

> Mao Zedong, the leader, sat out most dances; so many people wanted to chat. When he took the floor, it was with easy definiteness, as if he "gave the party line"

---

37. Li also notes that Jiang Qing already cared deeply about cultural matters at this time. He further comments that she was wearing a face mask at the concert, as she generally did at Yanan — people weren't sure if it was to protect herself from the dust or to protect them from any diseases she might have.

38. Strong, A.L. (1949). *The Chinese Conquer China*. New York: Doubleday & Co: 24.

to the band. Some people have said that he has no sense of rhythm; with this I disagree. He has a firm and delicate sense, and the rhythm is his own. He kept the friendliest contact with the music, yet never slavishly submitted. As his partner you had to pay close attention, yield watchfully, move at slight indications. But if you got his rhythm, he brought you out bang! with the band at the finish. It was in several ways a triumph to dance with Chairman Mao.[39]

Despite the high-level support enjoyed by the orchestra and its central role in the leadership's entertainments, its first few months of existence were not particularly stable. Part of the problem was that after all his hard work getting the orchestra established, Mr. He became quite ill.

"He Luting was spitting up blood," explained Mr. Li.

So, when Mr. Li arrived in Yanan later that autumn, he was made responsible for training the members of the six-month old orchestra.

"There was a talent problem," he said; and added, with a guffaw, "The Yanan Central Orchestra was just a bunch of kids put together to play Western instruments. These kids had never even seen a Western instrument in their dreams! I was a graduate of the Shanghai Conservatory — but I had to start with the piccolo and go all the way to the tuba, teaching them how to play!"

Mr. Li found the task of teaching virtually all the members of an orchestra how to play their instruments to be about as exhausting as it sounds. He also found it frustrating, since the orchestra members were by no means all as dedicated to the task at hand as he himself was. On the contrary, most of them found the process of learning Western instruments to be very difficult and many considered it a waste of time. Negotiations between the Communists and the Nationalists had by this point essentially stopped and Yanan was expecting to be invaded at any time; many of Mr. Li's orchestra members simply did not see much point in learning to play violin or oboe just then. With war preparations going on all around them, they had little desire to practice — indeed, Mr. Li found that if he didn't push them, they didn't study at all.

Controlling his mounting frustration, Mr. Li continued to work hard, studying instrument manuals by night and rising early every morning to give lessons in woodwinds, brass and strings. Then one day, when he felt he just couldn't take it anymore, he went for a long walk in search of He Luting. Although Mr. He was still unwell, he listened patiently as Mr. Li complained that the musicians were hopelessly slow and described the angst it caused him to see such good musical instruments going to waste on them. He also shared with Mr. He his latest brainstorm — to dump all the orchestra's current members and replace them with children who would learn more easily and willingly.

Once Mr. Li had finished venting, Mr. He pointed out the problems in his plan. Training an orchestra of small children in a wartime environment was not practical — who would take care of them? And, even if it were possible, it would take too long — the primary need for now was to learn, practice, and perform all at the same time. The

---

39. Strong: 25-6.

only practical solution was to continue working with the musicians who were already in the orchestra.

Mr. Li saw the sense in Mr. He's words and returned to his own cave somewhat mollified, deciding to look anew at his orchestra. Roughly speaking, the musicians could be divided into three groups. One group had some education, and worked harder than the others. They had rich life experiences and could write beautiful melodies in Chinese folk style. A second group had been drawn from the Party's culture work troupes and knew little more than how to hit gongs and drums; their immediate goal was to motivate peasants and workers to action and their long-term goal was to become cadres once the war ended. A third group consisted of peasants for whom joining the revolutionary army and getting free food was more than enough. They lived life one day at a time, ever aware that the next day might find them at the battlefront.

Having resigned himself to working with the current members of the Yanan Central Orchestra, Mr. Li decided to take a fresh approach by teaching them some basic music theory and harmony. Obviously, not all members of his orchestra would respond to this in the same way; the first group would be interested, the second group would not care, and the third group would do whatever it was told. The orchestra continued to play at the Saturday night dances and it also helped to put on an opera for both cadres and local people. Called *Lan Huahua*, the opera was a short, tragic tale about a young woman, evil landlords, and the valiant Communist Party's land reform policies.

"Nothing the Communist Party does is separate from politics," explained Mr. Li, who conducted *Lan Huahua* himself. "After seeing it, the people hated landlords."

Mao attended a performance of *Lan Huahua* and afterwards said, "It's very pleasing to the ear. It's a little bit like Soviet movies." [40]

Outside of his conducting and training responsibilities, Mr. Li managed to find more artistically fulfilling musical diversion when he was introduced to an American amateur violinist who worked in the medical unit of the US military's observation post. The American invited Mr. Li to play cello in a quartet that met in his cave at the US post, which was just outside the city's north gate. They played Haydn the first time and Mr. Li went back to play regularly, for as long as the Americans were in the area. Sometimes, to his delight, he was even invited to watch screenings of the American movies he loved so much.

As time went by, it dawned on Mr. Li that he was starting to understand the workings of the liberated area. He was also making many new friends and learning to focus on the positive aspects of his new existence. The best thing about Yanan was that he had never felt so free — for the first time in years, he could say whatever he wanted. Although Yanan's poverty was a major drawback, the Party took care of all physical needs, providing those who came to work at Yanan with shelter, clothing and food.

---

40. As quoted in Li Gang: 18. Li Delun also notes that, like many people at Yanan at the time, Chairman Mao's knowledge of symphonic music apparently came primarily from Soviet movies.

Shelter, of course, was a cave, and clothing was whatever was available, in Mr. Li's case an old US army uniform. However, food — which was most important to Mr. Li — was divided into three levels: big wok, medium wok, and small wok. Food made in the smaller wok was naturally better, and this was reserved for the highest-level leaders. The orchestra members ranked as medium wok, which meant that every meal had at least a little meat and when they performed, they got an extra ration. If, as occasionally happened, they gave five performances in one day, then they got five extra meals. This caused Mr. Li and others to joke that stomachs in Yanan were expandable and retractable — it was fine to be hungry, and it was fine to eat five meals in one day. In addition to extra food, orchestra members got a small stipend, which Mr. Li would use to buy dumplings at a market outside the south gate of the city.

Mr. Li's growing contentment was marred by only one thing: the absence of his girlfriend, Li Jue. However, about a month after his arrival, he bumped into Zhou Enlai at one of the weekly dances and Mr. Zhou asked if Li Jue had arrived yet. When Mr. Li explained that they were not yet married and she had delayed coming because she felt it would be like eloping, Mr. Zhou was incredulous.

"In this day and age, you're still thinking like that?" he asked. "Does she still want to come?"[41]

When Mr. Li replied that she did want to come — omitting the fact that Li Jue's parents didn't want her to marry him, since he was a musician and therefore had no future — Mr. Zhou said he would make the arrangements. Some weeks later, while Mr. Li was playing volleyball, a messenger rode up on horseback to deliver a letter from Zhou assuring him that his "lover" situation was in the process of being resolved. Mr. Li was extremely grateful both for the news and for the concern of a man as busy as Zhou Enlai and he carried the letter with him everywhere, until he lost it.

Unfortunately, just as Mr. Li was settling into his new life at Yanan, Yanan itself was becoming increasingly difficult to protect. Relations between the Communists and the Nationalists had so deteriorated that even the United States had given up hope of brokering a reconciliation or compromise. In January of 1947, General Marshall announced sadly that his mission had failed and he was returning home — where he would soon be made Secretary of State and become the architect of the Marshall Plan that helped to rebuild Europe from the devastation of World War II.

With Marshall and his efforts at reconciliation out of the picture, China's civil war heated up even further. The Nationalists set their sights on capturing Yanan, a victory that they believed would have major propaganda and psychological value. Well aware of the Nationalists' determination, Mao and his comrades decided it was better to abandon their base than to waste precious resources defending it. The abandonment would be scheduled and orderly and would take place gradually, so as not to excite notice. The departure of the Yanan Central Orchestra was scheduled for late February of 1947.

---

41. Luo: 162-3.

With preparations to leave the base underway, Chairman Mao met with several of the orchestra's leaders to talk about the importance of preparing for war. The peasants needed to be motivated to join the war effort, he told them, and merely playing symphonic pieces would not be effective towards this end.[42] Then, on the eve of the orchestra's departure, Zhou Enlai gave a report about the political-military situation to another group of orchestra leaders, which included Mr. Li.

The revolution is nearing its climax, Zhou explained; in three to five years, the Communists would finish off Chiang Kai-shek. Abandoning Yanan was part of the overall strategy that would bring victory to the whole country. The revolution would move from the caves of Yanan to the big cities and the arts and literature of the liberated areas would move with it. All the intellectuals and petty bourgeoisie would need to fundamentally change their thinking to reflect that of the proletariat. This change in thinking would not be easy — surrendering to the proletariat is like being reborn.[43]

Li Delun found himself deeply shaken by Zhou Enlai's words — a new era was truly dawning. When he had finished talking, Zhou asked Mr. Li and several others to join him for dinner, a meal that was particularly good since it came from the small wok and because all the animals that could not be taken on the march out of Yanan were being killed and eaten. At one point during the evening, Mao and his son appeared in the cafeteria and Zhou excused himself to say hello. When he came back, he brought up the issue of native versus foreign. If you just follow the old Chinese tradition, he explained, it is the same as following a dead person. If, on the other hand, you always follow the foreign way, then you are following imperialists. So, you must not go with the old dead tradition or the foreigner, but create a new way. This, in fact, is what Chairman Mao had just told him and it was something he wanted them all to remember. These words made a deep impression on Mr. Li, who would remember them for the rest of his life.

A mule train had been organized to carry the orchestra north — the musicians would walk and the mules would carry their instruments. It all looked fairly impressive, but unfortunately before they had even set off, one of the muleteers sat on a bass and ruined it completely. However, despite the somewhat inauspicious start, the trip was well-planned and Mr. Li and the other musicians soon fell into a comfortable pattern.

"Everything was very organized," explained Mr. Li. "We walked 40 *li* the first day, 30 *li* the second day, 40 *li* the third day, and 20 *li* the fourth day.[44] Every third day you could bathe, and every fifth day there was meat. The Communists can organize!"

There were two routes out of Yanan, to the northeast and the northwest, and the orchestra followed the northeasterly one. The journey took them through liberated

---

42. Li Gang, Huang Xiaofen (2001). Yanan Zhongyang Guanxuan Yuetuan chuangjian ji huodong shimo [The creation of the Yanan Central Orchestra from beginning to end] *Arts Today.com* January: 18.

43. See Luo: 163.

44. A li is about a third of a mile.

areas where they began to implement the Communist Party's land reform policies. These policies had been watered down in recent years, out of deference to the Nationalists during their peace negotiations; but now that all chance of compromise was over, the Communists pushed to eliminate all tenancy and to redistribute the land within each village so that everyone had an equal share. The orchestra's first involvement with this was in Jiaxian, an ancient and beautiful city on the side of a mountain.

"It was peaceful land reform, very peaceful," Mr. Li remembered. "We got the landlords to split up their land. Really, the landlords were often poor, too. They just had land — oftentimes there was nothing planted on it. Then, later, people said peaceful land reform was too rightist — the leftists came out and made it all chaotic."

Unfortunately, about a month after their departure, the Nationalist army started following the orchestra and the other Communists who had left Yanan.

"If the Nationalists saw anyone, they'd drop bombs," explained Mr. Li. "Once I hid in a little cave — I didn't want them to see me."

This close call made Mr. Li more safety-conscious and it occurred to him that at this point in time, he probably should not be trekking through the countryside in an American army uniform; he got rid of it and began wearing padded cotton clothes.

However, once they crossed the Yellow River into Shanxi Province, they were safe and could concentrate on other things, like the musical direction the orchestra should take now that it had left Yanan.

Unsurprisingly, nearly every member had an opinion on this topic and a hearty debate emerged when it came time to send a report back to Party headquarters.[45] Some of the less enthusiastic musicians believed that the orchestra should simply disband and go to the frontlines of the battlefield, or at the very least help the ambulance units. Mr. Li believed that they should continue training, although he acknowledged that the circumstances were not especially conducive to rehearsal. Some musicians complained that up until now the orchestra had only played for important people at Yanan — was this really a Communist orchestra or was it no different than a royal orchestra for VIPs? Still others complained about the women comrades, who they evidently felt were there more for show than for real work.

In the end, it fell to He Luting — who was still ill enough that he had to be carried on a stretcher — to filter through all these different ideas, decide on a direction and report back to the Party. His conclusion was that the orchestra existed to serve land reform and liberation. When it was new, it was important for its members to learn to play their instruments; but now that they had been playing them for some months, it was necessary to work at the same time they continued to learn. The orchestra would continue its onward march and its performances in support of land reform and liberation.

"We played every day, in the evenings," explained Mr. Li. "We did concerts with a little of everything, not whole symphonies. The orchestra was the dumpling skin —

---

45. See Luo: 170.

we held it all together, but there were lots of things inside. We did operetta, light opera, even a 'Liberated Don Quixote!' It was a spoken drama, by a Russian, but He Luting wrote incidental music for it. We played Schubert's military march and Mozart — I remember playing his *Serenade*."

The orchestra and other performers had three nights' worth of material, but since there was little entertainment other than local opera in the villages, the peasants would often ask them to perform everything they knew, and then do it again. Since the orchestra was in no particular rush to get anywhere, they would now and then agree to stay on, using the opportunity for a little relaxation.

"Sometimes we would play chess and sleep late," remembered Mr. Li. "We were very happy."

Mr. Li was even happier when his girlfriend Li Jue one day appeared out of the blue. Zhou Enlai had arranged for her to get to Yanan as promised, but by the time she arrived, Mr. Li had already left. Only the Peking opera troupe was left in Yanan and since she herself was an excellent Peking opera singer, she had performed several times, including once for Chairman Mao himself. The happy pair formalized their relationship by marrying and then continued walking north with the orchestra.

The going was somewhat tougher in the heat of summer and peasants who saw them pass by would look askance at them.

"The cases for our instruments were very rough," Mr. Li recalled with glee. "People thought they were coffins. In the summertime, they'd see us and say, 'In this heat, you aren't afraid of the stench?'"

In 1948, the orchestra arrived in Pingshan County, Hebei Province, where several other performing troupes had also congregated and the decision was made to merge the various troupes under He Luting's management. From Pingshan, they moved on to the provincial capital of Shijiazhuang where they settled for so long that they were actually able to rehearse. The enlarged ensemble was also able to stage an opera called *Chiye He*, or Red Leaf River, which was about the social changes in a village.

"The landlord comes and says the land is for him," explained Mr. Li. "He's very fierce. But it was the labor of the villagers that had cleared the land! The opera was land reform followed all the way up to real reform and liberation — it even had a bad cadre."

Then, at the very end of 1948, word came that it was time to liberate Beijing — the victory of the Communist Party under Mao Zedong was nigh. The orchestra was asked to get organized for the arts and culture workers' march into the city, one of several official marches that would signify the arrival of the People's Liberation Army and the liberation of Beijing. The orchestra entered the city from the west and walked beneath Marco Polo Bridge, the very spot where the war with Japan had ignited back in 1937. Mr. Li was extremely moved as he re-entered the suburbs of the city of his birth, overwhelmed by a sense of home-coming and by the magnitude of the effort it had taken to get there.

"It took us three years to get to Beijing with the orchestra — we walked for three years!" he recalled, half a century later.[46]

Despite the changes wrought by war, everything about Beijing seemed familiar to Mr. Li. As he breathed in the familiar scents and listened to the beautiful 'r'-accented Mandarin of the local people, he considered how he, like his hometown, had changed even as he stayed the same. When he left Beijing for Shanghai, he was a progressive young student in a fancy suit setting off to be a musician. Nearly a decade later, he had attained that goal, but had never envisioned that he would return to his hometown in the coarse clothes of a peasant, accompanied by a wife, a baby, and an orchestra of foot soldiers!

The Yanan Central Orchestra spent its first night in Beijing in a village near the Summer Palace and then moved on to Tsinghua University where the musicians were again able to practice and rehearse. They were warmly welcomed by the newly-liberated students, and the university orchestra soon invited them to a special performance of Schubert's *Unfinished Symphony*, conducted by their foreign teacher. When the performance ended, the students surrounded Mr. Li and peppered him with questions: What do you think about foreign music? Will we still have classical music under Communism?

Like all the other Communists entering Beijing to liberate its people, Mr. Li had been issued an "Entering the City Handbook" and instructed to use this — and only this — when responding to questions asked by the citizenry of Beijing.

Since, "Will there still be classical music under Communism?" was not a question in the handbook, Mr. Li was not free to answer it and the students were a little displeased at his avoidance. However, he gave them an indirect answer by leading the Yanan Central Orchestra in a performance that included works by both He Luting and Mozart. After all its years performing together on the road, the orchestra was actually better than the Tsinghua Orchestra and Mr. Li sensed that the students were quite moved to see these rough-looking men and women in army clothes giving such a beautiful performance.

On February 1, 1949, Mr. Li and all the members of the orchestra joined together with countless other arts and culture workers for a final, triumphant march into downtown Beijing. Their procession was headed by an American pick-up truck adorned with a painting of Mao Zedong. Because Mr. Li was one of the few Beijing natives involved, he was asked to give directions to the driver of the lead vehicle and therefore entered the city at the head of the parade. Li Jue was somewhere in the back, playing a drum, and his fellow orchestra members were walking with the other rank and file culture workers. The Yanan Central Orchestra's long march to Beijing was over and a new beginning was at hand.

---

46. In fact, it was two years, since Li Delun left Yanan in February of 1947 and arrived in Beijing in February of 1949.

THE FIRST NATIONAL CONGRESS OF ARTISTS AND WRITERS

Cultural propaganda work had served the Communist Party well in warfare and Party leaders did not forget it even as they stood on the threshold of victory (the war officially ended on October 1, 1949). The near-victorious Communists convened the First National Congress of Artists and Writers in Beijing on July 2 and was attended by a total of 753 people,[47] among them such musicians as He Luting, Li Delun, Tan Shuzhen, Ma Sicong and Zhou Xiaoyan. Because it had been held at the suggestion of the renowned scholar, poet and political activist Guo Morou, it was he who gave the keynote presentation on the struggle artists and writers would face as they worked together to build arts and culture for the people of New China.

Since attendees came from a variety of backgrounds, much of the meeting was devoted to summarizing arts and culture in China since the May 4th Movement of 1919. The writer Mao Dun discussed the state of culture in areas that had been controlled by the Nationalists and Zhou Yang gave an overview of culture in the areas under Communist control.[48] This review of the past was seen as crucial because it helped Congress attendees understand the differences between culture work in the Nationalist and Communist areas and also served to put them on the same page when it came to understanding what the official view of recent history would be.

The continuing importance that the future government would place on arts and culture work was underscored by the appearances of top political leaders at this First Congress. General Zhu De stopped by to offer his congratulations and Zhou Enlai came to give a speech, accompanied by his wife Deng Yingchao. While Zhou was addressing the Congress, footsteps were heard in the wings and Mao Zedong himself suddenly appeared on-stage. Delegates to the Congress leapt to their feet and erupted in cheers of "Long Live Chairman Mao! Long Live Chairman Mao!" Only when Mao moved to the podium, as though to make a speech did the cheering die down. Leaning over the microphone, Mao said simply, "The people need you, so we welcome you!"[49] Cheering once again filled the auditorium, lasting until Mao had exited the stage and Zhou was able to resume his interrupted speech.

Major speeches aside, a number of other reports were given, many of them focused on Mao's "Talks at the Yanan Forum on Arts and Literature." Indeed, Mao's "Talks" was held up as the general blueprint for all culture work: in the future, whenever any artist, writer, musician, or arts bureaucrat had doubts about the

---

47. Holm: 5.

48. For a general overview of the Congress, see Ming Yan (2002). *Ershishiji Zhongguo Yinyue Piping Daolun* [A Guide to 20th-Century Music Criticism in China]. Beijing: Renmin Yinyue Chubanshe: 221-2. Tan Shuzhen's account comes from our interviews and from Tan Shuzhen (1997). Nanwangde 1949 [Hard to Forget 1949] *Yinyue Yishu* 3: 5-10. Li Delun's account comes from Luo: 204-205. Zhou Xiaoyan's account is based on Sheila Melvin's interviews with her in August of 1998 and May of 1999.

49. This account of Mao's appearance at the meeting comes from Melvin's interviews with Tan Shuzhen. See also Tan: 6.

direction he should take in his art or in his approach to propagating art, it was to Mao's "Talks" that he should first turn for guidance.

When Congress representatives were not meeting in plenary sessions, they divided up into small groups for discussions about the future of their particular areas. Li Ling spoke about music in the Nationalist areas while Lu Ji discussed music in the liberated areas, especially Yanan. At least one speaker argued that symphony orchestras could not serve the workers, peasants and soldiers and should simply be disbanded or converted into culture work troupes. Another suggested that music education should be shortened to one year — living in an ivory tower for too long was not conducive to thought reform.

Evenings were devoted to banquets and entertainment, among them a gala performance largely organized by Li Delun and Li Ling that included Xian Xinghai's *Yellow River Cantata*. The orchestra was cobbled together with musicians from the Yanan Central Orchestra and the orchestra of the Peking Art Academy. It was conducted by Yan Liangkun, a choral conductor who had begun his studies with Xian Xinghai. Since there was not one musician who played viola, Mr. Li became the sole member of the viola section for the night. The evening was a long one — Mr. Li recalled it as lasting four or five hours — but Mao Zedong attended and sat through it from beginning to end.

Despite the full schedule of meetings and evening activities, the Congress allowed plenty of time for old friends to catch up, new comrades to meet, and for all the artists to discuss the future of their work in the soon-to-be-declared People's Republic. Unsurprisingly, Mr. Li was in the forefront of much socializing; in fact, after a few days, he began to play hooky from some sessions, and thus it was that he was in a teahouse when Mao Zedong made his unannounced visit. Although he was sorry to have missed Mao's appearance — the highlight of the Congress for many representatives — he had skipped the session in part because he was somewhat disappointed with the level of discussion at the Congress.

Indeed, ever since he had returned to Beijing, Mr. Li had been wondering what policies the new government would adopt when it came to such subjects as the relative merits of folk music versus Western music, professionals versus amateurs, and popularization versus raising artistic standards. Expecting serious discussion of these serious issues, he had been extremely excited about the Congress. Instead, he found that too much time was devoted to organizational issues, like the creation of the All-China Federation of Literary and Art Circles, which would include the Chinese Musicians' Association, to be headed by Lu Ji.[50] Speaker after speaker criticized formalism and talked about how intellectuals needed to learn from workers, peasants,

---

50. The Federation was tasked with the rather weighty mission of "mobiliz[ing] the nation's writers and artists to strive together for the flourishing of socialist literary and artistic creation so as to enrich the people's cultural life, enhance their mental vision, train new socialist human beings and encourage them to work for the building of a modern socialist motherland…and to unite with the people of all countries in the struggle against imperialism, colonialism, hegemonism and in the defense of world peace." See Liu, B. (1983). *Cultural Policy in the People's Republic of China.* Paris: Unesco: 29.

and soldiers and people from Nationalist-controlled areas needed to learn from those who had lived in Communist-controlled areas. Although Mr. Li said nothing at the time, he secretly felt that the delegates were treated well, but nobody really cared about their opinions.

In any case, Mr. Li continued to take good advantage of the opportunity to rendezvous with old friends and on one of his evenings out he had dinner with Tan Shuzhen. Mr. Tan filled him in on the news from Shanghai, including the whereabouts of their mutual foreign musician friends and acquaintances. Some, like the piano teacher Boris Lazareff and the composition professor Wolfgang Fraenkel, had opted to leave Shanghai for safer shores, but a surprising number had stayed on, including Mr. Li's cello teacher, Igor Shertzoff; the violinist, Josef Padushka; the voice teacher, Vladimir Shushlin; and Arrigo Foa.[51] In 1947, Foa had once again been made conductor of the Shanghai orchestra and his re-appointment had provided the opportunity for Mr. Tan's own return to the orchestra.

Like so many other long-suffering residents of Shanghai, Mr. Tan was delighted when the city was finally liberated by the Communists on May 27 and pleased with the announcement that General Chen Yi would be the city's mayor. One of Chen Yi's first actions after taking control was to invite the city's artists and writers to a meeting about the future of the arts under Communism. Mr. Tan had been among the invitees and found that General Chen had so much to say on the subject that he spoke from 2:00 in the afternoon until 8:00 in the evening, with only a short break for tea.[52] Weeks later, when it came time for Shanghai's 97-person delegation of artists and writers to depart for the Congress in Beijing, Chen Yi gave them a celebratory going-away banquet.

Naturally, Mr. Tan and Mr. Li also talked about the goings-on at the First Congress and the path that they expected music to take in the coming years. In fact, one of the reasons Mr. Tan had wanted this private dinner with Mr. Li was that he had been so nonplussed by the speakers who talked of disbanding the symphony orchestras and shortening music education to one year. Mr. Li had not attended the sessions that upset Mr. Tan, but he assured him that he had a pretty good sense of the Communist Party's cultural policy and that such ideas were extreme. Comforted, Mr. Tan devoted much of the rest of the meeting to a plan that he and other Shanghai musicians had hatched: getting He Luting appointed president of the Shanghai Conservatory.[53] He Luting was perfect for the job, Mr. Tan and many others thought, not only because of the high regard they held for his person and musicianship, but

51. Wolfgang Fraenkel left Shanghai in 1947 and settled in Los Angeles. He first worked in a Holly-wood movie studio playing, conducting and copying scores but then began to receive commissions and prizes for his compositions. Boris Lazareff went to the United States in 1948 and became a piano teacher. Vladimir Shushlin finally left Shanghai in 1956 to return to Moscow. He taught at the Moscow Conservatory until he died in 1978. See Chang Shuozong (chief ed.) (1997). *Shanghai Yinyue Xueyuan Da Shiji Mingren Lu* [A record of major events and famous people at the Shanghai Conservatory]. Shanghai: Shanghai Yinyue Xueyuan: 500-502.

52. See Tan: 5.

53. See Tan: 5-10.

because he had been at Yanan and the connections he had made there would likely serve Shanghai's music world well in the years to come.

Zhou Xiaoyan had also been invited to participate in the Congress as a delegate from Shanghai, an invitation that left her so taken aback that she nearly refused it.

"I didn't do anything for the revolution," she explained.

Indeed, Ms. Zhou had not spent her time in France learning about socialism, as had so many Chinese students who preceded her, but had dedicated herself to improving her voice. In this she had been aided by a fellow Conservatory graduate, the star pianist Li Xianmin. Ms. Li had graduated from the Conservatory and received a Boxer Rebellion Indemnity Scholarship to study in Belgium, where she attended the Belgium Royal Conservatory and then launched a career as a piano soloist. When the composer Alexander Tcherepnin returned to Europe from China, in 1937, he went to Brussels to visit her and before long he had obtained a divorce from his American wife and proposed to Ms. Li. The two were married in 1938 and moved back to Paris, where they set up house in the Latin Quarter, on the Rue Furstenberg, and became parents to three boys.

Tcherepnin and Li Xianmin treated Madame Zhou with great warmth and hospitality. They invited her to family gatherings and to parties attended by the French cultural elite and helped her find a voice teacher and choose a school. With all this assistance, Madame Zhou soon found herself living an exciting, Parisian life, albeit one tempered by war and by the tragedy of her brother's death from a botched appendix operation. More importantly, she made great progress in her studies.

Her voice designation was changed to coloratura soprano; she developed a French repertoire — Debussy, Ravel, Chausson, Fauré, Dubec; and within a few years could also sing fluently in English, German, Russian and Italian. After a time, she began to take private lessons in solfege and piano with Nadia Boulanger, the famous composition teacher and conductor, and to perform for the French public. One lucky break came when Boulanger invited her to sing as a soloist in a Bach cantata that she was conducting. Another came indirectly through the Chinese family with whom Madame Zhou roomed in Paris. The couple wrote an opera libretto based on a Chinese fairytale, which Tcherepnin liked well enough that he decided to compose music for it. A concert performance of the opera was scheduled for 1945, at the National Grand Theater, and was such a success that Madame Zhou was invited to give a concert of Chinese music in London. She was eager to accept the invitation, except for one problem — she didn't have any Chinese music.

Once again, Tcherepnin came to the rescue, providing her with a repertoire of songs by contemporary Chinese composers from his own personal collection and writing several Chinese-inspired tunes himself. Then, in 1947, came the professional highlight of Madame Zhou's time in Europe, when both she and Li Xianmin were invited to give a concert of contemporary Chinese music at the first Prague Spring Music Festival, with Madame Zhou singing works by Jiang Wenye, He Luting, Liu Xuean, and Tcherepnin and Ms. Li playing piano pieces by He Luting and Tcherepnin.[54] The Festival was attended by Copland, Bernstein, Shostakovich,

Menuhin, Oistrakh, Stravinsky and many other international musical luminaries whom Madame Zhou had never dreamed she would see, let alone meet. This performance led to more and by the time she finally got back to Paris, Madame Zhou found invitations to sing in the US, Sweden, Denmark, and Norway. Although she was tempted to go to the US, she knew in her heart that her education was at long last complete — it was time to go home.

After a joyous reunion with her family, and a few recitals in Wuhan, Madame Zhou made her Shanghai debut. Following the pattern she had established in Europe, she chose a program of both Chinese and Western music and her debut was such a success that she soon established a solo career in Shanghai. Eager to give back to the country she had left for so long, she also sang in numerous charity concerts and began to teach voice at the Conservatory. Thus, if Madame Zhou found it surprising that she had been invited to the First Congress of Artists and Writers, nobody else did and an American friend was able to persuade her to accept the invitation.

"That meeting changed my life," she recalled, explaining that from that time onward she felt that she had goals, dreams, direction — a whole new life — in front of her.

Zhou Enlai was acquainted with Madame Zhou's father, who had been lending quiet financial support to the revolution for some years, and he took the time to talk to her personally during his visits to the small group sessions.

"The first thing Zhou Enlai asked when we were introduced was, 'Have you put a tombstone on your brother's grave?' He remembered everything!" she exclaimed. "He told everyone how my little brother left a rich family to participate in the revolution. He told me, 'You should learn from your brother.' I said I was embarrassed, I'd done nothing. He said, 'It's never too late, as long as you stand by the people.'"

At one of the evening banquets, Zhou Enlai pointedly asked Madame Zhou to sing the French National Anthem, the *Marseillaise*. While she appreciated his asking her to sing in French — a subtle affirmation that her time spent in France was not wasted and that there would be room for foreign songs in revolutionary China — she was immediately flustered. In fact, she had spent so much time learning Debussy and Ravel that she could not actually sing the entire *Marseillaise!*

Sensing her embarrassment, the premier rescued her by starting to sing the song himself, in French. He was soon joined by many others among the delegates, and the banquet hall rang with the stirring notes and words of the *Marseillaise*.

Publicly inviting Madame Zhou to sing the French national anthem was an important enough gesture toward musicians who had studied overseas or studied Western music in China, but Zhou Enlai went even further than this. Indeed, behind the scenes at this First Congress, he sought out the French-educated violinist Ma Sicong to discuss the future development of music.

---

54. Jiang Wenye was born in Taiwan and studied music in Japan where he became well known in the 1930s. He returned to China in 1938 and later became a professor at the Central Conservatory. His compositions include symphonies, chamber music, and incidental music. Liu Xuean was a graduate of the National Conservatory who studied with Huang Zi and Xiao Youmei. He taught composition and wrote songs, movie music and incidental music.

"Mr. Ma, New China has been created on rubble," he said simply. "I would like to hear your thoughts on how to develop music in New China."[55]

Ma Sicong had plenty of thoughts on this topic. Over the past decade, he had travelled around the nation performing as a soloist and even worked for a time as conductor of the Taiwan Symphony Orchestra. He had begun to compose and had also devoted considerable energy to various educational endeavors. Mr. Ma knew from his experience that talent was the number one issue and this is what he told Zhou Enlai — China needed to train talent by establishing schools. Pleased with this response, Zhou Enlai said that his thoughts were the same, and he was therefore proposing to create the highest music institution in New China, to be called the Central Conservatory. This was glad news to Mr. Ma's ears, but it was followed by a request that would be hard to refuse — yet which he was not certain he wanted to accept.

"I want to place the burden of the preparatory work on your shoulders," said Mr. Zhou. "You can bring to it everything you learned in France. It's time for you to show us what you've got."[56]

It was, in fact, time for all musicians to show the Communist Party what they had and when the Congress drew to a close, they fanned back out across the country to begin laying the foundations for musical education and musical performance in a country about to be born.

55. For quote, see Ye Yonglie (2000). *Ma Sicong Zhuan. Aiguode panguozhe* [A biography of Ma Sicong, patriotic traitor]. Urumqi: Xinjiang Chubanshe: 161.
56. Ye: 161.

CHAPTER 6. NEW REALITIES AND NEW CHALLENGES

LAYING FOUNDATIONS AND DEALING WITH DIFFERENCES

The People's Republic of China was officially founded on October 1, 1949, when Mao Zedong stood on the rostrum of the Gate of Heavenly Peace, faced the crowd assembled in Tiananmen Square and declared: The Chinese people have stood up!

The new nation's artists and writers had already been briefed on what was expected of them, so they were able to set to work as soon as the celebrations were over. For classical musicians, this meant reviving existing music institutions and establishing new ones which together would serve as the basis for professional education and performance. At the same time, they had to continue hashing out their differences over the direction that classical music should take in Communist China.

The first new institution to be founded was the Central Conservatory of Music, which was formed by merging the Lu Xun Arts Academy music troupe with the music departments of several universities in Beijing, Nanjing, and Shanghai. It was one of many new flagship institutes of higher learning established in Beijing to train the nation's most talented students. Like the Central Academy of Drama and the Central Academy of Fine Arts, it came under the direct management of the Ministry of Culture. Although it was first located in Tianjin, in the mid-1950s it was moved to a spacious compound in downtown Beijing that had once been the estate of a Qing Dynasty prince.

Ma Sicong was leery of the administrative responsibilities involved in running a conservatory, so he did not initially accept Zhou Enlai's invitation to be its first president. But Premier Zhou was determined that Mr. Ma take the job. The renowned violinist's reputation would greatly enhance the Conservatory's own standing and his position as president would help send the message that the Communist Party needed and respected intellectuals, even those who came from capitalist or Nationalist backgrounds. So, when Mr. Ma finally accepted the position in 1950, Zhou gave him a salary that was about the same as Chairman Mao's and threw in many other perks, including two chefs — one to cook Chinese food and one to cook French cuisine — a spacious home, and a chauffeur-driven car. It was also made clear to Mr. Ma that the real management of the school would be left to Party members who had been at Yanan, like Lu Ji, the vice president and Li Ling, the vice dean.

Indeed, Mr. Ma was in some respects a figurehead, but this left him free to focus on such larger issues as establishing a curriculum and recruiting musicians who were overseas to come home and train New China's first generation of musicians. Huang Feili, a conductor who was then studying at Yale, recalled receiving his recruitment letter from Ma Sicong.[1]

"He wrote to me and said, 'New China has been established and things are good — come back.' The Korean War had started — it looked like it was the third world war. Also, I was married before I came — I hadn't yet seen my first-born child."

Mr. Huang made plans to go back, but his professor, Bruce Simon, tried to dissuade him as did the composer and professor Paul Hindemith.

"Hindemith said, 'What are you going to do there? Be a Communist? Don't go back. I'll help you go to Switzerland.' But, I told him the circumstances and he understood. He went upstairs and got some scores and some photos and signed them all. Then he said, 'When you go back, don't follow Huang Zi [in death].'"

With talented people like Huang Feili returning to teach, the Conservatory began to flourish. Separate departments were established for composition, voice, piano, and instrumental, with research, musicology and conducting added in 1953. A travelling performance group known as the Music Work Troupe was created for purposes of practice and propaganda. It participated in land reform and even went to North Korea to perform for Chinese troops fighting against the Americans.

Zhou Enlai's blessing was sufficient to ensure that the Central Conservatory would become China's premier institution of musical higher education, but Shanghai's conservatory was not forgotten. Because of its history and reputation, it was put under the control of the Ministry of Culture and made a branch of the Central Conservatory for several years. He Luting was named president, just as Tan Shuzhen and many other Shanghai musicians had hoped. Because the Conservatory's foreign teachers were gradually leaving China, Mr. He found himself having to hire many new professors. Like Ma Sicong in Beijing, he set out to find the best available, and frequently recruited musicians who had been educated overseas.

One of Mr. He's first hires was his old schoolmate Ding Shande, the country boy who had become one of the Conservatory's most accomplished pianists. Mr. Ding had begun to teach at the Conservatory back in 1937, but his long-held ambition was to

---

1. The authors interviewed Huang Feili at his home in Beijing in January of 2001. All quotes come from this interview.

study composition abroad. A chance to realize this had finally appeared in 1946 when the Nationalist government's education ministry held an audition to select several Chinese music students to study in France. The competition was tough and only five students were chosen to receive scholarships from the French government. Ma Xiaojun — the father of cellist Yo-Yo Ma — was one of them, but Mr. Ding was not. However, Mr. Ding did rate high enough to be selected as a self-paying student, which accorded him status and the right to change money at a preferential rate.

Mr. Ding was by this time a husband and father, but his wife offered to take their four children and move back in with her parents so her husband could fulfill his dream. Wasting no time, the grateful Mr. Ding wrote to his old schoolmate Li Xianmin and her husband Tcherepnin to ask for help arranging to study at the Paris Conservatory, and then boarded a cargo ship bound for France. When he arrived in December of 1947, he found that the Tcherepnins had not only done as he asked, but had also rented him an apartment. Like Zhou Xiaoyan before him, he soon became an ongoing beneficiary of their generosity.

Based on Tcherepnin's recommendation, Mr. Ding was accepted into the seminar taught by Conservatory composition professor Tony Aubin. The class had twelve students from around the world and they all critiqued each others' work; Mr. Ding was praised for his Chinese style, but told that his technique was too traditional. Aubin encouraged him to remedy this, in part by learning more about the music of French composers such as Fauré, D'Indy, and Franck. He took this advice and went even further by studying compositional analysis in Messiaen's class and score reading and composition with Nadia Boulanger.

Mr. Ding was thriving in Paris, but he was a family man and a patriot who had many reasons to go home. In August of 1949, he presented his *pipa* to the Tcherepnins in thanks for all their help and set sail for China.[2] While changing ships in Hong Kong, he saw in the paper that He Luting had been appointed head of the Shanghai Conservatory, and sent him a congratulatory telegram — the very first one Mr. He received. Mr. Ding then went to Beijing, where Mr. He happened to be attending a meeting. The two roomed together and stayed up chatting all night about their plans for developing music in the People's Republic. When they had both returned to Shanghai, Mr. He asked Mr. Ding to teach at the Conservatory and then made him the head of the composition department.

He Luting soon found that he had a gift for attracting good teachers. As he told his wife, "I don't have much talent myself. My talent is to bring people who have talent to the Shanghai Conservatory."[3]

---

2. Tcherepnin left Paris in 1948 to teach at De Paul University in Chicago, where he stayed until he gave up teaching to compose full time in 1964. He was invited to give a concert in the USSR in 1967, making him the second composer to be invited back after Stravinsky. Tcherepnin died in Paris in 1977, but his memory and music are still actively promoted by the Tcherepnin Society. Two of his three sons — Serge and Ivan — also became composers, with Ivan becoming well known for his work in electronic music at Harvard. The third son, Peter, is a businessman in New York.

Because of his success at recruiting, Mr. Ding was just one of many overseas educated professors to join the Conservatory faculty.

Yang Jiaren, who would ultimately become head of the conducting department, had studied piano with Mario Paci as a child and then gone on to major in choral conducting and music education at the University of Michigan. Li Cuizhen — the woman who could play all 32 Beethoven sonatas from memory — had completed the Conservatory's five-year curriculum in one year and then studied at London's Royal College of Music before returning to China in 1940.

Two overseas-educated violinists also joined the faculty. Chen Youxin, who was one of the first four Chinese musicians to officially join the SMO in 1938, had also studied at London's Royal College of Music in 1949. Upon his return to China in 1951, Mr. He made him the head of the Conservatory's instrumental department. Zhao Zhihua had studied in Shanghai with several SMO violinists before going to the US. He lived for a time in Austin and then went to the Boston Conservatory, where he studied with the concertmaster of the Boston Symphony until returning to China in 1951.

He Luting was also fortunate to have working for him the man who had expended so much effort lobbying on his behalf in Beijing — Tan Shuzhen. However, Mr. Tan himself was dismayed when he was told that he had been chosen as one of the Conservatory's vice-presidents.

"I just wanted peace," Mr. Tan recalled. "I wanted to play my violin and perform. But, Mayor Chen Yi gave an order — I was vice-president. I didn't want to do it, but they said this is an order from Beijing, you have to. I was just a violinist — I didn't understand yet that you can't refuse the Communist Party."

However, though he had not wanted the job, Mr. Tan soon grew to like his new position, and his life in New China.

"In 1949, life was much better. We had security, free medical care. We weren't afraid of losing our jobs. It was a good, peaceful time — no crimes, everything was clean. If a child found a dime, he would give it to a policeman."

Although he had to lay aside his dreams of being a violinist with the orchestra, Mr. Tan taught two violin classes of 16 students and was also at long last able to fulfill another dream he had been forced to put on hold — that of becoming a violin maker.

"I suggested that we start a small factory for instruments at the Conservatory — it was very difficult to find instruments. I sent people to northeast China to buy wood. They were gone for 6 months and brought back enough wood to make 100 violins. Then I gave the wood carvers samples — we started making violins and gave them to the students free of charge."

When Edgar Snow returned to China in 1960, he visited the Conservatory and its prosperous instruments factory. As he described it,

> Tan Shuzhen took me to see his factory, which was stocked with carefully selected varieties of pine, redwood, lapwood, ivory, ebony and horn. He himself had studied

3. Shi Zhongxin (2000). *He Luting Zhuan* [A Biography of He Luting]. Shanghai: Shanghai Yinyue Chubanshe: 165.

violin making in his youth from an old master, and now he also taught a conservatory course on the subject. I saw about a hundred skilled workers and student amateurs who were making and repairing violins, violas, cellos, oboes, clarinets, brass instruments, reeds and strings. Chinese are among the world's finest artists in wood, ivory, bone and metal; there is no reason to doubt their ability to excel in the making of musical instruments...." [4]

The Central Conservatory of Music in Beijing had Zhou Enlai as its champion and the Shanghai Conservatory had its history as the nation's first music school to protect it. However, the musicians who ran China's few professional orchestras found their work somewhat more complicated thanks to post-liberation politics.

The Yanan Central Orchestra was essentially deemed to have completed its historical mission and was merged into the newly-created China Central Song and Dance Troupe. Even so, it retained its status as a kind of "royal orchestra" and was still obliged to play for the top leaders at their traditional Saturday night dances. [5]

For Li Delun, this standing obligation had certain advantages, like the opportunity to observe the nation's top leaders and sometimes mingle with them. He found it amusing, for instance, that Marshal Zhu De — he of the "steady one-step" — was always the first to arrive at the dances and the last to leave. Chairman Mao never showed up until the middle of the evening, but his lateness bothered no one and the women always wanted to dance with him, even the female musicians in the orchestra. Zhou Enlai was still far and away the best dancer and also a popular partner. He always gave the orchestra specific requests and would sometimes stop to chat with Mr. Li, who never ceased to be amazed by the premier's memory — he could even recall how many brothers and sisters Mr. Li had.

At one dance shortly after liberation, Premier Zhou asked Mr. Li about the orchestra's journey from Yanan to Beijing. When Li Delun told him the details, Zhou Enlai cheerfully responded that he couldn't say the orchestra was the world's best, but it was certainly the first one ever to walk a thousand miles using donkeys to carry instruments!

However, while it was nice to chat with Premier Zhou every now and then, the obligation of performing on call for every event in Zhongnanhai was ultimately a burden which prevented Mr. Li from expanding the orchestra's repertoire or raising its level of playing. Indeed, time for playing any music at all was limited, since politics always seemed to take precedence — most of the musicians' time was spent listening to reports from leaders and studying such subjects as Marxism and Darwinism. Mr. Li's biggest dream was to conduct a complete symphony, but he could never seem to pull this off.

Although the orchestra did rehearse Schubert's *Unfinished Symphony*, it mostly just played dance tunes, works by He Luting, small pieces for political events, or a simple classical piece like the second movement of Tchaikovsky's *Violin Concerto*. Mr. Li

---

4. Snow, E. (1962). *The Other Side of the River*. New York: Random House: 568.
5. For quote, see Luo: 208.

thought he had covered every political base for a 1951 New Year's concert — the program included pieces related to the liberation war, the war against Japan, and the campaigns to "Resist America and Aid Korea" and "Oppose Corruption" — but was criticized by bureaucrats who said it had no political focus. His decision to perform Tchaikovsky's *1812 Overture* was even met by complaints that the music was too technical and not revolutionary enough.

"Is Beethoven's work poisonous?" Mr. Li would ask himself in frustration. "Will the ordinary people be poisoned if they hear it? Why can't we play symphonic music?"[6]

A further blow to Mr. Li's hopes of professionalizing his ensemble came later in 1951 when a small political rectification movement was started in arts and literature circles. Mr. Li's musicians were required to go to the countryside so they could better understand the lives of the peasants. When he balked over the lost rehearsal time, bureaucrats who knew little about Western music assured him that it would make them better musicians. This struck him as sheer nonsense. If you go to the countryside, you cannot practice, he replied — how can we raise our standards without practicing?

If politics made life difficult for the politically correct Yanan Central Orchestra, it created even more problems for the politically incorrect Shanghai Symphony.

Part of the opposition to the orchestra was simply based on the perception that a symphony was by definition an elitist institution that served the capitalist classes. Exacerbating this, however, were the Shanghai Symphony's origins as an orchestra created by, of and for foreigners — and the fact that it continued to have many foreigners in its ranks. Indeed, Arrigo Foa remained the orchestra's conductor and more than a quarter of its musicians were non-Chinese, including seven Russians, three Filipinos, an Austrian, a Hungarian and a Czech.[7] This situation infuriated many leftists, especially after the Korean War broke out in 1950 and almost anything foreign was perceived as unpatriotic. The orchestra was not permitted to play for events at which foreigners were present and when it performed arias from *Madame Butterfly*, there was an outcry over its alleged efforts to propagate imperialist culture.

"At liberation, the orchestra had a hard time to preserve itself," explained Wen Tan, a violinist who joined the Shanghai Symphony in 1953 and now serves as its archivist. "There were people who suggested that it be dismissed."

In the end, however, the symphony was not "dismissed," largely thanks to Shanghai's new mayor, Chen Yi.

"Mayor Chen Yi decided to preserve it," continued Wen Tan. "He said a symphony orchestra is very useful to our people so we must preserve it. If it is not desirable now, you can reform it."

Although the orchestra itself got a reprieve, life for its musicians remained difficult. Just as in the old days of war and inflation, they were so poorly paid that they

---

6. Luo Junjun (2001). *Li Delun Zhuan* [A Biography of Li Delun]. Beijing: Zuojia Chubanshe: 215.
7. Chen Xieyang (chief ed.) (1999). *The 120th Anniversary Album of Shanghai Symphony Orchestra (1879-1999)*. Shanghai: Shanghai Symphony Orchestra: 27.

could not survive on their salaries and thus had to moonlight recording music for films. But, unlike the old days, they had to turn 40% of their extra income over to the orchestra, as per order of Shanghai's Culture Bureau.[8]

Several of a series of political campaigns launched by the Communist Party shortly after liberation further complicated the position of both foreign and Chinese musicians. The "Resist America and Aid Korea" campaign that started with the Korean War targeted all those foreigners who remained in China, and anyone who had contact with them. This made life very awkward for anyone who had foreign friends or colleagues, as did so many musicians in Shanghai.

"After liberation, I couldn't keep in touch with Foa," Mr. Tan explained sadly. "Too many political movements. The last time I saw him he was on the streets, in a rickshaw — we didn't dare to greet each other."

The Resist America and Aid Korea campaign was succeeded by one aimed at domestic counter-revolutionaries, and then by the "Three Anti" campaign, which was meant to wipe out corruption, waste and bureaucratism and was targeted at Party members, officials and managers of factories and businesses.[9] As the conductor of Shanghai's orchestra, Arrigo Foa became a target of the Three Anti campaign.

"Foa was driven away in the Three Anti campaign," recalled Mr. Tan. "Someone called him a fascist and said he hit him during class. They said, 'You fascist, coming here to bully the Chinese.'"

Li Delun also recalled Foa's expulsion from China with sorrow.

"China called Foa a colonist — they had a big meeting to criticize him during the Three Anti campaign. They yelled slogans and kicked him out. But, he wasn't bad — he had a lot of Chinese students. He donated all his scores to the Shanghai Conservatory when he died."[10]

The broader political pressures were further complicated by the unresolved differences within music circles. Simply put, the music world was divided into two camps: those who believed that musical standards and technique were crucial to the development of music, and those who believed that the value of music was measured primarily by its political usefulness.

As was the case even before liberation, the two main representatives of these divergent points of view were the composers Lu Ji and He Luting. Whereas Lu Ji had previously argued that the most important function of music was to support the anti-Japanese resistance — and that the best musical form for doing this was song — he now saw its main purpose as serving the goals of Communist construction. He Luting, on the other hand, continued to argue that "we cannot use general political theories to

---

8. For figure, see He Luting. "Guanyu yinyue fangmiande qingkuang huibao (er yue, 1954) [A report on the situation in music, February 1954]." In He Luting (1999). *He Luting Quanji* [The Complete Works of He Luting]. Shanghai: Shanghai Yinyue Chubanshe: 126.

9. For campaigns, see Spence, J. (1999). *The Search for Modern China* (2nd ed.). New York: W.W. Norton & Company: 508-511.

10. Foa went to Hong Kong, where he conducted the orchestra now known as the Hong Kong Philharmonic, for many years. According to Tan Shuzhen, he died in Hong Kong in 1981.

substitute for specific music theory and technique...to experience life is very important for composers, but it cannot solve all problems of creativity.... Music is the art that most needs technical practice." [11]

In the autumn of 1953, the Second National Congress of Artists and Writers was convened in Beijing with the avowed mission of developing more creativity in the arts. Speakers at the Congress openly criticized much of the art that had been done in the first four years of the People's Republic as too formulaic. Art criticism was also taken to task for being too shallow and vulgar, with much of it seeming to be written by philistines. In his work report, the Party's deputy propaganda chief Zhou Yang stressed that creativity should be the most important aspect of arts leadership and urged that more and better work be created on a foundation of socialist realism. [12]

The Second Congress helped relax the general cultural atmosphere, but it had little direct impact on music circles. Indeed, by the beginning of 1954, He Luting was so frustrated with the situation that he sent a highly critical report to the Ministry of Culture in Beijing. [13] Mr. He's litany of complaints included funding allocated to the Shanghai Conservatory, which he claimed was so inadequate that some students got sick from the living conditions and poor nutrition and had to drop out. He was also upset about the nation's "abnormal" music education system which he said had regressed considerably since liberation. Missionary schools had previously been the best source of musically-trained students, but in the post-liberation process of converting them to public schools, music courses had been dropped. A music education system with professional-level conservatories and music departments but nothing underneath was a waste and was also detrimental to the Conservatory's recruitment efforts. Mr. He also bemoaned the treatment accorded to the Shanghai Symphony, and particularly to its foreign musicians. Orchestra musicians, he noted pointedly, are not like government cadres who sit in an office all day —— it took years of training and practice to become a good musician and if the Shanghai Symphony were allowed to decline too far, it would be impossible to rebuild.

Finally — and most controversially — Mr. He commented that the relationship between the leaders of the Musicians' Association and regular musicians was abnormal, even bad. In his view, the men who now led the association — i.e. Lu Ji — had never liked people from the Shanghai Conservatory and had targeted them for criticism ever since the days at Yanan. After 1949, musicians from Yanan's Lu Xun Academy had spread around the country and taken up leadership roles at major music institutions, bringing their bad attitudes with them — this was the main reason that China's music circles had been unable to unite once the country itself was united.

In He Luting's opinion, the men from the Lu Xun Academy who were now music circle leaders continued to adhere to old ideas and methods that were more suitable to

11. Shi: 177.

12. Ming Yan (2002). *Ershishiji Zhongguo Yinyue Piping Daolun* [A Guide to 20th-Century Music Criticism in China] Beijing: Renmin Yinyue Chubanshe: 222.

13. He: 126-131.

wartime conditions than to the task of developing music. While they were usually quite capable of making songs for the masses and were familiar with Chinese folk music, their level of music professionalism was not high and their knowledge of technique and theory was lacking. But, instead of acknowledging these flaws and trying to correct for them, they continued to emphasize political attitude over music theory. Indeed, they seemed to encourage the belief that if musicians simply went to the countryside to experience life and study politics, it would solve all the problems in music. Even worse, they created an atmosphere in which people who actually tried to master technique were seen to have political problems — Mr. He had actually seen young musicians practicing in secret for fear they would be criticized! Yet, ironically enough, when the time for a performance came, it was these musicians who were always placed in the front rows because they were the only ones who could play well.

When Lu Ji convened a meeting of the Musicians' Association in June of 1954, the discussion continued over the relative importance of technique and theory learned in Conservatory classrooms vs. political and social content that came from living among the people. He Luting gave a speech in which he expressed his views and later contributed a version of his comments to the official music magazine, *People's Music*. This further fueled the debate and the pages of the nation's major music journal were soon filled with articles both opposing and supporting his opinions. In the beginning, it was a measured debate by musicians who shared different views. However, little by little, the tone changed and inflammatory words like "bourgeois" crept in. Some writers claimed they could trace a line through everything Mr. He had ever written which demonstrated that he thought technique to be more important than anything else. The situation became even more ominous when some music circle leaders quietly began to compare Mr. He to Hu Feng.

Hu Feng was a well-known writer and editor who became the target of a nationwide criticism campaign in 1955 because of a lengthy essay he had written about the Communist Party's control of culture, which he said was so unremitting that it "exhausted" people to the point that they couldn't think straight. He also took issue with the Party's insistence on using Marxism to judge art, calling it "crude sociology" that was "not based on reality."[14] The campaign that Mao launched against Hu Feng was fierce, and the writer was jailed until 1979, as were other intellectuals accused of thinking like him or supporting him. If the whispered charges that He Luting was a "Hu Feng-ist" had grown louder, there is no telling what would have happened to him.

Mr. He understood the seriousness of his situation when he was called to Beijing and met at the airport by a car that took him directly to the Zhongnanhai leadership compound. He was ushered into a rectification and study meeting for leaders of the Musicians' Association that had been called by Chen Yi, who was now a vice premier with a portfolio that included cultural affairs. Chen Yi explained at the outset that the meeting was needed because the leaders of music circles were not united and there were too many conflicts. He hoped that the forum would give all attendees an

---

14. Spence, J. (1990). *The Search for Modern China*. New York: W.W. Norton & Company: 566.

opportunity to voice their opinions, which would be analyzed and discussed by the group.

True to form, He Luting was the first to speak, spilling his thoughts on a variety of topics, including the need to remember the important contributions of his teacher Huang Zi and not just those of the much-acclaimed Xian Xinghai and Nie Er. On the subject of the divisions in music circles, Mr. He stated bluntly that his "old friend" Comrade Lu Ji had done much work for music in China, but that he also had many faults. While every leader was entitled to have his own style, it was not proper for him to always believe that his way was absolutely right and that anyone who did not agree was wrong. Lu Ji then responded by suggesting that the differences between He Luting and himself concerned theory and point of view. Comrade He's evaluation of Nie Er and Xian Xinghai was too low and his opinion of Huang Zi and Xiao Youmei was too high, and he talked far too much about the technical aspects of music.

Once He Luting and Lu Ji had spoken, other participants expressed their views and the back-and-forthing went on for a week, until Chen Yi again took the podium to insist that the problem be resolved. Although he knew little about arts and culture, he did know this — some comrades in the audience were refusing to listen to others. There was no use in being too proud or in always telling others what to do. From his viewpoint, both Comrades He and Lu had strengths and weaknesses. He had heard them both speak, and he was disappointed. They did not criticize themselves; they just attacked each other and defended their own opinions. They refused to see the whole issue or to give up any part of their positions. It was his job to make them see clearly. He also added that the personal attacks on Comrade He were not right — all problems should be handled in the spirit of unity and of self-criticism.

He Luting respected Chen Yi and he responded to this well-intentioned reprimand by making a stab at self-criticism related to his own behavior at the meeting. However, he added that he could not disavow much of what he had said — to do that would be going against his own conscience, which was something he would never do.

And so the meeting drew to an end. Chen Yi had done his best to protect He Luting and to keep the situation from getting out of hand. But the differences between Comrades He and Lu — and among members of China's music circles more generally — had been papered over, rather than resolved. They would soon reappear, and in ever more virulent forms.

HELP FROM "BIG BROTHER"

Shifting political campaigns, deep-rooted philosophical differences, and the departure of many foreign musicians complicated the task of laying new musical foundations for the People's Republic. However, crucial assistance was soon provided by China's "big brother," the Soviet Union.

"Many experts were sent from the USSR when we were establishing the orchestras," explained Li Delun. "This was Zhou Enlai's arrangement. Some [East] Germans, too. Their influence was very great."

Indeed, the influence of Soviet experts was quite considerable in almost every area of New China's early development — over the course of the 1950s, approximately 10,000 Soviet and East European advisers came to work in China.[15] The new People's Republic of China government had decided to model much of its economy after that of the USSR, and Soviet experts came to help develop five-year plans for industrial development and to construct factories, bridges, power plants, exhibition halls, and more.

When it came to classical music, the Soviets were instrumental in building not only orchestras, but also ballet and opera companies and virtually the entire performing arts system. Soviet teachers started the first formal conducting classes and provided the model for China's conservatories. They also brought a detailed system of musical training and provided most of the text books to conservatories and music departments. The influence of Soviet advisers was such that it was soon apparent even in a musical institution as old as Shanghai's orchestra, where both the sound and the repertoire changed.

"At first, the biggest influence on classical music and the Shanghai Municipal Orchestra was Western," recalled Li Delun. "The programs, the sound, they were all Western. But, then it was more Soviet. The sound was too bright. USSR brass is different — the French horns have this big vibrato. The sound was so strong, so big."

The works of many Western composers were pushed aside in favor of compositions by such Russian composers as Tchaikovsky, Borodin, Rimsky-Korsakoff and Kalinnikov.

The influence of the Soviet musicians and the changes they implemented were not appreciated by all of China's musicians, among them Tan Shuzhen. In Mr. Tan's view, many of the Russian, Romanian and East German advisers sent to Shanghai were not really qualified to teach at the Conservatory or advise the orchestra.

"The young Soviets who came — they weren't so good. One of them had never heard a Kreisler or a Heifetz record! How could they teach us?!"

Mr. Tan was also unimpressed by their command of the general classical repertoire.

"The Soviets weren't so good at Beethoven and Mozart, not the younger ones. They had been closed for many years. They didn't even know Tchaikovsky that well — he was a capitalist!"

However, Soviet assistance was more welcomed by other musicians, especially up north in Beijing where the roots of classical music were not so deep as in Shanghai.

"Western classical music came to China in many different ways," recalled Wu Zuqiang, a composer and past president of the Central Conservatory in Beijing. "But,

---

15. Figure from MacFarquhar, R. (1997.) *The Origins of the Cultural Revolution, Volume 3: The coming of the cataclysm, 1961-66.* Oxford University Press and Columbia University Press: 280.

frankly, after the Revolution, it was the Soviet Union and Eastern Europe who had the most influence. Their important musicians came to help us establish a system. Of course, we had 'brotherly' relations and they came for political reasons, but music was separate. Many of us received great help from Soviet and Eastern European musicians."

Those who perhaps received the greatest help of all were the few fortunate musicians who were sent to train in the USSR or the nations of Eastern Europe.

As with the decision to send Soviet musicians to teach and train in China, the policy of sending Chinese musicians to study in the USSR was part of a much larger program that was announced in 1952. Candidates for advanced study in the USSR from all fields had to be strong political models, have solid professional skills and be no older than 35. In addition, they had to come strongly recommended and were required to pass tests in politics, general history and geography, as well as their areas of expertise.

When word of the new program began to spread in music circles, Li Delun's name was raised at once. Having been at Yanan, his political credentials were seemingly impeccable. He was, moreover, a graduate of the old National Conservatory in Shanghai and one of the very few conductors in the nation. And, he had just turned 35. Many people recommended him and he easily passed the first test. The next level of tests was administered by the Ministry of Culture and it was concerned exclusively with the propaganda of the Three Anti movement. Having just been through this, Mr. Li was virtually gleeful, since he knew exactly what to respond to every question.

Mr. Li, like everyone else, assumed that he had passed with flying colors and that he would be among those chosen to go. Thus did it come as a shock to discover that his application was held up because some in the Party hierarchy were questioning his loyalty — this, he soon discovered, was the ghost of his uncle who had turned traitor to the Japanese.

"It was a bit of a problem," Mr. Li explained. "But, I just had to write that I loved the country and all that — Zhou Enlai understood."

In the end, Mr. Li was chosen, along with the composer Wu Zuqiang and the soprano Guo Shuzhen, to be among the first group of nearly 2000 students who would go to study in the USSR. They all joined together for a year of intensive Russian language study in Beijing. As members of a select and politically important group, they were frequently addressed on political subjects by high-level guest lecturers, including Zhou Enlai, Liu Shaoqi, and Guo Morou. One after another, the speakers assured them that they would scarcely believe how modern and progressive the USSR was. Even better, they promised the students, the Soviet Union's today would be China's tomorrow!

Mr. Li enjoyed the language classes and the lectures, the only slightly discordant note being in the winter of 1953 when Stalin died. China was plunged into mourning at the passing of the revered Communist leader and Mr. Li, who was certain that all his Soviet teachers must be heartbroken, found it strange that they did not act that way at all.

As the year of language study drew to a close, Mr. Li and the other students prepared to depart. The government issued clothes to everyone, with each male receiving one winter and one summer suit, a leather jacket, a heavy winter coat and a Chinese-style Sun Yat-sen suit. Students were also given two suitcases each, along with a history of the Bolshevik Revolution and other important study materials with which to fill them.

In September of 1953, the time for departure finally arrived. Papers across the nation ran headlines announcing that "Li Delun and 1000 other students" had left for their studies in the USSR. Mr. Li's wife Li Jue had just given birth to the couple's third child — and first son — so it was a bittersweet parting at Beijing Station. Even so, Mr. Li was excited as he boarded the train, just as he had been back in 1946 when he left Shanghai Station en route to Yanan — another new chapter of his life was about to unfold.

After a two-day stop in Manchuria — where the students all changed into their matching suits for lectures on matters of etiquette, such as how to use a knife and fork — they boarded a Soviet train and trundled over the border, across Siberia, and into Moscow, where Mr. Li formally became a graduate student in conducting at the Moscow Conservatory.

Mr. Li's main teacher was a talented and famous conductor named Nikolai Anosov, for whom Mr. Li auditioned the first movement of Beethoven's *First Symphony*. Professor Anosov told Mr. Li that he knew how to conduct, but needed to work on his technique and develop a clearer pattern. Then, having dispensed this advice, he departed on a two-month conducting tour and left Mr. Li to study on his own.

Unsurprisingly, Mr. Li managed to make the best of the situation and was soon taking extra lessons with his piano professor. He also started to learn his way around the city.

> Scriabin's[16] house was right across the street — a memorial to him — I went every day to look there. Very few people went there, the director knew me. Also, I went to the Pushkin Museum every day. I followed school groups around and listened to their teachers. They had so many Rembrandts, so many beautiful paintings. I loved that — I especially loved Impressionism. Picasso, Cezanne. And, I went to so many orchestra rehearsals. Also, I discovered Glenn Gould! He wasn't famous at all. I heard him, and I knew at once. He put his hands in hot water before he played. Then he started to become very famous — there in Moscow, his reputation started.[17]

When Anosov returned after a few months, Mr. Li began his studies in earnest with the first symphonies of Beethoven and Tchaikovsky. Anosov nicknamed him "Doctor" and frequently asked him to demonstrate for the class; the two soon became friendly. Conducting opportunities began to present themselves. Right after the winter break, Mr. Li conducted the Moscow State University Orchestra and in

---

16. The Russian composer and pianist Alexander Scriabin, who was born in Moscow in 1872 and died in 1915.

February he led the Moscow Philharmonic Orchestra in a performance of Brahms *First Symphony* at the Moscow Conservatory Music Hall.

As Mr. Li became more immersed in the Soviet musical world, his respect for it deepened. He was astonished by the quality of the musicians and greatly impressed by the fact that Russians seemed to care equally about classical music and their own folk music. There was also a tremendous variety of performances — ballet, opera, comic opera, song and dance companies, choruses, orchestras, chamber groups and more. The music profession was extremely well organized. Every city had a music house that scheduled performances of both local and nationwide ensembles. The conservatory system was structured so that when students graduated, they were required to go to a local music house in a smaller city to work before they could move to a bigger city. This was looked upon as practical training for the graduates and also helped to maintain high performance standards throughout the country.

So enamored was Mr. Li of the Soviet music system that when a delegation of music leaders headed by Lu Ji came to Moscow in 1954, he shared his views with them quite frankly. He added that China's musical world really needed to open up a bit more — it was important that Western classical music be more widely introduced, including the works of the standard classical repertoire. Lu Ji, however, brushed off Mr. Li's suggestions with the reply that the most important role of music was to serve the workers, peasants and soldiers and that the best way to do this was through song, not orchestral music.

If the conversation with Lu Ji was a low-point of that year, a high point was the premiere of Shostakovich's *Tenth Symphony*. The performance of a new symphony by Shostakovich was a major event in the USSR and Mr. Li was as excited as everyone else.

"Shostakovich was very nervous," he recalled with a laugh, doing a quick imitation of the composer sitting stiffly, shivering, clutching himself, and scratching his head.

The symphony was widely praised by audience and critics alike and the reviews the next day were glowing, with one reviewer writing that it represented the heart of the Soviet people. But, though Mr. Li realized the symphony was a great piece of music, he also felt confused by it. When Anosov asked his opinion the next day, he tried to explain his feelings.

---

17. The Canadian pianist Glenn Gould performed in the great hall of the Moscow Conservatory on May 7, 1957. In fact, at age 24, Gould had already performed with the New York Philharmonic under Leonard Bernstein and had recorded Bach's *Goldberg Variations*, but he was unknown in the Soviet Union until this performance, after which he became an instant sensation. At a special concert he gave for students and teachers at the Moscow Conservatory, Gould performed works by Arnold Schoenberg, Alban Berg, Anton von Webern and Ernst Krenek, as well as Bach. Since the compositions of Schoenberg and other composers of atonal music were not played in the USSR, this concert was somewhat controversial. (For more on this, see www.robert.fulford.com/gould.html. Fulford's article originally published in *The Globe and Mail*, March 11, 1998.)

"I told him that I thought it had nothing to do with the modern USSR — the symphony was so dark, and the USSR's future was so bright. My teacher didn't say anything."

By 1955, Mr. Li's reputation was strong enough that he was invited to give a concert tour. When he arrived in the ice-shrouded city of Molotov for the first of the government-organized performances, he found himself battling apprehension as he wondered how the musicians would respond to him and what their playing level would be. However, when he reached the rehearsal hall, a wave of relief swept over him — the concertmaster was a Russian Jew who had played in the Shanghai Municipal Orchestra! He was a good musician, and Mr. Li remembered that he had sometimes asked him to join the small orchestra he organized to accompany theatrical performances. Also in the orchestra were the concertmaster's son, who had worked at the Voice of the USSR with Mr. Li, and a trombone player who had also been in the SMO. The three men were as happy to see Mr. Li as he was to see them, and privately revealed to him that they longed for the old days back in Shanghai. With these three familiar faces in front of him, Mr. Li relaxed and the rehearsal and concert performances of Beethoven's *Fifth Symphony* and Chopin's *First Piano Concerto* went well.

At the end of the tour, Mr. Li found his confidence enhanced, his reputation growing, and his wallet bulging with the 1500 rubles he had been paid, a hefty sum for someone who lived on a student stipend of 60 rubles a month. However, as soon as he returned to Moscow, he took his earnings and handed them over to the Chinese embassy, as per the regulations — the money was then put in a fund to buy Soviet tractors for Chinese peasants. The success of this first tour led to more opportunities — and thus more tractors — as Mr. Li found himself conducting in Siberia, Ukraine, Armenia and several Eastern bloc countries, including Czechoslovakia, where he participated in the Prague Spring Music Festival.

Mr. Li's last performance as a student in the USSR was at Moscow's Sixth International Youth Festival in 1957. The schedule called for him to conduct Chopin's *Second Piano Concerto* and Tchaikovsky's *Sixth Symphony*, outdoors in Gorky Park. The pianist was a 23-year old Chinese named Fu Cong, who was then studying in Poland.

Fu Cong — whose name is also spelled Fu Cong — was something of a celebrity in China, since he had taken third place in the 1955 International Chopin Competition, an important piano competition held in Poland every five years.[18] The young pianist was the first Asian to win a prize in a major international musical event and it pleased the leaders of New China, who were eager to rebuild their nation's international prestige after the years of decline under the warlords and the Nationalist Party.

Fu Cong's reputation in China was also enhanced by the fact that he came from a well-known family of Shanghai intellectuals. His father, Fu Lei, was a prolific translator who had rendered many famous French novels into Chinese, among them Romain Rolland's *Jean-Christophe*,[19] which became extraordinarily popular among

---

18. The first place winner was the Pole Adam Haraciewicz and the second place winner was Vladimir Ashkenazy.

young educated Chinese. Fu Lei was an involved — and strict — father who pushed his son hard and continued to try to steer his life and career even after the boy had gone off to Poland, mainly by way of numerous letters. In an essay published in 1957, he explained his son's early musical background, and how he had fostered it:

> [Fu Cong] had the good fortune to be taught for three years by Mario Paci, creator and conductor of the Shanghai Municipal Symphony Orchestra (forerunner of the present Shanghai Symphony Orchestra). Then he had several other teachers, none for very long. All thought he was a rebellious, difficult pupil — a boy of that age, after all, does not find it easy to stick to hours of practice. But Fou Tsong's love for music was so great that I found the severest punishment for slackness was to lock the piano and forbid him to play. He would look at the instrument and cry his eyes out.[20]

Because Fu Lei did not think that his son was diligent enough, he took him out of school and hired tutors for such subjects as math and English and himself taught him the Chinese classics, with a focus on narrative and pastoral poetry. When his son won a prize in the Chopin Competition, Fu Lei attributed this in part to his classical education:

> I too think that it is my son's knowledge and understanding of China's philosophy, ethics, poetry and art that has enabled him to appreciate the delicate, ethereal, sometimes agitated, sometimes pensive moods of Chopin. Besides the Chinese people have, through the ages, assimilated the best of whatever foreign influences have touched their culture....[21]

Speaking of his son's departure for Poland, Fu Lei wrote,

> He knows that he has taken only the first step in a rich limitless world of artistic opportunity. My hope for him — as I told him before he left for Poland, is this: "You must first of all be a man, then an artist, then a musician and lastly a pianist."[22]

Mr. Li was impressed by Fu Cong as a musician and a man, finding him to be extremely musical and also unafraid to voice his opinions on everything from art to politics. They talked about many things and both agreed that China was too closed and urgently needed to open more to the outside world.

Just before their collaborative performance was set to begin, Mr. Li somehow broke his baton, so he hurriedly called his professor and asked him to bring one. He thus conducted his very last concert as a student in the Soviet Union with Professor Anosov's baton, a memento so important to him that he managed to hold on to it for the rest of his life. After the performance, Anosov and his family took Mr. Li and Fu

---

19. Though *Jean-Christophe* has been little read in the West for many years, it was one of the books cited in Rolland's 1915 Nobel Prize award. The novel is about a young composer and is loosely based on the life of Beethoven.

20. See Retrospect (1980). *China Reconstructs* May: 52.

21. *Ibid.*

22. *Ibid.*

Cong to the famous Prague Restaurant for a celebratory lunch to which he invited a number of guests. Mr. Li was deeply moved by his professor's show of warmth and generosity and it was with a heavy heart that he presented him with an exquisite lacquer statue of Buddha and bid him farewell.

Mr. Li headed for Moscow's train station in early September of 1957, weighted down with bags, thoughts, and mixed emotions. His luggage had expanded well beyond the two suitcases originally issued him, since the Chinese embassy had eventually decided that it was too much work to collect the money earned by so many thousands of students and decided to let them keep it. Mr. Li had thus been able to buy a good supply of stereo equipment, recordings, and scores as well as many gifts for family and friends back home.

His thoughts, however, were in some ways even heavier than his luggage. He had learned much about the USSR and its musical world during his four-year sojourn and was still pondering it all. The country itself, he had gradually realized, was not the paradise of Chinese propaganda. On the contrary, corruption was rampant. In China, things were clear — every worker knew that to take a single sheet of office paper for your own use was wrong. But, in the USSR, corruption on a much larger scale was commonplace and petty bribes were required for everything from buying bread to entering a bathhouse. Drunkenness was a massive and visible problem and so was disillusionment, at least concerning the Stalin era. Even as a foreigner, Mr. Li could feel the darkness in people's hearts when it came to the dead Soviet leader, and he now understood why his Soviet language teachers had not seemed sad when Stalin's death was announced in Beijing back in 1953.

But, when it came to the USSR's musical world, Mr. Li was still full of nothing but admiration. It was true that the programs at many concerts had been less interesting than they could have; the political exigencies of the Cold War forced orchestras to limit repertoire from Western-born composers, and to over-emphasize the works of those born in what was now the East bloc. But, this aside, there was little to criticize about the quality of the orchestras, the structure of the music system or the vital role that music played in the life of the nation.

It would be hard to leave for good this vibrant, musical nation where he had made so many friends, conducted so many orchestras, and travelled so widely. But, waiting at the other end of the rail line would be Li Jue and their three children, his mother, and his many friends. Waiting also was the opportunity to fulfill the many dreams and ambitions that filled his head and his heart. Having learned so much in the USSR, there was now so much he could contribute to the building and development of China's own musical world!

Of course, he knew that there would always be those who opposed the foreign import of symphonic music. But for him personally, everything had been decided. He had been privileged to attend both the Shanghai Conservatory and the Moscow Conservatory.[23] He had conducted orchestras from Yanan to Leningrad — and beyond — and he knew for certain that he would spend the rest of his life working with the symphony orchestra. And, by helping to build orchestras, he would be helping to build

New China — as he had long known, there was no contradiction between music and revolution.

The Hundred Flowers

Political campaigns and philosophical differences had disrupted the development of music — and much else — in the early years of the People's Republic. But, by 1956, these seemed set to fade into the past, replaced by a new era of creative freedom and diversity in which a hundred flowers would bloom and a hundred schools of thought contend. Artists would be free to create, scientists to investigate, intellectuals to critique and everyone would benefit from the openness. This, anyway, was the vision that Chairman Mao presented in his famous "Hundred Flowers" speech made before a closed session of Party leaders on May 2, 1956.

As it turned out, the actual Hundred Flowers campaign would last only a few weeks, but its rhetoric remained alive and resurfaced intermittently over the next several years. When talk of the Hundred Flowers was ascendant, the cultural atmosphere relaxed and the arts began to blossom. Many musicians took great advantage of these periods of political thaw and even managed to continue creating and performing new works during the inevitable political frosts that followed.

It was in the spirit of the Hundred Flowers that the First National Music Festival was organized and musicians from around the nation gathered in Beijing in preparation for the September 1, 1956 opening ceremonies. An extended meeting of the Chinese Musicians' Association was held just prior to the festival, and on August 24, the 2000 association members in attendance decamped to the Zhongnanhai leadership compound and gathered in one of the courtyards. While the rank and file members grouped themselves into a formal pose, several association leaders went to formally invite Chairman Mao to join them for a pre-arranged photo session.[24]

They found Chairman Mao in the Huairentang chamber, where he generally received guests, engaged in conversation with Zhou Enlai, Chen Yi, Zhu De, Zhou Yang, and Xia Yan. Mao made no move to end the conversation, but instead included his new visitors and continued to talk. Like so many of the Chairman's impromptu thoughts, his words were recorded and ultimately immortalized, in this case as "Mao Zedong's Talk to the Leaders of the Musicians' Association." [25]

---

23. Mr. Li never wrote a dissertation and never asked for any sort of diploma or attendance certificate, so he never received one. Years later, friends suggested that he contact the Moscow Conservatory to get some kind of certificate, but he decided that, at the age of 80, he didn't really need it. For a conductor, he said, what you conduct is important, not what you hang on the wall.

24. For this account of how Mao came to give this talk, see Shi: 221.

25. For Chinese version, see Mao Zedong (2002). Tong yinyue gongzuo zhede tanhua [A talk to music workers], in *Mao Zedong Wenyi Lunji*. Beijing: Zhongyang Wenxian Chubanshe: 146-154. For English version, see Mao Zedong (1980). A talk to music workers. *Chinese Literature*, January: 82-91. All direct quotations are taken from this English version.

Mao's off-the-cuff remarks were rambling and repetitive, but still full of the raw power, colorful imagery, and historical references that characterized his speech. He began by explaining that the fundamental principles of socialist revolution were the same in all nations, but there were differences in minor principles and in the forms in which the fundamental principles were manifested. So, too, with the arts — the fundamental principles are universal, but artistic forms should vary among nations.

"Take the leaves of a tree," he opined. "At first sight they look much the same, but upon close examination each one is different. There is individuality as well as universality, dissimilarity as well as similarity. This is a law of nature and likewise a law of Marxism. This should also hold for composing music, for song and dance." [26]

In between such philosophizing — and segues into the respective virtues of Chinese cuisine and Western medicine — Mao made his major points about music in Communist China. Perhaps most significantly, he said that he found it perfectly acceptable for musicians to "apply appropriate foreign principles and use foreign musical instruments."[27] Learning good things from foreign countries was a necessity and would ultimately benefit China. It was fine to study foreign music and fine to use foreign musical instruments which, after all, are just tools. It was also perfectly acceptable to appreciate and to perform foreign music — indeed, much of the music of the Sui and Tang dynasties had come from foreign countries, and this had done nothing to harm Chinese music.

"You are students of Western things, 'Western doctors' so to speak," he said to the assembled musicians. "You are our treasures, and we should pay heed to you and rely on you." [28]

China especially needed these "Western doctors" to run its music schools, he continued, since asking "old-style minstrels" to assume such a responsibility wouldn't do. However, if it was fine to study and to enjoy Western music, China's "Western doctors" needed to be careful not to neglect or disparage China's own musical heritage.

> You have to learn many things from foreign countries and learn them well. You can thus broaden your horizon. But the Chinese people won't welcome any mechanical transplanting of things foreign into our Chinese art... The arts are inseparable from the customs, feelings and even the language of the people, from the history of the nation... Of course we favor music with a national character. As Chinese we would be in the wrong to do otherwise.[29]

In the process of incorporating foreign musical learning into Chinese traditions — and ultimately making them Chinese — it was also fine if musicians created works that were neither Chinese nor foreign in style, so long as there was an audience for them.

---

26. Mao: 82-3.
27. *Ibid.*, 83.
28. *Ibid.*, 90.
29. *Ibid.*, 83.

To be neither horse nor ass is also permissible. Mules are neither horses nor asses. The union of horse and ass is bound to change the form; total avoidance of change is impossible.[30]

In bringing his remarks to a close, Mao expressed his hope that the "controversy" in music circles could be resolved.

We must oppose dogmatism and conservatism. Neither·will do China any good. Studying things foreign isn't equivalent to copying them all. We learn from the ancients to benefit the living, and we learn from foreigners to benefit the Chinese people. [31]

The one sour note in Mao's generally forthright and encouraging speech came when He Luting interrupted to ask a question — his query was a legitimate one about the role of history, but to interrupt the Chairman while he was talking simply was not done. This unthinking act was one which Mr. He would have many occasions to regret, beginning the moment the meeting ended, when he was reprimanded by Zhou Enlai.

Since Chairman Mao had taken an hour out of his busy schedule to share his thoughts — while 2000 musicians waited for him outside in the blistering August sun — his words were quickly accorded the status of gospel. Like any gospel, they were open to interpretation. Musicians who favored the study of technique and the performance of foreign music alongside Chinese could find ample support for their stance in Mao's words. But, digging just a little deeper, so could those who emphasized the importance of works with national character or political content. Because of this ambiguity, Mao's comments did not resolve the controversy in music circles, but they did put a lid on it and help to maintain the status quo for several years.

The festival that followed the Musicians' Association meeting was a major cultural event intended to be a showcase for the new era. As one reviewer described it,

On the evening of September 1, 1956, the Concert Hall in Zhongshan Park, Beijing, had an air of festive anticipation. Three thousand musicians from all parts of the country had gathered there to launch the first national music festival in China's history. On the first night the program — vocal and orchestral — was richly varied and proved to be a very pleasing application of the principle: 'Let flowers of many kinds blossom!'[32]

To demonstrate the diversity of China's musical garden, some seven hundred pieces of music and song were presented at nearly 100 concerts. These included national salvation songs from the Japanese war era; *erhu* pieces by the late Liu Tianhua; Xian Xinghai's *Yellow River Cantata*; a 45-part *guqin* piece played on an instrument that dated to the Tang Dynasty (618-907AD); and Buddhist chants accompanied by cymbals and bells. Zhou Xiaoyan sang and the young pianist Fu Cong, home on vacation from his studies in Poland, gave a recital. The works of a number of

30. *Ibid.,* 90.
31. *Ibid.,* 89-90.
32. See (1957). The first national music festival. *Chinese Literature* 1: 194.

contemporary composers were performed, among them Ma Sicong's *Huai River Cantata* and tone poem *Song of the Forest*; He Luting's *Buffalo Boy's Flute* and *Evening Party*; and piano music by Ding Shande.

Folk music played an important role in the festival and the performance of representative songs from around the nation spurred much discussion. The topic was of special interest because of reform efforts already underway in traditional music, largely due to the pervasive influence of Western music and instruments. The biggest of these reforms was the creation of traditional instrument orchestras modeled after the Western symphony orchestra. Because most Chinese instruments were not suited for playing in ensemble in a large hall, they were re-designed to "improve" their pitch, volume, range and timbre. Brand new "traditional" instruments were even invented to stand in for Western instruments which had no clear counterpart among Chinese instruments. The *gehu*, for example, resembles an extremely large *erhu* to which a finger-board has been added; it is meant to function like a cello. Although the first traditional instrument orchestra had been founded in 1953, many more were established and refined in the late 1950s and early 1960s.

Indeed, this era was one of growth for musical institutions of all sorts. Conservatories were founded in Shenyang, in 1958; in Chengdu, in 1959; and in Xian, in 1960. Semi-professional orchestras and operas were established at work units throughout the nation — the Coalmine Workers Cultural Troupe, the Modern Opera Group of the China Railway Workers, and the Worker's Orchestra of the Peking Automatic and Electric Works. Professional symphony orchestras and ballets were founded in major cities, as were opera companies.

The development of "new opera," so called to distinguish it from traditional Chinese opera or Western opera, also made great strides. A major conference on new opera was held in early 1957 and attended by 170 opera performers, creators, and administrators.[33] Looking back on the short history of new opera, attendees agreed that it was an outgrowth of two traditions, Chinese opera and Western opera. Its roots lay in the May 4th movement and its primary development had come after the creation of the opera, *The White-Haired Girl*. But there was less agreement when it came to which of these bases — Chinese or Western — new opera should build on in the future. Debates sprang up as to how opera composers could best integrate Western methods with Chinese traditions; whether the singing style should be Western or native; and whether the performance style should follow that of Chinese opera or the Stanislavsky system.

None of these issues were definitively decided, but the meeting's spirit of openness helped make possible the composition and performance of many new operas between 1957 and 1963. Some leaned more heavily on China's traditional music, using singing styles borrowed from folk song and local opera. Perhaps the best example of this type is the extraordinarily popular *Third Sister Liu*, which premiered in 1959 and was made into a movie the following year. Others adhered more closely to the norms of

---

33. See Ming: 261-4.

Western opera, with continuous musical accompaniment, minimal spoken dialogue, and the use of motifs to identify the characters. This type was especially popular with composers in the late 1950s and early 1960s and included such operas as *Song of the Grassland*, *Blood and Tears of Hatred*, *Spring Thunder*, and the 1962 hit, *A Cloud Seeks Her Husband*.

With so much focus on the development of new opera, a number of Western operas were also performed in translation, including *Madame Butterfly*, *La Traviata*, *Eugene Onegin* and *Romeo and Juliet*. The Soviet Union's cultural influence was reflected in the tremendous popularity of two operas that are little known in the West, *The Young Guards*, by the Ukrainian composer Meitus, and *The Cloth Seller*, by the Azerbaijani composer Gadzhibekov.[34]

Important progress was also made in the performance and composition of orchestral music. Some of it was from the standard repertoire of Western classics. The Shanghai Spring Music Festival of 1962 featured pieces by Western composers that "ranged all the way from Bach and Beethoven to Johann Strauss"[35] and a *Peking Review* article published that same year reports blithely that "the music of the European classics from Bach, Mozart or Beethoven to the moderns through Debussy to Shostakovich is, of course, part of the daily musical nourishment of the people..."[36] But much of it was Chinese; the years 1959 to 1962 saw the premieres of roughly a dozen symphonies, six symphonic poems and 14 cantatas by Chinese composers, with Ma Sicong alone writing two symphonies, a tone poem, and a violin concerto.[37] Ding Shande and the Soviet-trained composer Zhu Jianer both wrote symphonies based on the Long March, which were premiered at the 1962 Shanghai festival.

Ding spent three years composing the five movements of his symphony, an undertaking for which he twice travelled to the provinces on the route of the Long March to interview veterans who had participated in it and peasants who remembered it. The symphony incorporates both the revolutionary songs sung by the Long March participants and the folk songs of the national minorities who lived along the route. Zhu Jianer's symphony, called *Epic of a Hero*, was written as the composer's graduation piece from the Moscow Conservatory and was the first choral symphony penned by a Chinese composer. For the choral parts, Zhu used five poems written by Mao Zedong over the course of the Long March.

But perhaps the most representative piece of this era is the work of two students at the Shanghai Conservatory, a violinist named He Zhanhao and a composition major named Chen Gang. The piece they composed is formally titled *Liang Shanbo and Zhu Yintai*, but is more commonly known in English as *The Butterfly Lovers*. It is a violin concerto in three parts based on a much-loved legend that is often referred to as "China's Romeo and Juliet." In writing it, the two composers were influenced both by

---

34. See Kagan, A.L. (1963). Music and the Hundred Flowers Movement. *The Musical Quarterly*: 425.
35. Chang Feng (1962). Biggest Shanghai Music Festival. *Peking Review* June 8: 18-19.
36. Li Yeh-tao (1962). Chinese Orchestral Music. *Peking Review* June 29: 14.
37. See Kagan: 428.

their study of foreign technique and their familiarity with China's own music. As He Zhanhao explains,

> I came from folk music and went to the Conservatory. So, I sang Yueju [Shaoxing opera] but played the violin. When I got to the conservatory, I studied foreign technique very hard. But, I asked, who am I studying this for? Am I going to play Bach and Beethoven for the peasants? I play it and they listen. I ask if it's good and they all nod their heads. I ask if they understand, they all say no. But they love to hear Yueju! Of course, the violin is very special and beautiful. So, this influenced our thinking — how could we use folk music with the violin? How could we nationalize the violin?[38]

He Zhanhao studied Western technique by day and listened to local opera at night. Thinking "to raise the level of Chinese music and bring Western and Chinese music together," he and several classmates began to adapt folk music to violin. They then went to factories and villages to play them and see how they were received. The welcome they received from their audiences encouraged them to write more, as did the support they got from fellow classmates and such professors as Ding Shande, who supervised their work.

"Sometimes we tried lots of different things," He Zhanhao continued. "Of course, inside we felt so young and not ready for this, but the leaders encouraged us. They told us, you all think Beethoven and Mozart are very great, but remember much of their music came from folk music, too."

Mr. He and Mr. Chen finally completed *The Butterfly Lovers* in 1959. The music they composed was unique in the way the violin uses the singing technique of *yueju*, which involves much portamento and different vibrato. They also adapted many other instrumental techniques from Chinese instruments and applied them to violin. Originally, they changed the ending of the story — when the two star-crossed lovers die and then turn into butterflies and fly off together — because they thought it was silly and superstitious, but their professors told them they were wrong to do this, since it was a romantic legend that came from the people. In May, *The Butterfly Lovers* was performed for the public in Shanghai's Lyceum Theater.

"And then suddenly everyone liked it!" recalled Mr. He. "The people welcomed it. *People's Daily* wrote an article called, 'Our Own Symphonic Music,' on May 27."

Of course, not everyone liked it — some considered its way of harmonizing Chinese melodies to be too simple and sentimental while some leftists decried the use of the "feudal" legend as inspiration. Nonetheless, audiences did love it, and the piece has stood the test of time. It is now a standard in the repertoire of Chinese orchestras and has also been performed by many orchestras around the world.

Because the new Chinese government was eager to demonstrate the progress it had made in many fields, including music, musical exchanges of various kinds were encouraged during this period. In 1958, China sent at least 12 companies with 580

---

38. The authors interviewed He Zhanhao at his home in Shanghai in January of 2000. All quotes come from this interview.

artists to twenty countries and in 1960 it sent 200 delegations to 48 countries.[39] Individual artists were also sent to participate in competitions, with pianists in particular making their mark in international concert halls. Fu Cong, of course, won the Chopin competition in 1955. Liu Shikun and Zhou Guangren — who, like Fu Cong, was a former Paci student — participated in the 1956 Liszt Festival. Liu took third place in the Liszt Festival and then entered the 1958 Tchaikovsky Competition in Moscow and placed second, behind Van Cliburn. Gu Shengying, a young graduate of the Shanghai Conservatory and a member of the Shanghai Symphony, won a gold medal at the 1957 World Youth Festival in Moscow and took top prize in women's piano at the 14th International Music Competition in Geneva in 1958. In 1962, a young pianist named Yin Chengzong who was studying at the Leningrad Conservatory won another second prize for China at the Tchaikovsky Competition, placing behind the tied first place winners Vladimir Ashkenazy and John Ogdon.

The success of Chinese pianists in prestigious international competitions was a source of pride and helped further other musical exchanges, including the visits of foreign companies and musicians to China. According to an article published in early 1957, there were "constant programmes of Western and other foreign music either live or on the radio — some played by Chinese orchestras with visiting conductors from abroad...[40] The world famous violinist David Oistrakh toured China in 1957, as did the Lambert Ballet. In 1961, a New Zealand pianist and professor named Frederick Page was invited to visit China for an entire month.

In Shanghai, he visited the Conservatory and the Symphony. Thanks to Mayor Chen Yi, both had been given permanent new quarters, the Conservatory in space it had once rented on Fenyang Road and the Symphony in a rambling garden home that had originally belonged to Sun Yat-sen's son. Page noted that the Shanghai Conservatory had a staff of 500 teaching 3000 full- and part-time students, including 700 advanced students enrolled in the five-year university-level course of study and 600 secondary-level students taking the seven-year course of study. He made special mention of the Shanghai Symphony, which was finally an all-Chinese ensemble since Huang Yijun had replaced Foa as conductor and the last foreign musician — V. Tarnopolsky — had departed in 1958.

Page wrote that,

> The Shanghai Symphony Orchestra is good, though I myself did not think it up to the standard of our National Orchestra. They play a standard 'Proms' repertory, Mozart *No. 40*, Beethoven *1, 3, 5* with *No. 6* in rehearsal; Dvorak *New World* and *Slavonic Dances*, Liszt *Les Preludes*, Tchaikovsky *4, 5, 6*, Khachaturian *No. 2*, Shosta-kovich *No. 11*, Debussy's *Petite Suite*; they are in touch with conductors and composers in Poland, Finland, Romania, East Germany, Japan, USSR. Their conductor has played in Moscow and Helsinki. They have a fine club house, with a new rehearsal hall, their own canteen, library, amusement facilities and so on. They

---

39. Kagan: 429.
40. See (1956). China's cultural relations with foreign countries in 1956. *Chinese Literature* 2: 230-1.

take very seriously their responsibilities towards their own composers; they are happy for new works to come forward for a tryout.[41]

In Beijing, he visited the Central Conservatory and on the eve of National Day attended a grand banquet in the Great Hall of the People at which "three orchestras play, a national instrumental, a western-style, a military band. The western-style orchestra plays Tchaikovsky waltzes ravishingly. The day itself brings band music of great solemnity..."[42] In summary, Page professed himself to be profoundly impressed by the vibrancy of the musical scene he witnessed:

> I have had a glimpse of the richness of China's musical life. Except for the Peking classical opera, all that I heard is virtually the result of the work of the last eleven years. They are pouring out music at the moment, fully conscious of the directive that music must serve people. They are reviving old operas, creating new forms of opera, experimenting with dance groups, taking up choral singing with immense enthusiasm. I had reservations about the quality of some of their new national songs, but none about the vibrancy and urgency of their singing. They are cultivating their old instruments, creating new ensembles; factories are turning out concert grands; theaters, concert halls, opera houses are packed.... What will happen when the music of the 20th century hits them?[43]

BLOOMING AND CONTENDING

Mao Zedong was evidently sincere in his desire to see the People's Republic enter a new era in which a hundred cultural flowers would bloom and a hundred schools of thought contend. Although many cadres opposed him, he worked hard for months to overcome their doubts and finally managed to get the Hundred Flowers officially launched in the spring of 1957. Once the campaign was in full swing, he continued working to convince intellectuals that they should not be afraid to speak openly about shortcomings they perceived in the Communist Party and its policies. The Hundred Flowers, Mao assured everyone, was to be "a movement of ideological education carried out seriously, yet as gently as a breeze or mild rain."[44] There would be no retribution, no struggle sessions, no humiliating public meetings.

Convinced that Mao meant what he said, intellectuals finally began to air their grievances and opinions on issues large and small. But as the criticisms piled higher and stung more sharply, Party officials who had opposed the movement in the first place became increasingly uneasy. Mao apparently also began to doubt the wisdom of the campaign and within weeks it was abruptly ended. In its stead came a new "anti-rightist" movement intended to single out and punish all those who had taken Mao at his word and criticized the Communist Party. By the time it was over, more than

41. Page, F. (1963). A musician's journal. *Arts and Sciences in China*: 13.
42. *Ibid.,* 9.
43. *Ibid*: 15-16.
44. Spence (2nd edition): 540.

300,000 intellectuals were declared rightists, a label that destroyed many careers and ruined many lives.

The end of the Hundred Flowers did not mean the end of the flowering of classical music development in the PRC. But it did mean that there would be as much contending — within music circles and with the ever-changing political environment — as there would be blooming.

Li Delun learned this first-hand in September of 1957 when he got off the train in Beijing after the week-long journey from Moscow. His wife and children were waiting eagerly to see him, but he barely had time to hug them before he was herded onto a bus that took him to a struggle session directed against a famous playwright. Mr. Li recognized this tactic as an application of the old dictum, "kill a chicken to scare the monkeys"; and wondered what he, as a monkey, could do to escape the same fate. Ultimately, he decided that the answer was nothing — if the Party wanted to declare him a rightist, it would find evidence to prove that he was just that.

As it turned out, nothing else happened to Mr. Li during the anti-rightist movement; but a few weeks later he was called in and presented with "A Report on the Mistakes of Comrade Li Delun," which detailed everything he had done "wrong" during his years as a student in Moscow.[45] Over several days, he was forced to sit and listen as he was questioned and criticized for many actions that he viewed as entirely innocent. Mr. Li's biggest mistake — aside from not realizing that he was under surveillance — had been speaking openly to Lu Ji when he visited Moscow in his capacity as head of the Musicians' Association. According to the report, Mr. Li had told Lu Ji that some of the leaders of China's music circles did little to help with music development in China. On the contrary, they did far too many things that had nothing whatsoever to do with music. Many didn't even understand music — they only knew simple notation and simple harmony!

His other principal "mistake" had been enjoying himself too much. "When he wanted to eat, he went to a restaurant," the report read, "And when he wanted to go out, he took a car — this is the lifestyle of the bourgeois class." [46] In fact, Mr. Li had earned so much money that he could have purchased a second-hand car; and as he sat listening to this review of his errors, he was thankful that he had not done so.

In the end, Mr. Li was not punished for his criticism of music circle leaders or his allegedly profligate lifestyle, but he was still angry. His own treatment aside, two incidents in the music world particularly upset him. The first concerned He Luting, who had come perilously close to being declared a rightist and apparently been saved only because Chen Yi once again intervened on his behalf. Mr. Li had read the *People's Music* article that had caused He Luting trouble earlier and that had once again come back to haunt him. He agreed with its honest summation of the issues that divided China's music circles and did not understand why it so upset others.

---

45. For report, see Luo: 288.
46. Luo: 288.

The second incident concerned a critique of Xian Xinghai's symphonies that was written by three musicians in the heady days of the Hundred Flowers and was published in *People's Music*. The musicians criticized technical aspects of Xian's symphonies, such as his heavy borrowing from famous works like *The Internationale*, and his poor orchestration, which they said often prevented audiences from even being able to hear his borrowed thematic motives.[47] Mr. Li was familiar with Xian Xinghai's work and he knew that the analysis was correct. In fact, he had conducted Xian's *Yellow River Cantata* while he was in Moscow and found the orchestration to be so poor that he had personally re-orchestrated the entire piece before the performance. But, since Mao had anointed Xian Xinghai as "the people's musician," the composer was supposed to be above all criticism. Wang Lisan, the article's main author, had therefore been branded a rightist.

The anti-rightist movement and his own "mistakes" left Li Delun in a kind of professional limbo, but his experiences would prove to be useful preparation for the future. Once the political dust had settled, he managed to be named conductor of the newly-formed Central Philharmonic Society.

The Central Philharmonic was created in 1956, one of the many new arts organizations of the Hundred Flowers. Although it was young and its musicians were inexperienced, its status as a national-level institution gave it strong potential and guaranteed visibility. It had an orchestra, a chorus, a corps of resident composers, a group of vocal and instrumental soloists and a handful of young conductors. Many of its members had been trained by Soviet-bloc experts and an East German had served as its conductor until the anti-rightist movement began. The Philharmonic was managed by Li Ling, the Cantonese musician who had studied at Yanan's Lu Xun Academy and worked in Chongqing and then Hong Kong, where he founded the Zhonghua Conservatory, before being appointed vice dean of the Central Conservatory.

Li Ling had the organizational skills and bureaucratic savoir-faire to build up the orchestra but he needed a talented and charismatic conductor with solid political credentials to help him. Likewise, Li Delun needed an orchestra with talented musicians, strong management, and institutional backing to help him realize his dreams of developing symphonic music in China. The two recognized the complementarity of their goals and began an easy and productive working relationship.

Li Delun's first task on the job was to lead the orchestra in accompanying the renowned violinist David Oistrakh. Preparing an inexperienced orchestra to accompany one of the world's most famous musicians was a daunting undertaking, but Mr. Li knew Oistrakh from Moscow and the two got along well. Their performance of Mozart's *A Major Violin Sonata* and Beethoven's *D Major Violin Concerto* was widely praised and later released as a recording.

---

47. See Luo: 289 and Ming: 258.

Mr. Li's true debut with his new orchestra came at the beginning of 1958, when he began to rehearse Tchaikovsky's *Sixth Symphony*. Although he had conducted the symphony many times in the USSR, the musicians of the Central Philharmonic had never performed it and Mr. Li found it necessary to draw deeply on his education and his life experience to help them understand it. It took a full month of rehearsals before the orchestra was prepared to play in public, but the effort was worthwhile — though only two or three performances had been planned, they were so well received that ten more were added. Since many in his audience were new to the music, Mr. Li established a life-long custom of giving an introductory talk before the start of each show.

"My concerts are lecture concerts," he explained. "We need to teach our audiences."

Li Ling and Li Delun's mutual determination to develop the young orchestra soon began to bear fruit. With his skill at navigating the bureaucracy, Li Ling convinced culture officials to give the Philharmonic an old movie theater which he cleaned up and re-christened as the Beijing Concert Hall. He then set the ambitious goal of giving a concert in the 1000-seat hall every week and achieved it by having the orchestra, chorus, solo singers, and solo instrument groups alternate performances. The Central Philharmonic soon became known for its regular Sunday concerts and for its outgoing conductor who talked to the audiences and did his best to make the music accessible.

Li Delun and Li Ling were generally happy with their progress in building the orchestra, although they were frustrated by the frequent interference of some culture officials who did not like them to perform foreign works. On one occasion, Li Delun had programmed Tchaikovsky's *Fourth Symphony* and was set to begin rehearsals when an official arrived, unannounced. On learning what the orchestra was rehearsing, the official pounded on the table and shouted, "Tchaik *Four*, Tchaik *Four*! Why always Tchaik *Four*? Why don't you rehearse Ma Sicong's pieces?"[48]

At the official's insistence, Li Delun had to cancel the Tchaikovsky and switch to Ma Sicong's *Second Symphony*. Although he had nothing against Ma's work, he wasn't prepared and the rehearsal went poorly. The incident left such a bitter taste in his mouth that he never again programmed Tchaikovsky's *Fourth Symphony*, and in the last years of his life regretted that he had never performed it.

Just as Mr. Li, the orchestra, and their audiences were settling into a routine, another major political movement came along: The Great Leap Forward.

The Great Leap began in part as a response to the 1957 agricultural harvest, which fell below expectations and had a negative impact on the government's plans for investment in industry. It disappointed Mao in particular because he saw it as a sign of the peasants' increasing focus on their own individual material wants, at the expense of the Revolution. Mao decided that what China needed was "continuing revolution" that would keep the masses forever mobilized in support of revolutionary goals. He sent urban-based cadres down to the countryside to encourage increased production,

---

48. Luo: 298.

in part by using the slogan "more, faster, better, cheaper." When the harvest did prove better in 1958, rural leaders decided that it was time to organize rural communes throughout the Chinese countryside, an undertaking of which they assumed Mao would approve. Peasants who only ten years earlier had farmed their own land as families were now grouped together in huge communes, required to collectively farm the land and even to cook and eat together at commune kitchens.

Soon, the whole nation was caught up in the excitement of the people's communes, a new social organization which had "appeared, fresh as the morning sun, above the broad horizon of East Asia."[49] Propaganda organs assured everyone that the communes would help enable China to hurry through the primary stages of socialism and catapult itself into the glorious state of communism.

While the peasants labored to raise agricultural production, urban residents were also encouraged to contribute by making steel for increased industrial production. This was done by donating household goods — cooking pots, decorative objects, metal fences — which were then melted down in so-called backyard steel furnaces, mostly amateur experiments that in fact produced little usable metal. Steel production was only the tip of the iceberg and the bureaucratic and social pressure to join the Great Leap Forward by doing "more, cheaper, better, faster" soon expanded into every sphere of economic and cultural activity, including music.

The Central Philharmonic at first simply increased the number of performances it gave for workers, peasants and soldiers. It also played *Madame Butterfly* for a China National Opera production, with only a month of rehearsals, and performed Shostakovich's *Eleventh Symphony*, with only a week to prepare. This was fast, compared to its usual preparation time; Mr. Li had to rehearse the orchestra morning, afternoon and evening to be ready. Even so, it soon became clear that such leaps were not great enough. Eager to do better, the orchestra's leaders held a meeting at which they wrote their goals down on paper and put them in a big red envelope: instead of doing 40 concerts a year, they would do 80. But soon after, they decided that merely doubling their annual performances at the drop of a hat was nowhere near ambitious enough. So, they doubled it again — to 160; and then again, to 320; and again, to 640; until they finally settled on the nice round number of 1200 concerts a year.

Twelve-hundred concerts sounded like a respectable goal to everyone, so it was this that was reported with great fanfare to the Ministry of Culture. And then, like hung-over revelers reviewing their champagne-inspired resolutions in the clear light of New Year's morning, the Philharmonic leaders sat back down and tried to figure out how they were actually going to achieve this.

For an orchestra like the Central Philharmonic, which needed a month just to rehearse one symphony, to suddenly give 1200 symphony concerts a year was clearly impossible. The only way to get close to the target number was to divide the orchestra into small groups and send them out to the factories and villages where they could sing or play a few songs, which would then count as a concert. Although this worked in

---

49. Spence (2nd edition): 549.

terms of achieving the Great Leap goal, it meant that the orchestra could hardly ever rehearse or perform together and was a big disappointment to Li Delun, who had better things in mind for his ensemble.

However, if this bothered Mr. Li, there was still more to come. One day, some of the more ardent Philharmonic members appeared banging drums and gongs and demanding to know what he was going to do to help them "catch America and surpass Britain." He replied that he had just finished his studies and wasn't going to surpass anyone; but within a few days they were back, insisting that he set a goal that would bring credit to the Central Philharmonic. Realizing that he had to surpass somebody, Mr. Li said the first thing that came to his mind — he would surpass Ivanov, the conductor of the Moscow State Symphony. Since Ivanov and the Moscow State Symphony had just toured China in May, everyone knew who the Soviet conductor was and the goal was deemed suitably heroic.

The Great Leap officially continued into 1960, but by 1959 the Central Philharmonic was freed from the monotony of giving 1200 performances a year because the Ministry of Culture ordered it to devote all its attention to preparations for a very important occasion: the celebration of the 10th anniversary of the People's Republic of China. The 10th anniversary was a major political and cultural event. Hundreds of activities were planned, including performances by the Czech National Orchestra and the USSR National Ballet. Preparing for such an occasion was not easy, since numerous Party officials had to sit in on rehearsals over a six month period and even the opinions of the musicians and the masses had to be solicited.

For the Central Philharmonic's concerts, Li Delun chose four standard Western classics — Beethoven *First*, *Third* and *Ninth Symphonies* and Prokofiev's *Seventh Symphony* — and the first symphony of Luo Zhongrong, the orchestra's resident composer. Then, as the anniversary drew closer, other events were hurriedly added, including a joint performance of Beethoven's *Ninth Symphony* with the Dresden State Orchestra and the creation of an orchestra of 500 to play Beethoven's *Egmont* and Li Huanzhi's *Spring Festival Overture*. To prepare for this latter event, Mr. Li had to take taxis all around Beijing to rehearse the different ensembles that would eventually be brought together for the mega-orchestra. In fact, both Mao Zedong and his guest Nikita Khrushchev attended the concert, so Mr. Li considered the effort to have been worthwhile.

The 10th anniversary National Day celebrations were a high point for the young Philharmonic, for the status of orchestral music in New China, and for the nation in general. But, like so many other high points, it was one which would soon prove ephemeral. Though few urban residents understood it at the time, the Great Leap Forward was going terribly wrong in the countryside. Indeed, as early as 1958, it had become obvious that agricultural production figures had been seriously exaggerated and that the country had not produced nearly as much food as central government leaders had been led to believe. Peasants across the country were beginning to go hungry and by 1959 they were eating leaves and grass, even as they were forced to turn over their meager grain production to the state, which then used it to feed city residents and to buy heavy machinery from the USSR. Between 1959 and 1962, upwards of 20 million peasants would starve to death.

The failure of the Great Leap coincided with — and contributed to — a sharp deterioration in China's relationship with its "big brother," the USSR. Mao and other senior Chinese leaders had been upset ever since Khrushchev made his "secret" criticisms of the late Stalin at the Soviet Communist Party's 20th congress in 1956 and their anxiety was compounded when the Soviet leader visited the United States in 1959. The Soviets, for their part, regarded the Great Leap Forward as too radical and thought China should take a more cautious approach to economic development.

Mao and Khrushchev managed to be courteous to each other during China's 10th anniversary celebrations, but just months later they were publicly criticizing each other by way of proxies, with China denouncing Yugoslavia and supporting Albania and the USSR doing the opposite. By the summer of 1960, the USSR took the drastic action of recalling all of its 1,390 foreign experts and advisers then working in China.[50] The loss of the Soviet advisers was a major setback for China, which had counted on their help in many important areas of industry, science, agriculture, and construction, not to mention culture. Even so, China had received much help from the more than 10,000 experts who had been sent since the program started and the government responded to its abrupt cessation with courtesy. Chen Yi even hosted a going-away banquet for all the recalled advisers.

The split with the Soviet Union had several implications for classical music in China. The first and most obvious was that China's conservatories, orchestras and music schools were now on their own. For the very first time, they would be without any long-term teachers or advisers from either Western or Eastern Europe.

Even more significant, if less immediately obvious, the USSR had served as kind of silent protector for symphonic music in China. Since the founding of the PRC, Chinese who supported the development of orchestras, conservatories, operas and ballets could always point to the example of their "big brother" when they wished to explain why such development was desirable, and even necessary. Critics of symphonic music had not been silent, of course, but there was little they could say when the Soviet model was proffered. But with the break in brotherly relations, the balance between critics and supporters of symphony orchestras and music slowly tipped toward the critics.

In this changed atmosphere, the critics grew louder. The Central Philharmonic seemed in danger of being marginalized, or even disbanded; Li Ling and Li Delun tried to raise its profile by touring the country to play pieces like *The Butterfly Lovers* and Tchaikovsky's *Fifth Symphony* for the masses. On a trip to Wuhan, they gave concerts in a tractor factory and many other similar venues, but were nonetheless taken to task by local officials who questioned what good this classical music did for the ordinary masses.

Li Delun and Li Ling wanted to expand the Philharmonic's repertoire, implement formal training programs for its musicians, establish a training institute for young

---

50. For figure, see Spence (2nd edition): 559.

people, and perform symphony concerts on a more regular basis; but their time was taken up in responding to questions about the usefulness of their orchestra. With the leftist winds blowing stronger, the realization of their goals seemed to recede ever farther away. Things looked brighter for a time, in 1961 and the first half of 1962, when the government made efforts to revive the Hundred Flowers and even released "Eight Articles on Literature and Art" designed to once again convince artists and intellectuals that the Party needed them. But then, in September of 1962, the situation again changed dramatically when Mao implored Party members and ordinary people alike "never to forget class struggle." [51]

"Class struggle" was a dreaded phrase for intellectuals, the polar opposite of "hundred flowers." It signaled clearly that Mao was once more rejecting the open and inclusive policies associated with the Hundred Flowers in favor of a combative and divisive approach to governance — and that they would again be the sacrificial lambs. Professional artists like Li Delun still hoped that they would be left alone, but in December Mao complained specifically about the theater arts. Mao's intent was for arts and literature to serve class struggle, not stay aloof from it.

Mao's complaints about the theater were not given major publicity in Beijing, but they were seized upon by the leftist mayor of Shanghai, Ke Qingshi, who almost immediately gave a speech encouraging Shanghai's culture workers to write about the "thirteen years" of the People's Republic, rather than the thousands of years of China's feudal past. His words were then dutifully echoed in print by a leading leftist ideologue and writer named Yao Wenyuan.

Yao followed this piece with more leftist articles on cultural topics and in May of 1963 suddenly decided to target the composer Claude Debussy in the pages of *Wen Hui Bao*,[52] a newspaper read primarily by intellectuals. Debussy came to Yao's attention not by way of music — he openly acknowledged that he knew nothing about Debussy or his music — but via a translation of Debussy's music criticism called *Monsieur Croche, the Dilettante Hater*. The translation was put out by the Music Publishing House as part of a Hundred Flowers project to translate and publish works by many important Western composers. Having seen the book, Yao wrote, he had several questions: Why were the publishers introducing and promoting the works of this bourgeois musician? What did they expect to come of introducing Western bourgeois music theory to China, especially impressionism?

Monsieur Croche is a loosely structured collection of Debussy's writings — themselves rather loosely written — that was first published in Paris in 1921. It includes music criticism, commentary, and a few essays in which Debussy makes flippant, even cutting, comments on such topics as the Prix de Rome, the

---

51. Mao's quote can be found in (1966). Hold High the Great Red Banner of Mao Zedong's Thought and Actively Participate in the Great Socialist Cultural Revolution. *Chinese Literature* 7: 8. This editorial was originally published in the *Liberation Army Daily* of April 18, 1966 and Mao made the comment in his address to the Tenth Plenary Session of the Communist Party's Eighth Central Committee.

52. For Yao's article, see *Wen Hui Bao*, May 12, 1963. For a detailed discussion of the article and the others that followed it, see Shi: 209-219.

administration of state opera houses, and Wagner's music. Monsieur Croche is a kind of alter-ego for Debussy who appears in eight essays and then disappears. It is he who voices some fairly extreme opinions, such as this disparaging reference to Beethoven's *Sixth Symphony*:

> Music contains so many impulses you could write a song about them. My favorite music is those few notes an Egyptian shepherd plays on his flute: he is a part of the landscape around him, and he knows harmonies that aren't in our books. The "musicians" hear only music written by practiced hands, never the music of nature herself. To see the sun rise does one far more good than hearing the *Pastoral Symphony*. What's the use of such incomprehensible art? Shouldn't all those complications be forbidden?[53]

This comment was controversial in the Europe of Debussy, but it seems unlikely to upset a Chinese leftist who believed that art should be created for the masses. Yao Wenyuan seems to have been more offended by Debussy's "bourgeois" background and lifestyle and the fact that he wrote "impressionist" music. That Debussy's roots were hardly typical bourgeois — his father joined the Paris Commune and was arrested and jailed after its fall — and that the composer himself called the "impressionist" label a "useful term of abuse"[54] mattered little to Yao, who in any case was primarily using Debussy to attack such supporters of Western classical music as the editors at Music Publishing House and to ferret out others.

While most of *Wen Hui Bao*'s more open-minded or musically-educated readers no doubt read Yao's essay with disdain and then moved on, the article riled He Luting so much that he could not put it out of his mind. Shortly after it was published, he called *Wen Hui Bao* and invited one of its reporters to come to his office so he could set the venerable newspaper straight on the subject of Debussy. Before the journalist had even sat down, Mr. He told him, in essence, that Yao's column was a misguided display of ignorance and that an influential paper like *Wen Hui Bao* discredited itself by publishing it.

When the reporter was finally able to take a seat, he took out his notebook and wrote down everything Mr. He said: Yao had taken Debussy's writing completely out of context. He did not understand when the composer was being ironic or sarcastic. He took sentences from *Monsieur Croche* and let his imagination run wild — the result was a joke. It was also absurd to use the standards of Marxism to judge the composer; Debussy had his limitations and Mr. He did not agree with everything he did or like everything he composed, but his ideas were unique for the era in which he lived.

At the end of the interview, the reporter asked Mr. He if he would write up his views for *Wen Hui Bao* to publish as a response to Yao's polemic. Mr. He, of course, had already gotten into serious trouble for voicing his opinions in print, but he saw no reason to hide his views on Debussy. He wrote a response called "A few requests for art

---

53. As quoted in Lesure, F. (1977). *Debussy on Music* (translated and edited by R.L. Smith) New York: Alfred A. Knopf: 47-8.

54. See Lesure: 48. Original article is, Conversation with M. Croche. *La Revue Blanche*, July 1, 1901.

critics," in which he commended Comrade Yao for taking the time to read about Debussy but added that it was unfortunate he had so badly misunderstood *Monsieur Croche*. Unfortunately, Comrade Yao was clearly unfamiliar with the arts activities in turn-of-the-century European bourgeois society and did not understand impressionist painting or music. When one is unfamiliar with a subject, Mr. He noted, one should be very cautious and study harder to get the truth. The bulk of his response was then devoted to parsing Yao's interpretation of *Monsieur Croche*, and explaining what Debussy had actually said and what Mr. He thought he meant.

After his response was published — under the pseudonym Shan Gu[55] — the editors of *Wen Hui Bao* invited Mr. He to attend a meeting about Debussy. Mr. He assumed that it was a Hundred Flowers type of discussion and again aired his views freely. He talked about the importance of studying Debussy and of learning about foreign culture in general. He suggested that in evaluating the past, it was wise to use an historical viewpoint rather than an ideological one, while in arts education it was necessary to recognize the importance of the bourgeois artistic legacy. As for Debussy's music, it was a bit like the paintings of the famous artist Qi Baishi — it showed lots of interest in life, but little struggle. It was poetic and based on Debussy's feelings about nature, not a direct attempt to imitate the natural world.

About a week later, *Wen Hui Bao* ran another article on Debussy — and then another and another. While a few were defenses of the composer and his music, most simply branded him as a bourgeois impressionist. It soon became clear to He Luting that the paper was running a smear campaign. Yao Wenyuan wrote that Debussy didn't truly understand the French peasants — he thought their lives were idyllic, when in reality they were a constant struggle of blood, sweat and tears! The landlords were constantly cheating them — how could they possibly feel peaceful? Another critic noted that Debussy's instrumental work — suggestive of such things as the dialogue between wind and sea — was written for rich old ladies who sat around and ate all day.

After each article was published, a journalist would come to He Luting's home or office to record his response. What about Qi Baishi's paintings, asked Mr. He — by painting shrimp, insects and leaves, how did he help the revolution? Debussy was dead — no one could ask him now what were his class feelings. One could only acknowledge that he was a very influential composer. After the publication of an article called "What is Music?" Mr. He told the reporter that by the standards of that article, only *The Internationale* could really be called music. What would be the point of a concert if it was simply the performance of *The Internationale*, over and over? In the current climate, he concluded, if you criticized Debussy, you were right; and if you didn't, you were accused of worshipping the West.

55. The journalist suggested using a pseudonym. He Luting originally intended to use his own name, but then decided that it would be too harsh for someone of his reputation and position to criticize Yao Wenyuan's opinion directly. Barbara Mittler points out that the pen name he chose — Shan Gu — was that of a poet-official from the Northern Song Dynasty, Huang Tingjian (1045-1105), who was known for remonstrating the government.

Mr. He was asked to write another article after this conversation, but declined. Slowly but surely, he was beginning to suspect that he had been trapped; later, he was told that everything he said was reported back to high-level officials in Shanghai, some of whom were delighted that he had finally "come out of hiding." Frustrated and exhausted, he announced that he was requesting a two-year leave of absence from his Conservatory duties so he could read, write and compose.

With He Luting refusing to speak, the wave of anti-Debussy articles died down but the incident further deepened the split in China's divided music circles. It was soon followed by a campaign known as *san hua*, or "the three -izes," an effort to nationalize, revolutionize and "mass-ize" music in China. In other words, all music was to be Chinese, have political content, and be acceptable to the masses.

Uncertain how to implement these directives, radicals began to attack the piano because it was seen as the instrument most representative of Western bourgeois culture. Piano professors came under great pressure and some conservatory students refused to continue with their piano lessons. As the movement accelerated, some professional musicians put away their Western instruments and switched to Chinese instruments or took up such peripheral jobs as selling concert tickets. Some amateur musicians began to sell — or even destroy — their much beloved instruments out of fear that they would be criticized for owning them. A small campaign was even launched against a popular song book called *Two Hundred Famous Foreign Songs*, which was faulted for including "soft," sentimental songs like an extremely popular Indonesian lullaby that was subsequently banned.

"China had no classical music — this came from Europe," explained Li Delun. "But, we had the 'three -izes.' What were we supposed to do? 'Revolutionize' — even Beethoven was criticized, Shostakovich. 'Mass-ize' — even ordinary people in the West don't listen to classical music all the time! This was very difficult, but you still had to do it. It was very hard to be a person then."

Once again, culture officials organized meetings in an attempt to resolve the issues that were causing conflict in the music world. He Luting and Li Delun both attended one such meeting in August of 1963. This time, Zhou Enlai addressed the attendees and urged them to consider the roots of the problems that continued to plague their work. He Luting again spoke out, complaining among other things that in the thirteen years of New China's history, only five foreign operas had been performed — and this considering that even one or two a year would not be enough! Other musicians complained privately that all they did every day was talk about the "three -izes," and that everyone was afraid to touch anything foreign. However, radicals at the meeting had complaints about other things, like uppity Central Conservatory students who called Beethoven and Tchaikovsky "Old Bei" and "Old Tchai," as if they were respected friends. This was no way to refer to the "two tigers," one bourgeois and the other feudal! [56]

56. For meeting, see Shi: 222 and Luo: 344.

Like Chen Yi before him, Zhou Enlai had done his best to help musicians find common ground, but failed. All further efforts to broker peace then fell by the wayside when the Ministry of Culture itself was attacked by Chairman Mao, who publicly complained that it was ignoring the presence of feudal elements in the arts and failing to do its job. He added, cuttingly, that if the Ministry did not shape up, its name should be changed to the "Ministry of Emperors, Princes, Generals and Ministers," or the "Ministry of Gifted Scholars and Beautiful Ladies," or the "Ministry of Foreign Dead People."[57]

Mao addressed the subject of culture again in December of 1963, when he wrote "Two Instructions Concerning Literature and Art," which included the ominous message:

> Problems abound in all forms of art such as drama, ballads, music, the fine arts, dance, the cinema, poetry and literature, and the people involved are numerous; in many departments very little has been achieved so far in socialist transformation. The "dead" still dominate in many departments... Isn't it absurd that many Communists are enthusiastic about promoting feudal and capitalist art, but not socialist art?[58]

On December 18, the Ministry of Culture organized another meeting, this one about how to respond to Mao's criticisms.[59] Once again, the issue of symphonic music came up, with many in the room criticizing it. One person called it a "tiger," and another said pointedly that musicians who played foreign music could not be on the same level as those who played national music. He Luting replied angrily that they were talking like warlords; but Li Delun sensed that the wind was blowing from the wrong direction, and decided to take a different tack.

Yes, he agreed, there was a need for a revolution in symphonic music — and in China's own traditional music, too, which still had many feudal and backward elements. But critics of symphonic music should not be afraid of this "foreign tiger" because China had the weapon to fight him, and that weapon was Marxism! He added that it was absurd to say that everything from the West was bad — what about the microphone he was talking into? Was it bad because it was Western? As for those who thought that musicians who played Western music did not belong on the same level as those who played Chinese music — fine. The next time Li Delun and his colleagues met them, they would allow all the traditional music players to be seated first. If there were then no seats left, the symphony orchestra musicians would sit on the floor or remain standing — but they would not for a moment be told that they were any less revolutionary than performers of traditional music!

57. MacFarquhar: 385.
58. Mao Zedong (1967). Two instructions concerning literature and art. *Chinese Literature* 9: 11-12.
59. For an account of this meeting, see Luo: 346-7.

CHAPTER 7. THE CULTURAL REVOLUTION

On November 10, 1965 an article entitled "On the new historical opera *Hai Rui Dismissed From Office*" was published in Shanghai's *Wen Hui Bao*. The article was less a review than a scathing critique and its author was none other than the anti-Debussy crusader who had so angered He Luting with his inaccuracies and generalizations — Yao Wenyuan.

This time around, the target of Yao's poisoned pen was Wu Han, a renowned scholar of the Ming Dynasty who was also a vice-mayor of Beijing. It was Wu Han who had written the play, *Hai Rui Dismissed From Office*, at the request of one of Beijing's Peking opera companies. The play had caused no problems when it was performed. Mao Zedong himself had attended and commented, "The play is good, and Hai Rui was a good man! *Hai Rui Dismissed From Office* is written pretty well [too]."[1] Mao further underlined his pleasure by inviting the actor who played Hai Rui home for dinner and sending Wu Han a personally inscribed copy ovice-mayorf the fourth volume of his own collected works.

The historical Hai Rui was a Ming Dynasty official who even in his own lifetime was renowned — and detested — for his austerity, honesty and bluntness. On one famed occasion, he sent a memorandum to the Jiaqing Emperor telling him that he was vain, cruel, selfish, suspicious and foolish, and also a failure as a father, husband and ruler. Unsurprisingly, this led to his arrest, but he came back to serve under two more emperors, including Wan Li, to whom he wrote a memorandum recommending the severest penalties to stop official corruption. By way of

---

1. MacFarquhar, R. (1997). *The Origins of the Cultural Revolution, Volume 3: The coming of the cataclysm, 1961-66*. Oxford University Press and Columbia University Press: 251-2.

example, he reminded the reclusive emperor that in the reign of the Ming Dynasty's first ruler, officials guilty of serious embezzlement were killed and their skin was then peeled off and made into balloons filled with grass for public display.[2]

It is unlikely that Mao would have suffered being told he was a failure as a father, husband and ruler any more than the Jiaqing Emperor did. But, at one point in 1959, he went through a phase of feeling frustrated that none of his officials or fellow leaders spoke honestly to him. To push them to speak more openly, he suggested that they model themselves after Hai Rui. When Mao's suggestion was made known, propaganda officials asked Wu Han to write several essays about Hai Rui's courageous insistence on speaking out, even to the point of defying the emperor. These essays were published and presumably inspired the Peking opera company to produce an opera about the honest official.

Thus, when intellectuals and officials across the country read or heard about the *Wen Hui Bao* article criticizing *Hai Rui Dismissed From Office* in November of 1965, many were confused and some were downright miffed. Why would the important newspaper and its star leftist writer devote precious space to a scathing analysis of a four-year old play written by a senior official and esteemed historian?

Anyone reading the piece would have understood PRC politics enough to know that it could never have been published without high level backing. Most readers would certainly have recognized that the article was at the very least an attack on Wu Han. Some must have suspected that the unfortunate historian was merely a convenient target and that those responsible for the polemic actually had something much bigger in mind, like the start of a new movement or the unseating of senior officials. But, no matter how attuned they were to the intricacies of Chinese politics, few officials or intellectuals who read the blistering editorial could have recognized it for what it was: the opening salvo in The Great Proletarian Cultural Revolution.

Indeed, though hardly anyone knew it at the time, it was Jiang Qing herself who had travelled to Shanghai under a cloak of secrecy and arranged for Yao Wenyuan to write the anti-*Hai Rui* diatribe. Chairman Mao knew of his wife's efforts and supported them — he even reviewed some of the countless drafts of Yao's article. Jiang Qing and Mao each had their own reasons for wanting to launch a cultural revolution and each found it convenient to use *Hai Rui* and its author Wu Han — who would die in 1969 as a result of unending persecution — as the launching pad for their plan.

For Jiang Qing, the publication of Yao's essay and the start of the Cultural Revolution was like a political coming-out party. Many of Mao's colleagues had not approved of his marriage to the former actress and it had been tacitly agreed long ago, back at Yanan, that she would stay out of politics. The agreement had held until the early 1960s, when Jiang Qing began trying to involve herself in cultural affairs. Her primary focus was Peking opera, the most widely-performed of the more than 350 different kinds of Chinese opera. Peking opera drew her attention because of its

---

2. Anecdotes come from Huang, R. (1981). *1587: A Year of No Significance.* New Haven and London: Yale University Press: 135 and 154. Chapter five is a fascinating discussion of Hai Rui's career.

popularity, because Mao had shown particular concern with it, and because it was easily labeled "feudal," with its stereotyped roles, plots based on legends and history, and stylized performance. But, her worries about feudalism and other negative influences also extended to other art forms. When she saw *Hai Rui* in 1962, she had apparently disliked it and tried to get Beijing officials to start a criticism campaign against it. Her efforts were thwarted, so she went to the friendlier, more leftist environment of Shanghai where several revolutionary operas had already been staged.

Of course, Jiang Qing was the wife of China's most powerful leader — a sensitive position in many nations — and she knew that many of her husband's colleagues wanted her to keep away from affairs of state. She therefore found it useful, even necessary, to insist that in assuming this new role she was merely trying to be a good wife, in this case by helping her husband to clear away the "anti-socialist poisonous weeds" that were threatening to overgrow China's cultural garden. Her goal in helping to launch, and then lead, the Cultural Revolution was, in her words, to be "just a plain soldier, a sentry of the Chairman patrolling on the ideological battle front."[3] However, if this was the official explanation for her entry into politics, other observers saw it differently.

"It was all a power struggle, all politics," said Li Delun. "She hadn't done anything, she hadn't participated in anything, she had no standing. So, she decided she'd make a Cultural Revolution."

Chairman Mao's true reasons for wanting to start the Cultural Revolution are presumably more complex than his wife's — he was, after all, the undisputed leader of China and it is not immediately obvious why he would consider it beneficial to plunge the nation he led into total chaos and attack the Communist Party of which he himself was chairman.

Culture certainly had something to do with it. Mao, of course, had long placed tremendous emphasis on literature and the arts, and the propaganda uses to which they could be put. Like his wife, he had also been growing increasingly upset about certain trends in China's cultural world, including the preponderance of traditional and "feudal" stories. Mao had also changed his opinion about *Hai Rui Dismissed From Office*, perhaps due to his wife's influence. By 1965, he evidently had come to the conclusion that it was a direct attack on his own leadership and that the figure of Hai Rui was actually a stand-in for Peng Dehuai, a general who had written a letter to Mao in which he implicitly criticized the Great Leap Forward.

However, no matter how upset Mao was about the number of ghosts on opera stages or the true intentions of the author of *Hai Rui*, this does not explain why he deliberately launched a new revolution less than three decades after the triumph of the Communist revolution which he himself had led.

To account for his actions, historians and other observers offer a variety of explanations. Perhaps the most popular is similar to Li Delun's view of Jiang Qing's motives: that it was all about power. Mao had tired of his president, Liu Shaoqi, and

---

3. MacFarquhar: 439.

may even have suspected that he was after Mao's own job. But, since Liu had not actually done anything wrong, Mao couldn't attack him directly. Instead, he did it in a round-about manner by unseating officials to whom Liu was close, starting with the hapless Wu Han and moving up through the bureaucracy to such officials as Deng Xiaoping. He then closed in for the kill, targeting the president himself, using his alleged support of bourgeois culture as an excuse. By 1968, Liu Shaoqi was expelled from the Communist Party and denounced as "the big renegade, traitor, and scab...the arch-criminal who opposed the exercising of proletarian dictatorship over the bourgeoisie in the realm of culture and art,"[4] and by 1969, he was dead in jail.

Another commonly offered explanation is that Mao genuinely feared the death of his revolution. He was a true revolutionary and could not bear to see all his plans crushed to death by a mammoth bureaucracy. He may also genuinely have feared that capitalism could make a comeback in China, and that "bourgeois" culture was the first sinister sign of its incipient return. Likewise, he knew himself well enough to realize that he was best as a wartime leader, not a peacetime administrator, and sensed that he could be usurped if he allowed the status quo to be maintained. Thus, for reasons both ideological and self-serving, he decided to start a new revolution, this one in the realm of culture.

Still others point to the great shock Mao sustained when Khrushchev criticized the dead Stalin. Mao, they argue, was desperately afraid that he would meet the same fate as Stalin after his death — or maybe even the same fate as Khrushchev, who was thrown out of office. His fears were compounded by the dramatic failure of his efforts to reach the state of communism faster than the Soviet Union through the Great Leap Forward and the people's communes. The Cultural Revolution, they argue, was the aging Mao's last-ditch effort to make a dramatic contribution to communism, one which would ensure that China surpassed the USSR and forever secure his own reputation as one of the world's great Communists.

Other explanations are more prosaic — and unlikely — including the suggestion that Mao allowed his wife to start the Cultural Revolution because he wanted to distract her from a romantic affair he was having at the time.

Whatever their true motivations, the fact is that Mao Zedong and Jiang Qing together started the Cultural Revolution, and the publication of the article "On the new historical opera *Hai Rui Dismissed From Office*" was their opening gambit in what would become a bloody political upheaval.

Recognizing the editorial's inherent dangers, Beijing officials stalled before permitting it to be reprinted and even then tried to couch it as an academic debate, but their efforts were to little avail. The editorial's late-November re-publication in both *Beijing Daily* and *People's Daily* set off an exchange of views that grew more acrimonious and leaned further left as the months went by. Meanwhile, Mao left Beijing and kept largely out of sight, while Jiang Qing moved to solidify her position.

---

4. See (1969) Mao Zedong thought forever sheds its radiance. *Chinese Literature* 6: 96.

In the early months of 1966, she began working as cultural adviser to the People's Liberation Army, which was headed by the fawning and ambitious Lin Biao. She informed the nation that there was a sharp struggle in China's cultural world and that since 1949 Mao's policies had been consistently thwarted by the dictatorship of a sinister anti-Party, anti-socialist black line whose adherents favored art and literature that was either bourgeois, revisionist, or dated from the semi-colonial era of the 1930s. Fortunately, however, the PLA was willing to help in the battle to "destroy blind faith in Chinese and foreign classical literature." [5]

Newspapers began to prepare the nation for the new revolution with editorials like one that appeared in the *Liberation Army Daily* in mid-April, entitled "Hold High the Great Red Banner of Mao Zedong's Thought and Actively Participate in the Great Socialist Cultural Revolution":

> The struggle to foster what is proletarian and liquidate what is bourgeois on the cultural front is an important aspect of the class struggle between the proletariat and the bourgeoisie, between the socialist road and the capitalist road and between proletarian ideology and bourgeois ideology. The proletariat seeks to change the world according to its own world outlook, and so does the bourgeoisie. Socialist culture should serve the workers, peasants and soldiers, should serve proletarian politics, and should serve the consolidation and development of the socialist system and its gradual transition to communism. Bourgeois and revisionist culture serves the bourgeoisie, serves the landlords, rich peasants, counter-revolutionaries, bad elements and Rightists, and paves the way for the restoration of capitalism.

By May, the nation's key cultural officials had been removed from office and Lin Biao — who would soon become Mao's heir-apparent — had popularized the formulaic description of Mao as "our great teacher, great leader, great supreme commander and great helmsman." Students jumped on the bandwagon and protests spread to universities. Some of the revolution's more radical supporters decided to use the students, and issued them red arm bands that declared them to be Red Guards. With a title and a uniform, the Red Guards quickly found themselves a mission: to destroy the "four olds" of the "exploiting classes" — old customs, old habits, old culture and old thinking — and promote the "four news" of the proletariat. Violence began to erupt as the definition of the "four olds" was broadened and soon led to public attacks against intellectuals who could be accused of "feudal" thinking, who had a specialization or a habit that could be called "bourgeois," a Western education, or a fondness for China's traditional culture — in other words, virtually any educated Chinese. Mao, whose relationship with intellectuals had long been fraught with difficulties, was perfectly happy to see them attacked.

Upset by the escalating violence, Zhou Enlai and Liu Shaoqi consulted with Mao but received from him only the vaguest of guidance. Acting in what they considered to be the best interest of the nation and the Party, they sent work teams into the

---

5. Spence (2nd edition): 572.

universities to try to quell the unrest. The burgeoning revolution, however, found supporters in many segments of officialdom and society and its momentum was increasingly difficult to hold back.

Some supporters no doubt genuinely believed that a cultural revolution was necessary to prevent the return of capitalism to China. Others, especially the young, had been brought up in a world dominated by Chairman Mao and simply accepted whatever he said or did as right. Some knew the whole enterprise was absurd but were afraid to speak out against Mao and Jiang Qing, since at the very least that would have meant political death. And many people probably cared little about the revolution's ideological justification, but saw in it an opportunity to advance their own interests, political and otherwise; to escape a dead-end job or a boring university curriculum of politics and manual labor; or even to exact revenge on a society or an individual by whom they felt slighted.

In any case, by the summer of 1966, the Cultural Revolution was so well underway that no one could stop it. As the *People's Daily* put it on June 1,

> For the last few months, in response to the militant call of the Central Committee of the Chinese Communist Party and Chairman Mao, hundreds of millions of workers, peasants and soldiers and vast numbers of revolutionary cadres and intellectuals, all armed with Mao Zedong's thought, have been sweeping away a horde of monsters that have entrenched themselves in ideological and cultural positions. With the tremendous impetuous force of a raging storm, they have smashed the shackles imposed on their minds by the exploiting classes for so long in the past, routing the bourgeois "specialists," "scholars," "authorities," and "venerable masters" and sweeping every bit of their prestige into the dust....Facts have eloquently proved that Mao Zedong's thought becomes a moral atom bomb of colossal power once it takes hold of the masses. The current great cultural revolution is immensely advancing the socialist cause of the Chinese people and undoubtedly exerting an incalculable, far-reaching influence upon the present and future of the world. [6]

In July, Mao reappeared, famously floating down the Yangzi River for two hours in an effort to demonstrate that he was strong and capable of leading, even if he was getting older. The next month, the Chinese Communist Party met and officially endorsed the Cultural Revolution. Then, on August 18, Mao appeared in military uniform before tens of thousands of screaming Red Guards in Tiananmen Square and accepted from them one of the red armbands that was their insignia. It bore the words "Red Guard," in his own calligraphy. Henceforth, the Red Guards adopted as their guiding philosophy Mao's teaching that, "In the last analysis, all the truths of Marxism can be summed up in one sentence: 'Rebellion is justified.'"[7]

---

6. (1966) Sweep away all monsters. *Chinese Literature* 7: 65. This editorial was originally published in the *People's Daily* of June 1, 1966.

7. (1966) New masters of the stage — a survey of the Peking stage during China's National Day celebrations. *Chinese Literature* 12: P. 91-99

With rebellion as the clarion call, normal functioning of the nation virtually ceased, especially in urban areas. Schools shut down, factories fought each other with guns, and humble professors and high level officials alike were paraded through the streets wearing dunce caps and shameful placards. Among the earliest figures to be publicly humiliated and punished were cultural leading lights against whom Jiang Qing held some grudge. They included the playwright Tian Han, who had penned the lyrics to the national anthem, and Zhou Yang, Mao's one-time cultural spokesman who had become the Party's deputy director of propaganda. Priceless artifacts of China's cultural heritage — temples, tombs, museums, ancient buildings — were plundered or destroyed because they were "old." Some of these artifacts were large — such as portions of the Great Wall — and some were small, like the cemetery in Shanghai where Mario Paci's tomb had been maintained since his death by a former student.[8] Provincial governments were replaced with revolutionary committees and Red Guards tried to take over virtually every organization in China, from the railroads to the Foreign Ministry. Despite the efforts of a few sober men like Zhou Enlai who did their best to mitigate the chaos, the nation slipped so far into an abyss of death and destruction that by the autumn of 1967, even Mao Zedong and Jiang Qing acknowledged that the marauding groups of Red Guards had to be reined in. The violence then ebbed, but the Cultural Revolution itself would last for the rest of Chairman Mao's life.

CLASSICAL MUSIC'S DARKEST HOUR

"When the Cultural Revolution came, we thought it was a minor movement," recalled Tan Shuzhen. "We didn't know that it would last ten years. We never thought some people would die — many people would die."[9]

For Mr. Tan, as for so many others, the dawning realization that the new movement would be different from all the others came when he answered a knock at his door and found standing before him, wearing a red armband, not a stranger but someone with whom he was well acquainted. However, though he immediately recognized the young violin student, Ni, he did not recognize the expression on the young man's face.

"This Ni, his father was a good friend of mine. I helped arrange for his entry to middle school. Then when he wanted to go to college, six professors refused to accept him. I went to the Party leaders and said I thought he was talented — the Party secretary said, well let him in. That was about 1963."

---

8. According to Dong Guangguang, the student who looked after Paci's grave was Y. Y. Pan.

9. A detailed account of Tan Shuzhen's Cultural Revolution experiences can be found in *The Gentleman from Shanghai*, a video in which Mr. Tan tells the story of his life. The video is produced by the Hopewell Foundation and its executive producer is Walter Scheuer. Some of the quotes in this section come from the videotape or are very similar to Mr. Tan's statements in that video. Sheila Melvin watched the video with Mr. Tan in his home in Shanghai and he retold the story as they watched, and sometimes added supplementary comments.

Although Mr. Tan was an old family friend who had done Mr. Ni more than one good turn, the young student-turned-Red Guard was not there on a social matter.

"He accused me of dressing like a Westerner," explained Mr. Tan.

Dressing like a Westerner had been normal enough in Shanghai for decades. But by the mid-1960s, many people were wearing Mao suits and the political climate was so malevolently anti-foreign and anti-bourgeois that the once innocent act of wearing a three-piece suit could be construed as an unforgivable offense. In Shanghai and other cities, bands of young Red Guards roamed the streets with scissors, cutting up the clothes of anyone dressed too fashionably, snipping off the hair of women with permanents or men who used hair oil, and beating up any victim who resisted their actions.

Once Ni had made his initial accusation against his erstwhile family friend and mentor, other Red Guards from the Conservatory came in quick succession.

"The whole string class came in, and took my wife's diamond ring and my Rolex watch."

Most of Mr. Tan's valuables, including his violins, were taken away. However, the Red Guards evidently didn't feel like lugging all his books away, so they simply taped up the bookcase that held his precious collection of foreign-language novels and tomes about the violin. Back at the Conservatory, they posted malicious "big-character" posters that contained more accusations against him.

"They said I didn't make violins, I was lying. They said I was trying to destroy China's traditional music."

Criticisms even more damning than his sartorial style, violin-making ability, or musical tastes soon followed.

"Once there was a large meeting in a grand hall to criticize me — they grabbed my hair. They said I was a member of the Nationalist Party. They kneeled me down, they beat me. But I said I cannot confess to something I didn't do. They pushed me down the stairs, but I had to work the next day."

Before he knew it, Mr. Tan was locked up like a common criminal, his jail the Conservatory in which he had spent more than 17 years as a teacher and vice-president.

"For nine months I was confined in a closet under the stairs — a dark room, and it smelled bad. No lamp. I was allowed to come out sometimes to do some work or go to the toilet."

After nine months, the conditions of Mr. Tan's captivity improved slightly and he was allowed to work — but not as a musician.

"I had to go around and repair the toilets — 122 toilets. I used to go to the fifth floor toilet to try if I could see my home. I couldn't see it, but it was the right direction."

Although Mr. Tan's family lived only blocks away, he was not allowed to see them, except on one occasion when a Red Guard who was watching him let his daughter and grand-daughter visit for five minutes.

"My grand-daughter called me grandfather and when I heard this, I broke out in tears. We were treated like criminals, like animals, like prisoners. We weren't allowed to talk. So when I heard this, I cried. My daughter didn't say anything. I just told her, tell your mother I am fine. I could not say they beat me often."

Survival under such conditions was understandably difficult, but Mr. Tan sought solace wherever he could find it.

"I used to put my watch under my pillow. It was a very great comfort to listen to it."

He credited his ability to withstand the humiliation, loneliness, and pain largely to his love of his family and his faith in God.

"I just thought of my family. I wanted to see them again.... I never thought to commit suicide because I'm a Christian. I just thought, 'The sun will come out. It's night, but the sun will come out, eventually.'"

If the night was dark for Mr. Tan, it was even darker for many others at the Shanghai Conservatory. In the first terrible years of the Cultural Revolution, many Conservatory professors and their family members responded to the cruelty and abuse heaped upon them by resorting to the ultimate act of suicide.[10]

The first professor to end his life as a response to the Red Guards' abuse was Lu Xiutang, an *erhu* master in the traditional music department who killed himself on August 31, 1966. A week later, Yang Jiaren, the University of Michigan graduate who became head of the Shanghai Conservatory's conducting department, killed himself together with his wife, Cheng Juoru, who was the principle of the Conservatory's middle school.

Another three days passed and then the pianist Li Cuizhen killed herself. Ms. Li had moved to Hong Kong in the late 1950s, but He Luting and others at the Conservatory had written to invite her back and she once again decided to return.

"I am very attached to the conservatory, you know," she told a friend. "I was trained there and I have worked there. It is really the most important thing in my life apart from the children. Many of my colleagues were fellow students when we studied there together. They all wrote to me. My students wrote to me. The Party secretary wrote to me. Everybody said I was needed at the conservatory, so I came back."[11]

Ms. Li was praised for her decision to return, but her loyalty was forgotten when the Cultural Revolution began. Instead, she was accused of being a "counter-revolutionary academic authority" by Red Guards who tortured her both mentally and physically.

"They made her crawl on the ground, they covered her with ink, they made her call herself names," remembered Mr. Tan. "She had no political problems, only she

---

10. Some of this information comes from Chang Shuozong (chief ed.) (1997). *Shanghai Yinyue Xueyuan Da Shiji Mingren Lu* [A record of major events and famous people at the Shanghai Conservatory]. Shanghai: Shanghai Yinyue Xueyuan: 451-503. These pages contain brief summaries of the lives of renowned Conservatory professors who died before 1994, including those who committed suicide in the Cultural Revolution.

11. Quote is from Cheng, N. (1986). *Life and Death in Shanghai*. New York: Grove Press: 57. Cheng refers to Li Cuizhen as Li Zhen.

liked to wear Western clothes. One night she put on all her best clothes and make-up and wrote a note: 'I need a rest.' Then she turned on the gas."

These first suicides and double-suicides at the Conservatory were like the opening of a floodgate.

"One violin professor, Zhao Zhihua, killed himself with his wife," said Mr. Tan. "They had two children, 10 and 6, and they wrote a note to their daughter: 'In the morning, you won't have a mother or father. Take your brother to your grandmother.' Then they turned on the gas and killed themselves."

Mr. Zhao was the violinist who had studied in Austin and Boston. He was soon followed in death by a fellow violinist, Chen Youxin, who had headed the Conservatory's instrumental department and also been one of the first four Chinese musicians to officially join the SMO.

As the Cultural Revolution wore on, the suicides at the Conservatory piled up so rapidly that a sick gallows humor spread among professors, many of whom were no doubt themselves struggling against the impulse to end their earthly suffering.

"One professor couldn't stand the criticism and decided to hang himself," recalled Mr. Tan. "He got a rope and hanged himself but the rope was uncomfortable. So he went to get a towel to put over the rope — his wife saw him and stopped him. We heard about it and we all laughed — he didn't hang himself because it hurt his neck! But, later he did kill himself with sleeping pills. He couldn't do labor because he was sickly, so he had to write big-character posters. One day he wrote one character wrong and the guard in charge told him it was a big mistake, he'd better correct it. That night he killed himself."

By the time the first few years of the Cultural Revolution were over, 17 Conservatory professors, spouses and students had been driven to take their own lives.[12] Others, like middle school piano professor Wang Jiaen, died during imprisonment or forced labor, and still others because they were locked up and denied treatment for serious illnesses. Another early, double suicide in Shanghai that reverberated through music and intellectual circles around the country was that of Fu Lei and Zhu Meifu, the parents of the pianist Fu Cong. Fu Lei had been publicly criticized and declared a rightist back in 1957 and Fu Cong had been forced to return to China to participate in the rectification movement for overseas students. He apparently saw the writing on the wall and when he graduated from the Warsaw Conservatory the following year, he went to London and sought political asylum. This caused great consternation to Chinese government officials, although in the more enlightened months of the early 1960s parents and son were able to correspond, thanks to the intervention of Zhou Enlai and Chen Yi. Fu Cong was thus able to tell his

---

12. The number 17 comes from Tan Shuzhen. The composer Zhu Jianer puts the number at 18. *Shanghai Yinyue Xueyuan Da Shiji Mingren Lu* [A record of major events and famous people at the Shanghai Conservatory] lists 20 professors who died during the Cultural Revolution era, but some died from maltreatment or untreated illness rather than suicide.

parents when he married Zamira Menuhin, the daughter of violinist Yehudi Menuhin, and the delighted Fu Lei was even able to write to the Menuhin family.

However, when the Cultural Revolution began, Fu Lei and Zhu Meifu were fiercely persecuted from the start. Fu Lei seems already to have been in despair by the early summer of 1966, when he wrote in his last letter to his son. "Your mother is always optimistic and believes she will see you again some day. But I have already given up hope and I know I'll never meet you again."[13] In late August and early September, Red Guards from the Shanghai Conservatory searched their house for three days, looking for letters from Fu Cong, whom they viewed as a traitor. They then forced the sleep-deprived couple to stand on a bench in the doorway of their home wearing dunce caps. Fu Lei's premonition that he would never again see his son was made true on September 3, 1966, when his wife took poison and then hanged herself and he took poison and then sat at his desk to await death.[14] Fu Cong did not learn of his parents' joint suicide until November, when a French friend told him the tragic news.

Professors and established intellectuals like Fu Cong's parents were most likely to be criticized and tortured by the Conservatory's Red Guards, but students and recent graduates also sometimes fell victim. One such unfortunate was Wang Xilin, a troubled composer who graduated from the Shanghai Conservatory in 1962. By his own account, he ran into problems in 1963 because he objected to the policy of art serving politics.

"Symphonic music was supposed to serve politics, the ordinary people were supposed to understand it," explained Mr. Wang. "The atmosphere was terrible that year when I made a two-hour speech opposing 'nationalization' and 'mass-ization.' Of course they let me talk — this is the way the Communists do it. They let you talk, and then they crush you! It's always the same way. We didn't understand, when we were young — we just loved the Party."[15]

As punishment for voicing his unorthodox opinions, Mr. Wang was sent to perform labor in Shanxi province, where he was supposed to change his thinking.

"They wanted me to completely remold myself. I labored and read Mao Zedong's work — you can't understand. Whatever was dirtiest and most difficult, they wanted me to do. I couldn't handle it. The pressure was very great — I had a breakdown. I screamed all night. I was a rightist. At a big meeting, they all said I was so bad. 'Knock down Wang Xilin! Knock down Wang Xilin!' I felt like a rat on the street, everyone yelling to beat me. It was terrible. Struggle sessions were a great invention of the Communist Party. You had to stand there straight for a long time — six hours. Sweat poured off you and your legs shook till you would fall over. I was in a mental hospital for six months."

---

13. Fu Lei's words are as quoted by Fu Cong in Tan Aiqing (1980). The homecoming of pianist Fou Tsong. *China Reconstructs* May: 50.

14. Kraus: 93.

15. Sheila Melvin interviewed Wang Xilin twice at his Beijing home in April and July of 2000. All quotes are from these interviews.

When the Cultural Revolution actually began, Mr. Wang was locked up.

"We all slept on the floor. We were bad people, all in one room. We couldn't have contact with anyone. In the day, they struggled against us — and they hit our ears. My left ear still has problems. They hit you with the right hand, so the left ears got hurt the worst. My tooth was knocked out, too. I had to stand on a tiny stool — you couldn't fall off it. Everybody spat at you and hit you and shouted at you. They struggled against me for a long time."

The darkest moment of his travails came on October 28, 1968, when he was awoken around midnight.

"They called me out — they said, do you want to pee. Then they blindfolded me and put a towel in my mouth and tied my hands behind me. They made me walk to the countryside; we walked very far. There were two or three of them, my jailers — I couldn't see. Then they put me in a hole and started burying me. I thought they were going to bury me alive. Then they pulled me out — they were just trying to scare me. Then they dragged me to a room. I couldn't see anything. They said I had to answer truthfully. They pulled my pants down and hit me for two hours. I was so thirsty. The next day my skin was raw — my clothes stuck to it. But I had to go to work the next day. They had this all planned. Even after I was released, I still wasn't free. I decided to escape. But, how would I escape? So, then they took us around to all the villages and took turns struggling against us. There were 10 or 20 of us. This treatment — because we spoke the truth. I didn't steal anything, I didn't hurt anyone. This is when I started thinking about expressing all this in music."

Musicians who were singled out for abuse by Red Guards reacted to the similarly abysmal treatment accorded them in a variety of ways. Some, like Tan Shuzhen, found strength in God; some despaired and sought escape in death; some, like Wang Xilin, broke down under the mental and physical torture. But perhaps only one responded by fighting back with the same fierceness as his attackers' — He Luting.

Mr. He's old nemesis Yao Wenyuan had become one of Jiang Qing's closest affiliates after he wrote the editorial criticizing *Hai Rui* — a member of what would later be called the Gang of Four. He had neither forgotten his run-in with He Luting nor forgiven him for daring to defend Debussy. On the contrary, it seems he had merely been biding his time until he could take his revenge.[16]

Big-character posters criticizing Mr. He appeared at the Conservatory early on — he was a missionary for bourgeois liberalization, he tricked young people into following the heretical revisionist position, and so on. But on June 8, 1966, Mr. He knew the real trouble had begun when he and his wife heard on the radio that both *Liberation Daily* and *Wen Hui Bao* contained full page articles detailing how revolutionary faculty and students at the Conservatory had identified the anti-Party, anti-socialist element He Luting. Similar articles were published in the June 9 papers, and these were then re-published around the nation via the Xinhua News Agency. His

16. This account of He Luting's experiences is largely drawn on Shi Zhongxin (2000). *He Luting Zhuan* [A Biography of He Luting]. Shanghai: Shanghai Yinyue Chubanshe: 230-257.

"poisonous" attack on critics of Debussy was revisited and Shanghai Communist Party secretary Zhang Chunqiao — another of Jiang Qing's "Gang of Four" cohorts — labeled Mr. He's defense of Debussy the most serious counter-revolutionary incident prior to the Cultural Revolution. When enough articles had been published, they were collected and released as a book called *Collection of Articles Criticizing He Luting*.

Life became increasingly unpleasant for He Luting and his wife Jiang Ruizhi, who was principle of the Conservatory's elementary school. Mr. He's daughters were worried and confused, too, as were his friends and neighbors. When he went out on the street, people would spit at him and call him a counter-revolutionary monster. Red Guards ransacked their house, dragged Mr. He and his wife to a middle school classroom and forced the couple to kneel on desks while they beat them with belts. After the beating, they made Jiang Ruizhi kneel on the floor so they could chop off her hair, and then they ran away. The couple was just preparing to escape when the Red Guards returned to commit one last act of cruelty, dumping ink all over their heads and faces.

True to form, He Luting did not take any of this lying down. Instead, he went home and wrote "My First Big-Character Poster" and posted it at the Conservatory. On the poster, Mr. He called the accusations against him baseless and went on to refute many of them with specific evidence. It did no good, of course, and he soon found himself locked up. The next two years were an endless round of struggle and criticism which culminated in two massive struggle sessions which many Chinese intellectuals remember with awe to this day. [17]

The first was organized by the Shanghai Revolutionary Committee's command center for attacking He Luting and was held on March 13, 1968. It was unusual both because of the size of the crowd mustered to attend it and because Zhang Chunqiao had decided to use it as a pilot for his plan to broadcast major struggle sessions, live. Televised struggle sessions would be more humiliating for the victim and would also be a practical application of the old saying, "kill a chicken to scare the monkeys." So, all across Shanghai, work units gathered their employees together to watch the struggle against He Luting unfold on live TV.

The session began predictably, when Mr. He was dragged on stage by two big Red Guards and forced to bow his head and shoulders in a submissive manner while the assembled crowd shouted slogans: Knock Down the Anti-Communist KMT official He Luting! Knock down Chiang Kai-shek's running dog!

This was followed by a direct, inquisitorial dialogue designed to make Mr. He admit his guilt. But instead of showing fear and defeat, as he was supposed to, Mr. He straightened his shoulders and stared angrily ahead whenever the Red Guards relaxed their grip. Neither did he answer the questions posed him in the humble and contrite manner expected — instead, he publicly defended himself.

---

17. Xiao Ding and Xu Ying (1995). Bu pa yaomode ying gutou: Wenge chijian He Luting [Hard bones against the devil: He Luting in the Cultural Revolution]. Jiang Ruizhi (chief ed.), *Lun He Luting* [On He Luting]. Shanghai: Shanghai Yinyue Chubanshe: 74-82.

When asked why he had attacked the proletarian headquarters in 1963 — a reference to his defense of Debussy — he told his questioner that Yao Wenyuan was not right about everything. Another question referred to a statement Mr. He had reportedly made — that the Nationalist Party had attacked him, the Japanese had attacked him, and now the Red Guards were attacking him, too. Such language was clear heresy, since it put the Red Guards on the same level as the Japanese and the Nationalists, but Mr. He simply acknowledged that he had said it and added that it was true. The enraged Red Guard questioning him informed Mr. He that if he continued to behave this way, he would die. Mr. He replied that before he died, he had two requests — he wanted to finish his seven-section orchestra piece and he wanted to clear himself of all these false accusations against him.

Mr. He's defiant attitude was unheard of and was more than anyone on Shanghai's Revolutionary Committee could swallow. Within two weeks of the session, he was branded an active counter-revolutionary element, officially transferred to the custody of the city police and locked up in a real jail. At the same time, planning began for a second televised criticism session that would be so well organized it would be certain to break and humiliate the stubborn old musician. Investigators were sent everywhere He Luting had ever lived to gather "evidence" against him. To ensure that the session would go smoothly, several run-throughs were held.

By the end of April, the Revolutionary Committee was ready to try again and Mr. He was once more dragged into the glare of klieg lights before thousands of people shouting slogans. On this occasion, Zhang Chunqiao decided to oversee the live broadcast himself. He delegated the task of running the criticism session to Yu Huiyong.

Yu was a graduate of the Shanghai Conservatory who had gone on to become a professor of composition in its National Music department. He seems to have long felt slighted by his colleagues who taught Western classical music and over the years grew stridently leftist. By the early 1960s, he had come to Jiang Qing's attention and she gradually grew to depend on him for musical advice. At the time of the criticism session, Yu was leader of the Shanghai Conservatory's Revolutionary Committee and soon afterwards he was given the important job of heading Shanghai's Culture Bureau.

Yu Huiyong must have been eagerly awaiting the opportunity to humiliate his former boss, since he dug right in when He Luting was dragged out. As Mr. He listened to one spurious charge after another, he was startled to notice that his wife, two of his daughters and several nieces from Hunan (who had defended him to the investigators sent from Shanghai) were also on the stage. Only his middle daughter was missing, an absence which he thought odd — it would be years before he found out that she had killed herself after watching his first televised struggle session.

Trembling with rage at the sight of his family and the absurdity of the charges, Mr. He tried several times to grab the microphone out of Yu Huiyong's hand, but did not succeed. However, his chance to reply came during the culmination of the session, when Yu Huiyong demanded outright that he admit his guilt.[18]

"I am not guilty," replied Mr. He.

"You opposed Mao Zedong," countered Yu Huiyong.

"I sang the praises of Chairman Mao! At Yanan, I arranged *The East is Red* for a chorus. After liberation, I wrote songs like *Long Live the People's Leader* and *Chairman Mao Comes to Tiananmen.*"

"In Chairman Mao's 1956 meeting with music workers, how did you desperately oppose him, right to his face?"

"I already wrote this in my self-confession. When Chairman Mao talked about matters of tradition, I interrupted."

"How did you have the monstrous audacity to do that?" Yu Huiyong shouted. "You counter-revolutionary!"

"Your accusations are false!" He Luting shouted in response. "Shame on you for lying!"

At these words, a powerful Red Guard stepped forward and grabbed the microphone away — nobody ever dared to speak that way during a struggle session.

But before the surprised Red Guard could react, He Luting grabbed the microphone back.

"Shame on you for lying! Shame on you for lying!" he repeated over and over before the stunned live audience and a television audience that was no doubt equally shocked — and awed — by his brazen courage.

Yu Huiyong was wise enough to realize that it would be a mistake to punch the frail old man standing before him on live television, so he ordered the Red Guards to twist his arms. They twisted so hard that Mr. He collapsed on the stage in pain, but when they let go, he stood back up, and repeated his curse of shame in a voice choked with pain.

All the planning and preparation of Shanghai's top revolutionaries had once again failed to prevent the struggle session from flying out of their control. Up in the control booth, the live broadcast was cut off at the order of an angry Zhang Chunqiao, who also abandoned his plans for the live broadcast of future struggle sessions. Non-televised public struggle sessions against Mr. He continued and after each one he would go back to his cell and write an essay refuting whatever charges had been made against him. Meanwhile, in Shanghai and throughout the country, cowed intellectuals who had seen or heard of He Luting's courage took heart, inspired by the example of a man who maintained his integrity and sense of self-worth in this most nonsensical time.

The Shanghai Conservatory had the highest Cultural Revolution death toll of any musical institution in China, but musicians at the Shanghai Symphony naturally suffered, too. The pianist Gu Shengying had joined the orchestra in 1955 when she was 18 and had then gone on to become famous when she gave her prize-winning performances in Moscow and Geneva. But Ms. Gu came from an intellectual family — their home library had more than 20,000 volumes[19] — and her father had been a high

---

18. Dialogue from Shi: 255-6.
19. Kraus: 141.

level official in the Nationalist Party. In the anti-rightist campaign of 1957, he was declared a rightist and exiled to distant Qinghai Province. Given this family background and her own career as a classical musician, Ms. Gu was a natural target for Red Guards.

"They beat her. They made her kneel," remembered Tan Shuzhen.

According to Wen Tan, Ms. Gu herself was able to cope, but her mother was not.

"Her mother was so depressed," he explained. "She didn't leave the house. She didn't want to live."

On January 3, 1967, Ms. Gu, her mother, and her younger brother gathered together in their home and gassed themselves. Their husband and father did not learn of their deaths until years later, when he was allowed to return from exile.

Perhaps even more horrifying is the fate of Lu Hongen. Mr. Lu was originally a timpanist with the orchestra but in 1952 he was made assistant conductor and later promoted to resident conductor. He is said to have been a demanding musician who was outspoken with his opinions on music and other subjects. When the Cultural Revolution came, he continued to speak his mind and by some accounts had a mental breakdown. Whether due to genuine rage, mental distress, or both, one day in 1968 he took a copy of the "Little Red Book" and tore it to pieces. The "Little Red Book," known more formally as *Quotations from Chairman Mao*, was a pocket anthology of Mao's writings compiled by Lin Biao that was memorized by virtually everyone and treated as sacred. To destroy one was a crime considered so severe that Lu Hongen was shot in the head.

"Lu Hongen dared to speak. He was a Catholic," explained Wen Tan. "The Gang of Four wanted to secure their own positions so they wanted to kill a few people — kill a chicken to scare the monkeys."

TWO PATHS OF ESCAPE

The suffering of musicians in Shanghai was arguably the most extreme of anywhere in the nation — or at least it seems that way when measured in terms of their collective response. Shanghai was the birthplace of Western music in modern China. It had more musicians who had studied overseas or been taught by resident foreigners. The Shanghai Conservatory was headed by He Luting, who had for so many years gone head-to-head with leftist radicals who criticized the systematic teaching of Western music in China. And Shanghai, of course, was the city from which the Cultural Revolution itself was launched.

But Beijing's music world was also torn apart by Red Guards who routinely criticized, humiliated, and tortured their victims. They also fought against each other, with rival factions struggling to gain control of such places as the Central Conservatory and the Central Philharmonic, each proclaiming that it alone was loyal to Mao Zedong and his teachings. Most musicians who came under attack in this confusing, demoralizing and dehumanizing atmosphere simply tried to stay alive and keep sane. But, like He Luting, Central Conservatory president Ma Sicong took a different approach, one that shocked and amazed all who heard of it: he escaped China.

By the time the Cultural Revolution began, Ma Sicong was spending much of his time teaching and composing at home. So it was there, in his comfortable courtyard house, that he first learned about the new political movement from a student who showed up for a lesson without his violin and explained sadly that he would no longer be able to study.[20] Like so many other victims, Mr. Ma was at first reasonably sanguine about the news because he assumed he had little to fear. When some Conservatory students posted criticisms of him, he responded evenly by writing his own posters expressing warm support for the Cultural Revolution. However, a few days later, Mr. Ma was called to the Conservatory for a meeting and unexpectedly found himself surrounded by hundreds of students shouting, "Down with the stinking bourgeois experts!" and "Long live Mao Zedong!" When one student mistakenly cried, "Long live Ma Sicong!" the others turned on him. The scene was so absurd and had such a nightmarish quality that Mr. Ma could hardly believe it was real — but it was.

Within a few days Mr. Ma was informed that he was being sent for a prolonged period of "study training." Together with 16 colleagues and about 500 other members of China's arts and culture elite, he was locked up on the grounds of the Communist Party School — the same place where Matteo Ricci is buried — which was then serving as "a sort of concentration camp for intellectuals and prominent cultural figures."[21] The inmates were divided into military style groups for study and discussion, with spare time spent writing big-character posters. It was a tedious existence, but they were not badly treated by the soldiers who guarded them and Mr. Ma later thought this was actually President Liu Shaoqi's way of protecting them, before he himself was overthrown. However, about 50 days later, in the middle of August, a truck bearing the words "Reserved for Black Gang" was sent to pick up Mr. Ma and his colleagues and take them back to the Conservatory.

When they arrived, they were pushed out of the truck in front of an untold number of people who stood waiting to criticize them. Someone dumped a bucket of glue over Mr. Ma's head — the industrial glue used to stick big-character posters to the outside of buildings. Someone else affixed a dunce cap to his head that read "Ox-ghost and snake-demon" and hung a placard round his neck that said "Ma Sicong, agent of the bourgeois opposition." Still others began to paste random big-character posters and insulting slogans to his hat and person, like one that read "blood-sucking ghost." He was then handed a pot and a stick and ordered to march around the campus banging on it while erstwhile students and other "revolutionaries" hurled abuse at him and spat in his face.

Mr. Ma's colleague, Zhao Feng, who was vice president of the Conservatory, fared even worse — he was made to don a sheep skin coat in the brutal August heat,

---

20. This account of Ma Sicong's sufferings during the Cultural Revolution is drawn from Ma Sicong (1967). Cruelty and insanity made me a fugitive. *Life Magazine*, June 2.

21. Ma: 27.

with the wool worn outside to demonstrate that he was a wolf in sheep's clothing. Liu Shikun, the renowned pianist who had placed second in the 1958 Tchaikovsky International Piano Competition, was also included in the group; Liu had married the daughter of Ye Jianying, the general who bought the instruments for the Yanan Central Orchestra, in 1962 but since Ye himself had many problems during the Cultural Revolution, he was not able to protect his son-in-law. Red Guards would soon twist his wrists with the aim of preventing him from ever playing the piano again. When the day was over, Ma Sicong and the others were locked in a low building that had once been used to store pianos. One side of Mr. Ma's small room was all glass, so passersby could see him at any time — he was told that since he was an animal, he would be displayed and treated as such.

Every morning, Mr. Ma and his fallen colleagues were woken up at 6:00 AM and forced to read Mao's *Selected Works* or important newspaper editorials. From 8:00 AM until noon, they cleaned toilets, moved piles of rocks, or chopped firewood, and in the afternoon composed self-criticisms. Each morning and evening they were also required to sing *The Howling Song*, which went like this:

> I am an ox-ghost and snake demon.
> I am an ox-ghost and snake-demon.
> I am guilty, I am guilty.
> I committed crimes against the people,
> So the people take me as the object of dictatorship.
> I have to lower my head and admit to my guilt.
> I must be obedient.
> I am not allowed to speak or act without permission.
> If I speak or act without permission,
> May you beat me and smash me.
> Beat me and smash me. [22]

The rest of each day brought different tortures. Sometimes they were forced to hang their heads and crawl on the floor like animals, sometimes they were ordered to stand facing a wall for hours on end, and sometimes a Red Guard would come in and up-end everything in their rooms. One night Mr. Ma had just laid down to sleep when two Red Guards, a young man and a young woman, entered his room and told him to get up. The young man took off the brass-buckled belt which was a standard part of the Red Guards' military-style uniform — and a favored instrument of torture — and

---

22. The Chinese version of this song can be found in Luo Junjun (2001). *Li Delun Zhuan* [A Biography of Li Delun]. Beijing: Zuojia Chubanshe: 379. This English translation is taken from Wang Youqin. *Student attacks against teachers: the revolution of 1966.* Humanities.uchicago.edu/faculty/ywang/history/1966teacher.htm.

Interestingly, Wang notes that, of the many teachers he interviewed who were regularly forced to sing this song, none of them could remember all the words. Ma Sicong gives a shorter version of the song in his *Life Magazine* article and calls it *The Howl of the Black Gangsters*. He also notes that the song ends on the seventh note with a crescendo, to make it sound ugly.

began beating Mr. Ma with it mercilessly while the young woman slapped him in the face and spat at him.

Other incidents of random torture were not even mentioned by Mr. Ma in an account he wrote of this terrible time, but were later recalled by Zhao Feng and Liu Shikun: the time when a flute player whom Mr. Ma knew threatened to kill him with a knife; the time a Red Guard beat Mr. Ma's shaved head with a board full of nails; the time a revolutionary worker forced him to bend down and eat grass, since the surname "Ma" also means "horse."[23]

August of 1966 was the worst month for many artists and intellectuals, with September a close second. When the initial insanity waned a bit, Mr. Ma was left to his own resources much of the time and was allowed to spend nights and weekends at home. But this was a less attractive arrangement than it sounds, since his family had fled Beijing because of Red Guard attacks and was still on the run in southern China. Nearly everything he owned had been confiscated or destroyed, except for 14 unpublished scores secreted with friends and the treasured 18th-century Gamiu violin which was hidden at his chef's home. And even though his family and belongings were gone, his house was not empty — two families had moved in and 60 Red Guards were also staying there.

Unable to bear her father's suffering — which included several suicide attempts — Mr. Ma's daughter, Ma Ruixue, took matters into her own hands.[24] With the help of relatives, she put together a bold and dangerous plan to flee China. In November of 1966, she came back to Beijing and with the assistance of the family chef, Jia Junshan, managed to meet her father and tell him of her plan. Mr. Ma did not want to flee his own country. Up until the Cultural Revolution, he had been on friendly terms with both Zhou Enlai and Mao Zedong. He had been well-respected and well-treated and he had held many high-level political and professional positions. However, his current existence was increasingly unbearable to him and in the end his daughter persuaded him that he could just leave for a short rest, and then return.

To carry out the secret plan, Mr. Ma got a sick note from his doctor that entitled him to a week's rest and then disguised himself as a worker, the big bag of tools he carried serving to hide his precious violin. His daughter dressed in the uniform of a Red Guard and together they took a train south to Guangzhou, where his wife and son awaited them; a third daughter, who was married with children, chose to remain in Beijing. In the area of Guangzhou, they made contact with a shadowy man known to them as Doghead who specialized in smuggling people to Hong Kong by boat. For the

---

23. For these accounts, see Ye Yonglie (2000). *Ma Sicong Zhuan. Aiguode panguozhe* [A biography of Ma Sicong, patriotic traitor]. Urumqi: Xinjiang Chubanshe: 209.

24. For an account of the Ma family escape written by his daughter, see Mai Zi and Ma Ruixue (eds.) (2002). *Ma Sicong Zui Hou Ershi Nian* [Sitson Ma's Last 20 Years]. Guangzhou: Guangdong Renmin Chubanshe. This section is also supplemented with information from Ye Yonglie (2000). *Ma Sicong Zhuan. Aiguode panguozhe* [A biography of Ma Sicong, patriotic traitor]. Urumqi: Xinjiang Chubanshe. For obvious reasons, Mr. Ma does not provide any names in his own account of his escape and the details he offers are sketchy.

astronomical sum of 50,000 Hong Kong dollars, he agreed to get the four family members out of China and into Hong Kong.

After several weeks spent hiding at various locations in Guangdong Province and more than one aborted start to the journey, Ma Sicong and his family clambered into a rowboat in the dead of night. It took them to a small, motorized vessel that held a total of 13 people. The boat was so overloaded that the only luggage they were permitted to bring was Mr. Ma's violin. Even so, the cabin was too crowded; he and his family had to lie out on the stern to help balance the load.

Waves splashed across them throughout the harrowing night-long journey across the sea that separated China from Hong Kong and the freedom and sanity it represented. There were a few close calls with search lights, but no patrol boats spotted them and by dawn they had reached a rocky shore. Groping his way to the top of a slippery boulder, still grasping his violin, Mr. Ma took off the little badge bearing Mao Zedong's image that was then worn by everyone in China and tossed it into the sea.

Once the Ma family had made it safely to the home of a relative, late that evening, events moved quickly.[25] The next morning, January 17, the relative went to the US Consulate to ask that Ma Sicong and his family be granted asylum in America. Soon thereafter, the British consul and a deputy American consul came to interview them. They had many questions, and came back on each of the two following days. However, by the third day all the Hong Kong newspapers were headlined with news of Ma's escape and the consular officials announced that they had already contacted President Johnson — it was time to leave for the United States. The entire family was brought to the US consulate for haircuts, new clothes, and travel documents, which gave them the surname Li. They were transferred to CIA custody and given first class tickets on a plane bound for Washington.

Because Britain feared that Communist Party operatives would organize riots in Hong Kong if word of Ma Sicong's asylum were announced, the family's arrival in the US was kept secret for several months. When it was finally revealed, there were riots in Hong Kong anyway, and a frenzy in the US press. Dong Guangguang, Ma Sicong's sister-in-law, recalled the press conference that he gave from their house in New York in April of 1967.

"You should have seen it, the reporters coming by bicycle and motorcycle, so many people at 12:00. And the reporters kept saying 'Mao Zedong' instead of "Ma Sicong' — Mao Zedong has escaped from China! My husband kept correcting them."

Many international publications covered the defection of the French-educated violinist and composer and *Life* magazine ran a first person account by Mr. Ma, called "Cruelty and Insanity Made Me a Fugitive."

---

25. This account of Ma's experiences in Hong Kong draws on an essay by his daughter, Ma Ruixue: *Weijiliya de shenmi xiaowu* [The secret little house in Virginia]. Mai Zi and Ma Ruixue (eds.) (2002). *Ma Sicong Zui Hou Ershi Nian* [Sitson Ma's Last 20 Years]. Guangzhou: Guangdong Renmin Chubanshe: 50-63.

However, if Ma Sicong's immediate troubles were over, they were only beginning for many of those he left behind. His *Life* magazine article was translated into Chinese, published in Red Guard newspapers, and spread around the country. Red Guards from the Central Conservatory marched to Beijing's foreign embassy district in direct defiance of orders from Zhou Enlai and burned a straw effigy of Ma holding a violin in one hand and a record in the other. The Ministry of State Security labeled his disappearance "Special Case 002," after the number of the boat in which he was thought to have fled. The Central Conservatory's Red Guards then began to hunt down everyone who had contributed to this audacious escape. In the end, they collected "evidence" — whether real or created — against more than 50 members of the extended family and its associates, many of whom had no idea that the Ma family was planning to escape China. [26]

The first person to be arrested was Jia Junshan, the family chef who had helped Mr. Ma and his daughter to rendezvous. He was arrested in June, although the only "evidence" the Red Guards managed to collect against him was a dinner menu for the Ma family. There was never a charge, a trial or a verdict, but he was jailed for four years, until he had a stroke and was released to the care of his family, still technically a prisoner until his death in 1978. The next to be arrested were Ma Sicong's brother-in-law and his wife, who had helped Mr. Ma's daughter to contact Doghead. Another brother-in-law was sentenced to five years in jail and six years at hard labor for allegedly helping with the escape strategy. With both brothers jailed, there was nobody to care for Mr. Ma's mother-in-law, and she died.

Mr. Ma's own brother, Ma Siqi — the one who had first taken him to France — had known nothing about the escape plan, but was implicated because his sister-in-law and niece came to Shanghai and had lunch with him while they were on the run from Red Guards. Ma Siqi was poor and seriously ill. When the Red Guards came to search his house for evidence, they found that he and his wife used cut up squares of newspaper as toilet paper. Although many families did this, the finding was used as further evidence of his crimes — the paper could have had Mao's name or image on it. Ma Siqi and his wife lived under surveillance for three years, but their children did not fare so well. Their 30-year-old daughter was detained as an active counter-revolutionary and was so upset at the prospect of being jailed that she had a heart attack and died, right in the Public Security Bureau office. One of their sons was sentenced to 12 years in jail and another — who was in middle school at the time — was sentenced to nine years.

Ma Sicong's second older brother, Ma Siwu, had also been in France with Mr. Ma as a youth. While there, he had fallen in love with his French landlord's daughter, married her, and returned with her to Shanghai, where he became a university French professor. Since his wife spoke no Chinese and they had no children, they lived a very

---

26. This account of what happened to Ma Sicong's relatives and friends back in China is drawn entirely from Ye: 286-299.

private life. Neighbors remembered them walking their dog together every evening, his wife beautifully dressed and wearing high heels in pre-Cultural Revolution years.

Ma Siwu had known nothing of the escape plan and had not seen his brother or his sister-in-law for some time. Since there was no evidence against him, he was left alone — until early 1968, when Ma Sicong was convicted of treason *in absentia*. After that, Red Guards began putting up big-character posters that called Ma Sicong a traitor and accused Ma Siwu of having planned the entire escape. As the months passed, more posters went up, with more detailed — and entirely fabricated — allegations. When Red Guards asked Ma Siwu for his response, he simply replied that there was nothing he could say. Then, on July 10, 1968, he came home quite late from work and took one last walk with his wife. The next morning, he kissed her goodbye, went to his office — and jumped off the roof of the building. Upon hearing the news, Ma Siwu's wife screamed with such anguish that all the neighbors came running, though there was little comfort they could offer. After obtaining the Chinese government's permission to leave — she was by then a Chinese citizen — she sold all her belongings and returned to France, carrying her husband's ashes. All of her own family had died except for one sister, and she herself soon died of grief and loneliness.

The litany of Red Guard-inflicted tragedies that followed in the wake of the Ma family's departure goes on — even the doctor who wrote him the sick note was sentenced to 8 years in jail, though he knew nothing of the plan to escape. By the time the investigation was complete, people had been arrested or investigated in Beijing, Shanghai, Nanjing and around Guangdong Province — everywhere one of the family members had visited on their long journey away from China. Though Ma, his wife and two of their children were safe in the US — and the third daughter miraculously escaped persecution in Beijing — this was the legacy of their departure with which they would have to live for the rest of their lives.

Li Delun's Cultural Revolution experience was not so dramatic as Ma Sicong's, although it began in much the same way and also had a surprise ending. The start of the movement was a time of intense mental confusion for Mr. Li, as he found himself branded a "black element" and essentially came to believe in his own guilt. Ordered by some of his erstwhile colleagues — now self-proclaimed revolutionary leftists — to write confessions regarding his various bourgeois crimes, Mr. Li willingly complied. Cooperation, however, did little good and the Philharmonic's offices were soon full of big-character posters criticizing him, some of them even written in desperation by his own children. Members of the Philharmonic's Cultural Revolution work group repeatedly searched his house for evidence against him, confiscating such random proof of his "guilt" as two ornamental knives from Helsinki, two of his daughter's dolls, and a book in which his checkered family history was recorded. He was forced to get rid of his much-loved cat, since keeping a pet was one of his bourgeois crimes, and a photo of himself with Oistrakh on which the Soviet violinist had written many kind words was burnt. His wife, Li Jue, also came under attack and she was locked up by Red Guards from the Central Ballet.

Inevitably, Mr. Li was declared a member of the so-called "black gang" of reactionary or bourgeois authorities. He was locked up with 18 other alleged black gang members in a "cowshed," actually an apartment just across from his own. For the next few months, their daily life consisted of writing confessions, attending criticism sessions directed at them, and toiling alongside construction workers. They slept, ate, and labored together like a chain gang; passing students would spit and throw rocks at them when they walked to get their food.

After a few months, Mr. Li and his other black gang colleagues were allowed to return home. Since the orchestra was not functioning, Mr. Li had nothing to do but walk around Beijing reading the big-character posters plastered everywhere. When he had read all those within walking distance, he bought a bike and rode out to the universities, where the posters were most extreme. Reading the posters that disfigured the city did not help him achieve his goal of understanding the Cultural Revolution any better, but it did make him a better bike rider — distances that used to take him forty minutes to cover now took only twenty.

Indeed, as he rode around the city, Mr. Li found himself gradually becoming more interested in bicycles than politics. He would spend hours a day just watching them go by and soon he started hanging out at a local bike repair shop. Since it was widely rumored that no artist would ever be able to work professionally again, it occurred to Mr. Li that bicycle repair could be a good way to support his family in the future. He began helping out at the shop and when he went home he would take his own bike apart and put it back together, over and over. He wandered around the wholesale markets, and even bought a used Phillips bike for the considerable sum of 90 yuan. Soon, he could tell the make of any bike at a glance, and even knew what kind of steel had been used in its manufacture.

After a full day of watching and tinkering with bikes, Mr. Li would buy vegetables and go home to cook dinner for his children. His wife was still locked up at the Central Ballet, and was only allowed home on Saturdays. On Saturday nights he would prepare an extra-special meal and the family would all gather round and wait for her return — these few nights eating together as a family were the moments for which he lived.

Mr. Li's new life of fixing bicycles and aimlessly roaming the city looked set to continue indefinitely until suddenly, on April 20, 1967, he found himself plucked from this surreal existence in the same incomprehensible manner that he had been thrust into it. On that day, a radical editorial writer named Qi Benyu who was then in Jiang Qing's good graces stopped by the Central Philharmonic and inquired about Li Delun.

"Every time I see him rehearse and perform, he's always covered in sweat," said Mr. Qi. "He shouldn't be 'black gang.'"[27]

With these few words Mr. Li was set on the path to exoneration and could again look forward to a future in which he was a musician, rather than a bicycle repair man. He was happy about this change in his status, but he was also confused — why should

---

27. Luo: 387.

the fact that he sweated when he conducted redeem him of his supposed counter-revolutionary crimes? He did not have long to wonder because just weeks later he learned the answer — Jiang Qing needed him. Or, more to the point, she needed his skills as a conductor and a musician.

JIANG QING AND MODEL OPERAS

It is generally the destructive aspects of the Cultural Revolution that are discussed whenever the era is mentioned. This is understandable, even proper, because so many innocent people suffered and died for no justifiable reason and because such vast damage was inflicted upon China's cultural heritage. But, the stated intent of the Cultural Revolution — however poorly realized — was not simply to destroy, but also to create.

Because Chairman Mao had taught that, "Without destruction, there can be no construction," the destruction came first. But, the *quid pro quo* of smashing the "four olds" was building the "four news," which encompassed the creation of a new proletarian culture. This new, government-mandated culture was to include a transformed, proletarian version of many art forms, but its most significant realization was in music because this was the area in which Jiang Qing concentrated her energies and political ambitions.

The start of Jiang Qing's involvement in efforts to reform and revolutionize music and musical theater pre-dated the Cultural Revolution by several years. In fact, her very first public speech in all her years as Chairman Mao's wife was given at the 1964 Festival of Peking Opera on Contemporary Themes. "Our operatic stage," she told the assembled actors,

> ...is occupied by emperors and kings, generals and ministers, scholars and beauties, and, on top of these, ghosts and monsters! It is our view that opera on revolutionary contemporary themes must reflect real life in the fifteen years since the founding of our Chinese People's Republic, and that images of contemporary revolutionary heroes must be created on our operatic stage. This is our foremost task.[28]

Other radicals were of the same opinion and several such operas had already been produced and were showcased at the festival. Three in particular caught Jiang Qing's attention: *The Red Lantern*, *Shajiabang*, and *Taking Tiger Mountain by Strategy*.

The Red Lantern was a Peking opera adaptation of a Shanghai local opera that was based on a film called *There Will Always Be Successors to the Cause*.[29] It tells the story of a revolutionary railway worker named Li Yuhe and his mother and daughter, who are

---

28. Jiang Qing (1967). On the Revolution in Peking Opera — Speech Made in July 1964 at Forum of Theatrical Workers Participating in the Festival of Peking Operas on Contemporary Themes. *Chinese Literature* 8: 119-120.

29. See Wan Kung (1977). How our revolutionary operas and ballets were produced" *Chinese Literature* 6: 68.

actually related to him by common politics rather than blood. They use a red lantern to communicate with other revolutionaries in a Japanese-occupied town and when Li Yuhe and his mother are tortured to death, the young girl carries on and successfully delivers a secret code to fellow guerillas.

Shajiabang was also based on a Shanghai local opera, called *Sparks Among the Reeds*. Jiang Qing happened to see it during one of her stays in Shanghai and liked it well enough to bring the script back to Beijing and give it to the Number One Peking Opera Company with the suggestion that they re-mount it as Peking opera. Her idea was, of course, accepted and the opera was produced in time for the Festival; its name was changed to *Shajiabang* by Chairman Mao himself when he saw it that July.

Like *The Red Lantern*, Shajiabang takes place during the war against Japan. It is set in a lakeside village outside Shanghai called Shajiabang, where 18 soldiers from the Communist Party's New Fourth Army have gone to recover from wounds received while fighting the Japanese. When the Japanese come to attack, the villagers hide the Communist soldiers in the lake — they breathe through reeds — and together the soldiers and villagers repel the enemy.

Taking Tiger Mountain by Strategy also came from Shanghai, where the Shanghai Peking Opera Company adapted it from a movie that was itself based on a novel called *Tracks in the Snowy Forest*. It is set after the victory against Japan, during the last years of the civil war. A gang of bandits made up of former Nationalist soldiers have entrenched themselves on Tiger Mountain and are terrorizing the local community. The People's Liberation Army arrives to organize resistance to the bandits; a heroic scout platoon leader named Yang Zirong disguises himself as a bandit and enters the enemy's fort. His bravery and cunning enable the PLA to defeat the bandits and all the locals are won over to the Communist cause.

The leftist winds that produced these revolutionary Peking operas affected all the arts alike, even including ballet. Because it was seen as so thoroughly bourgeois, the effort to adapt the vocabulary of classical ballet — "which can at best express despair, sorrow, debauchery and madness, the neurotic psychology of the dying exploiter classes"[30] — and make it "express the soaring, confident and militant spirit of the proletariat"[31] was widely hailed. Again, Jiang Qing supported and even cultivated these efforts early on, believing them to be important examples of the practical application of Mao's dictums, "Make the past serve the present and make foreign things serve China" and "Weed through the old to bring forth the new." The two ballets with which she was most closely involved were *The White-Haired Girl* and *The Red Detachment of Women*, both first performed in 1964.

Like so many of these early revolutionary productions, *The White-Haired Girl* originated in Shanghai but was based on earlier work, in this case the Yanan-era opera of the same name. In the years since, the opera had been revised, re-made as a play and filmed several times. It had even been produced as a ballet in Japan and was performed

---

30. (1970). A revolution in ballet. *China Reconstructs*, October: 10.
31. *Ibid.*

in Beijing by a Japanese company on two occasions, in 1957 and in the early 1960s. The Chinese version of the ballet came out of the Shanghai Dance School.

The Red Detachment of Women evolved from an opera that was first performed on the southern island of Hainan in 1959 and then made into a film which won a prize at an international film festival in Moscow in 1961. As with *Shajiabang*, it was Jiang Qing who brought the story idea to Beijing and suggested that it be adapted, in this case by the Central Ballet of China. The ballet has two main heroic characters, the male Communist cadre Hong Changqing and the female worker Wu Qinghua who together establish an all-women's armed detachment to fight the Nationalists in the 1930s. As a Cultural Revolution-era description puts it,

> Hong Changqing is a fine political cadre and representative of the people's army built and led by Chairman Mao, a Communist armed with Mao Zedong Thought. He firmly follows Chairman Mao's teaching that "political power grows out of the barrel of a gun" and carries out and defends Chairman Mao's proletarian revolutionary line. That is, with Mao Zedong Thought he guides the enslaved people's anger and hatred against the landlord class onto the revolutionary road to destroy the old world and emancipate mankind. On the battlefield he is a fearless commander and fighter who is not afraid of hardship or death. On the enemy's execution ground he is a towering proletarian hero who says, "I'm not afraid to have my head cut off, for I know communism is the truth." Hong Changqing crystallizes the qualities of the proletariat, the people's army, and the Communists.[32]

To create a ballet that could convincingly convey the idea that "political power grows out of the barrel of a gun," choreographers borrowed liberally from Peking opera, folk dance and acrobatics. They nixed romantic *pas de deux* in favor of furious group dances by rifle-toting ballerinas dressed in army uniforms and passionate, athletic solo performances in which the female lead expresses "her flaming hatred for the oppressors and her touching identification with the oppressed."[33] The ballet's composers, Wu Zuqiang and Du Mingxin, also trolled widely, and

> ...did not let themselves be restricted by the makeup of the western orchestra but used the percussion and other traditional musical instruments of Peking Opera. The bold combination of the western orchestra's range of sound and volume with lively national color enriches the music's power of expression and gives it a unique style popular with the workers, peasants and soldiers.[34]

"Clarity" and "simplicity" were the guiding precepts for the theme melodies which were played whenever the heroes appeared, with clarity meaning that the melody must convey the heroes' most noble characteristics and simplicity meaning that the music should be easily understood and remembered, as well as be suitable for dancing.[35]

---

32. *Ibid.*, 9-10.
33. *Ibid.*, 13.
34. *Ibid.*, 16.

When the ballet was performed in Beijing in 1964, the accolades were loud. Among the praise-givers was Chairman Mao himself, who said of it, "The orientation is correct, the revolutionization successful, and the artistic quality good."[36] Jiang Qing was subsequently lauded for having "successfully stormed the most stubborn fortress of art till then so tightly controlled by the Western bourgeoisie.... The choice of the ballet as a first target of attack in carrying out the policy of 'making foreign things serve China' is actually a significant beginning in the remoulding of the world's theatrical stage with the thought of Mao Zedong."[37]

Once the Cultural Revolution started and the bureaucratic ranks were purged of those who opposed her, Jiang Qing was able to focus on further revising and developing these pet musical projects that had begun to premiere in 1964. The revisions were arduous — sometimes lasting years — and Jiang Qing apparently involved herself with the smallest details, as this 1968 account of her work with the creators of *The Red Lantern* indicates:

> Day and night, Comrade Jiang Qing fought by our side. We shall never forget her selfless labor for the revolution, her serious earnest attitude towards the arts, her meticulous revolutionary spirit. In staging *The Red Lantern* she checked and planned everything carefully — from selecting the script to every detail of the story, every gesture, every aria, every line sung, as well as lights, scenery and make-up. She even discussed with us where the patches should be placed on the grandmother's clothes and where to buy the brightest shade of red woolen thread binding the girls' braids.
>
> Comrade Jiang Qing frequently came to our rehearsals and gave specific directions. At one dress rehearsal she went backstage and gave several important instructions on the make-up of Li Yuhe. After the necessary changes were made, just before he went on stage, she checked him again. Only when she was satisfied that his make-up was correct did she let him make his entrance.
>
> In the execution scene, Li defies the Japanese chief of military police with these words: "You can't kill all the Chinese people, all the Chinese Communists. I advise you to think it over." Comrade Jiang Qing wanted Li to concentrate all his furious hatred for imperialism in the second "you." She studied enunciation carefully herself and read the word for the actor several times to show him how it should be done.
>
> I remember one dress rehearsal in 1964. Comrade Jiang Qing pointed out that in the scene, "Bitter History of a Revolutionary Family," a line in an aria sung by the grandmother — "Li Yuhe dodged and hid with the orphan he saved" — was damaging to the image of a revolutionary hero and must be changed. We never expected that at two in the morning we would receive a telephone call from Comrade Jiang Qing. She had thought of how to change the line. Make it: "Li Yuhe

35. *Ibid.*, 13.
36. *Ibid.*, 9.
37. Wu Xiaoqing (1969). A great victory in 'making foreign things serve China. *Chinese Literature* 5: 80.

dashed about for the revolution," she suggested. What a world of difference in those few words! They raised the entire level of Li Yuhe's thoughts and emotions.[38]

Li Delun experienced Jiang Qing's "meticulous revolutionary spirit" firsthand once she decided to use him for her projects. For instance, after *The Red Detachment of Women* had been performed numerous times, Jiang Qing suddenly decided that the introduction of the ballet was not bold enough and did not adequately reflect the main character's heroism. She asked Li Delun to lead a composers' group tasked with changing it and suggested as models three pieces of foreign music: Sarasate's *Zigeunerweisen*, or *Gypsy Airs*; Brahms' *Hungarian Dance No. 5*, and Aaron Copland's theme song for the film version of Steinbeck's novel, *The Red Pony*. Part of the process of creating a new theme involved watching foreign movies, and since *The Red Pony* was one of Jiang Qing's favorites, she and the group watched it time and again, often with Mr. Li serving as translator. This work was all done on Jiang Qing's schedule and she would frequently call Li Delun and other musicians to her offices in the middle of the night.

"We had meetings every night: this part isn't right, that part isn't right," recalled Mr. Li. "I'd fall asleep. She'd call me, LI DELUN! I'd wake up and say, 'Chairman Mao said it's alright to sleep during meetings.' He did say that, and then she couldn't criticize me!"

By mid-1966, Jiang Qing's pet productions — which also included a symphonic work based on *Shajiabang* — were already referred to as "model revolutionary theatrical works," "model revolutionary operas," or, more simply, "model operas."[39] Then, on May 31, 1967 her efforts in creating these model operas were officially acknowledged by a *People's Daily* editorial which declared:

> Holding high the great red banner of Mao Zedong Thought, Comrade Jiang Qing has advanced bravely to participate in this performing arts revolution. She has created, for the first time in history, eight shining-star models for Peking opera, ballet and symphonic music. She has captured the most stubborn citadel of theater arts, Peking opera; surmounted the highest peak of performing arts, ballet; and that of the most sacred "pure music," symphony.[40]

The "eight shining-star models" included five Peking operas — *The Red Lantern*, *Shajiabang*, *Taking Tiger Mountain By Strategy*, *On the Docks* and *Raid on White Tiger Regiment*; two ballets, *The Red Detachment of Women* and *The White-Haired Girl*; and the *Revolutionary Symphonic Music "Shajiabang"*.[41] All underwent lengthy revisions overseen by Jiang Qing and her colleagues and came to share certain key characteristics designed to "inspire

---

38. Wen Wei-ching (1968). The course of a militant struggle. *Chinese Literature* 12: 103-4.

39. The term "model" in association with these revolutionary operas first appeared in a *Liberation Daily* article of March 16, 1965, entitled "Seriously Study the Peking Opera *The Red Lantern*." It contained the sentence, "This is an outstanding model of the revolutionization of Peking opera." See Ming Yan (2002). *Ershishiji Zhongguo Yinyue Piping Daolun* [A Guide to 20th-Century Music Criticism in China]. Beijing: Renmin Yinyue Chubanshe: 312.

40. See Melvin, Sheila and Cai, Jindong (2000). Why this nostalgia for fruits of chaos? *The New York Times* (Arts and Leisure) October 29.

men to struggle... [to] make hatred of oppression shine through the tears in the audience's eyes." [42]

The shared characteristics included plots that tended to be stilted and propagandistic. Sentimentality of any sort — even to the extent of having characters who were related to each other by marriage or birth — was not permitted. If the absence of family bonds, romantic love, and the fear of such things as torture and death seemed unrealistic, this was of no matter. Indeed, Chairman Mao himself had said that, "life as reflected in works of literature and art can and ought to be on a higher plane, more intense, more concentrated, more typical, nearer the ideal, and therefore more universal than everyday life." [43]

Since Mao had said that art was supposed to reflect the real lives of the people but was also supposed to be nearer the ideal than ordinary life, the model operas combined "revolutionary realism" with "revolutionary romanticism." [44] In practical terms, this meant that they were dominated by heroic characters who were portrayed as utterly flawless, fearless, and selfless. [45] Every tool of the production was used to underline their heroic nature — pleasing vocal notes, graceful movements, flattering make-up, gentle lighting, even the placement of the heroes' names at the top of the programs. By contrast, the heroes' enemies — be they Japanese, Nationalists, landlords, or the bourgeoisie — had no redeeming characteristics whatsoever. To underline their evil nature, they were made to act like buffoons, to sing the least pleasing arias, to dance the most ungraceful parts. Even when alone on-stage, the villains stood off center in poor lighting and, in film versions of the operas, they were shown in lighting so shadowy it was virtually black and white. Their names were printed at the bottom of the program, separated by several inches from those of the heroic characters and the actors who played these roles were the last to take a bow, which in any case was generally met by catcalls and boos.

The music of the model operas also shared common traits, despite the different genres. One of these was composition by group and another, interestingly enough, was the use of Western instruments. Jiang Qing had attended an experimental art school as a young girl and been introduced to Western instruments and some Western music.

---

41. More revolutionary theatrical works were created and tested throughout the Cultural Revolution. Some of these attained the status of "model opera" and some did not.

42. Hung Yu (1965). Ah Chia on "The Red Lantern." *Chinese Literature* 5: 101.

43. See *Liberation Army Daily* Editorial, April 18, 1966 (1966). Hold high the great Red Banner of Mao Zedong's Thought and Actively Participate in the Great Socialist Cultural Revolution. *Chinese Literature* 7: 11.

44. *Ibid.*

45. The concept of the heroic character was such an obsession with Jiang Qing that a formula known as the "three prominences" or "three emphases" was developed to summarize it. These "three emphases" of plot development were that positive characters had to be emphasized; among the positive characters, heroic characters had to be emphasized; and among heroic characters, the main hero had to be emphasized. See (1974). Model Revolutionary Theatrical Works Future Popularized and Developed. *Chinese Literature* 8: 101 and Mittler, B. (1997). *Dangerous Tunes: The Politics of Chinese Music in Hong Kong, Taiwan, and the People's Republic of China since 1949.* Wiesbaden: Harrassowitz Verlag: 85.

She even studied piano, but stopped after three months because she disliked her teacher's habit of hitting her wrists with sticks when she got the tempo wrong.[46] This seems to have been the limit of her studies, until the early 1960s when she tried to teach herself to read music. In the eyes of musicians like Li Delun, her knowledge of Western music was not worth mentioning.

"She couldn't understand anything," Mr. Li said dismissively of his musical work with her. "She couldn't understand a fart! All she could do is pick the colors of the costumes: 'That green isn't right.'"

However, if she was no expert on Western instruments or music, she still had opinions which only became stronger as time went on.

Some of these were particularly silly. On one occasion, she told Li Delun that she didn't like trombones and did not want them played anymore. Mr. Li could not envision his orchestra without trombones, so he hurriedly responded that it must have been the tuba whose sound she so disliked. His fast thinking saved the trombones, but caused the tuba to disappear from China's orchestras for the remainder of the Cultural Revolution. Later, Jiang Qing again tried to ban the trombone, but Mr. Li persuaded her to let him keep two.

More fundamentally, like many before her, she apparently became convinced that Western instruments in general were superior to Chinese instruments. Specifically, she deemed their sound to be more "heroic," a quality which was crucial to the model operas. The music for the model Peking operas was thus revised to include a small Western orchestra. Musicians were seated in a pit, instead of on-stage as was the norm in Peking opera, and they used printed parts instead of playing from memory. Musical balance, such as that between voice and instrumental music and between Western and Chinese instruments, was another obsession. Worried that the percussion instruments used in Peking opera were too loud, she had them confined to a small, sound-absorbing structure in the orchestra pit, which soon became known as a "pigeon cage." Some gongs and cymbals were even made with a new metal alloy that was supposed to temper their sound.[47]

Once the original eight model operas had been anointed by *People's Daily*, they quickly filled the nation's stages and airwaves. Although each production was associated with the group that created it, they were also performed by local operas, ballet companies and symphonies, or transplanted into other art forms from around the country. Model opera music blared from loudspeakers in parks and playgrounds, restaurants and stores, even in farm fields and moving trains. Students and workers used scores and production guides to mount their own productions, which followed

---

46. Witke, R. (1977). *Comrade Chiang Ch'ing* [Jiang Qing]. Boston, Toronto: Little, Brown and Company: 53.

47. Jiang Qing's obsession with balance led to what some musicologists call the "four emphases" for orchestral music. These were that among choralists and instrumentalists, the choralists should be emphasized; among Chinese instruments, the *jinghu*, *erhu* and *pipa* should be emphasized; among these three instruments, the jinghu should be most prominent; and among Western instruments, the string instruments should be emphasized. See Mittler: 95, note 284.

the originals even down to the size and color of a patched cloth sack carried by a peasant in a passing stage appearance. Several of the operas were translated into the language and theatrical style of China's minority peoples, such as Uighurs and Tibetans, so more non-Chinese speakers would be exposed to them.

The extent to which model operas saturated the nation was exacerbated by the absence of virtually all other entertainment. Private television sets were practically unheard of, and radio stations were banned from playing any foreign music and most Chinese music. No new feature films were made during the first years of the Cultural Revolution, leaving the film-going public to watch Soviet classics like *Lenin in October* and *Lenin in 1918*; Albanian and Romanian films about fighting the Nazis; and North Korean films about fighting the Japanese, or the wildly popular North Korean sob story, *The Flower-Selling Girl*. Even in the early 1970s, when some Chinese films were again produced, they were outnumbered by documentaries like the 1973 offerings *New Techniques in Metal Pressing, Synthetic Wool, Introducing a Good Strain of Paddy*, and *Removing Coaldust from Chimney Smoke*.[48]

With high- and low-brow entertainment alike so severely curtailed, model operas permeated the nation's collective consciousness. Virtually everyone could sing the main arias to any of the operas or hum the main themes. Some could sing every song, recite every word of dialogue, mimic every gesture — and still can, to this day. The heroes and villains of the model operas became cultural reference points and the performers of the heroic roles achieved stardom on a level that can only be compared to a Hollywood actor like Marilyn Monroe in her heyday or perhaps a pop star like Elvis in his — absolutely everyone knew that Tong Xiangling was Yang Zirong in *Taking Tiger Mountain By Strategy*.

To support the performance of model operas on such a wide scale, it was necessary to train countless performers and musicians. Thus, where zealous young revolutionaries were destroying pianos and violins just a few years earlier, now they were eagerly studying them in the hope of participating in the model opera productions, which all used at least some Western instruments. Since the conservatories were not functioning and most schools did not have music programs, young musicians learned to play their instruments from friends, relatives, neighbors, or professional musicians who moonlighted as tutors. Although they were not allowed to play concertos or symphonies in public, they could still practice etudes and other training techniques and some learned to play classical masterpieces in private. At the same time, they gained a deeper understanding of traditional Chinese music, since model operas were largely based on Peking opera music and folk songs. The training of so many young people in both Western instruments and Chinese music was unprecedented in China's history. Though its purpose was revolutionary, its greatest impact was on music and would only be understood when the Cultural Revolution finally ended.

---

48. (1973). New Scientific and Educational Documentary Films. *Chinese Literature* 6: 106.

REVOLUTIONIZING SYMPHONY

Like her attack on the citadel of Peking opera and the fortress of ballet, Jiang Qing's surmounting of that "most sacred 'pure music,' symphony," began several years before the start of the Cultural Revolution. Its focus was the Central Philharmonic, which at the time was barely managing to stay alive.

The virtual banning of foreign music had robbed it of its bread-and-butter repertoire, and there were few Chinese symphonic pieces that could replace the foreign classics. When even foreign instruments began to be condemned, many of the Philharmonic's musicians took up Chinese instruments to demonstrate their revolutionary patriotism. Li Delun thus faced the unenviable task of conducting a symphony orchestra that could not play most Western classical music and was full of musicians who were rapidly trading in their violins for *erhus*.

Recognizing that the Central Philharmonic's life was on the line, its Party Secretary Li Ling organized what was internally referred to as "survival month," in March of 1964. Billed publicly as "spread symphonic music month," this was essentially a last-ditch effort to popularize the orchestra with ordinary people and convince the cultural leftists that a symphony orchestra really could serve the workers, peasants and soldiers. It consisted of dozens of small performances led by Li Delun in factories and villages throughout the Beijing area.

At the start of each survival month show, Mr. Li would humorously introduce the instruments and the music. He got around the fact. that virtually all the instruments were foreign in origin by emphasizing the importance of the gong — an instrument that is to this day made almost exclusively in China and is possessed by orchestras everywhere. It was still possible to play a few small foreign pieces, like Beethoven's *Egmont* overture, so Mr. Li gave these a politically correct spin — *Egmont* was about a national hero in the Netherlands, at a time when the country was about to be invaded by Spain.

This road show was well-received by audiences and seemed certain to help ensure the orchestra's survival, except for one unfortunate incident. The single piece of symphonic music which was known and loved by nearly all the peasants and workers for whom they performed was *The Butterfly Lovers*. But, by 1964 the work that had been praised just five years earlier as China's "own symphonic music" was already black-listed alongside the music of Tchaikovsky and Debussy because it was viewed as a love story for rich people. However, since none of this black-listing was official, audiences did not know about it and the Central Philharmonic was not allowed to say anything. This meant that when the crowds shouted to hear *The Butterfly Lovers*, the orchestra could neither play it nor explain why.

Usually, Mr. Li was able to distract the audience in some way or another, but on one occasion the peasants were so determined to hear the piece that they grew angry and began throwing rocks, forcing the musicians to flee for safety. When word of the incident got to higher level officials, it was not the rock-throwers who got in trouble but Mr. Li and the orchestra. To make amends for making the peasants unhappy, they were forced to go back and apologize — even though they still couldn't play *The Butterfly Lovers*, and still couldn't say why.

Worried that this incident could sabotage all their hard work, Mr. Li decided to arrange a medley of revolutionary songs played in historic sequence, during which Chairman Mao's picture would be projected on the back of the stage. The medley was a success with audiences — at the grand finale, *Sailing the Seas with Our Great Helmsman*, everyone would stand to sing along, and then shout, "Long live Chairman Mao!" Since it was both politically correct and palatable to the peasants, Party leaders were also happy and finally seemed to accept Mr. Li's long-held conviction that a symphony orchestra could be revolutionary.

Although survival month appeared to have worked, the orchestra still found itself engaged in as much political study as music making. Maestro and musicians alike had to read Mao's works before they started to rehearse and then take frequent study breaks. Usually, they would study one section of the *Selected Works*, play a piece of music — which oftentimes had itself been composed for purposes of political propaganda — and then try to tie the two together. It was also considered essential for them to feel the music politically and to demonstrate their feelings as they played. For instance, when they rehearsed or performed an especially sorrowful song from *The White-Haired Girl*, the musicians were all supposed to look pained. One of the violinists just couldn't manage to play and look anguished at the same time — he said playing a violin was playing a violin — and as a result was soundly criticized for not having any feelings for the proletariat.

This, then, was the situation at the Central Philharmonic in late 1964, when word came that Jiang Qing wanted to visit. If some in the Philharmonic were apprehensive or unhappy upon hearing the news, Li Delun was not — he was delighted. Indeed, he immediately viewed Jiang Qing's interest as a crucial opportunity for the orchestra and decided that they would stage their "survival month" program for her.

When Jiang Qing arrived at the Philharmonic, Mr. Li introduced the instruments of the orchestra and his musicians played a short song on each.[49] Jiang Qing listened and occasionally offered comments. She liked the viola, she told them, but did not like the folk song played on it because it was too soft, too sentimental, too evocative of lords and ladies in gardens. Chinese opera, she noted, was much more powerful than folk songs. She occasionally asked a question, and inquired whether all the musical instruments were made in China. With his customary finesse, Li Delun replied that all the instruments could be made in China — in fact, they could even be made in China and then exported. Impressed by this reply, Jiang Qing declared that although the instruments were Western in origin, Chinese people could make them and play them, so they could certainly be used to serve the workers, peasants and soldiers.

---

49. For this story, see Luo: 361-366.

"Bourgeois music must die one day," she added. "But we must not die with it. We must blaze a trail of our own."[50]

Having learned about the instruments, Jiang Qing asked Mr. Li to explain "symphonic music." Mr. Li replied that it was simply the works played by a symphony orchestra — symphony, concerto, overture, rhapsody, suite and many other types. He started to explain the structure of a symphony, but she interrupted him. Over the years, Mr. Li came to believe that Jiang Qing was incapable of listening to other people talk — after three minutes, she would think of something else and change the subject.

The subject to which she changed on this and many other occasions was revolutionary operas.

"The music of our Peking opera is very rich," she said. "Symphonic music should try and make adaptations from Peking opera."[51]

She then told them about the revolutionary opera *Shajiabang,* and invited them to attend a dress rehearsal of it the next day.

Jiang Qing's visit made a major impression on many members of the Philharmonic. As Lu Gongda, a Central Philharmonic cellist who became a musical adviser to Jiang Qing, described it in an article published in 1967,

> Comrade Jiang Qing, courageous standard-bearer in the great proletarian cultural revolution, came to us in the Central Philharmonic Society, bringing Chairman Mao's warm concern. With the torch of Mao Zedong's thought she lighted the fire of the cultural revolution and fanned the flames of the revolution in symphonic music.[52]

Li Delun began to ponder the implications of her visit as soon as she had left. Peking opera — like symphonic music — had been under heavy attack for several years but had once again begun to thrive since Jiang Qing brought her revolution to it. How, he wondered, could they revolutionize symphonic music in a similar way and ensure its survival?

The next day the entire Philharmonic boarded buses and went to see the rehearsal of *Shajiabang.* When it was over, Jiang Qing had Mr. Li called backstage and asked his opinion of it.

"It was terrific!" he replied.[53]

Jiang Qing then asked what he intended to do with the Philharmonic, and he promptly replied that while *Shajiabang* had great expressive strength as an opera, he thought the accompaniment was a bit thin — it would be even better with a symphony orchestra. His answer struck the jackpot — Jiang Qing loved the idea, but asked Mr. Li if he was sure they could come up with a suitable symphonic score. He was not sure, he said; but they could try with a few pieces and see how it worked.

50. Lu Kung-ta (Lu Gongda) (1967). A revolution in symphonic music. *China Reconstructs* September: 18.
51. Lu: 18.
52. *Ibid.*
53. Luo: 363.

Deeming this a workable plan, Jiang Qing told Li Delun to go ahead with it — if she liked the results, she would send the opera's star singers to perform with his orchestra.

When Mr. Li went back to the Philharmonic and reported this conversation to his colleagues, there was general, though not universal, agreement that Jiang Qing had thrown them a life-line. A model opera creation group was formed, technically an assembly of equals but actually headed by the Philharmonic's resident composer Luo Zhongrong. The seven creation-group members would suggest ideas, Mr. Luo would write the music, the group members would critique his work, and then Mr. Luo would rewrite.

In the end, the creators of China's first revolutionary symphonic work decided to take a page out of Peking opera, which had throughout its history assimilated various kinds of folk music. Broadening on this idea, they "weeded through the old to bring forth the new," considering numerous aspects of Chinese and Western musical and visual culture as possible material for the symphony. As Lu Gongda explained in his 1967 article,

> To better bring out the ideas of people's war and portray the heroes better and more adequately and vividly, we refused to be limited by the convention of bourgeois symphonic music that the theme must be expressed solely through musical images. We added whatever art form could serve proletarian politics well, including traditional Chinese instruments, voices and chorus, recitation, a backdrop with projected scenes. The Peking opera *Shajiabang* contains many beautiful singing passages portraying the heroes of the New Fourth Army and the Party underground workers. These are now part of our symphony. Skillfully woven together, these different media form a complete production with symphonic music as the main part. The singing is still in Peking opera style, and Chinese cymbals, gongs, drums, the hu chin (a kind of fiddle) and sona (brass horn) have been added to the orchestra. All these have now become integral components of the *Shajiabang* symphony.[54]

The dress rehearsal of Act Two, which they had decided to set first, was held in the auditorium of the Central Conservatory in March and attended by Jiang Qing.

"Very good," she told Mr. Li and the orchestra at its conclusion. "It's really not bad."[55]

Jiang Qing instructed the New China News Agency reporters in attendance to report that the work was a beneficial experiment in nationalizing symphonic music. She then turned to Mr. Li and asked if they could do the entire opera. When he replied in the affirmative, she suggested that the finished piece premiere on the October 1 National Day holiday. Mr. Li agreed, and then went back to the Philharmonic to inform all his colleagues that they had to compose an entire revolutionary opera in six months.

---

54. Lu: 19.
55. Luo: 364.

Not everyone in the orchestra was supportive of this plan. Some thought Li Delun was just trying to get into Jiang Qing's good graces and did not understand that his ultimate goal was always to save the orchestra. Others objected to the project on principle — they were a symphony orchestra, not a Peking opera troupe or political propagandists. As Lu Gongda warned, in his politically-slanted account,

> The Party authorities in our organization who were taking the capitalist road had tried to stop us from composing a new revolutionary symphony. Now they tried to disrupt and keep people away from our rehearsals by scheduling many big concerts. They told the singers, "Singing in the Peking opera style will ruin your voice." Citing foreign conventions, they opposed the use of Chinese instruments, spoken commentaries and the performers dressing and making up according to their roles. Their aim was to turn our symphony away from reflecting Chairman Mao's thinking on people's war and class struggle and keep it in the realm of "pure music" without a definite theme, a clear-cut stand, or national characteristics. The flames of our revolution were being extinguished by these criminals![56]

This opposition notwithstanding, the Central Philharmonic went ahead with the plan and began setting the rest of the revolutionary opera to symphonic music. Jiang Qing followed the entire process and occasionally offered words of encouragement.

"Only some 20 really good works were composed during the rise of capitalism, and not many more in all the several thousand years of feudal society," she told them at one point. "Let's not worship things blindly. By putting in several years of hard work, we can produce a number of works." [57]

Buoyed by these words of wisdom from on high — and by the belief that creating revolutionary music was their only means of survival — the creation group carried on and finished in time for National Day. Because the completed symphonic *Shajiabang* was only 40 minutes long, not enough for a whole concert, Mr. Li needed to program another piece alongside it. Hearing of the problem, Jiang Qing herself suggested that a symphony concert should have something foreign in it, so Mr. Li and the Philharmonic were able to perform an overture and Liszt's *First Piano Concerto*. Thus it was that China's first revolutionary symphony was paired with Liszt, played by Liu Shikun, and premiered before an audience of workers, peasants, and soldiers sprinkled with famous Peking opera singers to whom Jiang Qing had sent tickets.

The *Revolutionary Symphonic Music "Shajiabang,"* as Jiang Qing personally named it, opens with an overture in praise of Chairman Mao and the Communist Party. It has "the marching song of the New Fourth Army as the theme melody and full

---

56. Lu: 19. Lu Gongda jumped out the window of his Central Philharmonic office in 1968; Li Delun's son had just stopped in to see his father and was outside the building when Lu landed. He picked Lu up and got help, but Lu's spine had been driven into his brain and he died later that afternoon. Lu's suicide followed the fall from grace of Qi Benyu, the man whom Jiang Qing had sent to call Li Delun back to work as a conductor. Qi was accused of belonging to a "May 16th corps" allegedly trying to overthrow Mao Zedong and Lu was charged with being his associate.

57. *Ibid.*, 20.

orchestration to express the heroism of the army as it fights the enemy on both sides of the Yangzi."[58] A chorus sings over the music:

> Red flags fly,
> The bugles sound,
> Hills and rivers echo.
> Drive out the Japanese invaders
> Wipe out the traitors,
> Defend and save our country!
> Sons and daughters of China,
> To battle, singing valiantly!
> The Guomindang [Nationalist] reactionaries won't fight,
> They betray our country for gold and office.
> Pointing the way forward,
> Chairman Mao and the Communist Party
> Lead the war of resistance...

The chorus then assumes the role of militant soldiers, waving their flags against imperialism, and a narrator explains the plot of the story. A painted backdrop descends to show the lake around which the story is set, as a folk melody is played on Chinese instruments. Then, with solo singing in Peking opera style and chorus singing in Western harmony, the story unfolds to the accompaniment of symphonic music. Heroic characters, such as the underground Party worker and tea house owner Sister Ah Qing, are accompanied by violin and clarinet, which were intended to emphasize heroic qualities. The Japanese enemy, by contrast, is indicated by the bassoon and lower brass instruments.

The concert was a success and instantly transformed the Central Philharmonic from a near pariah into a model ensemble with the same high status as the other performing arts groups who had premiered model operas. It was soon performing *Revolutionary Symphonic Music "Shajiabang,"* in factories and villages everywhere. Mr. Li was happy that his gambit had worked — he no longer had to worry about his orchestra's survival, or his own. But every now and then, he wistfully recalled the plans he'd had for developing symphonic music when he returned from Moscow. This, apparently, was no longer in the cards. However, he was so busy conducting that he had little time to dwell on past dreams.

"Every day, we played *Shajiabang,*" recalled Mr. Li. "I could conduct it upside down. Even the musicians could play it with their eyes closed."

The success of the symphonic *Shajiabang* sparked efforts to create more revolutionary works using Western musical instruments and symphony orchestras, like the Shanghai Symphony's adaptation of *Taking Tiger Mountain by Strategy*. The two of

58. *Ibid.*

these that originated at the Central Philharmonic and came to be widely performed were "The Red Lantern" With Piano Accompaniment and The Yellow River Piano Concerto.

Like the symphonic version of *Shajiabang*, "The Red Lantern" With Piano Accompaniment included Peking-opera style singing and was a joint effort of the Central Philharmonic and the China Peking Opera Troupe. It was premiered in July of 1968 by Yin Chengzong, the young pianist who had won second prize in the USSR's 1962 Tchaikovsky Competition.

Although Yin was a classically trained pianist, he had adapted well to the musical exigencies of the Cultural Revolution and become an ardent member of the Central Philharmonic's "Mao Zedong Thought Propaganda Team." To celebrate the 25th anniversary of Mao's Talks at the Yanan Forum on Literature and Art in May of 1967, he even brought a piano to Tiananmen Square and played music from *Shajiabang* there, in the open air.[59] He spearheaded the effort to write piano music for *The Red Lantern* and explained his inspiration in writing:

> My comrades and I have often discussed the question: Is it possible to make the piano serve the workers, peasants and soldiers? We looked at it this way: The piano was created by working people. Why can't it serve the working people, proletarian politics and socialism?... The successful revolution in Peking opera was like a clap of spring thunder shaking the whole world. It gave us courage and inspiration. We thought: Armed with Mao Zedong's thought and under the leadership of Comrade Jiang Qing, the literary and art workers could break through the most stubborn fortress such as Peking opera. What other fortress can't we conquer?[60]

Yin sent a tape of his efforts to Jiang Qing and soon became a member of her inner circle of favored artists. The premiere of "The Red Lantern" With Piano Accompaniment was a gala affair attended by 10,000 people and held at the Great Hall of the People. Mao Zedong, Jiang Qing, Zhou Enlai and Lin Biao were all in the audience and went on stage together at the end to congratulate the "revolutionary and literary art fighters" who performed it. Performers, dignitaries, and audience members alike then burst out singing *The East Is Red*, *Sailing the Seas Depends on the Helmsman* and *The Internationale*, followed by hearty cheers of "Long live Chairman Mao! A long, long life to Chairman Mao! We wish Chairman Mao a long, long life! A long, long life!"[61]

With the piano version of *The Red Lantern* a success, Yin Chengzong and Jiang Qing decided to try out a symphonic version. Although this never attained the status of "model opera," its preview performance did provide the occasion for Li Delun's final rehabilitation when Jiang Qing invited him onstage and publicly called him a "hero" for the meritorious service he had rendered in creating model operas. Mr. Li was

59. Yin Cheng-tsung (Yin Chengzong) (1968). Be revolutionary cultural workers, always loyal to Chairman Mao. *Chinese Literature* 9:15.

60. Yin: 13.

61. (1968). Chairman Mao and Vice-Chairman Lin Piao Attend Musical Performance. *Chinese Literature* 9: 3.

relieved to be completely rehabilitated, even though he still had no idea what he had done wrong, or what he had done right, for that matter. Speaking privately with friends, the best he could come up with was that during the Hundred Flowers movement, people were in big trouble if they criticized their leaders, while during the Cultural Revolution, they were in big trouble if they did not.

The Yellow River Piano Concerto, an adaptation of Xian Xinghai's famed Yellow River Cantata, was created by Yin Chengzong and several other musicians under Jiang Qing's guidance. At her suggestion, Yin and three fellow members of the Yellow River composition team travelled to the banks of the Yellow River to prepare for the task of writing the concerto. They lived in caves, rowed with the boatmen and interviewed peasants about the war against Japan. Then, according to Yin Chengzong's own account, they went back to Beijing to compose China's first revolutionary piano concerto with the idea that it should express:

> Chairman Mao's concept of people's war. To reflect this we broke with the old western conventions that a concerto must consist of highly formalistic movements and decided to write four organically linked sections.... We made full use of the richly expressive concerto form with the piano accompanied by other instruments. Guided by Chairman Mao's directives that we should make the past serve the present, make things foreign serve China, and evolve the new from the old, in the boatmen's song we adapted the western cadenza technique to depict the tumultuous river and the boatmen's victory over the rapids.... We also made use of traditional techniques of such Chinese instruments as the zheng and the yangqin to enliven the melodies and bring out the youthful exuberance of the liberated area.... Finally, at the suggestion of a soldier, we added the melodies of The East is Red and The Internationale to evoke the splendid image of China's working class and broad masses fighting for the liberation of all mankind on the side of all oppressed nations and peoples of the world.[62]

The concerto finally premiered in 1970 and was an instant success. It is the only one of the model symphonic works created under Jiang Qing's guidance that still remains in the regular repertoire of Chinese orchestras. It is even performed on occasion by orchestras outside China, although when Harold Schonberg reviewed it for The New York Times in 1973, he panned it as "movie music. It is a rehash of Rachmaninoff, Khachaturian, late romanticism, bastardized Chinese music and Warner Brother climaxes."[63]

Schonberg's comments notwithstanding, the Yellow River Concerto helped introduce Western-style orchestral music to millions of Chinese who heard it live or watched it on film. Like the other model symphonic works and the model operas in general, it ultimately proved more important in promoting Western-style music than revolution. And, as Jiang Qing said of all the model operas, "Although they still have

---

62. Yin Cheng-chung (Yin Chengzong) (1974). How the piano concerto "Yellow River" was composed. Chinese Literature 11: 101-2.

63. Kraus: 149 and Witke: 459. Quote is from The New York Times of October 14, 1973.

shortcomings and areas which need further adjustment, at least they have caused a sensation and shocked the world!"[64]

64. Witke: 392.

CHAPTER 8. MUSIC AND POWER

The model operas had certainly "caused a sensation" and may even have "shocked the world." They also served as the catapult for Jiang Qing's leap to the highest echelons of political power. Having started out in the early 1960s as a mere cultural advisor to the army, by 1969 she was an important member of the governing Politburo and her power in cultural matters was unmatched. But by the early 1970s the political situation in China was changing, especially on the international front.

China's relationship with the Soviet Union had remained tense throughout the 1960s and showed no signs of improving. On the contrary, the Chinese leadership was increasingly worried about the build-up of Soviet troops on their shared border. As a result, even while government propaganda organs continued to spout the militant anti-capitalist and anti-imperialist rhetoric of the Cultural Revolution, the leadership began quietly seeking ways to improve their nation's relationship with the West.

In April of 1971, China sent its ping-pong team to Japan to participate in the Thirty-First World Table Tennis Championship, an event in which the US team was also playing. Friendly overtures from one of the American players were reciprocated by the Chinese and within a week the shocked Americans found themselves in Beijing as guests of the Chinese government. Zhou Enlai received the young Americans in the Great Hall of the People and even offered them a welcoming toast. The decades of hostile non-communication that had followed the Communist victory were over and an era of "ping-pong diplomacy" had begun.

Just three months after the ping-pong team's visit, the United States national security advisor Henry Kissinger arrived in Beijing, sent by President Nixon on a top-secret mission to meet with Premier Zhou and plan an official state visit. When Kissinger's trip ended, President Nixon himself informed the American people that he would travel to China within the next year.

Zhou Enlai was the strongest and most visible proponent of this friendlier policy towards the US and its implementation served to strengthen his position within the leadership. This left some leaders feeling threatened — particularly Jiang Qing — but he used the leverage he gained to push for more contact with the West. Just as he had done way back at Yanan, he once again turned to classical music as a tool for furthering his diplomatic goals.

When Kissinger scheduled a second visit to Beijing in October of 1971, Premier Zhou suggested to Li Delun that the Central Philharmonic should perform for him.

"Premier Zhou said to me, 'Kissinger's German. You should play Beethoven,'" recalled Li Delun.

This was Zhou's second attempt to use Beethoven's music for diplomatic purposes, the first being the visit of the West German foreign minister some months earlier. That concert never took place because it was scuttled by Jiang Qing's musical advisor, Yu Huiyong. Yu by now was based in Beijing as vice-director of the powerful "culture group" that oversaw all cultural activities and he refused to give the Central Philharmonic any time to rehearse.

"We wanted to show our revolutionary state to the whole world!" continued Mr. Li. "But, what could we do? We couldn't do ballet, because the women don't wear enough clothes. Drama — you had the problem of a script. So, it was orchestra. Orchestras are well organized, the men are in formal clothes and the women's skin is covered — who cares about the content?!"

Premier Zhou, in fact, did care about the content. He even asked Li Delun to explain all nine Beethoven symphonies to him and to provide him with written materials for follow-up study. Wishing to keep his interest private, the premier asked Mr. Li not to drop the materials at the West Gate of the Zhongnanhai leadership compound, as was normal practice, but to leave them at the State Council where he had a private office away from prying eyes.

Once a Central Philharmonic concert had been added to Kissinger's itinerary, Jiang Qing and Yu Huiyong decided that they had better call Li Delun in to discuss it. Jiang Qing asked Mr. Li which Beethoven symphony the Philharmonic played best. When Mr. Li replied that it was the composer's *Fifth*, Yu Huiyong objected that this was an unacceptable piece of music for Communist China because it was about fatalism. Mr. Li next suggested the composer's *Third Symphony*, but Yu also objected to this, proclaiming it to be about Napoleon. Having been shot down twice, Li Delun decided to keep quiet and Jiang Qing then turned to Yu Huiyong, who suggested that Beethoven's *Sixth Symphony* was acceptable because it was about nature. Mr. Li considered replying that the *Sixth Symphony* wasn't so much about nature as it was about landlord's property, but thought the better of it. Later, when Zhou Enlai got wind of the discussion, he commented privately to Mr. Li that he didn't see anything wrong with Napoleon: he was a Jacobin revolutionary who created the Napoleonic Code which destroyed the special powers of the feudal classes![1]

Jiang Qing and Yu Huiyong would undoubtedly have preferred that the Beethoven performance not take place. But, Zhou Enlai had the upper hand when it came to international affairs and he cared so deeply about the Kissinger visit that he was not about to let Yu Huiyong stymie his musical plans again. Unable to derail the concert, Yu could only make sure that the Philharmonic performed Beethoven's politically palatable *Sixth Symphony*, instead of the *Fifth Symphony* which it played best.

Jiang Qing also made certain that Kissinger was treated to a model Peking opera performance as a counterbalance to the orchestral concert of bourgeois music. Kissinger was, presumably, polite at the time, but he later described the model opera as "an art form of truly stupefying boredom in which villains were the incarnation of evil and wore black, good guys wore red, and as far as I could make out the girl fell in love with a tractor."[2]

Nixon was not German, so when he arrived on his state visit in February of 1972, he was not treated to a Beethoven symphony. Instead, he heard a special rendition of *Home on the Range*, which was apparently played either at his own request or at that of someone in his delegation.[3] He was also taken to a model opera by Jiang Qing herself, in this case *The Red Detachment of Women*. Nixon was not impressed by Jiang Qing, who sat next to him at the performance, calling her "abrasive and aggressive" and expressing surprise that she asked him hostile questions even as the ballet was being performed.[4] However, while Kissinger again called the performance "stupefying,"[5] Nixon confessed to actually enjoying it.

"I had not been particularly looking forward to this ballet," he wrote, "but after a few minutes I was impressed by its dazzling technical and theatrical virtuosity. Jiang Qing had been undeniably successful in her attempt to create a consciously propagandistic theater piece that would both entertain and inspire its audience. The result was a hybrid combining elements of opera, operetta, musical comedy, classical ballet, modern dance, and gymnastics."[6]

The Nixon visit ended with the signing of the Shanghai Communiqué. A triumph of diplomacy and determination brokered by Zhou and Kissinger, the Communiqué enabled China and the US to finesse the many differences that separated them and provided a foundation for a stable relationship in the absence of formal diplomatic relations. Since it contained a provision calling for more "people-to-people contacts and exchanges" in "science, technology, culture, sports and journalism,"[7] it also gave

---

1. For Mr. Li's thinking see Luo Junjun (2001). *Li Delun Zhuan* [A Biography of Li Delun].Beijing: Zuojia Chubanshe: 406. For Zhou's comment, see Luo: 407.

2. Kissinger, Henry (1979). *White House Years*. Boston: Little, Brown and Company: 779.

3. See Schonberg, Harold C. (1973). Philadelphians play committee music. *The New York Times* September 18.

4. Nixon, Richard (1978). *The Memoirs of Richard Nixon*. New York: Grosset & Dunlap: 570.

5. Kissinger: 1068.

6. Nixon: 570.

Zhou more opportunities to use music for diplomatic purposes. The premier and those who shared his views took advantage of the evolving situation to push for a broader opening to the West and in effect inaugurated an era of classical music diplomacy.

Zhou started quietly by inviting the American pianists Frances and Richard Hadden to perform in Beijing. The three had known each other in pre-liberation days, when the Haddens were socialist sympathizers who lived in Wuhan, and had maintained intermittent contact over the years. The Haddens' joint recital was not open to the public but it was nonetheless a milestone since it marked the first classical music performance by foreigners since the start of the Cultural Revolution. Some months later, Zhou also made it possible for the general public to hear foreign music for the first time in five years when he gave China's central radio station permission to play Romanian folk music to mark Romania's national day. Jiang Qing was not happy about this and Li Delun recalled her saying that no one should ever assume that "decadent sounds" could be played on Chinese radio just for diplomatic reasons.[8]

The first public performance of foreign music by foreigners came at the beginning of 1973 when the Swiss cellist Henri Honegger performed in Beijing and Shanghai.

"He played six Bach suites," Li Delun recalled. "Everybody in the audience kept completely still. Things were opening up a little."

Honegger was followed by the London Philharmonic Orchestra and its conductor John Pritchard. The London Philharmonic performed five times before capacity crowds in Beijing, Shanghai, and Guangzhou, giving those fortunate enough to be allotted tickets the chance to hear Beethoven, Brahms, Dvorak, and Haydn for the first time in years. Next came the Vienna Philharmonic and its conductor Claudio Abbado. The Vienna Philharmonic gave four concerts for more than 20,000 people and its final performance included *The Yellow River Piano Concerto* with Yin Chengzong as soloist and members of the Central Philharmonic joining the orchestra.

The London and Vienna Philharmonics were two of the world's greatest orchestras, but Zhou's real goals were diplomatic and he was most intent on improving relations with the US. Consequently, the most important event in this musical diplomacy was the September 1973 visit of the Philadelphia Orchestra under Eugene Ormandy.

The tone of the visit was set when the Central Philharmonic Chorus welcomed the renowned American orchestra's 105 musicians and 35-person entourage by singing *America the Beautiful*, in English. This open-hearted gesture was planned by Li Delun and approved by Zhou Enlai, to the great displeasure of Yu Huiyong. It moved many of the Americans to tears and seems to have eased any anxiety they may have had about

7. As quoted in Spence, Jonathan (1990). *The Search for Modern China*. New York: W.W. Norton & Company: 632.

8. See Luo: 405 for Jiang Qing's comments. Attacking music with the phrase "decadent sounds" (*mimi zhiyin*) has a very long history in China, dating back to the Han Dynasty. For a discussion of this, see Jones, Andrew F. (2001). *Yellow Music: Media Culture and Colonial Modernity in the Chinese Jazz Age*. Durham and London: Duke University Press: 114-117.

visiting Communist China. Indeed, on one occasion a group of musicians laughingly surrounded Mr. Li and told him that he was being ambushed by capitalism. On another, a wealthy octogenarian donor who had travelled to China with the orchestra pointed at the trip sponsor from Pan Am and dead-panned to Mr. Li, "He's a capitalist — shoot him!"[9]

The congeniality of the atmosphere was such that one afternoon the entire Philadelphia Orchestra went to the Central Philharmonic to observe rehearsals. Mr. Li welcomed them with a short history of the orchestra and then led it in playing *Moon Reflected on Erchuan Spring*, a piece originally composed by the blind folk musician Ah Bing and arranged for orchestra by the composer Wu Zuqiang. Whether out of courtesy or genuine interest, Ormandy expressed great appreciation for the piece and asked for a copy of the score. Embarrassingly, Mr. Li was forced to evade his repeated requests, since he could not give the score to a foreigner without Jiang Qing's permission.

The next piece was Beethoven's *Fifth Symphony*, which Mr. Li had finally managed to program even though it was just for a rehearsal. After leading the Central Philharmonic in the first movement, Mr. Li proffered his baton to a surprised Ormandy and asked if he would conduct the second movement. *The New York Times* music critic Harold Schonberg had travelled to China with the orchestra and he described what followed:

> Mr. Ormandy stood up, doffed his jacket and necktie, went to the podium and brought down his baton. The orchestra responded. It was very much in the Ormandy manner — full, resonant, singing. The Central Philharmonic sounded like a different orchestra, suddenly playing with confidence and rhythmic assurance. A glowing Mr. Ormandy paid tribute to Mr. Li for having trained so fine an orchestra.[10]

When the rehearsal was over, the orchestras exchanged gifts, with the visitors presenting many scores of works by American composers, a set of Philadelphia orchestra recordings and some instruments, including a clarinet, trumpet, and flute. The Chinese reciprocated with so many Chinese musical instruments that Schonberg said they "came forth as though a loaded camel train were discharging its cargo." [11]

The Philadelphia Orchestra was scheduled to perform six concerts, four in Beijing and two in Shanghai. The first two Beijing concerts went off without a hitch. At the first, the orchestra played Mozart's *Haffner Symphony*, the American composer Roy Harris' *Third Symphony*, and Brahms' *First Symphony* with the *March of the Workers and Peasants* and *Stars and Stripes Forever* as encores. The French president Pompidou had arrived in Beijing the same day as the orchestra, so Zhou Enlai and other leaders were not in attendance, but many music world insiders had been given tickets, as well as

---

9. Luo: 412.

10. Schonberg, H. (1973). Ormandy, unexpectedly, leads Peking orchestra. *The New York Times* September 16.

11. *Ibid.*

specially selected workers, peasants and soldiers. Their collective response to the concert was described by Schonberg in a story that ran on the front page of *The New York Times*:

> One thing was certain: He [Ormandy] has never played to a more polite or attentive audience. There was dead silence during the performances of the three symphonic pieces, and everybody listened with a force that was almost palpable. There was no coughing, no whispering, no shifting around. The feeling of concentration was almost frightening.[12]

The third Beijing concert suddenly became complicated when Jiang Qing unexpectedly announced that she would attend, together with other high level radicals such as Yao Wenyuan and Wu De. When Ormandy heard the news, he changed the program to include the *Yellow River Piano Concerto*, the score for which he had obtained several months earlier through the US State Department and tried out at New York's Saratoga Music Festival. Originally, the orchestra had also planned to play Beethoven's *Fifth Symphony* but through her interlocutors Jiang Qing asked that this be changed to Beethoven's *Sixth*. This caused some consternation on the American side, since there had been no previous mention of Beethoven's *Sixth* in any discussion of the programs to be performed and they had not brought the parts. Not knowing of Yu Huiyong's proclamations regarding Beethoven's symphonies, they were understandably confused as to why the composer's *Sixth Symphony* was suddenly so much preferable to his *Fifth*. However, Ormandy obliged and the orchestra borrowed the parts from the Central Philharmonic.

With Jiang Qing in attendance, the concert was a major event and the sense of anticipation was high among audience and musicians alike. All went well with Beethoven's *Sixth* and the *Yellow River Concerto*. The bowings on the Central Philharmonic's parts for Beethoven's *Sixth* were different from those used by the Philadelphia musicians, but they adapted with few problems. The soloist for the *Yellow River Concerto* was Yin Chengzong — whom Schonberg described as having "not only a sure grasp of technique but also a rich, velvety tone and a great deal of temperament"[13] — and the performance was a tremendous hit with the audience.

But when the orchestra played Respighi's *Pines of Rome*, Li Delun sensed that Jiang Qing was unhappy. This was not good news for him — the program selections of foreign orchestras were submitted in advance and it was Mr. Li's job to write a summary of each piece which the leadership depended on in granting approval for the performance. He had been obliged to help nix two of the pieces Ormandy proposed — Strauss' *Don Juan* and Debussy's *Afternoon of a Faun*, but had foreseen no problem with the Respighi. However, Jiang Qing had apparently expected the music to be about pine trees, and only pine trees. When she heard the part that sounds like a military march drawing closer and growing louder she became increasingly agitated. This

12. Schonberg, H. (1973) Philadelphians a "Big Success" in their first concert in China. *The New York Times* September 15.

13. Schonberg, H. (1973). U.S. group plays for Mao's wife. *The New York Times* September 17.

didn't sound like pines, she told Li Delun — it didn't even sound like a forest! What kind of music was this?![14]

At the intermission, Jiang Qing went back stage to meet with Ormandy and to thank him both for the concert and for his support back in 1940, when he had been involved in a benefit to raise money for the medical service of China's Communist Eighth Route Army and its Canadian doctor, Norman Bethune. Ormandy apparently decided that her friendliness meant he could speak openly, so he mentioned that he had heard Russian music was not allowed to be played in China. Though clearly taken aback by this implicit criticism, Jiang Qing lied smoothly that Chinese orchestras often played Tchaikovsky and Mussorgsky and that the Philadelphia Orchestra was welcome to play their works, too.[15] Ormandy pressed on, explaining that he had in fact wanted to play Tchaikovsky but had been told it would not be permitted. Jiang Qing assured him that he was mistaken, the conversation ended, and she returned to her seat to listen to the rest of the concert. Ormandy concluded with the encore piece *March of the Workers and Peasants* and the response, according to Schonberg, was "overwhelming, with repeated volleys of rhythmic clapping... by far the most enthusiastic response the Philadelphia Orchestra has so far encountered on its visit to China." [16]

Despite the general atmosphere of good cheer, it was apparent to Mr. Li that Jiang Qing's displeasure over the *Pines of Rome* together with Ormandy's innocent questions about Russian music had left her in a bad humor. She even declined to go back stage to meet the members of the orchestra, although after a long chat with Yu Huiyong she changed her mind, which meant that the Philadelphia musicians — who had already been taken back to their hotel — had to return to the sweltering theater so Jiang Qing could shake their hands and give each of them a gift: some powdered sweet-scented osmanthus flour used to flavor porridge. She also presented Ormandy with two ancient *qin* scores from her personal collection. *The New York Times* made much of this gift, stressing its rarity and the fact that it came from her own library, but Li Delun and other Chinese present were less impressed by this than they were amused by the fact that Ormandy examined the Chinese scores upside down until Jiang Qing corrected him.

The Philadelphia Orchestra gave one more concert in Beijing and visited the Great Wall before heading down to Shanghai. Some of its members also got acupuncture treatments, which had become a mini-fad among the musicians after a member of the stage crew tried the treatment for a sore elbow and then raved about it. A sumptuous banquet followed the last Beijing concert and many toasts were offered by visitors and hosts alike. Ormandy seems to have summed up the general feel of the trip when he said, "The orchestra has been happier than on any other trip it has ever

---

14. See Luo: 414.

15. Li Delun was under the impression that the American pianists Frances and Richard Hadden had told Ormandy that he should not program any Russian music, since they had been told not to.

16. Schonberg, H. (1973). U.S. group plays for Mao's wife. *The New York Times* September 17.

made." [17] According to Schonberg, "Mr. Ormandy was not merely saying polite things. The general feeling among the players is that this indeed was the greatest trip the orchestra has ever made. The hospitality has been 'positively overwhelming,' many friendships have been made." [18]

The Philadelphia Orchestra's visit to Beijing thus ended on a high note, an apparent diplomatic success for Zhou Enlai and a musical success for all concerned.

THE RADICALS' REVENGE

When the Philadelphia Orchestra departed China, Zhou Enlai moved on to other issues. In addition to his numerous domestic and international responsibilities, he had a difficult personal battle to fight since he had been diagnosed with cancer in 1972.

But Jiang Qing was evidently unable to put Zhou's classical music diplomacy out of her mind. Culture was her turf, the justification for all her power, and she had spent years developing the model operas and striving to eliminate all vestiges of "feudal" and "bourgeois" art. Yet, in less than a year, three foreign orchestras had given public performances in Beijing. Although she had job security as long as Mao lived, the Chairman was not in good health and was at any rate becoming somewhat mercurial when it came to cultural issues. The domestic political situation had also changed in ways that were not necessarily to her advantage.

Mao's designated successor, Lin Biao, had been a close ally of Jiang Qing's, the man who first gave her an official position as cultural advisor to the army back in the early 1960s. But in the autumn of 1971 a plane on which he was travelling had crashed in Mongolia, allegedly as he was fleeing after a failed coup attempt that would have involved Mao's assassination. Lin Biao's death and his purported plot had shocked the nation and had many ramifications for intra-Party politics, among them an initial strengthening of Zhou Enlai's position.

The Lin Biao incident was followed just a few months later by the death of Chen Yi. Chen Yi and Mao had once been so close that they critiqued each other's poetry, but when Jiang Qing and Lin Biao launched a campaign against Chen in the early years of the Cultural Revolution, Mao did nothing to stop it and even chimed in with his own wild accusations. Zhou Enlai's efforts to protect Chen Yi had been in vain, and he was still in disgrace when he died in January of 1972.

However, when Mao was asked to approve the eulogy to be read at Chen's funeral, he pointedly crossed out all mention of the general's "mistakes." Then, on the day of the funeral, he shocked everyone by getting out of bed at 1:00 in the afternoon and announcing that he would attend the ceremony. Since time was short, Mao did not even bother to dress — he just put on a silk robe, slippers and a coat and insisted on leaving at once, despite the biting January cold and his own poor health. When he

---

17. Schonberg, H. (1973). Philadelphians play committee music. *The New York Times* September 18.
18. *Ibid.*

arrived, he invited Chen Yi's wife and children to join him in the VIP reception hall. With tears in his eyes, he told Chen Yi's widow "Chen Yi was a good comrade."[19]

In the eyes of some observers, Chen Yi's death — together with Lin Biao's betrayal and death — marked an important turning point in the Cultural Revolution. Although it was not over, its force began to ebb and soon afterwards Mao started to rehabilitate some people who had been imprisoned and struggled against for years. This included not just political leaders like Deng Xiaoping, whom Mao brought back to power in early 1973, but also intellectuals and artists — among them He Luting.

Mr. He had by this time been locked up for nearly six years and had written 64 rebuttals of the charges leveled against him. Despite his long imprisonment, he had not been forgotten by the old guard Beijing leadership. Premier Zhou first broached the subject of his incarceration in a private meeting with Zhang Chunqiao and brought it up again at a dinner with Jiang Qing and Yao Wenyuan.[20] The Premier's mild inquiry was met with resistance by Yao, but Zhou persisted, reminding him that He Luting had made many significant contributions to the revolution. He Luting's *Song of the Guerillas* was very important, he added — if the charges against the composer could not be resolved, they should just be forgotten.

Soon after Premier Zhou's inquiries, Mao Zedong himself apparently spoke to Zhang Chunqiao about Mr. He, reminded of the old musician by a letter from his childhood schoolmate who also happened to be Mr. He's older brother. Chairman Mao did not listen to any prevarications — when Zhang Chunqiao started to respond, Mao reportedly cut him off and told him to end the struggle against the old musician. "He wrote the *Song of the Guerillas*," Mao is said to have added. "Isn't that still good?"[21]

Mao's about-faces on Chen Yi and He Luting, and Zhou Enlai's involvement in bringing both about cannot have made Jiang Qing happy. Chen Yi had directly criticized the excesses of the Cultural Revolution back in 1967 and Jiang Qing had been instrumental in his downfall. Similarly, her close comrades Zhang Chunqiao and Yao Wenyuan had engineered He Luting's humiliation and imprisonment. Mr. He's release was a slap in the face to Zhang and Yao, and less directly to Jiang Qing herself.

Jiang Qing responded to the changing situation in various ways, including at least partly successful efforts to taint Mao's perception of the loyal Premier Zhou. When it came to the "bourgeois" music that Zhou Enlai promoted for diplomatic purposes, she first tried to learn more about it. Following his example, she turned to Li Delun for her education. But whereas Premier Zhou deferred to Mr. Li's expertise and listened like a willing student, Jiang Qing told him what she wanted to learn and how she wanted to be taught.

---

19. For this account and quote see Li Zhisui (with Anne Thurston) (1994). *The Private Life of Chairman Mao*. New York: Random House: 545-6. After the Cultural Revolution ended, a towering statue of Chen Yi was erected on the Bund in Shanghai; the statue is so large and so prominently placed that foreign tourists often assume it is Mao Zedong.

20. See Luo: 407.

21. See Shi Zhongxin (2000). *He Luting Zhuan* [A Biography of He Luting]. Shanghai: Shanghai Yinyue Chubanshe: 273.

She requested tapes of Brahms' *First Symphony* and Rachmaninoff's *Second Piano Concerto*. She did not like the Brahms, but was so enamored of the Rachmaninoff that she asked for more copies to pass on to others. Next, she asked Mr. Li to organize a tutorial on the history of classical music. However, she stipulated that there be no Schumann or Brahms and that she would only listen to the music of other bourgeois composers if they lived in the era when the bourgeoisie was rising to its peak (and was thus a progressive force when compared to feudal society). This meant that Beethoven was acceptable, but not Tchaikovsky, Debussy, or any modern composers like Schoenberg, since they came from the era when the bourgeoisie was in decline.

These ground rules made the subject essentially impossible to teach; Mr. Li was not unhappy when she asked someone else to take over management of her musical education and assigned him the task of organizing a "Criticize Soviet Revisionism" group. This project, which focused on the revisionist tendencies in Soviet music, seems to have been tied to Yu Huiyong's failed effort to organize a major campaign to criticize Tchaikovsky. Although its purpose was criticism, it gave Mr. Li and his colleagues a welcome opportunity to immerse themselves in Soviet music.[22]

At Li Delun's request, Jiang Qing also permitted the Central Philharmonic to rehearse ten foreign symphonies beginning in 1972. Mr. Li had been singularly dissatisfied with his orchestra's performance of Beethoven's *Sixth* during the second Kissinger visit and he told Jiang Qing of his unhappiness. While Jiang Qing certainly did not support such performances of "bourgeois" music, if the Central Philharmonic was to play Beethoven for foreigners, she wanted them to play it well.

It is unclear why Jiang Qing initially adopted this non-combative stance towards Zhou's classical music diplomacy, even to the point of attending the Philadelphia Orchestra's concert and presenting its musicians with token gifts. But in the weeks following the concert, she changed her stance. Most of the impetus for the change certainly lay in the shifting battle-lines of her quiet power struggle with Zhou. But it was further spurred by the translations of several *New York Times* articles which she came across in internal files in the weeks following the Philadelphia Orchestra's visit.

The articles, written by Schonberg, were very positive on the subject of the Philadelphia Orchestra's visit to China. But Schonberg called Wu Zuqiang's *Moon Reflected on Erquan Spring* "a rather saccharine piece in which an Oriental melody was placed over a conventional Western diatonic harmony."[23] His comments on the *Yellow River Piano Concerto* that Jiang Qing had been instrumental in creating were even more scathing. Aside from panning it as "movie music" and "a piece of trash," he noted that the Philadelphia musicians had dubbed it the "Yellow Fever" concerto.[24] He also commented more generally that Chinese composers "may have thought they were adapting Chinese music their own way, but what has come forth, as in *Yellow River* and

---

22. See Luo: 408.

23. Schonberg, H.C. (1973). Ormandy, unexpectedly, leads Peking Orchestra. *The New York Times* September 16.

24. Schonberg, H.C. (1973). Yin spoke only Chinese, Ormandy only English. *The New York Times* October 14.

The Red Detachment of Women, is a bland and even vulgar eclecticism with every cliché of the Socialist Realism style."[25]

Schonberg had already left the country and there was nothing Jiang Qing could do to get back at him for his comments. But the anger she felt — combined with her lingering displeasure over the *Pines of Rome* and Ormandy's queries about Russian music — evidently fuelled her unhappiness about Zhou Enlai generally, and his classical musical diplomacy in particular. She and her radical colleagues found an outlet for this displeasure in the upcoming visit of a Turkish pianist and violinist who had been invited to perform in Beijing in October in honor of Turkey's national day.

Given that three major orchestras from the US and Europe had performed publicly in China in the previous six months, the visit of two musicians from Turkey should not have been a controversial event. As usual, Li Delun was asked to provide the leadership with a musical summary of the proposed program, but since he was busy, he passed the job off to Professor Huang Xiaohe, a musicologist at the Central Conservatory. Professor Huang turned in a long and thorough summary; the relevant bureaucrats sat on it for weeks before sending it back with orders that he condense it considerably and return it within three hours. This hastily abbreviated summary then began to circulate among the highest levels of the Chinese leadership.

The program was not rejected — Jiang Qing, Zhou Enlai, Hua Guofeng and other top leaders initialed their approval of it. But Jiang Qing added the comment, clearly directed at Li Delun, that any Chinese music played in China had better be revolutionary; if the Central Philharmonic wished to present any folk or classical music, it had to have special approval and she did not want to hear anything more like *Moon Reflected on Erchuan Spring*.

Yao Wenyuan seems to have read Professor Huang's summary more closely than Jiang Qing, since he hit on a paragraph that was certain to cause any good cultural radical to take umbrage. Apparently without thinking much about politics, Professor Huang had written that the proposed repertoire was standard for soloists, that most of the works had no deep social content, no clear story, and no descriptive title — the music simply expressed the change and contrast of emotions. So, generally speaking, the pieces were all relatively healthy and cheerful.

To state that any music had no deep content was naturally anathema to cultural radicals — in their view, all music had social and class content. Even if a composition was absolute music that had no descriptive title or clear story line, it still reflected the composer's thinking and his class stance. Yao Wenyuan therefore appended a rhetorical question to the program: Did absolute music really just express emotional changes and contrasts and have no social content? This, he noted ominously, was a theoretical question that needed further study.

Since a comment had been added, the program was recirculated and Jiang Qing read it again, noting that she agreed with Comrade Wenyuan's comments. For good measure, she also jotted down her opinion that the music of Schumann and Brahms

---

25. *Ibid.*

was like sobbing and that some works by bourgeois composers were so difficult to understand that they sounded like someone going crazy! Certainly it was not possible to say that such music could have no deep social content without a class position. Indeed, even composers of program music could deviate from what the title of their pieces suggested, as was the case with that *Pines of Rome* that the Philadelphia Orchestra had played. Comrade Li Delun needed to provide the Central Committee with correct material and not let it be misled.

What had started out as a simple invitation was now a complicated political struggle. Since the intended concert date came and went while the proposed program circulated, it was also an embarrassing diplomatic gaff. Trying to get hold of the situation, Zhou Enlai issued a new invitation to the musicians. But since that was technically a new event, the program had to be circulated for approval yet again. Zhou tried to jump-start the process by noting that he himself had no problems with the chosen music, but Jiang Qing declined to take his lead. Instead, she upped the ante by writing that from now on China should either receive fewer arts groups from capitalist countries, or else receive none at all, because their visits could have very serious results. This comment was clearly an attack on Zhou Enlai and the initiative he had taken in expanding ping-pong diplomacy into classical music diplomacy; but the premier did not take the bait. Instead, he wrote that not to receive any such delegations was impossible; and the recital went ahead.

Since this had all been an internal, written discussion among leaders it should have ended with the concert. But Jiang Qing did not let it rest. Instead, she and Yu Huiyong went to the press to start a "discussion" about "music without titles," or absolute music. This so-called discussion was in fact a minor campaign and its underlying purpose was to discredit Zhou Enlai and the musical — and political — opening to the West which he had spearheaded.[26]

With the undeclared campaign underway, articles about absolute music and whether or not it had social and class content suddenly began to appear in the national press. Three of the more important ones were written by "Chu Lan," a pseudonym for one of four writing groups that functioned as propaganda machines for Jiang Qing and her radical colleagues. Like so many Chinese nom de plumes, "Chu Lan" was a pun, in this case on an old idiom which could be reinterpreted as meaning, "comes from Jiang

---

26. The oddly-themed campaign to criticize Lin Biao and Confucius which began in January 1974 was also partly aimed against Zhou Enlai. The campaign included some critical allusions to Confucius' use of music, like "All contending classes understand that if they want to seize political power and consolidate it, they must first control ideology. The use of music figured prominently in the many programmes Confucius advanced for ruling the country and the people." The criticisms of Confucius's use of music were no doubt intended as criticisms of Zhou Enlai's use of music. (For quote, see Xu Xialin (1974). Confucius' Reactionary Ideas About Music. *Chinese Literature* 8: 95.) Zhou Enlai was also criticized for having allowed foreigners to make two documentaries which were subsequently interpreted as critical of China. One was about the London Philharmonic's visit to China and the other — against which a major criticism campaign was launched — was a general documentary by the Italian filmmaker Michelangelo Antonioni.

Qing."[27] Chu Lan's writing was largely managed by Yu Huiyong and was recognized by readers as the voice of the radical leaders on art-related subjects.

Chu Lan did not pull any punches. The discussion about absolute music, he wrote, was of vital importance.[28] It was not an academic discussion, it was not merely criticism of bourgeois classical music, and it was not a simple debate over whether or not a piece of music should have a title. Instead, it was an exposure of the fact that some people, even after the experience of the Proletarian Cultural Revolution, still held the bourgeois counter-revolutionary revisionist belief that music has no social content. Indeed, the discussion of absolute music had made it very clear that there were still people — i.e., the unnamed Zhou Enlai — who worshipped the West and wanted to revive the old. As one of the articles put it,

> Summed up bluntly: The current tendency to idolize the foreign and revive the ancient in the realm of music is aimed in essence at negating the Great Proletarian Cultural Revolution, attempting to reverse the wheel of history, and reviving the practices of the sinister revisionist line in literature and art. This tendency stems ideologically from the theory of human nature.[29]

As the propaganda machine revved into gear, dozens of articles echoing the thoughts of Chu Lan suddenly began to appear in papers throughout the country. At first the criticism was largely limited to absolute music, but then Jiang Qing complained in another internal memo that she had also criticized bourgeois music with titles — like the *Pines of Rome* — and that only if such music were included could the campaign be complete.[30] Unsurprisingly, Yao Wenyuan wrote that he completely agreed with Comrade Jiang Qing — this was a critical struggle in the area of music between the proletariat and the bourgeois, the Marxists and the revisionists and it included both titled and untitled music. Indeed, even some of the dreaded Debussy's works had titles!

Once Jiang Qing's complaints were made known, the campaign broadened somewhat to include all bourgeois music. As one *People's Daily* editorial explained,

---

27. See Ye Yonglie (2000). *Jiang Qing Zhuan* [A biography of Jiang Qing]. Ulumuqi: Xinjiang Renmin Chubanshe: 697-8. Chu Lan's writing appeared in "two papers and one periodical" — *People's Daily, Liberation Daily* and *Red Flag*.

The other three writing groups were Liang Xiao, a reference to Beijing and Tsinghua universities where the writers were based; the Shanghai-based Luo Siding, a pun on a saying of Lei Feng — *zuo yige yong bu sheng xiude luo siding* — which means to be a screw that never rusts, i.e. someone who always works for the Party no matter what; and Tang Xiaowen, a pun on *dangxiao wen*, or writing from the Communist Party School where the group was based. The groups were all created in the early 1970s. In Beijing, it was often said, "*xiaobao kan dabao, dabao kan liangxiao,*" meaning the little papers look to the big papers and the big papers look to Liang Xiao.

28. See Ming Yan (2002). *Ershishiji Zhongguo Yinyue Piping Daolun* [A Guide to 20th-Century Music Criticism in China]. Beijing: Renmin Yinyue Chubanshe: 306.

29. See Witke, Roxanne (1977). *Comrade Chiang Ch'ing* [Jiang Qing]. Boston, Toronto: Little, Brown and Company: 459.

30. See Luo: 423.

Marxist-Leninists hold that all musical works, as a form of ideology, "are products of the reflection in the human brain of the life of a given society." There is no music that is merely "a form of the flow of sounds" without any content; for a composer has clearly in mind what he wants to praise or oppose and what content and mood he means to convey, whether he gives his work a title or not. For example, when the German bourgeois composer Beethoven was asked the meaning of his *Sonata No. 17*, a composition without a title, he replied: "Please read Shakespeare's *The Tempest*." That play, we know, preaches the bourgeois theory of human nature.[31]

In-house criticism groups at work units throughout the country echoed these ideas in their own publications. The workers' criticism group of the Tianjin port declared that the moment musical notes became a melody, they possessed class content. Indeed, they wrote, there was no music in the world that rose above class and no melody that did not relate to social life. The workers' criticism group at a Beijing instrumental factory declared that the idea that music has no class concept was a product of counter-revolutionary humanism — every kind of music served a certain class.[32]

The campaign against absolute and other bourgeois music was still in full swing in May of 1974 when Li Delun received a letter from the Philadelphia Orchestra. Mr. Li had managed to get Jiang Qing's permission to give Ormandy the score for *Moon Reflected on Erquan Spring* before he left China and the letter informed him that Maestro Ormandy wished to conduct the piece at year-end concerts in Philadelphia, Baltimore and the District of Columbia. The orchestra's public relations department hoped that Mr. Li could provide it with more information about the music to help American audiences better understand the piece.

Mr. Li could not reply to such a request on his own and Yu Huiyong refused to advise him, so he wrote directly to Jiang Qing. She responded by asking the Culture Group and the Ministry of Foreign Affairs to discuss the situation and report back to her. The Minister of Foreign Affairs responded pragmatically that since the Americans already had the score, they should be allowed to perform it, assuming there were no political or ideological problems with the music.

But Yu Huiyong disagreed. Countermanding the foreign ministry, he ordered Li Delun to write a letter to Ormandy telling him that the arranger of the piece thought his own work had serious problems of artistic and social content and did not want it performed — if such a performance were to take place, it would not improve the friendship of the Chinese and American people. The arranger of the piece, of course, was Wu Zuqiang, who had never said any such thing — he did not even know that the Philadelphia Orchestra was planning to play it. Mr. Li wrote the letter as ordered and Yu Huiyong then re-wrote it with stronger wording and told Mr. Li to sign it. The

31. Zhao Hua (1974). Do musical works without titles have no class character? *Chinese Literature* 4: 90. This was originally a *People's Daily* editorial.

32. See Ming Yan (2002). *Ershishiji Zhongguo Yinyue Piping Daolun* [A Guide to 20th-Century Music Criticism in China]. Beijing: Renmin Yinyue Chubanshe: 308.

letter was sent off to Philadelphia, where it presumably caused some dismay, and nothing more was heard from the Philadelphia Orchestra.[33]

THE END OF THE NIGHTMARE

The campaign against absolute music faded away after a few months without doing any real harm to Zhou Enlai or anyone else, but it did mark the end of the era of classical music diplomacy. No more foreign orchestras would perform in China for the duration of the Cultural Revolution. Even so, the broadening of China's musical boundaries did not come to a complete end, thanks to help from an unexpected corner: Mao Zedong.

By 1975, Mao once again seemed to be reconsidering the path that the Cultural Revolution had taken. He even complained to Deng Xiaoping that there weren't enough operas and that any new play or book or film was heavily criticized for the tiniest fault.

"There are too few model plays," he complained. "Moreover, even the slightest mistakes are dealt with by criticism. There is no more blooming of a hundred flowers. The others cannot bring up their opinions; that's no good. There is a fear of writing articles, writing plays, novels, poems, and songs." [34]

In making these complaints to Deng Xiaoping, Mao was preaching to the choir. Deng had never been a fan of Jiang Qing or her model operas, and Mao's dissatisfaction encouraged Deng to air his own opinions more openly. He publicly complained that the model operas had become so dominant that it seemed there was a policy to "let a single flower blossom." He also called the depiction of class struggle in the operas "one-sided thinking in terms of absolutes." [35]

A few weeks later, Mao voiced his changing viewpoint even more strongly when he wrote that the Party's cultural policy needed adjusting. Over a period of time, he suggested, cultural activities should be expanded so that writers would produce more poems, novels, essays and critiques. Just because a writer had made a mistake in the past did not mean he would make it again. With the exception of serious counter-revolutionaries, the Party should help its intellectuals to reform.[36]

---

33. Mr. Li wrote to Ormandy in 1977 to tell him that the situation had changed and it would be alright to play *Moon Reflected on Erquan Spring*. The letter is still in the Philadelphia Orchestra's archives, but Ormandy did not program the piece.

34. See Kraus: 237. (Original source is, Verbatim Record of Chairman Mao's Talks with Comrade Deng Xiaoping in early July, 1975. Document of Central Committee 15: 101 February, 1979).

35. Xin Hua (1976). Mass debate on revolution in literature and art. *Chinese Literature* 6: 104.

36. See Ye Yonglie: 743. Also, Kraus, Richard C. (1991). Arts policies of the Cultural Revolution: the rise and fall of culture minister Yu Huiyong. In William A. Joseph, Christine P.W. Wong, and David Zweig (eds.), *New Perspectives on the Cultural Revolution*. Cambridge: Council on East Asian Studies/Harvard University: 237. The original source is, Full Text of Chairman Mao's Written Statement of July 14, 1975, Document of the Central Committee 15: 101-102 (February 1979).

A vehicle for both Mao and Deng to convert opinions into policies soon appeared via *The Pioneers*, the first big feature film since the start of the Cultural Revolution. Jiang Qing was unhappy about the movie because it had been made without her involvement and because she saw it as a veiled expression of support for Zhou Enlai.[37] The day after it was released, in early 1975, she issued orders that prevented its further distribution and banned all reviews. Yu Huiyong — whose title was now Minister of Culture — then released a list of the ten major ways in which the movie was "seriously wrong politically and artistically,"[38] and *The Pioneers* all but disappeared.

Normally, that would have been the end of it, but the film's writer boldly decided to send letters to both Mao and Deng asking that the criticisms of his movie be reconsidered. Deng made certain that Mao saw the letter and on July 25, Mao scribbled his opinion on Deng's copy: "There is no big error in this film. Suggest that it be approved for distribution. Don't nitpick. And to list as many as ten accusations against it is going too far. It hampers the adjustment of the Party's current policy on literature and art."[39] Mao's response was said to have particularly upset Jiang Qing and she did everything she could to downplay it, but *The Pioneers* returned to the theaters.

Members of the music world then decided to try the same tactic by writing to Mao directly about an important occasion: the 40th and 30th anniversaries, respectively, of the deaths of Nie Er and Xian Xinghai. The music of both composers had been largely ignored during the Cultural Revolution, in part because they had worked with writers who were labeled counter-revolutionary, but mainly because Jiang Qing preferred revolutionary music with which she herself was directly associated. Many musicians considered this both disrespectful and ridiculous, so when Xian Xinghai's widow visited Beijing they urged her to write to Mao and request permission to hold a joint memorial concert for her husband and Nie Er. Again the letter was brought to Mao's attention by Deng Xiaoping and again the Chairman's response was positive: go ahead and have a concert.

Mao's response sent Beijing's music circles spinning — at long last they could perform something other than a model opera! Not surprisingly, it also angered Jiang Qing and her radical colleagues, who saw both the request and Mao's response as a move against them. Therefore, while Li Delun and other members of the concert-organizing group were eager to make it a major cultural event, Jiang Qing and her cohorts were just as eager to diminish it. When the organizing group suggested a big

---

37. *The Pioneers* tells the story of the oil workers who successfully opened up the Daqing oil field, which Chairman Mao had praised as an example for all Chinese industry. In the film, part of the workers' success is attributed to their intensive study of Chairman Mao's essays "On Contradiction" and "On Practice." Both essays were closely associated with Premier Zhou, since he had encouraged their widespread study, and it was this that evidently led Jiang Qing to interpret the film as a tacit expression of support for Zhou. For a discussion of *The Pioneers* and Jiang Qing's role in criticizing it, see (1977) A Grave Struggle Around the Film *The Pioneers. Chinese Literature* 1: 94-104.

38. *Ibid.,* 96.

39. *Ibid.,* 100.

venue for the concert, the cultural radicals moved it to a smaller one; when the organizing group secured an agreement to have it televised, the radicals told the newspapers not to write about it. Jiang Qing even tried to control the content of the program, demanding that the words to any songs with lyrics by writers with bad political backgrounds be changed. This was not a new strategy; she had previously ordered that new lyrics be written for Nie Er's *March of the Volunteers* — China's national anthem — because the original had been written by Tian Han, who had been denounced and died in prison in 1968.

In the days before the concert, Jiang Qing suddenly got "sick" and the organizing group was told that since she would be too ill to attend, no other central level leaders could be invited. The vice minister of culture even informed Mr. Li that he could not invite Xian Xinghai's widow, who had written to Mao in the first place; but Mr. Li convinced him to change his mind at the last minute. Mr. Li also skirted the directive that no central level leaders be invited by extending an invitation to Zhou Enlai's wife, Deng Yingchao, who replied that both she and her husband were too (genuinely) sick to attend, but would be certain to watch it on television.

Despite the best sabotage efforts of Jiang Qing and her supporters, the concert in memory of "the people's composers" was a resounding success. For many in the audience, it must have seemed like a trip down memory lane as they once again heard the songs by Nie Er and Xinghai that had inspired them to fight the Japanese and support the Communists. The concert was broadcast nationwide and was such a hit with musically-starved Beijing audiences that three additional performances had to be added in the 10,000 seat Capital Coliseum, the venue Mr. Li had originally requested. Jiang Qing was predictably outraged and Mr. Li was in trouble once again, this time for having had the temerity to invite Zhou Enlai's wife to the concert.

Li Delun was by this point thoroughly fed up with his collaboration with Jiang Qing and he had no regrets about having issued the invitation. His feelings were only strengthened when Premier Zhou Enlai died from cancer on January 8, 1976. Because Jiang Qing and her colleagues had been targeting the popular premier for several years, they did everything possible to ensure that his death would receive minimal attention. Even Chairman Mao did not issue any kind of public statement celebrating the life or mourning the death of the man who had worked for him loyally for so many decades. Although protocol required a major state funeral, the government issued orders that life and work should go on as normal, even to the point of insisting that the Central Philharmonic keep to its scheduled model opera performances.

Premier Zhou's body was laid out in the Taiwan Room of the Great Hall of the People, as he requested, and his body was scheduled to be cremated on January 11. Deng Xiaoping was assigned to give the eulogy at the funeral ceremony. Despite the lack of official encouragement and the bitter cold January weather, millions of mourners turned out to pay their last respects by watching the funeral cortege cross the city. As one account described it,

It was somber and cold that day. Long before dusk, when the hearse was to emerge from Beijing Hospital to begin its solemn procession to the Babaoshan Cemetery of Revolutionaries, knots and knots of people, including parents carrying babies in their arms, began to collect on the sidewalks. Several million turned out. Every inch of the pavement westwards to Babaoshan was occupied, sometimes three or four deep, with a huge crowd collected at Tiananmen Square. Black armbands were everywhere. Women of all ages wore in their hair home-made heavy white paper chrysanthemums. The cortege moved slowly, very slowly, to the refrains of a funeral march. As it approached, subdued sobbing turned into unrestrained wailing all along the capital's main thoroughfare, usually roaring with traffic and now oppressively muted except for the whisper of the crawling vehicle and the sound of people weeping.[40]

The Premier's ashes were put aboard an airplane and scattered across the vast lands and rivers of the nation he had loved and served for so long.

Zhou Enlai's chosen method for the disposal of his body only served to enhance the respect and love that people felt for him — and the dissatisfaction that many harbored over the rather perfunctory send-off he had been given. When the traditional Qingming Festival for honoring the dead came in early April, the sorrow over Zhou's death, the anger over his send-off, and the general weariness with the Cultural Revolution suddenly became volatile. Crowds of people began pouring into Tiananmen Square to leave flowers, wreathes and poems in honor of "the People's Premier" at the base of the Monument to the Peoples' Heroes. Official demands that they cease and desist only caused more people to flood into the area; Yu Huiyong visited the Central Philharmonic to tell its members not to go, but Mr. Li and his musicians went anyway. Poems honoring Zhou were glued to the lamp posts and strung from the pine trees that border the square, like this one called *So Much Grief and Rage on Earth*:

> At Qingming, we mourn our dear premier even more,
> Yet in the papers, no mention of your name.
> The people's deep grief can never be suppressed,
> As in crowds we gather at the Martyr's Memorial.
> With flowers we try to express all that is in our hearts;
> Hot tears fall and wet our clothes.
> Why has the spring come so late this year?
> Because of so much grief and rage on earth.[41]

Other poems were veiled criticisms of Jiang Qing and her cohorts, who were blamed for the premier's perfunctory funeral and deeply resented for a multitude of other reasons. One of the best known was called *Heads Raised We Unsheathe Our Swords*:

40. Fang, Percy Jucheng and Fang, Lucy Guinong J. (1986). *Zhou Enlai — A Profile*. Beijing: Foreign Languages Press: 4.
41. The Tiananmen Poems (A Selection) (1979). *Chinese Literature* 3: 6.

In our grief we hear the devils shrieking;
We weep while wolves and jackals laugh.
Shedding tears we come to mourn our hero;
Heads raised we unsheathe our swords.[42]

And some, like *On a Certain Woman*, were barely veiled at all:

This woman is really crazy.
She even wants to be an empress!
Look at yourself in the mirror
And see what you are.
Whoever dares attack our premier
Is like a mad dog barking at the sun.
To hell with you![43]

As mourners read these poems aloud to each other and copied them into notebooks, Jiang Qing and her fellow "wolves and jackals" became increasingly uneasy. On the evening of April 5, they sent troops into Tiananmen Square to clear away the tributes, and those who were posting them there. In the fighting that ensued, hundreds — perhaps thousands — of mourners were arrested and some were beaten and killed. With Mao himself at death's doorstep, Jiang Qing and her henchmen moved to solidify their own power.

Within days, they had accused Deng Xiaoping of instigating the "counter-revolutionary riots" at Tiananmen Square and stripped him of all his official posts. In the criticism campaign which ensued, "the unregenerate capitalist roader" was specifically taken to task for disliking the model operas and trying "to rehabilitate the art and literature of the landlord class and the bourgeoisie." [44]

By May Day, Deng himself was the prime subject of theatrical celebrations, which included a dance called *Reversing Correct Verdicts Goes Against the Will of the People*; a Peking opera called *Beat Back the Right Deviationist Wind*; and a children's play called *Denouncing Deng Xiaoping*.[45] The Central Philharmonic was told to provide the background music for a documentary film criticizing Deng, but Mr. Li checked himself into a hospital so he would not have to be involved with it. Aware that his life was likely to become even more difficult, he began weeding through his diaries and other papers to cleanse them of anything that might prove harmful. In the process, he came across the score to Shostakovich's *Tenth Symphony*, the one he had heard so long ago in Moscow and considered oddly sorrowful.

"When I looked at the score again, suddenly, I understood — it was so great. He was expressing everything the Soviet people must have felt, and everything we had gone through in the Cultural Revolution."

---

42. *Ibid.*, 3.
43. *Ibid.*, 13.
44. Xin Hua (1976). Mass Debate on Revolution in Literature and Art. *Chinese Literature* 6: 102 and 104.
45. See Theatrical Performances Over May Day (1976). *Chinese Literature* 7: 124.

Less than six months after the events at Qingming — on September 9, 1976 — Mao Zedong himself was dead. If his death produced less intense mourning than Premier Zhou's had (and even some relief) it created far more anxiety as people everywhere wondered what would happen next.

Fortunately, the aftermath of Mao's death proved calmer than his life. At 3:00 in the afternoon on September 18, the nation ceased all work for three minutes and listened silently as whistles sounded and bells tolled. Hua Guofeng peacefully assumed power and, on October 6, ordered the surprise arrests of Jiang Qing, Yao Wenyuan, Zhang Qunqiao and their comrade Wang Hongwen. The four radical leaders were labeled a "Gang of Four," charged with having perpetrated the innumerable crimes of the last decade, and vilified throughout the nation and the world. The Cultural Revolution was over.

With Mao dead and the "Gang of Four" jailed, the Chinese government grappled with the task of explaining why the Cultural Revolution happened and assigning responsibility for the many crimes that had taken place. Rather than acknowledge the ultimate accountability of the Communist Party, the leadership chose to lay blame primarily on individuals who were safely jailed or dead. Jiang Qing was at first painted as the arch villain, variously labeled "the political pick-pocket," "the careerist and swindler," and the "counter-revolutionary double-dealer who knew how to veer with the wind."[46] The model operas she had masterminded were too popular to be discredited, but her role in creating and producing them was deliberately diminished and she was tarred with the same feudal, bourgeois brush that she had used against so many others.

"She is an out-and-out executioner of proletarian literature and art," declared one exposé, "a trumpeter of feudal, bourgeois and revisionist wares, a witch trying to resurrect zombies both Chinese and foreign."[47]

With no apparent irony, she and her Gang of Four colleagues were accused of using the arts as a means to promote a counter-revolutionary line and restore capitalism, the same specious accusations that they had used to bring down so many others:

> Their line in literature and art was an important component of their extreme Rightist political line aimed at seizing power in the Party and government, overthrowing socialism and restoring capitalism. The gang's first step in this direction was gaining control over literature and art.... Step by step they established a fascist dictatorship in literary and art circles, ignoring instructions from the Party Central Committee and Chairman Mao... The gang of four learned all the despotic measures used by Chiang Kai-shek, Hitler and the Inquisitors of medieval Europe.[48]

---

46. See Chiang Ching (Jiang Qing) (1977), The political pickpocket (article written by the Mass...). *Chinese Literature* 2.

47. See An Exposure of Jiang Qing (collectively written by the propaganda team of Dazhai Brigade) (1977). *Chinese Literature* 2: 119.

48. Hua Wenying (1977). The "Gang of Four's" Revisionist Line in Literature and Art. *Chinese Literature* 7.

Jiang Qing and the other members of the Gang of Four were finally put on trial for their crimes in 1980, accused of "persecuting to death" an estimated 34,800 people and of having "framed and persecuted" 729,511 others.[49] Jiang Qing refused to acknowledge any guilt or regret at her trial, defiantly insisting that she had only been implementing her husband's wishes.

"I was Chairman Mao's dog," she told the judges. "Whomever he told me to bite, I bit."[50]

She shouted at witnesses, called the judges fascists, and was so disruptive that she was thrown out of the courtroom more than once. Zhang Chunqiao was quietly stubborn, refusing to answer any questions put to him by prosecutors, while Yao Wenyuan and Wang Hongwen were more cooperative. When the trial ended, Jiang Qing and Zhang Chunqiao were both sentenced to death — albeit with two years' reprieve, to allow them to repent — while Wang Hongwen got life imprisonment and Yao Wenyuan 18 years. Jiang Qing shouted so loudly when she heard the sentence of death pronounced against her that she did not initially hear of the reprieve; only after it had been repeated to her did she calm down, knowing that it meant she would never be executed.[51]

While there were few who would argue that it was proper to put Jiang Qing and her collaborators on trial and punish them, most Chinese certainly saw that the Cultural Revolution could never have happened without the compliance and support of other leaders, most prominent among them Mao Zedong. The delicate process of apportioning to Mao the blame he deserved, without vilifying him or discrediting his entire reign, was handled by Deng Xiaoping, who had returned to power after the fall of the Gang of Four. In 1981, the Communist Party issued a Central Committee resolution which stated at the outset that the Cultural Revolution "was initiated and led by Mao Zedong."[52] In an interesting twist, the resolution claimed that the theses which Mao used as a basis for initiating the Cultural Revolution were inconsistent with his own "Mao Zedong Thought." Mao had become "arrogant" and "confused right with wrong and the people with the enemy" in starting the Cultural Revolution, which was "an error comprehensive in magnitude and protracted in duration." However, terrible as it was, it did not negate Mao's many achievements — or the authority of the Communist Party — since "after all, it was the error of a great proletarian revolutionary."

---

49. Spence: 680-1.

50. Meisner, M. (1986). *Mao's China and After, A History of the People's Republic.* New York: The Free Press: 462.

51. Jiang Qing committed suicide in 1991 and Wang Hongwen died of cancer in 1992. Yao Wenyuan finished his term and was released in 1996 and Zhang Chunqiao was given medical parole in 2002. Both Yao and Zhang live quietly in Shanghai.

52. See Schoenhals, Michael (ed.) (1996). *China's Cultural Revolution, 1966-1969, Not a Dinner Party.* Armonk, New York: 296-303. The original is from the Central Committee of the Communist Party's, Resolution on certain questions in the history of our party since the founding of the People's Republic of China.

REBUILDING AND RECONCILIATION

On March 26, 1977, Li Delun led the Central Philharmonic in a triumphant performance of Beethoven's *Fifth Symphony*. The demand for tickets was so high that eleven more performances had to be added.

"Papers all over the world covered it," recalled Mr. Li. "'China played Beethoven — their policies are really changing.'"

The first concert was broadcast nationwide and for many music lovers around China it came as the final proof that the Cultural Revolution was truly over.

"They played Beethoven's *Fifth*," remembered Xu Ximing, head of the Shanghai Music Lovers' Association, who listened to the broadcast in Shanghai. "It is about the light that comes after a period of great difficulty, so it was very appropriate."

If the performance marked the musical end of the Cultural Revolution, it also signified that the time for re-building had begun. Despite all Li Delun's efforts, politics had so dominated music in the thirty years of the Central Philharmonic's existence that it had rehearsed only 20 different programs since its founding.[53] The end of the Cultural Revolution seemed to present one last opportunity to move forward; so, Mr. Li dusted off his old dreams and began proposing new plans — a regular concert season; a new concert hall to replace the old facility, which had been irreparably damaged by the 1976 Tangshan earthquake; new instruments; regular musical check-ups for players; educational outreach activities to spread symphonic music; and more foreign exchanges.

Of all these plans, it was the last that proved easiest to realize. So many renowned foreign musicians were eager to perform and teach in China that it was like the 1950s all over again, except this time the musicians were from capitalist democracies instead of Communist brothers. The first to arrive was Seiji Ozawa, who was then conductor of the Boston Symphony Orchestra. Although Ozawa is Japanese, he was born in China and was so anxious to return that he managed to arrive in Beijing in November of 1976, just weeks after the fall of the Gang of Four. Because there were still many who objected to the idea of a "capitalist" conductor leading a "proletarian orchestra," Ozawa was not invited to conduct, but Li Delun was instructed to give him a warm welcome. The two soon developed a strong rapport and Ozawa shared with Mr. Li his wish that he could conduct the Central Philharmonic on his next visit.

This wish came true in May of 1978, when Ozawa was invited to lead the Central Philharmonic in a performance of Chinese, Japanese and Western music. Unfortunately, Mr. Li was not permitted to play host on this occasion because new officials at the Ministry of Culture had decided to go after some of those artists who had achieved national prominence under the Gang of Four.

Borrowing a page from the book of those whom they sought to repudiate, they first organized a large public criticism session of Yu Huiyong and several model opera

53. Luo: 478.

stars who had assumed political positions. Yu Huiyong had apparently been hoping that he would escape prosecution, but once he was named as a major follower of the Gang of Four at the 11th Communist Party Congress in August of 1977, he lost hope. On August 28, he found a bottle of Lysol disinfectant in a courtyard bathroom and took it home with him. That night, he wrote a note in which he acknowledged that he had been wrong in following the Gang of Four, apologized for it, and said that only death would absolve him of his guilt. Around 8:00, he finished writing and swallowed the Lysol. He was still breathing when he was discovered, but he died in the hospital three days later.[54]

Li Delun was not nationally denounced, but culture officials nonetheless launched an investigation of him and sent a team over to the Central Philharmonic with orders to remove him from his posts. Mr. Li had not anticipated this and as he looked back on the previous decade, he felt sad, tired, and ill-used.

"It was all a power struggle, all politics — Jiang Qing just used music...We were all used by her, to give her something to do. I worked hard, but in my heart it was difficult."

With the political tide turning against him and no job to do at the Philharmonic, Mr. Li acted on the advice of friends and once again checked himself into the hospital. This time the decision proved a life-saving one — although he had not thought he was sick, doctors discovered a malignant tumor on his kidney. Because it was small and was removed early, he was given a good prognosis for his physical recovery. However, his political recovery looked at best uncertain; all the doctors could do for him in this regard was prevent the Ministry of Culture's eager investigators from continuing to hound him even as he lay in his sick bed recovering from surgery.

Mr. Li was fully recovered, physically, by Ozawa's 1978 trip, but not politically. When the Japanese maestro repeatedly asked to see him, officials lied by saying that Mr. Li was sick. When Ozawa wanted to visit anyway, they changed their line and said that he was far away in the south of China. The conductor Han Zhongjie hosted Ozawa in Mr. Li's absence, and Ozawa startled everyone by asking if he could stay at Han's house instead of in a hotel. Officials agreed to the request and Ozawa lived with Han's family in their spartan apartment and ate homemade *jiaozi*, or dumplings, for dinner. The concert he conducted provided a big boost to the Central Philharmonic and its musicians.

"He brought freshness to us," Han later told a reporter. "His conducting is so passionate and impressive to both the orchestra members and audience that many music students have made him their idol and imitate his conducting." [55]

When Ozawa's visit was over, culture officials apparently felt guilty about having lied to him, so they sent Mr. Li to the south and told him to write a letter to Ozawa when he got there. They never sent for him to come back, so Mr. Li was still in

---

54. See Dai Jiafang (1995). *Yangbanxi de Fengfeng Yuyu* [The Trials and Tribulations of Model Operas]. Beijing: Zhishi Chubanshe: 249–250.

55. In interview with Chen Jie (2004). From hutongs to who's who. *China Daily* February 26: 13.

this quasi-southern exile in early 1979 when Deng Xiaoping himself announced that Ozawa would be returning to China yet again, this time with the entire Boston Symphony Orchestra. As preparations for the visit got underway, Mr. Li's friends and colleagues began to call for his return to the helm of the Central Philharmonic. Their cries soon grew loud enough that Politburo member and future secretary-general of the Communist Party Hu Yaobang heard them and intervened with the Ministry of Culture, which then permitted Mr. Li to return to his job.[56]

Ozawa's tour with the Boston Symphony generated great excitement. The US and China had just established full diplomatic relations and the visit was the first by an American orchestra since the Philadelphia Orchestra in 1973. Of equal importance was the deep admiration and respect that many Chinese had for Ozawa as an Asian conductor who had triumphed on the international stage and who clearly cared a great deal about their country. Crowds clamored to get tickets to the four concerts split between Beijing and Shanghai. Ozawa opened three Beijing rehearsals to the public and drew thousands of listeners, among them 1700 musicians from around the country.

At its first Beijing performance, the program included Gershwin's *An American in Paris*, Berlioz's *Symphonie Fantastique*, and Wu Zuqiang's *pipa* concerto *Little Sisters of the Grassland* with the renowned *pipa* player Liu Dehai.[57] At one concert the orchestra played Liszt's *First Piano Concerto* with the pianist Liu Shikun, whose hands Red Guards had tried — unsuccessfully — to permanently cripple. And at the grand Beijing finale, 217 musicians from the Boston Symphony and the Central Philharmonic jointly performed Beethoven's *Fifth Symphony* before a stadium audience of 18,000.[58]

The Boston Symphony's tour was followed almost immediately by a visit from the renowned violinist Isaac Stern. This was to be Li Delun's first major performance after his enforced two-year absence and he and the orchestra were determined to perform well and learn as much as they could. They even held public practice concerts featuring the Brahms and Mozart violin concertos that Stern was scheduled to play.

"We were prepared," recalled Mr. Li. "But the scores were all a mess — they were from the Zhonghua Symphony and had been hand copied in the 1940s, and there were many mistakes."

However, when Stern arrived and the real rehearsals began, Mr. Li realized that, despite their preparation, they lacked rhythmic precision. Stern, too, felt that something was amiss:

> As I entered the rehearsal hall in Beijing, I found it jammed with people who, it quickly became apparent, knew music. Also immediately apparent was the rather limited approach of both the conductor and the orchestra to Western music; they

---

56. Hu Yaobang was also involved in Fu Cong's rehabilitation, recommending that he be welcomed back to China since he had left under special circumstances.

57. A recording of Ozawa leading the Boston Symphony in *Little Sisters of the Grassland* was released by Philips in 1979.

58. Tan Aiqing (1979). Music and friendship — the Boston Symphony Orchestra in China. *China Reconstructs* July: 8.

were unaccustomed to playing with varieties of color and passion. There was a distinctly stiff, technical, old-fashioned approach to the way they played.

The immediate problem was how to deal with the conductor without causing him to lose face in front of his orchestra. Before the rehearsal, I spent a few minutes alone with him, going over the salient points in the music. In the presence of the orchestra, I made it clear — with a smile, a joke, a friendly gesture — that I was not trying to be a big shot and had not the least intent to cut the conductor down. To the contrary, I was trying to build them all up; there was a difference, and all orchestras can sense it. In the case of the Central Philharmonic, both the conductor and the players recognized immediately that when I asked them to do this or that, I was not teaching them how to play; I was making them feel individually capable of accomplishing more than they were doing now.[59]

Stern was accompanied by a camera crew throughout his visit and when he got back to the US the footage was edited to make a film called *From Mao to Mozart: Isaac Stern in China*. The film — which won a 1980 Academy Award for best documentary — shows Stern passionately instructing the Central Philharmonic while Li Delun stands at his podium, listening intently. But, it also supports Stern's contention that his advice was offered with such sincere good will that no one was offended; indeed, Mr. Li considered Stern's visit to be like a shot of adrenaline, a chance for young musicians who grew up during the Cultural Revolution to see true professionalism first hand. When Stern departed for Shanghai, he and Mr. Li promised each other that they would one day perform together again.

Stern's visit was followed in October by that of the legendary Herbert von Karajan and the Berlin Philharmonic. The trip got off to an inauspicious start when an improvised gangway built to accommodate the orchestra's Lufthansa DC-10 collapsed, seriously injuring a cellist and an oboe player. But Karajan decided at once that the orchestra would remain in Beijing and the show would go on despite the accident. He went ahead with all scheduled events, including a trip to attend a Central Philharmonic rehearsal to decide whether its musicians were good enough to join the Berlin Philharmonic on stage. When he proclaimed himself satisfied, 36 members of the Central Philharmonic were chosen to play Beethoven's *Seventh Symphony* with the Berlin Philharmonic. Mingling during rehearsals, two Central Philharmonic members and a violinist from the Berlin Philharmonic discovered that they had all lived in Harbin in the 1930s and 1940s and even studied with the same violin teacher, Vladimir Trachtenberg. The violinist, Helmut Stern, was a German Jew and he credited China with saving his life. [60]

The Berlin Philharmonic was extremely well-received by audiences and critics alike. One reviewer wrote that Brahms *First Symphony* had been played in Beijing many times by both local and visiting orchestras but "none caught the grandeur of the work

59. Stern, Isaac (with Chaim Potok) (1999). *My First 79 Years*. New York: Alfred A. Knopf: 246.
60. For Helmut Stern, see Luo: 480 and Liu Xinxin and Liu Xueqing (2002). *Haerbin Xiyang Yinyueshi* [The history of Western music in Harbin]. Beijing: Renmin Yinyue Chubanshe: 189-90.

so well as von Karajan... the audience was electrified from the very beginning when the strings sang out in a glowing and sonorous tone to the high-spirited horn call near the end."[61] Karajan was so pleased with his orchestra's visit that he suggested further exchanges, which is exactly what the Central Philharmonic was hoping for. He told the Chinese press that he was amazed at the character and precision demonstrated by the Philharmonic musicians, especially since their average age was only mid-thirties and they had not been able to play Western music for much of their adult lives. He also praised Li Delun's musical talents and publicly promised to invite him to conduct the Berlin Philharmonic. Finally, he proposed that the Berlin Philharmonic work with the Ministry of Culture to stage and film Puccini's *Turandot* in the Forbidden City, where the opera's mythical story is set.[62]

Unfortunately, nothing came of his proposals; the Ministry of Culture flatly refused to consider the idea of using the Forbidden City to stage an opera, especially with a foreign orchestra. It also balked at the invitation to Li Delun, which was seen as demonstrating a hegemonistic attitude on the part of Karajan and Germany since it named a particular conductor rather than requesting the Ministry to send whomever it wished. Eager to demonstrate its sovereign right to make such decisions, the Ministry declined on Mr. Li's behalf and informed the Germans that Huang Yijun at the Shanghai Symphony would conduct the Berlin Philharmonic instead. Mr. Huang did not want to accept an invitation meant for his friend, but Mr. Li urged him take advantage of the once-in-a-lifetime chance, so he did.

In June of 1980, Mr. Li and the Central Philharmonic hosted the pianist Dong Guangguang and the violinist Ma Sihong, the younger brother of Ma Sicong. Both had left China for the US more than three decades earlier and built successful careers as performers and teachers. They had married in 1954 and eventually settled in New York, where they founded the Siyo Music Society to introduce classical music to New York's Chinese residents. The couple had not been back to China since they first left, so their trip was full of emotional reunions with surviving family members. Ms. Dong also used her visit to discover the fate of her piano, the beloved Steinway that had once belonged to Paci. It had been taken over by the government filmmaking company, she learned, and only after several years of pleading and prodding was her nephew finally able to get permission for her to take it out of China. Ms. Dong had the piano shipped to New York and then discovered that it was too big to fit in the couple's city apartment.

"But, I thought, 'I'm not going to give up that piano again!" explained Ms. Dong. "So that's why we bought our house — I bought it with specifications for the piano."[63]

Mr. Li conducted the Central Philharmonic for Dong Guangguang's performance of Brahms' *First Piano Concerto* and Han Zhongjie conducted for Ma Sihong's

---

61. Zhao Jinglun (1980). Berlin orchestra and von Karajan acclaimed. *China Reconstructs* February: 42-43.

62. For Karajan's comments, see Zhao: 43.

63. Miss Dong stayed in touch with the childhood sponsor who had given her the gold bar with which she bought the piano; he had moved to Brazil and was preparing to celebrate his 100th birthday at the time of our interview with Ms. Dong.

performance of Brahms' *Violin Concerto*. The couple then went to Shanghai, where they gave a concert with the Shanghai Ballet Orchestra and a nostalgic joint recital at which they played the same program in the Lyceum Theater as they had in 1946, just before they first left China.

Li Delun was delighted with all the opportunities to work with visiting musicians, but bothered by his inability to implement most of his other ideas for improving and professionalizing the Philharmonic. Foreign exchanges were very important, but the foreigners came and went — real and lasting change would have to come from within the organization and would require greater financial support from the Ministry of Culture. Instead, the Philharmonic found itself under increasing pressure to earn its own way. In 1979, it was so busy recording music for movies in order to make money that it performed only four different programs. Inspired by the Berlin Philharmonic — which did forty different programs in a year — Li Delun implemented a firm policy of daily morning rehearsals, with all revenue-making activities limited to afternoons and Sundays. This plan proved successful and in 1980, the Central Philharmonic performed 26 different programs, more than it had in its entire history. As important as the quantity was the variety, with the orchestra at long last free to play Debussy, Bartok, Stravinsky and even some contemporary pieces.

Mr. Li also made slow progress on his plan for building a new Beijing Concert Hall, although it required him to be intimately involved in every aspect from budgeting to design. It took eight years, passed through the hands of three different culture ministers, and cost nine times the original projection, but in 1986 the 1200-seat Beijing Concert Hall was finally completed. The opening of the new hall — the first professional concert hall in China — was a gala affair, with many dignitaries in attendance to hear Yan Liangkun conduct the Central Philharmonic Society in Xian Xinghai's *Yellow River Cantata* and the last movement of Beethoven's *Ninth Symphony*, "Ode to Joy." As the major force behind the hall's revival, Li Delun addressed the audience and shared his hope that the hall would be a major venue for serious music and a music activity and education center for all Beijing.

Rebuilding at the Shanghai Symphony proceeded in much the same way as at the Central Philharmonic, except that it was slower. Having spent so many years making amends for having been too open and capitalist in pre-liberation days, Shanghai and its cultural institutions were once again in a position to feel embarrassed, this time for having been the excessively leftist launching pad of the Gang of Four. Thus, for the first few years after the Cultural Revolution, the Shanghai Symphony did not play any major work of Western music unless it had been performed in Beijing first. The logistics of rebuilding were also more complicated since the Shanghai Symphony had not been accorded the same special treatment as the Central Philharmonic. Conductor Huang Yijun had been replaced by Cao Peng and many of its musicians had been seconded to local opera troupes to play model operas during the Cultural Revolution.

However, the Shanghai Symphony's deep musical foundations assured that it would rebuild successfully, even if it took some time. Huang Yijun was asked to return to the podium within weeks of the fall of the Gang of Four and veteran musicians were called back. The orchestra benefited from some of the same foreign exchanges as the Central Philharmonic and its audiences returned in the burst of excitement about classical music that followed the end of the Cultural Revolution and the visits of so many world famous musicians. When it gave a series of concerts celebrating the 215th anniversary of Beethoven's birth in 1985, the ticket lines stretched around the block and many people had to be turned away.

In 1984, Chen Xieyang replaced Mr. Huang as conductor and in 1986 he became music director, assuming full responsibility for the orchestra's artistic and business affairs. This was an important move because it was the first time that a practicing musician was put in the top management position, a job which had previously been given to Communist Party cadres at all orchestras. Mr. Chen then set about further professionalizing the Shanghai Symphony, making it the first orchestra to sign employment contracts with its members, the first to establish a development foundation, and the first to set up a music lovers' association.

China's education system was especially hard hit by the Cultural Revolution. For ten years there had been no open entrance exams, no formal graduations, no teaching of a standard non-political curriculum. Red Guards had destroyed school records, burnt text-books, and beaten, abused and murdered teachers at schools throughout the country. The return to normal functioning thus took longer at institutions of music education than it did at the orchestras. Although music educators began picking up the pieces as soon as they could, regular enrollment in the conservatories did not begin until 1978. The Central Conservatory led the way and the announcement that it was re-opening and accepting students based on merit was carried in *People's Daily*.

"I can't tell you how enthusiastic I was," recalled the composer Guo Wenjing. "Just imagine — a genuine call for students in a big governmental newspaper! It was a unique event!"[64]

The Conservatory recruited students in Beijing, Shanghai, Chengdu and Guangzhou but received far more applicants than expected.

"In 1978, 18,000 people applied and we accepted 100," explained the composer Wu Zuqiang, who was then the head of the Conservatory's composition department. "But then we accepted 100 more — we had nowhere to put them, but it was such a shame!"

That nobody had anticipated such a high demand for professional-level music education is unsurprising. The conservatories had been shuttered, the professors locked up in "cow sheds," and the entire Western classical canon banned for the better part of a decade. It must have seemed that relatively few people would be seeking to spend their first five years of post-Cultural Revolution life mastering counterpoint, learning to play Beethoven, or singing Puccini. But, in fact, Jiang Qing's radical culture policies had not caused bourgeois music to "die," as she had predicted when she visited

---

64. See Kouwenhoven, Frank and Schimmelpenninck, Antoinet (1997). Guo Wenjing — a composer's portrait. *Chime*. Spring/Autumn: 18.

the Central Philharmonic. Instead, these policies had given it new life, creating an entire generation of musicians who had a basic grounding in both Chinese and Western instruments and a passionate desire to obtain a formal music education.

Those accepted to the Conservatory's first post-Cultural Revolution class included farmers, factory workers, shop assistants, a fire fighter, a forest ranger and a milkman who had somehow managed to pursue their musical goals even as they labored at these proletarian occupations.[65]

"I wouldn't change a single selection," said Wu Zuqiang, speaking of the Conservatory's first composition class. "They were all great. You look at Tan Dun, Chen Yi, Zhou Long, Qu Xiaosong — they are so successful."

Tan, Chen, Zhou and Qu came from different regions of the country and diverse family backgrounds but all were musically talented youths who had been sent to the countryside to do physical labor during the Cultural Revolution. They had continued to develop their musical interests even as they planted rice or carried rocks — Tan Dun started an orchestra with largely homemade instruments that included tree branches and farming tools and Chen Yi played revolutionary songs mixed with Paganini passages for the farmers' children. Their respective talents were then noticed and each was brought back to a city in order to work as violinist, conductor, or composer for troupes that performed model operas. When the Central Conservatory re-opened, they sent in their applications and were selected from among the 18,000 other applicants. Then, as Wu Zuqiang put it, they "worked very hard... and, as I've often told them, they caught up with the good times. It was easy to connect with the outside world."

Indeed, in the first five years after the Central Conservatory re-opened, more than a thousand foreign artists came to give master classes or guest lectures.[66] The first to stay for a prolonged period was the British composer Alexander Goehr.

"Alexander Goehr built the bridge," said Guo Wenjing, who was also accepted into the first post-Cultural revolution class. "He is the great missionary. All composers mention him. The conservatory has had exchanges ever since."

During his 1979 stay, Goehr introduced New Music from the Second Viennese School to the avant-garde. His subject was not without controversy — some people still opposed the teaching of 20th-century music, especially atonal — and at the last minute he was almost asked to give a general discussion of classical music history instead, but those who thought students should be exposed to the new prevailed.

The Chinese-born composer and Columbia University professor Zhou Wenzhong also came early on and proved to be of special importance not only for his teaching but because he founded the Center for US-China Arts Exchange, which later became instrumental in helping young Chinese composers to study in the US. Goehr and Zhou were followed by other influential foreign composers including Gyorgy Ligeti, Isang Yun, Toru Takemitsu and George Crumb.

---

65. See Tan Aiqing (1983). Renaissance in music education. *China Reconstructs* October: 63-65.
66. For the number of visiting musicians, see Tan Aiqing: 63.

Many performers of classical music also came to help train the Conservatory's instrumentalists, including some of the world-renowned musicians who travelled to Beijing to perform. Among them was Yehudi Menuhin, whose daughter had been married to, and divorced from, the pianist Fu Cong. Menuhin described his impressions of the recovering music education system in his autobiography:

> The musical establishment operates a highly organized sieving system of regional and national competitions, for teachers and students, so that the best of China's talent was present. I thought the players remarkably well prepared but interpretatively immature, hardly surprising, perhaps, as they had been cut off from the rest of the musical world for so long. There was however, in compensation, a great sense of fraternity among them all, formed during the years of oppression when they had to practice in secret and faced prison if caught... Over several days I sat in the big hall packed with aspiring violinists and listened and advised.[67]

In 1982, Menuhin taught at the Central Conservatory again and brought with him more than 50 of his own students. He continued to return in subsequent years and was eventually named an honorary professor.

The Conservatory did not just wait passively for the outside world to come, but reached out to it by sending delegations overseas. Importantly, it also made efforts to contact the nation's two famous musician defectors, Fu Cong and Ma Sicong.

Fu Cong had settled in Europe, become a renowned concert pianist on the international circuit and eventually lost all contact with his homeland. In 1977, he managed to track down his brother, the only member of his family still alive and living in China. Later that same year, Wu Zuqiang led a delegation from the Central Conservatory to London. Fu Cong passed a message through a friend asking Wu to leave his address if it would be permissible for Fu Cong to visit him. Then, in Fu's words,

> When I found Wu's address waiting for me when I got back I went that same night to see him in his hotel. I had met many people from China in Britain, but I was particularly excited to see Wu, because in agreeing to see me he represented my country officially. The whole delegation attended a concert I gave in the Queen Elizabeth Hall. That night I played as my final encore [He Luting's] *Buffalo Boy's Flute*, the Chinese tune I like most, to express my deep love for China and my Chinese friends.[68]

After meeting Wu Zuqiang in London, Fu Cong wrote directly to Chinese leader Deng Xiaoping telling him that he wished to return to China to visit his brother and to do something for his country. When his parents were posthumously rehabilitated, he returned for their memorial service and seven months later went back to give lectures at the Central and Shanghai Conservatories. He also discussed his original decision not to return to China, telling a journalist,

---

67. Menuhin, Yehudi (1996). *Unfinished Journey: Twenty Years Later*. New York: Fromm International Publishing Corporation: 408-9.

68. Tan Aiqing (1980). The homecoming of pianist Fou Tsong. *China Reconstructs* May: 50.

294

In December 1958 I graduated. If I returned to China I knew my situation would be impossible. Both my father and I would have had to expose each other. This was unthinkable. We would never do that. So I was forced to leave. About my leaving I always felt full of regret and anguish. After all, I'm one of millions of intellectuals in China. They all suffered terribly in the cultural revolution, but I escaped this. It seemed so unfair. I felt uneasy, as if I owed something to all my friends.[69]

Fu Cong also published a collection of the many letters his father had written him. The letters were full of Fu Lei's advice on being first "a man, then an artist, then a musician and lastly a pianist."[70] The letters became extremely popular among college students who were themselves looking for advice in their fast-changing nation.

The Conservatory's efforts to re-establish a connection with its former president, Ma Sicong, were far more complicated. Fu Cong had defected as a young man while already overseas and had remained quiet about his reasons for leaving and his opinions about the situation in China. As he later told a reporter, "All these years I've followed this principle: Never allow anyone to use me to harm my country and never do anything dishonorable for personal gains."[71] For these reasons, and because of the compassion many felt for him due to his parents' joint suicide, it was relatively easy to rehabilitate him.

Ma Sicong, on the other hand, was an established cultural figure who had secretly fled the country and then publicly made critical statements about China, most notably in the *Life* Magazine article. He had been tried for treason *in absentia* and declared guilty. Immediately following the verdict, he had essentially been rendered *persona non grata* — his music ceased to be played, his work was removed from textbooks, and his name was expurgated from the dictionary of Chinese musicians.

So, while the vast majority of intellectuals who were persecuted in the Cultural Revolution were rehabilitated at the end of 1978, he was not. Behind the scenes many people argued in his defense — his only "crime," after all, had been to escape persecution that all agreed had been unjust — but others argued that he should have stayed and suffered like everyone else, and then pointed to his *Life* Magazine article and the several trips he had made to Taiwan as proof of his disloyalty. Zhao Feng — the Conservatory vice-president who had been made to dress as a wolf in sheep's clothing — was appointed president of the Conservatory.

Mr. Ma, meanwhile, had settled into his new life in the US, but not with much peace. He and his wife moved from Virginia to Maryland and then to Philadelphia, where their daughter lived. Mr. Ma learned to drive and to do housework. He composed and gave concerts in the Chinese community, with his wife playing piano. The most popular of all his compositions was *Thinking of Home*, an irony that was not lost on him. When Henry Kissinger made his first secret visit to Beijing in July of 1971,

69. Tan Aiqing: 49.
70. See Retrospect (1980).*China Reconstructs* May: 52.
71. Tan Aiqing: 51.

Zhou Enlai quietly availed himself of the opportunity to deliver Mr. Ma a personal message. He had two big regrets in his life, the Premier reportedly told Kissinger, one of which was that Ma Sicong had been forced to leave China in his old age, a circumstance which made him very sad.

Upon returning to the US, Kissinger relayed the message to Mr. Ma, who was so moved by the premier's words that he retreated to his room and cried for many hours.[72] When he learned of Zhou Enlai's death in 1976, he became so depressed that he stopped composing for a time. But when the Cultural Revolution ended and the rehabilitation process began, he started to hope that he would be invited back. Many signs seemed to point in his favor, particularly Fu Cong's return and the invitation issued to his brother, Ma Sihong. But, the months and years continued to pass with no word of his rehabilitation and no invitation to return.

Wu Zuqiang, who succeeded Zhao Feng as Conservatory president, visited Mr. Ma and his wife in the US in 1984 and behind the scenes he and other school officials pushed for a positive decision on Mr. Ma's case. These efforts finally bore fruit at the Chinese new year of 1985 when a hundred newspapers around China carried the same headline: Ma Sicong had been completely rehabilitated by the Ministries of Culture and State Security. Wu Zuqiang called Mr. Ma in the US to give him the long-awaited news and Mr. Ma, by all accounts, was very happy. He and his wife made tentative plans to return to China for good, but first decided to travel around Europe. When their vacation was over, they continued to talk about buying tickets for China but still did not do so. Wu Zuqiang called again in 1986 to invite Ma Sicong to be a judge in a youth violin competition, with all expenses paid by the Conservatory. Still, Mr. Ma did not return. In 1987, he was hospitalized with heart disease; he continued to talk about going back even as he lay in hospital. Finally, on May 20 of that year, Ma Sicong died in Philadelphia, never having managed to muster the mental, physical and emotional strength to return to China.

Ma Sicong had been gone from China for nearly twenty years at the time of his death, but he was still widely mourned. The tenth anniversary of his passing was commemorated in Beijing with a concert of his most important violin pieces and in 2002 the Guangzhou Museum of Art opened a Ma Sicong Memorial Hall. The hall displays many of Ma's possessions — including his piano and violin — and commemorates him for being the first Chinese musician to hold a recital in modern China and the first to compose music for the violin, and for his efforts as a music educator.

Like the Central Conservatory, the Shanghai Conservatory reopened in 1978 with an abundance of talented applicants from which to choose. It, too, had many foreign visitors. Isaac Stern was among them and considerable time in the film *From Mao to Mozart* is devoted to interviews with Tan Shuzhen. But, the rebuilding process was arguably even harder at the Shanghai Conservatory than elsewhere because so

---

72. Ye Yonglie (2000). *Ma Sicong Zhuan. Aiguode panguozhe* [A biography of Ma Sicong, patriotic traitor]. Urumqi: Xinjiang Chubanshe: 329.

many of its professors had died — and because the humiliation and torture that had driven them to their deaths had come from within the Conservatory. Thus, in addition to finding replacements for professors lost to suicide, it was also necessary to allay the bitterness and anger that weighed on many who survived. The 1979 decision to re-instate He Luting as president did much to help with this process.

Mr. He was by this point 75 years old, but he had been determined to get his old job back ever since his release from prison in 1972. In the intervening years, Mr. He had gone through a period of intense emotional struggle. Naturally, he was grief-stricken when he learned that his second daughter had killed herself back in 1968. But he also felt tremendous sorrow — and even guilt — over the suicides of so many Conservatory professors.

"He Luting had asked many people to come back from Hong Kong," recalled the composer Zhu Jianer. "He felt so much guilt. He felt terrible when he came out of jail and learned of all who had died."

Mr. He apparently felt worst about the pianist Li Cuizhen, because he had worried about her from the start, knowing that her love of beauty and enjoyment of pretty clothes could get her in trouble. When he heard how she had died — dressed in her best clothes and carefully made up — he cursed himself for not having tried to help her remain strong in the face of the Red Guards.

But if Mr. He was angry at what happened to him — and furious at what happened to others — he was still determined to contribute whatever he could to the development of music in China. The Conservatory's revolutionary leaders gave him a small desk in the music research room and made it clear that he was not wanted, but he went to work anyway. When the Cultural Revolution ended, he went to Beijing without permission to demand that the officials at the Ministry of Culture give him his job back. His ultimate reinstatement as Shanghai Conservatory president was a cause for celebration in intellectual circles nationwide. A special concert of his own music was held to honor him in Shanghai when he reassumed his post and a similar concert was held in Beijing in 1983 to celebrate his 80th birthday.

Upon returning to the leadership of the Conservatory, Mr. He first presided over a memorial service for the many professors who had committed suicide or died in captivity. Then he got back to work, using his position as a platform for promoting his views on music and music education. He emphasized the importance of preserving Chinese tradition even as imported techniques and theories were adopted to make Chinese music better. He repeatedly stressed that the purpose of a musical organization was not to earn money, but to make music and improve people's culture level — if the government's goal was to make money, it should invest in factories, not music. Finally, Mr. He once again began to gather the most talented people available to administrate and teach at the Conservatory, starting with Ding Shande, Zhou Xiaoyan and Tan Shuzhen who were all re-appointed to their former positions as vice-presidents.

Like his colleagues, Tan Shuzhen willingly returned to the Conservatory, trying to put out of his mind the memory of the many months he spent locked in one of its closets and the years he was forced to spend fixing its toilets.

Since faith had sustained Mr. Tan in his years of suffering, he concentrated on forgiveness in its aftermath. Mr. Ni, the young violinist turned Red Guard who had first criticized him, was at the top of Mr. Tan's list.

"After the Cultural Revolution, he tried to avoid me, but I told the other students, I don't care. He did not do it voluntarily. It was the moment. They were my best students — the second person who came to criticize me, I'd known him since childhood. If you hate someone, you hurt yourself first. He doesn't feel it."

Mr. Ni went on to become a violin teacher in the US and Mr. Tan came to look upon him as a "very good friend."

The Red Guard who had repeatedly beaten Mr. Tan was sentenced to eight years in prison. Then, one day Mr. Tan saw him riding a bike.

"I wanted to forgive him, but he didn't dare to talk to me. Let bygones be bygones. Forgiveness will make me happy, make me have peace of mind."

But if Mr. Tan could forgive those who hurt him, he could never quite come to terms with the fact that so many of his friends and colleagues had taken their own lives.

"It's all so cruel. But if they had my thinking — they didn't have to die, they just had to endure. When I was little, I listened to mother tell me Bible stories. All those who died were younger than me — they'd still be alive. They were intellectuals. But if they had only studied the Bible — or Buddhism, or Confucius. If you don't want to believe in God — but..."

Mr. Tan left his sentence hanging, just as the personal and collective memories of the needless suffering, death and destruction caused by the Cultural Revolution would always be left hanging over those who experienced it. Even so, the post-Cultural Revolution rebuilding process succeeded, the spirit of reconciliation triumphed, and China's music world — like the nation itself — entered a new era.

CHAPTER 9. THE NEW ERA

When Yehudi Menuhin visited Beijing in 1979, he brought with him a violin and bow as a gift for the Central Conservatory of Music.

Conservatory president Zhao Feng accepted the violin and noted that in bringing a musical gift, Menuhin was following a tradition begun by Matteo Ricci all the way back in 1601. However, the clavichord that the great Jesuit brought had been kept in the palace and was of no use to the common people. The violin presented by Mr. Menuhin, promised Zhao Feng, would not suffer that fate but would instead play a key role in training young Chinese violinists.[1] Menuhin's gift, in other words, was not just an echo of the past but also a herald of the future.

Indeed, Menuhin was not in Beijing to spread his religion like Ricci and the many missionaries who followed with organs, harpsichords and violins. Nor was he there to gain commercial or diplomatic favor, like Lord Macartney and his German band. He was not even there on a quasi-diplomatic musical mission, like Eugene Ormandy and the members of the Philadelphia Orchestra. Instead, he was in Beijing simply to play, teach, and share the classical music he loved with the people of China.

For most of its history in China, classical music existed to serve non-musical goals. But having survived the turmoil of the Cultural Revolution — and emerged the stronger for it — classical music has become an integral part of China's culture. Major cities across the country are now home to state-of-the-art concert halls and opera houses. The nation's top leaders regularly attend orchestral concerts and Western operas and proclaim their love for the music of Mozart and Beethoven. China is one of the world's top producers of musical instruments and a major source of the pianos and violins used around the world. So many millions of

---

1. Fu Hu (1980). Yehudi Menuhin's Chinese Debut. *Chinese Literature* April, p. 124.

Chinese children study these instruments that there is a shortage of teachers. Chinese composers and musicians regularly receive the international classical music world's top prizes and it is unlikely that there is a single conservatory in the West that does not have a roster peppered with Chinese names or a major orchestra in America without a Chinese musician in it. The dominant theme of the past quarter century is the internationalization of China's classical music world and its integration with the global music community. Indeed, music world insiders increasingly look to China and wonder what role it will play in the future development of classical music worldwide.

In the most optimistic scenarios, the global status of Chinese musicians and the growing number of world class music venues in major cities will help spread a love for classical music to a broader population. China will then become not only a producer of instruments, musicians and composers, but of audiences who fill concert halls, purchase (legal) recordings made by top international orchestras, and travel around the world to attend opera and music festivals. In more pessimistic scenarios, classical music in China will succumb to the same pitfalls that some critics think it has in much of the West — individual and corporate greed; an excessive emphasis on stardom; bad management; poor music education; and governmental and societal indifference.

A convincing case can be made for either scenario — with the most likely being some combination of the two — but the future is at best uncertain. What is certain is that the development of classical music in China has no parallel anywhere. Having survived conditions that would be unimaginable in the US or Europe, it entered a period of growth that continues to this day. It is certain to carve its own unique path moving forward.

As Chairman Mao told the leaders of the Musicians' Association, when "foreign things" are assimilated "they must be transformed and become Chinese."[2] The transformation of classical music in China has been one not just of new faces and new sounds, but of the fundamental ways in which classical music relates to society. It is by looking at these fundamentals that one can best understand how classical music has evolved over the past three decades, and how it is likely to evolve in coming years.

MUSIC AND MODERNIZATION

The basic standard for judging all our work is whether it helps or hinders our effort to modernize.
— Deng Xiaoping, speaking to the
Fourth Congress of Artists and Writers in 1979.[3]

If there weren't classical music, there wouldn't be modernity.
— Li Delun.

---

2. Mao Zedong (1980). A talk to music workers. *Chinese Literature*. January: 83-91.
3. Deng Xiaoping (1979). Speech Greeting the Fourth Congress of Chinese Writers and Artists, October 30 (english.peopledaily.com.cn/dengxp).

The concept of modernization is a powerful force in China, one that is strongly linked with the West. Most historians date the beginning of China's modern era to the Opium War, its first major interaction with the nations of Europe. Various attempts at modernization that followed the war — from the self-strengthening movement of the 1860s to the May 4th Movement of 1919 — have looked to the West (and Japan) as a model. So strong is the association between the West and modernity that the very word "modern" was transliterated into Chinese as *mo deng*. It became common parlance in the early 20th century and is still used to this day.

Given this perceived connection between the West and modernity, it is unsurprising that Western music has been similarly viewed as modern since it was first introduced. Crowds gathered to look at the clavichord brought by Matteo Ricci because they were fascinated by the sight of a keyboard instrument. Emperors Kangxi and Qianlong studied Western music in part because they admired its technologically advanced instruments and remarkably accurate system of notation. School-songers saw it as a progressive force and May 4th intellectuals who promoted Western-style music believed it would help to modernize Chinese society and people.

The Communists largely accepted this view of Western music as modern. Zhou Enlai saw its value as a tool of modern diplomacy. Mao grouped Western music with the "modern things" that must be learned from foreign countries. He even conferred on conservatory-trained musicians the title of "doctors" while denigrating traditionally-trained musicians as "minstrels." Jiang Qing included symphonies and concertos among her model operas and encouraged composers to incorporate Western musical instruments and techniques into Chinese opera.

This assumed link between modernity and the West survived the Cultural Revolution and its aftermath. When Deng Xiaoping came to power he pushed the "four modernizations" — industry, national defense, science, and technology — as the governing creed and set the country on a mad rush to modernize, largely by looking to the West for models, advice, and support.

By the 1990s, local governments had begun to use classical music as a means of projecting a modern and progressive image. Unsurprisingly, this trend started in Shanghai which, one official explained, needed "to distinguish itself not only for its industry, commerce and finance but also for its culture" [4] if it wished to join the ranks of the world's great cities. Looking for visible ways to demonstrate that it was advanced culturally as well as economically, Shanghai decided to build an opera house.

"If you want to find the level of a city, you ask if they have an opera house," explained the composer Xiao Bai, expressing a widely held view. "If they do, it's a progressive, developed city."

Since the opera house was intended to serve as visible proof of Shanghai's advanced cultural level, the city wanted it to be modern and visible. It allocated prime

---

4. The official was Chen Zhili, when she was deputy secretary of the Shanghai Municipal Party Committee. See Melvin, Sheila (1999). A rage for opera houses (Oh, and opera, too). *The New York Times* May 30.

real estate right next to the Shanghai government headquarters and built the Shanghai Grand Theater at a cost of $157 million dollars. The stunning, French-designed glass and steel structure immediately fulfilled its main function of demonstrating Shanghai's modernity and enhancing its prestige. It also became a magnet for the world's top orchestras, operas, and ballets and has significantly enriched the city's musical life.

The completion of the Grand Theater in 1998 also had the effect — perhaps not entirely unintended — of making leaders in other cities extremely jealous, especially those in Beijing. Indeed, for months after it opened, it was common to see a sharply dressed Shanghai official proudly pointing out such design features as the Grand Theater's cascading crystal chandeliers or retractable stage to an awestruck Beijing official who was trying hard to keep his jaw from dropping. It was not long before Beijing dusted off plans for its own grand theater, which was originally scheduled to open in 2004 but has been delayed until at least 2005.

Beijing's National Grand Theater stands near the Great Hall of the People in the Tiananmen Square area on land that was originally set aside by Zhou Enlai back in 1958 — political movements and the inability to agree on a design or a budget then stalled construction for the next 40 years. Since it is being built in part to prove that Beijing can do things bigger and better than Shanghai, the National Grand Theater is budgeted to cost nearly $400 million and is intended to have four auditoriums instead of three. It was also designed by a French firm and is even more modern and striking in comparison to its surroundings, a glass and titanium dome surrounded by a lake and lawns and entered through an underwater tunnel; supporters call it a "water pearl" while detractors label it a "duck egg."

The opera house fad has spread to other cities whose leaders are also determined to demonstrate that they are modern and advanced. Hangzhou, Wenzhou and Nanjing have all held design competitions for architecturally outstanding, three-hall theaters just like Shanghai's. Other cities have chosen to build or modernize concert halls, including Guangzhou, Chengdu, and Shanghai's Pudong New Area.

The construction of so many new venues has brought a renewed focus to the ever-pressing issue of arts management, itself a modern concept. It first became the subject of attention in the early 1990s by way of reforms at the Beijing Concert Hall. The Central Philharmonic Society did not prove adept at managing the Concert Hall which Li Delun had worked so hard to see re-built and soon after it reopened in 1986, it devolved into a venue for fashion shows and movies. Mr. Li repeatedly urged the Philharmonic's administrators to use the facility for serious music, but to little avail. In 1993, they finally decided to get if off their hands by leasing the entire space to a business man named Qian Cheng.

Mr. Qian implemented a new management strategy which he described as using culture to support culture. Instead of waiting for arts organizations to rent the hall, he recruited ensembles, made profit-sharing arrangements, and sometimes even acted as producer. So successful was his approach that the number of performances held in the Concert Hall increased nearly ten-fold in five years. Qian then used the increased revenues to undertake more ambitious projects. He founded the respected performing arts magazine *ArtsToday.com*, began a series of weekend teaching concerts, and established a popular summer music camp for children. Within a few short years, the Beijing Concert Hall became the serious music center that it was intended to be, greatly improving the situation for classical music in Beijing and becoming a model for concert venues throughout the country. Mr. Qian achieved enough of a celebrity status to be profiled in a 1999 China Central Television special that celebrated 20 key figures in the era of "reform and opening," and his achievements were even written about in *The Wall Street Journal*.

Unfortunately, few other concert halls have reached the level that the Beijing Concert Hall attained under Mr. Qian's leadership. Indeed, even though local governments invest huge sums of money in building or renovating concert halls and opera houses, they budget paltry amounts for arts management. The Shanghai Grand Theater had only two people in charge of programming when it opened in 1997 and neither had much experience. Part of the reason for the delayed opening of the National Grand Theater in Beijing is that it has not even been decided whether the Beijing government, the Ministry of Culture, or some other bureaucratic entity will manage the facility.[5] There is plenty to criticize in this approach, but the "build it and they will come" philosophy has worked well enough to satisfy Shanghai's government and will likely do the same in Beijing.

Like leaders in many countries, Chinese officials channel far more money to structures intended to house the arts than they do to the arts themselves. But recognizing that modernity and advanced culture require more than just buildings, many cities have also begun to support all kinds of international arts festivals. The most ambitious and successful of these is the Beijing International Music Festival which was founded in 1998 by the German-trained conductor Yu Long, a grandson of the composer Ding Shande. The Festival has brought scores of top-level international orchestras, operas and soloists to perform in Beijing and also provided a stage for numerous Chinese performers.

With so many individuals, leaders, and local governments attracted to classical music in part because of its association with modernity, it is unsurprising that the institutions of classical music themselves have felt pressured to modernize. The initial push to update both organizational structures and attitudes came from the Ministry of Culture, which began insisting that arts organizations earn more of their keep almost as soon as the Cultural Revolution ended.

In the beginning, many musical and other organizations found themselves unable to adapt to the new environment. A number of opera and ballet companies virtually ceased to perform while orchestras cut their concert schedules and accepted any revenue-earning opportunities that came their way. Poorly-paid musicians found

---

5. See (2004). Guojia Dajuyuan Mianlin San Da Kunrao [The national grand theater faces three big difficulties]. *Zhongguo Qingnian Bao* [China Youth Daily] Feb. 26. The other difficulties are setting standards as to who can perform in it and the deciding whether to classifiy it as an enterprise — which means it assumes greater responsibility for its finances — or a government body.

work moon-lighting. In 1993, journalists counted 600 professionally trained musicians playing in Beijing's joint venture hotels, most of them from such renowned institutions as the Central Philharmonic and the Central Conservatory.[6] Since these musicians got paid the same whether they attended orchestra rehearsals or not, many skipped them and the quality of play suffered. Audiences lost patience and turned to even more modern forms of entertainment, like television, karaoke, disco, and bowling.

The situation perhaps reached its nadir in 1993 when a company on far away Hainan Island offered to buy the Central Philharmonic Society on condition that it change its name to "The Hainan/Central Symphonic Orchestra."[7] The proposal — the equivalent of an unknown Hawaiian company offering to purchase the National Symphony Orchestra in Washington, DC — sent shock-waves through China's culture circles. The subsequent revelation that the Central Philharmonic was in such bad straits that it was seriously considering the deal caused such an uproar that the central government was forced to acknowledge the problems in classical music. As a stop-gap measure, President Jiang Zemin ordered that the equivalent of US$100,000 in immediate aid be given to the stricken orchestra.

The general crisis then helped spur the Ministry of Culture to implement further reforms which gradually began to have an effect. Subsidies to arts organizations were tied to the number of performances they gave, a measure which forced everyone to get back on stage. The practice of paying all performers the same salary — even if they never performed — was also dropped in favor of a low base pay supplemented by rehearsal and performance bonuses. The custom of assigning musicians to orchestras, singers to operas, and dancers to ballets and guaranteeing them lifetime employment was also ended. Instead, orchestras and other performing arts groups were allowed to hold auditions, hire employees on contract, and require them to pass tests in order to keep their positions. A number of orchestras, operas and ballets were also reorganized and given new names; the Central Philharmonic Society, for example, became the China National Orchestra in 1996.

Once music organizations were given more control over their own destinies, they began to implement their own modernizing reforms. Major orchestras created the position of artistic director, unifying most of the artistic decision-making power in the hands of one person. Artistic directors — often foreign-trained Chinese conductors with extensive overseas experience — then began to make changes aimed at bringing their practices in line with international norms.

They assigned positions based on talent rather than seniority and held blind auditions for open seats. They broadened their repertoire beyond Beethoven and the other Romantics to include 20th-century composers, contemporary composers, and pops. They established regular season schedules, worked to stop the common practice of giving away tickets, and started subscription concert series. They founded

---

6. See Zhao Gang (1993). Classical Musicians Moonlight at Hotels. *China Daily* March 24.
7. See Mao Jingbo (1993). One note of sympathy for Central Symphony read: Good promotions, carefully chosen pieces and devoted musicians are the keys to the revival of symphony. *China Daily* April 23.

membership associations and newsletters, established foundations to solicit corporate donations, and set up boards of directors. Starting with the Shanghai Symphony, they even began recruiting foreign musicians, primarily for their woodwind and brass sections, which are generally considered to be weak in China.

Opera companies looked to co-productions with overseas operas to help them modernize and raise their standards. Lead performers, directors, and set designers now often come from overseas. Starting with a 1995 production of *Turandot* by the China Central Opera Theater, they also began to abandon the Communist tradition of singing in Chinese translation so the "masses" could understand. Instead, singers now struggle to learn Italian, French, and German so they can sing the librettos in their original language as is standard practice in most of the world.

Like orchestras and operas, China's conservatories have also received government pressure to modernize, primarily by taking in more revenue. To help in this goal, they have been permitted to charge tuition, a policy change which has encouraged many to expand enrollment. The result is that China is now home to some of the world's biggest conservatories. These fast-growing institutions have modernized their approach to teaching by building on the foreign exchanges that began in the late 1970s. The Shanghai Conservatory Zhou Xiaoyan Opera Center, for instance, now holds an intensive three-week opera master class every summer at which young singers from around the nation study with coaches from New York's Metropolitan Opera. In 2002, it added a one-time master class with Itzhak Perlman for young violinists. Both were organized by Madame Zhou and the Conservatory with the support of the Culture Institute of the Committee of 100, a New York-based organization of prominent Chinese Americans, and are likely to be followed by similar collaborative teaching efforts.

Another means of modernizing curriculum and teaching approaches is by hiring as professors Chinese musicians who have extensive overseas experience, forward looking ideas about music, or both. This is particularly noticeable in the composition departments of the Central and Shanghai Conservatories where the renowned composers Guo Wenjing, Ye Xiaogang, Qu Xiaosong and He Xuntian now teach.

Guo Wenjing, who heads the Central Conservatory's composition department, encourages young composers not to focus exclusively on Western music but to also learn the fundamentals of Chinese music and listen to the work of contemporary Chinese composers.

"In the past we venerated so deeply anything coming from the West that we tended to overlook our own culture in the act," he explained. "In higher music education, Chinese compositions were practically ignored in favour of Western music. At present the situation is already different.[8]

---

8. See Kouwenhoven, Frank and Schimmelpenninck, Antoinet (1997). Guo Wenjing — a composer's portrait. *Chime*. Spring/Autumn: 47. The authors also interviewed Mr. Guo twice in Beijing. Quotations without other attribution come from these interviews.

In his own compositions, which are played frequently in Europe and increasingly in the US, Mr. Guo uses "Western technique and Chinese material" but he hopes to free himself even from these constraints.

"I want to get rid of Western influence, and I want to get rid of Chinese influence," he says. "I can't do this completely, of course, but I have a goal."

He Xuntian and Qu Xiaosong both teach composition at the Shanghai Conservatory. Mr. He is widely known in China for his long hair, wide-ranging style, free thinking, and success. In the 1990s, he spent two years in Tibet researching the music for a new-age, Tibetan-inspired collaboration with the singer Dada Wa called *Sister Drum* which sold more than 2 million copies in 50 countries. Qu Xiaosong teaches with Mr. He at the Shanghai Conservatory where he fills his students with his often iconoclastic ideas about music.

"Conservatories give you the vegetables, but how you finally make the dish is up to you," says Mr. Qu. "European music is only one part. Students should understand Chinese music, too. Chinese and Western music are so different — and of course there is African music, Indian music, so many different traditions. We should not just study Western music from the end of the 18th century to the beginning of the 20th century."

These highly individual — and artistically and commercially successful — professors are inculcating young composers with decidedly modern ideas about music.

"I think a good composer shouldn't think about the audience," says Qu Xiaosong. "He shouldn't think about anything but the music. An artist's first responsibility is to art — if you are responsible to art, you are responsible to society."

Mr. Qu's opinion represents a sharp break from the past in the PRC, where the mass appeal of music has always been of paramount importance. It echoes, however softly, the disdain for audience tastes that is associated with certain contemporary composers in the West, a modern attitude faulted by some critics for the general decline in the popularity of classical music since the 1960s. Indeed, it even raises the question as to whether increasing modernization is likely to help or harm the development of classical music in China.

But, Mr. Qu's opinion notwithstanding, the majority of Chinese composers do think about their listeners and have proven quite successful at engaging their interest. He and his contemporaries in composition and performance have been hired by China's conservatories and orchestras because they bring new thinking, new energy, and new direction.

The purpose of modernization in China is to make the nation strong and put it on an even footing with the West — or maybe even surpass it. Music has long been promoted in service of this goal, but in the past 25 years it has made tremendous strides in modernizing itself. Indeed, one day it, too, may stand on an even footing with the West — or maybe even surpass it.

MUSIC AND SOCIETY

> At present, some parents are hoping beyond all hope that their children will change their lives through studying the piano, experts said.
> — *China Daily*, April 6, 2004.

Western classical music holds a special status in contemporary Chinese society that goes well beyond the musical. This derives from its history as a sophisticated import enjoyed by emperors, intellectuals, and revolutionaries alike; its modern and progressive image; and the sense that it is in some ways superior to China's own music because it is more scientific, or heroic, or international.

Individual leaders use classical music to enhance their own images. Former president Jiang Zemin was photographed at the performances of so many international orchestras and operas that it is probably safe to say that he attended more classical concerts during his term in office than any recent American president has in his. Jiang took every opportunity — even in the middle of business meetings or banquets — to demonstrate his knowledge and appreciation for music by singing or playing piano. He even let it be known that he had assuaged his sorrow over the death of his predecessor Deng Xiaoping by staying up all night listening to Mozart's *Requiem*. The *Requiem* then reminded him of a poem by Du Mu and the music and poetry together, according to one account, "evoked a feeling which is difficult for ordinary people to understand."[9]

"Ordinary" people may indeed find it difficult to understand the feelings that Mozart's *Requiem* evokes in a Chinese president, but they nonetheless understand the prestige that is associated with classical music. Gone are the days when, in Tcherepnin's words, "The Chinese student who decides to take up music as his profession does so...not because his parents or relatives know anything about western art or western musical instruments" but because he loves it so much that he is willing to pursue his lonely dream "against the will of his family."[10] On the contrary, it is now oftentimes parents who push children to learn Western instruments, especially the piano. Indeed, in 2004, the *Shenzhen Daily* reported the astonishing — and perhaps somewhat exaggerated — news that there are 38 million children studying piano in China.[11]

"Parents always have endless dreams for their children, no matter whether they're talented or not," one Shanghai paper noted in 2000. "And for many of those parents, the piano, seen as the instrument of the aristocracy, is the foundation on which their dreams are built."[12]

---

9. (1997). Jiang Listens to Requiem to Mourn Deng Xiaoping. *Hong Kong Ta Kung Pao*. March 1. (As translated in FBIS, March 3, 1997.)

10. Tcherepnin, Alexander (1935). Music in Modern China. *The Musical Quarterly*, Vol. XXI, No. 4, October: 397.

11. See *Shenzhen Daily* (2004). Boy startles music world. March 30. (www.newsgd.com)

12. Sun, Claudia (2000). "Aristocratic" piano scales new heights of popularity. *Shanghai Daily* March 3: 9.

In the mid-1980s, this "piano fever" reached such a pitch that piano factories could not begin to meet demand. Getting a piano was a matter of waiting for years or using back-door connections and bribes. Some people even bought pianos for investment purposes only, certain that both demand and price would continue to rise so that owning a piano was "better than putting their money in the bank."[13]

The availability of pianos is no longer an issue. As Edgar Snow predicted back in 1960, China now excels at making musical instruments and has become one of the biggest producers of pianos and violins.[14] Guangzhou's Pearl River piano factory is the second largest manufacturer of pianos in the world — it made 200,000 in 2000 — and its instruments can be found in the homes of middle class families from Beijing to Baton Rouge. But, even as the problem of sufficient piano supply has been resolved, it has led to a new shortage of professional teachers.

To meet this demand, piano training centers and schools have sprung up across the country. Some are headed by famous pianists, like the Liu Shikun Piano Arts School which is headquartered in Hong Kong and has branches all over China.[15] The music publishing industry, which was almost bankrupt after the Cultural Revolution, is booming from the demand for piano method books. A graded test system was introduced in 1998 to better measure students' progress; critics claim that this creates too much pressure and leads children to study only one or two pieces of music so they can pass to the next level, but the system is popular with parents eager to quantify their children's accomplishments.

The most talented students naturally seek to attend conservatory, as do many of those who are somewhat less talented, and the conservatory system is now booming.

"Chinese music education is developing pretty well," said Wu Zuqiang. "The Central Conservatory is one of the ten biggest in the world and our students are all over the world. There are nine conservatories and they all have elementary schools... But, it's still not enough."[16]

The growth in music education is such that the Sichuan Conservatory in Chengdu — a city not well known to most Westerners — boasts a new building with 800 practice rooms and a plan to increase its enrollment to 10,000 within the next few years.

Clearly, the millions of young men and women studying piano and other instruments are not all going to be the next darlings of the international concert circuit like the 21-year-olds Lang Lang, who was the best-selling classical pianist of

---

13. Ruo Ming (1987). Piano fever. *China Reconstructs* January: 45.

14. See *People's Daily* (2001). China ranked one of world's top piano producers. January 4 (english.peopledaily.com.cn).

15. Liu Shikun's artistic and political stars rose in the immediate aftermath of the Cultural Revolution, but began to fall in the early 1980s when he was divorced from his wife, the daughter of Ye Jianying. He was subsequently accused of smuggling and other economic crimes during the anti-spiritual pollution campaign in 1983. He was never jailed, but he fell out of favor for much of the 1980s and then made another comeback in the 1990s.

16. The conservatories are in Chengdu, Wuhan, Tianjin, Shenyang, Xian, Beijing (2), Shanghai, and Guangzhou.

2003, and Li Yundi, the first-prize winner of the 2000 Chopin Competition. But they, and their parents, have hopes.

Indeed, some parents will do almost anything to help their child in his musical studies. Lang Lang's parents played classical music for him while he was still *in utero* and spent half their annual income to buy him a piano before he turned two. His father, an *erhu* player, then quit his own job when Lang Lang was eight years old so he could spend a year and a half coaching him for the entrance exams to the Central Conservatory's elementary school. After Lang Lang was accepted, he moved with him from Shenyang to Beijing to coach him and care for him as he continued his studies. Li Yundi's parents, too, sacrificed heavily for their son's piano playing, spending their life savings to buy him a piano when he was seven. They also moved across China from Chongqing to Shenzhen so Li could follow his piano teacher, Dan Zhaoyi

If the success of Lang Lang and Li Yundi is exceptional, the dedication of their parents is not. Indeed, since China has only nine conservatories, children who are accepted often must leave home and move to a new city. It is not uncommon for one parent to go with the child in order to handle all the mundanities of daily life so the child can devote himself entirely to practicing for the next decade or more. While such children may become accomplished instrumentalists, they may also graduate from Conservatory unable to fry an egg or wash a pair of socks. The pressure on them to succeed is tremendous; where some rise to the occasion, others have nervous breakdowns. From a musical viewpoint, they are generally so driven to succeed as a soloist that they have little inclination to participate in chamber music or orchestral training.

"The purpose of music education here is for everyone to become a soloist; there's no interest in ensemble or even orchestra," complained the composer and Shanghai Conservatory professor Qu Xiaosong. "There is a narrow understanding of music."

Indeed, this "narrow understanding" is as much a feature of classical music in China as is its special status. And, like its status, it is related to classical music's origins as an import and to the fact that it is often harnessed in pursuit of aims that go well beyond the musical.

It leads to a preference for extravaganza, like productions of *Aida* that get bigger and more sensational each time. A 2000 production staged in Shanghai in cooperation with a US company was billed as the "world's most spectacular staging" and included the Shanghai Symphony and the Shanghai Broadcasting Symphony; a 500-person chorus; 60 ballet dancers; 1000 walk-on actors; 300 acrobats; and a number of elephants, camels, lions, tigers, boa constrictors, white horses, and parrots. Staged again in 2003, it included all of the above plus trained dogs, galloping horses, a fire-eater, a fireworks show and a "half-time" performance by kung-fu students from the renowned martial arts center at Shaolin Temple. [17]

17. For description of 2000 production, see Zhang Qian. (2000). *Aida* debuts in Shanghai. *China Daily* October 13: 9. Description of 2003 production comes from personal correspondence with an audience member, Anne Stevenson-Yang.

This love of extravaganza, combined with a rather grandiose perception of classical music's power, led the Chinese government to invite the "Three Tenors" — Pavarotti, Domingo and Carreras — to give a mega-concert in Beijing in support of China's (successful) bid for the 2008 Olympics. The June 2001 joint event drew then-President Jiang Zemin and a host of other political leaders as well as 100,000 people who paid between US$200 and US$2000 for the 23 different classes of tickets — and this in a city where the average worker doesn't earn much more than US$2000 in a year. It also led officials to finally agree to a performance of *Turandot* "on-site" in the Forbidden City as Karajan had suggested back in 1979. The $15 million 1998 mega-production was performed by the Maggio Musicale Fiorentino under the baton of Zubin Mehta and directed by the acclaimed film director Zhang Yimou.

The narrow understanding of music means that most audiences continue to prefer works from the standard romantic repertoire, like Beethoven and Tchaikovsky. Early music from the West — like baroque — is rarely performed and neither are the works of Western contemporary composers. Until quite recently, the works of contemporary Chinese composers also fell into this vacuum. While *Aida* fills stadiums, a 1998 performance of *Faust* in Shanghai led several reviewers to declare that Chinese audiences were not ready for Gounod's music.

It also contributes to a dearth of chamber music performances. Although some conductors and composers are now working to develop chamber music (and the Shanghai Symphony has held an excellent series of Sunday night chamber concerts for some years now), they have their work cut out for them. Indeed, the narrow understanding of classical music sometimes leads to problems with audience etiquette, as happened at a 1999 chamber concert in Guangzhou that sent shivers down the spines of many music world insiders.

Because the concert was given by the renowned Julliard String Quartet, it drew a large crowd, most of whom had evidently never before attended a chamber concert and many of whom clearly did not often attend classical concerts of any sort. It got off to a bad start when late-arriving audience members forced their way into the concert hall after the performance had started and then climbed over seats to get to the best ones. The situation quickly went downhill when "the entire audience dispersed after the first work, interpreting the brief break as an intermission."[18] The Julliard musicians were so upset by the audience's departure that "they argued among themselves as to whether the concert should go on." They decided to continue, but "during the second half of the programme, Smetana's *From My Life* quartet, the performance was halted by a beeper in the audience. The musicians were willing to finish only after order was restored."

The concert was quickly dubbed an "incident" by local media, who pointed out that similar behavior had occurred at performances by the Borodin Quartet and by the pianists Fu Cong and Kong Xiangdong. All three major newspapers "expressed grave

18. This account of the concert and all quotes come from (1999). Guangzhou's quest for cultural refinement set back after night of musical chairs. *South China Morning Post* February 22.

concern as to who was responsible for the 'impropriety' and what should be done to prevent future embarrassment." The vice governor even got involved, suggesting that the program should specify the number of movements for each work to help cut down on the ill-timed applause between movements. Other commentators blamed theater managers for not enforcing rules and promoters for not educating the audience.

The "narrow" understanding of classical music also affects orchestras. As in the West, the number of people who regularly attend classical concerts is only a small percentage of those who potentially could, based on income and population. Many people simply have no interest, while some stay away because they fear that they will embarrass themselves by revealing their unfamiliarity with the music or with concert etiquette.

It contributes to an unfortunate snobbery that favors foreign orchestras and performers over Chinese. There are many people in China who will pay small fortunes to hear Jose Carreras sing a few arias and folk songs in the Shanghai Grand Theater or the Vienna Philharmonic play in the acoustically-atrocious Great Hall of the People, but would never consider going to a recital by a top-rate Chinese opera singer or a concert by the China Philharmonic.

It also affects the understanding of orchestra musicians and other performers. At the opera master classes held at the Shanghai Conservatory in 2000, several of the Metropolitan Opera coaches were stunned by the singers' lack of basic musical knowledge. In one class of singers who had considerable talent and training, most students did not even know in what century Mozart lived. Such basic information about a composer and the era in which he lived is crucial to an understanding of music style, but widely absent among Chinese performers who nowadays focus on technique to the exclusion of all else.

Indeed, the present-day lack of a broad and deep cultural understanding to underpin technical music studies was a pet peeve of pioneering musicians like Li Delun and Tan Shuzhen.

"The quality of musicians isn't good enough," complained Mr. Li. "They can play, but they don't understand. The Japanese are like that, too. They get every note right, but they don't understand the music. They need to understand the culture and the history, foreign and Chinese. Otherwise, you are just a machine."

Tan Shuzhen attributed the problem not only to individual education, but to the system.

"Chinese conductors' and musicians' understanding of Western music is very shallow," he said. "Since liberation there has been no planning. Like Beethoven — they know the *Fifth* and the *Ninth*, but none of the others. It won't change. It gets worse and worse — there's no system."

But if the problems of narrow understanding are many, most have a silver lining. Audiences may demonstrate a preference for big events and a narrow range of composers but in this they are not so different from audiences in many countries. The more important point is that Western opera is very far removed from the cultural background of any Chinese, yet *Aida* — with a few special effects and a lot of extras —

311

can draw a stadium crowd of 50,000. Likewise, Guangzhou audiences may demonstrate behavior that is inappropriate for chamber music, but at least they have enough curiosity about classical music to go to a performance by the Julliard Quartet (although members of the Julliard Quartet apparently thought otherwise).

While the number of people who regularly attend orchestra concerts may not be high as a percentage of population, it is still enough to fill the halls. Equally important, the crowds at a symphony concert in China are not the members of the well-heeled blue- and grey-hair set one sees in the US, but a refreshing mix of old and faithful music lovers and curious youths from a range of economic brackets. For many urban youths, attending a classical concert is considered a fun night out or a smart choice for a first date.

Indeed, attending a classical concert during the adopted (and adapted) Christmas-New Year holiday festivities has become *de rigueur* for fashionable young people in the cities. The Christmas-New Year season is now the busiest and most profitable time of the year for orchestras and musicians. Concert tickets sell out the moment they go on sale; the halls are full night after night; and scalpers do a flourishing business. In provincial cities, orchestras often provide entertainment at lavish Christmas banquets in five-star hotels and then return to the concert hall for a series of New Year concerts. The live broadcast of the Vienna Philharmonic's New Year's concert has even become a holiday ritual for many Chinese families, who now start off the calendar new year with a heavy dose of Strauss.

The popularity of piano and other instrument studies also provides symphony orchestras with a steady stream of new audience members.

"One makes three," said Wu Zuqiang. "When a child studies, his parents study too."

Indeed, the parents of music students are so fond of attending concerts with their children that there was a mini-uproar in Beijing several years back when a major concert hall implemented height restrictions to keep kids out.

Classical music also draws new listeners through other art forms. Ballet has grown so popular that in Beijing it sometimes seems possible to see *Swan Lake* performed by a different Russian ballet company every month. Broadway musicals such as *The Sound of Music* and *Phantom of the Opera* now draw big crowds in cities like Shanghai and Beijing. Once again, classical music is even being used in an effort to re-invigorate Peking opera. The organizers of the high-profile production *Royal Concubine Yang of the Tang Dynasty* — among them Mei Baojiu, the son of Mei Lanfang — decided to create a "symphonic Peking opera" because they saw it as a way to entice more young people to watch Peking opera.

"Peking Opera artists have been trying hard to attract audiences, especially the young, back to the theater," noted one article about the production. "Traditional operas are being directly challenged by films, television, computer games, live shows in bars and other kinds of entertainment. Combining the opera with a Western symphony orchestra has been considered a potential solution." [19]

And, as if all these factors did not suggest enough potential, there is the simple fact of population. Symphony orchestras are located in big cities, many of which have populations well in excess of 10 million, so the potential for audience growth is virtually limitless, assuming that more resources are channeled into music education and outreach efforts.

When it comes to performers, the problem of cultural and educational depth is not one likely to be resolved soon — children who begin studying classical music before they are born and enter conservatory at the age of eight do not have much free time to read books, or learn about the era in which Mozart lived, let alone have the kind of life experiences that Li Delun and Tan Shuzhen had. Indeed, this "shallowness" may be one of the reasons that so many Chinese prodigies have failed to fulfill the potential of their early years.

But, cultural understanding is of little use without technical ability and in this regard China is currently producing some of the world's best young musicians. With the tremendous opportunities that befall the most talented of these will come ample opportunity to grow as performers — and people — and to share this growth at home. Moreover, as Chinese composers become ever more important in contemporary classical music, a Chinese cultural background may become more of an advantage than a disadvantage.

As Lang Lang told an interviewer in China, "I hope to present classical music to all people — I mean everyone. I have some communicating work to do. For example, telling my personal experiences to youngsters who love to play the piano, as well as those who know little about music but intend to get to know it. I will play more and more Chinese music. I hope in ten years when you walk along the street, everyone can tell you something about Beethoven, Chopin, and Tchaikovsky, as well as our own Chinese composers."[20]

MUSIC AND POLITICS

> There is in fact no such thing as art... that is detached from or independent of politics.
> — Mao Zedong in his 1942 Talks at the Yanan Forum on Arts and Literature.

The end of the Cultural Revolution did not mark the end of the Chinese government's involvement in the performing arts either in terms of support or control.

In the early years of rebuilding after the Cultural Revolution, Deng Xiaoping and like-minded leaders tried to stay away from direct interference. So long as art could be said to support the cause of modernization, it was generally considered to be acceptable. But when many artists took advantage of their new-found freedom to experiment with new forms and styles, the cultural leftists were distressed. They pressured Deng to curb it, and in 1983 he finally succumbed, condemning the

19. (2003). Peking opera gets a makeover. *China Daily* August 8.
20. (2004). Music prodigy Lang Lang. *China Pictorial* March. (www.rmhb.com.cn/chpic)

"corrosive influence of decadent bourgeois ideology" and vowing to "clear away cultural contamination" [21] through a campaign against "spiritual pollution."

When the anti-spiritual pollution campaign got underway, students and workers alike were forced to attend Cultural Revolution-style meetings at which they read articles declaiming against the "decadent, moribund ideas of the bourgeoisie." Artists and writers who had stood out because of their critical or experimental work — or even their long hair or Bohemian clothing — came under attack. The compositions of Tan Dun, the Central Conservatory student from Hunan, were banned from being performed for six months after his string quartet *Feng-Ya-Song* was excoriated in the pages of *People's Music*.

"I was denounced as a running dog of capitalism," he explained to a journalist in 1997. "Because of my boundary-less thinking, my music made people nervous. They didn't know how to appreciate it, and they encouraged young people to think of it as poison."[22]

Fortunately for artists like Tan Dun, the anti-spiritual pollution campaign itself also made many high-placed people nervous and was quietly allowed to whither away, the last campaign of its kind. But the absence of campaign-style interference does not mean that classical music, or any other performing art, has become "detached from or independent of politics."

On the contrary, the Chinese government remains the nation's largest sponsor of the performing arts. Virtually all musicians, singers, and even composers are government employees. They belong to a *dan wei*, or work unit — a symphony orchestra, an opera house or a conservatory — just as state-owned factory workers do. The work unit then belongs to a local government bureau or a national level administration or ministry.

In Beijing, for instance, the China National Symphony belongs to the Ministry of Culture, the China Philharmonic to the State Administration of Radio, Film and Television, and the Beijing Symphony Orchestra to the Beijing Culture Bureau. Until recently, the Shanghai Symphony and the Shanghai Opera House came under the Shanghai Culture Bureau and the Shanghai Broadcasting Orchestra came under the Shanghai Bureau of Radio, Film and Television; but the two bureaus have been merged into the Shanghai Culture, Radio, Film and Television Administration Bureau, leaving the city with only one cultural overlord. In the provinces, an orchestra can belong either to a provincial bureau, like the Sichuan Broadcasting Symphony Orchestra, which comes under the Sichuan Provincial Bureau of Radio, Film and Television, or a local bureau, like the Wuhan Orchestra, which comes under the Wuhan City Culture Bureau.

This diversity of official overlords may be confusing enough, but the reality is even more complex. Bureaucratic lines often blur in the Chinese system of

---

21. Quotes taken from notes of the Second Plenum of the 12th Central Committee, Oct 11-12 1983.

22. As quoted in Cameron, Lindsley (1997). A Marco Polo going backward at full tilt. *The New York Times*, November 2.

government, especially on the local level, and individual leaders may also exercise power over areas that are technically outside their purview. This means that professional arts organizations on the local level may effectively report not only to their official overlord but also to the local Propaganda Bureau, the vice-mayor or vice Communist Party secretary in charge of culture, and even the mayor, governor or Communist Party secretary, should any of these officials choose to interest themselves in cultural affairs.

Government control of the performing arts has its good points, as does the plethora of potential overlords. Orchestras and other arts organizations may be pressured to make money, but they are not allowed to go bankrupt. Musicians are often badly underpaid, but they are provided with housing, medical care and even musical instruments. If one bureaucracy cannot come up with the money for an overseas tour or a special event, another one may. Arts organizations that manipulate the system well can get extra support or special privileges. Individual leaders can also provide great help. Former president Jiang Zemin saved the Central Philharmonic by ordering that it immediately be given cash from government coffers, an action that no US president could manage. Music-loving vice premiers, governors, and Party secretaries regularly channel resources to support their favored orchestras, operas, or performers.

But this financial and administrative dependency also means that orchestras and other arts groups still sometimes find themselves treated as tools for policy and propaganda. They are required to perform for political events and to have their repertoire for such events approved — even chosen — by bureaucrats. In the major cities, an orchestra's public concerts will far outnumber its political performances, but in second-tier cities it is the other way around. Indeed, in some interior cities, tickets to the ever-popular New Year concerts are not even sold to the public, but are reserved exclusively for the leaders themselves or handed out to individuals and work units whom particular bureaucrats wish to thank and reward.

The ability of individual officials to involve themselves in the arts also creates the danger that some leaders may come to view an orchestra essentially as a toy or a hobby, treating them in much the same way as Qianlong did his little ensemble of eunuch musicians. Even the country's top orchestras are sometimes asked to play at personal parties for high-level leaders or their off-spring, an invitation they cannot refuse. Indeed, when Jiang Zemin was mayor of Shanghai, he not only sat in on the Shanghai Symphony's rehearsals but even conducted it!

The Shanghai Broadcasting Orchestra experienced the double-edged nature of leadership support when a Shanghai vice-mayor who had risen from the ranks of the former Bureau of Radio, Film and Television began channeling support to the bureau's orchestra, the Shanghai Broadcasting Symphony. The orchestra received supplementary funding and was essentially made the house orchestra of the Shanghai Grand Theater (which, in fairness, was largely funded by the Bureau of Radio, Film and Television). Flush with cash and newfound prestige, it renovated rehearsal facilities to international standards and hired the American-trained conductor Hu

315

Yongyan to return to China as its music director. He in turn did an excellent job of raising the orchestra's profile and standards by recruiting players from North America, creating a Friends of the Symphony group, organizing outreach activities, and considerably improving marketing and sales. The orchestra prospered for several years — until the supportive vice-mayor stepped down in a government turnover. Trouble then set in at the Shanghai Broadcasting Orchestra, where budget cutbacks led to management changes, staff reductions, the cancellation of planned concerts, and the departure of Hu Yongyan.

Government control of the performing arts — and its often nebulous nature — also creates conflicts. Such was the case in 2000 when the State Administration of Radio, Film and Television decided to reinvent its second-tier China Broadcasting Symphony Orchestra as a first-tier orchestra.

The orchestra hired the returned conductor Yu Long, who was already renowned for his success with the Beijing International Music Festival, and he went about implementing changes to bring it in line with international standards. The orchestra's name was changed to the China Philharmonic Orchestra; blind auditions were held for all seats; and salaries were tripled. Drawn by the possibilities of high pay and bright prospects, many of the best players in China auditioned, including dozens from the China National Symphony (the former Central Philharmonic), of whom forty or so were ultimately hired.

The departure of so many of its musicians to the upstart China Philharmonic decimated the ranks of the once august China National Symphony. It also caused considerable controversy, with some seeing it as an unfair attack on its bureaucratic owner, the cash-poor Ministry of Culture, by the cash-flush State Administration of Radio, Film and Television.

"These are terrible things!" said the outspoken composer Wang Xilin at the time. "Four years ago, they made the China National Symphony; and now they are destroying it. This is using political and economic methods to destroy art. Art has its own laws — you can't use politics to control it. And the way artists must depend on politicians — this is shameless."

Others, however, were more sanguine about the situation, including the re-named National Symphony's long-time conductor, Li Delun.

"I think it's good," said Mr. Li. "They can help each other forward. They'll attract the best players from around the country. It is feudal societies that keep people in one place; there should be movement. Musicians can go to different orchestras — talent exchange is a good thing. We need to break the old system. And if the standards rise for everyone, this is good, too."

The China National Symphony itself had implemented similar reforms several years earlier when it changed its name and hired the returned conductor, Chen Zuohuang. Since the reforms included blind auditions, testing and the like, but were not accompanied by dramatically increased salaries, they caused considerable resentment, particularly among musicians who lost their seats or jobs.

When Chen set about the difficult task of rebuilding after the exodus to the China Philharmonic, these spurned musicians and other disgruntled orchestra personnel apparently decided to get their revenge. They found a channel through a journalist from the official New China News Agency and plied her with all manner of negative stories about Chen. She then wrote an article called "The Real Story of the Disintegration of the China National Symphony Orchestra" and got it published in a legal issues magazine called *Golden Sword*.[23]

"The Real Story" was in actuality a vicious personal attack on Chen, filled with inflammatory accusations from unnamed sources and written in hyperbolic language. Chen was accused of nepotism, financial irregularities, and musical ineptitude and was even faulted for having his underwear washed by a hotel laundry. The article was so detailed that it could not have been written without the cooperation of the orchestra's management and so extreme that it would have required the tacit approval of the Ministry of Culture. Its publication caused an even greater stir in music circles, especially when Chen Zuohuang responded to it by submitting his resignation and leaving China.

Chen was replaced by Tang Muhai, a graduate of the Munich Academy of Music who had been selected by Karajan to open the Berlin Philharmonic's fall season in 1983. This good fortune had led to guest conducting jobs across Europe and a 12-year conducting position in Portugal. But Tang, too, had difficulties with the orchestra's Ministry of Culture-appointed management and after only a year he boarded a plane to Europe and publicly swore that he would return only if the orchestra manager was replaced. When this did not happen, Tang took a new position with the Finnish National Opera, and the China National Symphony found a third expatriate Chinese conductor to lead it in as many years. He is the affable and energetic Li Xiaolu (a grandson-in-law of Tan Shuzhen), who also leads orchestras in Maine and Connecticut.

If orchestras are sometimes treated as political tools, so are individual artists, especially the star performers. In the 1980s, many local culture bureaus did all they could to prevent talented musicians from leaving the country to study overseas. They feared — usually rightly — that the musicians would not return and the government's investment in their education would be lost. China has become much freer over the past decade and such hardball tactics are harder to employ. Instead, smart local governments now entice top performers to remain in China by using golden handcuffs that may include free apartments, generous salaries, and plentiful high-profile performance opportunities. In turn, the performers must participate in political functions at the government's beck and call, even if this involves canceling a long-standing domestic or overseas obligation. And, like athletes who work as corporate sponsors, they must always consider their public image and never undertake any musical activity that might demean their status or embarrass the government.

---

23. See Melvin, Sheila (2000). Battle of the orchestras in Beijing. *International Herald Tribune* September 13: 12.

Even performers who are not citizens of China are expected to adhere to the unwritten rule that one never embarrasses the Chinese government. The world famous cellist Yo-Yo Ma discovered that, when he was banned from performing in China because of his involvement with the music for the film *Seven Years in Tibet*. Ma has long been a hero in China and the ban was subsequently lifted, but the message it sent was loud and clear. Most foreigners are not held to the same standards as those applied to ethnic Chinese, but with the right amount of money they can still be seduced into behaving as propaganda arms of the Chinese government, as the "Three Tenors" were.

Of course, conflicts — and even control — are not always bad. The creation of the China Philharmonic, for instance, has been a boon to China's musical world and there are few who would now argue that it was not for the best. But there were no winners in another conflict born of the nebulous nature of government control of the arts — and of the ever-growing and equally opaque links that both have with commerce.

"The Concert Hall Incident," as it became known, began innocently enough when the Beijing Concert Hall was shut down for fire code violations in the early months of 2001. The violations were in the process of being corrected when the Concert Hall's charismatic, nationally-known manager Qian Cheng left his office for a lunch meeting with the director of the China National Symphony on April 15 and simply never returned. That evening, the economic crimes division of the Beijing Public Security Bureau appeared at the Forbidden City Concert Hall, another poorly-run venue which Qian had leased and turned into a success. Accompanied by two employees of the China National Symphony, they informed Qian's colleagues that he had been placed under house arrest, and proceeded to remove all records that pertained to the finances of the Beijing Concert Hall from 1994 to 2000.

Beijing's newspapers were ordered not to write about Mr. Qian's disappearance, but a Guangzhou newspaper ran a daring report about "the incident." It discussed allegations that Qian had embezzled money but also claimed that the National Symphony had begun trying to break the lease and get the Concert Hall back from Qian as soon as it became profitable. In the view of Qian Cheng's supporters, the accusations of financial impropriety were part of the National Symphony's attempt to reclaim its Concert Hall and Mr. Qian's only "crime" was financial success that excited the greed and jealousy of his National Symphony landlords.

Qian Cheng's disappearance and the prolonged closure of the Beijing Concert Hall dealt a serious blow to the city's musical life. Scores of concerts were cancelled or postponed, *Arts Today.com* ceased publishing, the Concert Hall's numerous educational and outreach activities came to an end, and the facility that was one of the Chinese capital's major performance venues remains shuttered — and all without any official acknowledgement of a problem other than fire code violations. Late in 2003, it was announced that renovations to improve the Concert Hall's acoustics would begin in 2004.

An incident similar to that involving the Beijing Concert Hall occurred in Shanghai that same year when a gregarious businessman named Chen Bangke disappeared on his way to a meeting and was subsequently accused of a variety of unspecified economic crimes. Mr. Chen, who went by the English name of Bonko, was a great opera lover who parlayed his passion into support for Shanghai's cash-strapped opera company. Indeed, the state-owned freight-forwarding company that Bonko managed became virtually the sole supporter of opera in Shanghai from 1996 until 2001, including productions of *Aida*, *Faust*, and *Flying Dutchman*. His support was considered so important at the time that Zhou Xiaoyan commented wryly, "If Bonko stops, opera stops."

Indeed, Bonko did more than just write checks — he also acted as producer, deciding what operas would be staged, who would direct them, and who would perform in them. Performers for the starring roles were recruited by him from overseas, necessitating many trips to Europe. His office at the freight-forwarding company was full of photos of himself standing on stage with opera casts in Shanghai and around the world. Some in Shanghai's arts world resented Bonko's hands-on style, while others simply saw it as a matter of he who pays the piper calls the tunes. When he disappeared, his supporters claimed that his arrest was the result of a business dispute that had nothing to do with opera, while his detractors claimed it was connected to his excessive use of company money on opera productions and the purchase of paintings by artists such as Picasso.

Whatever the truth, this incident, like that of the Beijing Concert Hall, underscores the shaky foundations on which China's music world stands. The China National Symphony was given a re-built concert hall, but not the money or expertise to run it properly. The Shanghai Opera House was rightly obliged to perform in order to keep its subsidies, but was not allocated enough money to actually stage operas. Each then had to find an unorthodox solution to its particular problems, which worked for a time but then (for different reasons) backfired. To be fair, the nature of government control of music and the other arts does not often lead to such public brouhahas, unexplained disappearances, and arrests but it does create other conflicts.

Perhaps most important, it hurts the process of modernization and professionalization which the government itself is encouraging. An orchestra that might be called to perform at a political or quasi-political function on a moment's notice finds it very difficult to plan its season. This, in turn, hurts advance ticket sales, marketing, and cooperative ventures with outside performers. It also creates morale and personnel problems within orchestra ranks, an issue that is especially problematic now that major orchestras all have foreign members and work regularly with foreign guest conductors and soloists. There has been at least one instance in which foreign musicians banded together and refused to play at a political performance that was scheduled on short notice. Since the Chinese musicians had no choice but to attend, they were naturally unhappy about the foreigners' protest. Some music directors try to forestall such problems by specifying contractually that foreign musicians do not have to play for political events. But, if this exemption mollifies the foreigners and prevents walk-outs, it does little to pacify Chinese musicians, especially since foreigners receive significantly higher pay.

The insistence that politics, broadly defined, comes first also sends the message that the music itself is secondary, which does little to aid efforts to improve an orchestra's artistic level. Violinists of a major Shanghai orchestra were unhappy to be issued $50 instruments for an outdoor performance because leaders were more worried that the real instruments, which are mostly government-owned, might get wet if it rained than they were about the quality of the music — or about the musicians themselves. The repertoire for political events is also generally undemanding, which further undercuts efforts to improve.

Although it is not common, politics can sometimes cause censorship. The outspoken composer Wang Xilin has perhaps had the most problems with this. He was, for instance, told that his *Guo Shang* could not be played because it uses the same word — *shang* — as a controversial 1988 television documentary called *He Shang*, or *River Elegy*. Officials had no problem with the music itself and would have permitted its performance under a different title, but Wang refused to change it.

Slightly more common than censorship is repertoire editing, or padding, by government officials. For instance, officials might ask that a planned program of American music be changed or postponed during one of the recurring periods of US-China tension. Or, they might require an orchestra to play equal numbers of Chinese and foreign pieces around a major national holiday. An orchestra planning an international tour is likely to have its program choices closely scrutinized, and sometimes changed, since it is seen as representing China to the outside world.

The Chinese Communist Party has used the performing arts as a political tool for as long as it has existed. This politicization of the arts reached a destructive extreme during the Cultural Revolution and the Party has since ceded considerable control to the forces of the market and the judgment of artists. This relaxation of control in favor of modernization, professionalization, and economic independence in music and the other arts is likely to expand as China continues on the path of modernization.

But, a belief in the intrinsic power of art — and music in particular — to influence people's thinking and behavior is deeply ingrained in China's traditional culture and has been thoroughly absorbed into Communist ideology. Overlaying this is a belief that government has the right — even the moral obligation — to control the arts if it deems this to be for the good of the people. Add to this the cultural tendency, exacerbated by Communism, to use political connections in pursuit of one's own goals — be they commercial, artistic, or both, as seems to have happened at the China National Symphony — and it becomes apparent that Mao's proclamation regarding the link between art and politics is as true today as when he made it more than sixty years ago. There is no such thing as art that is independent of politics in China — and there probably never will be.

MUSIC AND NATIONALISM

> Great musical activity is going on in China. The Chinese composer has under his hands one of the richest sources of native music. He has the world's most populous country to support him. The more national his product, the greater will be its international value.
> — Alexander Tcherepnin, in his 1935 essay *Music in Modern China*.

> Of course, we favor music with a national character. As Chinese, we would be in the wrong to do otherwise.
> — Mao Zedong, in his 1956 speech to leaders of the Musicians' Association.

Nationalism in China is a complex, controversial, and occasionally combustible force. It dates, roughly speaking, to the late 19th and early 20th centuries when the Chinese government was finally forced by its interactions with the West and Japan to accept the modern concept of nationhood. Prior to that, the imperial view was simply that China was the center of the world — all under heaven, as it was sometimes put — and the other lands of the earth were occupied by tributary states or barbarians. China's inherent superiority was so thoroughly assumed and its cultural pride so deep that there was no need of a special term to describe it.

Once China began to acknowledge that it was but one nation among many, the concept of nationalism was promoted as a means of sustaining its deep cultural pride and cohesiveness. But in assigning a name to what had previously been a given, the promoters of nationalism were acknowledging the defeat of China's former superiority complex. So it is that Chinese nationalism includes both insecurity and pride, xenophobia and patriotism, in an ever-changing mix. Where American nationalism exaggerates its country's achievements and ignores its failures, Chinese nationalist rhetoric revels in every detail of the nation's various "humiliations" at the hands of the West and Japan.

The conflicting strains and anti-Western tendencies that run through Chinese nationalism make it a difficult force to harness. Well aware of its incendiary nature, the People's Republic has suppressed it over the years almost as much as it has supported it. Even so, the shadow of nationalism has long hovered over diplomacy, politics, and many other fields of endeavor, including music.

In music history and musicology, its presence has been so strong and unpredictable that until quite recently the history of Western music in China could not be written about with any semblance of objectivity. The result is that even though Western instruments and music theory dominate the curriculum of China's conservatories, few people (even musicians) have an accurate understanding about how classical music came to China and became a part of its culture. The role that missionaries played in spreading it has been purposefully ignored, that of path-breaking educators and composers like Xiao Youmei and Huang Zi deliberately underplayed in favor of the "revolutionary" composers Nie Er and Xian Xinghai, and the contributions of professional foreign musicians cast in a negative light. This distorted version of history has been transmitted to foreign scholars, many of whom have blithely accepted it without considering that it may be a politically tainted distortion of the past.

This process is easiest to see in discussions of the Shanghai Municipal Orchestra and Mario Paci. Until the late 1950s, the Shanghai Symphony still had foreigners in its ranks, but by the early-1960s visit of the New Zealand musician Frederick Page, the process of denigrating their contributions had already begun. Page was told the story of Paci's refusal to let Xian Xinghai conduct the Municipal Orchestra, but in a greatly dramatized version.

"The European conductor of the Shanghai Symphony Orchestra in the late 1930s tore the manuscript [of the *Yellow River Cantata*] in two, before the orchestra, when it was put in front of him," Page related in his account of his visit. [24]

Paci, of course, had done nothing of the kind — according to Xian Xinghai himself, Paci had revoked an invitation to conduct Beethoven's *Eighth Symphony* because of opposition from members of the orchestra related to Xinghai's role in protests at the National Conservatory. Indeed, Xinghai did not even write the *Yellow River Cantata* until he was in Yanan in 1939, four years after the cancelled conducting invitation.

The anecdote as related to Page is clearly intended to imply that Paci was a racist who treated Chinese unfairly. The truth, of course, is that he treated orchestra musicians of all races badly at times, but was a great supporter of Chinese musicians and composers. Indeed, among the few of Paci's papers that his wife was able to take with her when she left China in 1949 were scores of music by He Luting, Ding Shande and Tang Xueyong. Ding had inscribed the score, "To my dear teacher Maestro Mario Paci," while Tang Xueyong wrote, "A Mon ami Maître Paci, son admirateur."[25]

Page visited China in the lead-up to the Cultural Revolution, but such politically-tainted distortions continue to be repeated and accepted as truth. Annette Schimmelpenninck and Frank Kouwenhoven, two scholars who write with great passion and knowledge about the works of contemporary Chinese composers, fall into this trap when they relate that Tan Shuzhen "was invited to turn the pages for a Western soloist and made such a good impression that he and some others were eventually accepted as Chinese members in the ensemble."[26] This story, which is false, was told to them by a folk song teacher at the Shanghai Conservatory. They further state that "Paci could hardly claim to be a missionary for the ordinary Chinese"[27] and seem unaware of his extensive teaching of Chinese pianists, his efforts to bring Chinese into the concert hall, his support of Chinese composers, his efforts to start a conservatory, or his integration of the orchestra. Even an anecdote told them by Ding Shande about how the Conservatory students were allowed to go to concerts but had to sit "up in the gods with only a poor view of the stage" is interpreted as evidence of "the deep rift between native and foreign communities in China."[28] In fact, the

24. Page, Frederick (1963). A musician's journal. *Arts and Sciences in China*: 15.

25. These scores were given to the authors by Floria Paci Zaharoff.

26. Schimmelpenninck, Antoinet. & Kouwenhoven, Frank. (1993). The Shanghai Conservatory of Music. *Chime*, No. 6, Spring: 66.

27. *Ibid.*, 66.

Conservatory students sat up with "the gods" not because they were discriminated against as Chinese, but because Paci allowed them to buy deeply discounted tickets, a fact that Ding Shande would no doubt have mentioned had he been questioned further.

This politically influenced version of history is also promoted by Richard Kraus, the author of *Pianos & Politics in China*, an insightful account of the political nature of Western music in the PRC that focuses on the piano. Kraus essentially casts Paci and other foreign musicians as agents of imperialism in the same manner that many PRC historians do. Paci's positive contributions are ignored and the integration of the orchestra, for which Paci himself obtained funding from Italy, is denigrated because the Chinese musicians were paid less than the foreigners — a situation which still exists today, even though the orchestras have been entirely under Chinese control for more than fifty years. Kraus also states that the Chinese musicians "had no social interaction with the European musicians,"[29] which again is utterly false. He faults Paci for having "bitterly disappointed Xian Xinghai"[30] but does not mention the Chinese musicians whom Paci invited to perform as soloists with the SMO, the composers whose works he premiered, the countless Chinese piano students he taught — often for free — or any of the many other ways he worked to share classical music with Chinese people.

While such accounts as these fit neatly into a black-and-white, nationalistic version of pre-liberation Shanghai as a battleground for the struggle between pompous imperialists and repressed Chinese, they are simply not supported by the historical record or the accounts of Chinese musicians who lived through the era. The truth of this distortion is increasingly acknowledged by Chinese scholars and a number of important histories of Western music in China in the pre-liberation era have been written in the past decade.

However, while it is now permissible to write objectively about Western music in the pre-liberation era, the subject is still controversial. This was demonstrated in 1999 when the Shanghai Symphony decided to celebrate its 120th anniversary by publishing an album, hosting ceremonies, and generating publicity. Objections to this celebration soon sprang up from musicologists and other intellectuals — generally Beijing-based — who believed that the orchestra should date its founding to 1956 when it took on its current name. They argued, in essence, that the era in which the orchestra was exclusively foreign or foreign-dominated did not count. The Shanghai Municipal Band and the Shanghai Municipal Orchestra, in their view, were separate, imperialist institutions which could not be considered precursors of the Shanghai Symphony Orchestra. Other musicologists and historians — usually Shanghai-based — responded that this was nonsense and traced the development of the orchestra over the 120 year period to demonstrate its continuity. They also noted that many hospitals

---

28. *Ibid.*, 66.
29. Kraus: 5.
30. Kraus: 74.

and universities that had been founded by foreign missionaries saw no need to eliminate their missionary past from the historical record; some even used their original names. The Shanghai Symphony ignored objections and went ahead and feted itself; it is planning another celebration and another album for its 125th anniversary in 2004.

Nationalism has also been a powerful, if changeable, force in music creation and composition from the early 20th century until today. School-songers used Western tunes to set Chinese texts and convey Chinese values "in order to awaken the national spirit."[31] May 4th intellectuals like Xiao Youmei pushed for the creation of a national music that would be a combination of Chinese melodies with Western harmony and musical forms. Spirit and emotion were its most important aspects — so long as these were nationalist in character, there could be many different kinds of "national music."

But as the 1930s wore on and China became engulfed by war, fewer composers shared this sort of broad-mindedness. "Revolutionary" composers like Nie Er and Xian Xinghai came to see music and nationalism as inextricably linked, its primary purpose being to inspire resistance to Japanese imperialism. So did virtually all their peers, even if they disagreed on aspects of this approach, as did Lu Ji and He Luting.

When the Communists came to power, their urge to control virtually every aspect of public and private life took over and they turned nationalism in music from a natural tendency into a requirement. Nationalism was made one of the "three -izes" that were intended to be the basis of all musical composition, the others being that the music be revolutionary and understood by the masses. Nie Er and Xian Xinghai were anointed as role models, and their portraits were hung prominently in conservatories and concert halls across the land.

But when it came to how, exactly, music should be nationalized, the directives were inconsistent and constantly changing. Perhaps the classic example of this is the treatment of He Zhanhao and Chen Gang's violin concerto, the *Butterfly Lovers*. When the concerto was first performed in 1959, it was hailed by *People's Daily* as "our own symphonic music" and widely praised for its successful symphonic adaptation of a Chinese melody and legend, but by 1964 it had been unofficially banned because of its "feudal" content.

When the Cultural Revolution began, the rhetoric of nationalism was subsumed in that of revolution. With few exceptions, music had to tell the story of a revolutionary hero who triumphed over the Japanese, the Nationalists, or the bourgeoisie. Despite these supremely narrow constraints, composers responded to the challenge and music is considered to be the strongest aspect of the model operas. For example, in the model Peking operas for which Yu Huiyong was the lead composer, he used traditional Peking opera and enhanced it with folk music, *quyi* storytelling, and concepts from Western opera like musical motifs used to introduce specific characters. He also successfully combined the symphony orchestra with Chinese

---

31. See Gerlinde, G. (1998). Early 20th-century "reforms" in Chinese music. *Chime*. Spring/Autumn: 119.

instruments. Indeed, Yu's music, and that of the model operas as a group, is a supremely successful example of nationalism.[32]

When the Cultural Revolution ended, the revolutionary version of nationalism that the model operas embodied was abandoned. The operas themselves were not condemned because too many important people, like Mao Zedong and Zhou Enlai, had praised them and too many millions of people had enjoyed them. However, the operas themselves were so over-performed that they were temporarily shelved.[33] This meant, in effect, that the Chinese government had spent the better part of three decades mandating that music have national or revolutionary content yet all there was to show for it were a few pieces from the 1950s. Orchestras dusted off their copies of *Butterfly Lovers* and a few pieces by such composers as Luo Zhongrong and Zhu Jianer, but mostly they played the works of Western composers like Beethoven, Tchaikovsky, Schubert and Debussy.

Unsurprisingly, some culture officials and critics were upset by the turn to Western music.

"People asked, why don't you perform Chinese pieces?" explained Li Delun. "I said, It's not that we aren't performing them, it's that there aren't enough good pieces yet! They make it seem like if you don't play Chinese music, you don't love China."

In the relative artistic freedom that followed the Cultural Revolution, composers were for the first time in decades largely free to follow their own creative instincts. But, it took some time for many to adjust.

"In our first year at the Conservatory, most of us continued to write pieces with a strongly revolutionary flavor," Guo Wenjing explained in an interview. "Tan Dun composed a violin piece called *I Dreamt of Chairman Mao*, and Qu Xiaosong wrote a string quartet based on one of Xian Xinghai's songs, *Let's Go Behind Enemy Lines*."[34]

Once it became apparent that the political situation had truly changed, students stopped writing politically motivated pieces. Instead, they queued for courses on 20th-century music taught by visiting professors like Alexander Goehr and immersed themselves in such basics of formal composition training as harmony, counterpoint, form, analysis, and orchestration.

---

32. The subject of Yu's positive contributions to the development of Peking opera is still so controversial that several books on the subject have been banned.

33. Some of the model operas began to be performed again in the mid-1980s. Those set in the pre-liberation era — especially *The Red Lantern*, *Shajiabang*, *The White-Haired Girl*, *The Red Detachment of Women* and *Taking Tiger Mountain By Strategy* — are now part of the standard repertoire for Peking opera and ballet companies in Beijing and Shanghai and are big crowd pleasers that are often taken on tour. The model symphonic operas *Revolutionary Symphonic Music "Shajiabang"* and *Revolutionary Symphonic Music "Taking Tiger Mountain by Strategy"* have also been performed in Beijing and Shanghai in recent years, although they are not standard repertoire for any orchestras. For more on the revival of the model operas, see Melvin, Sheila and Cai, Jindong (2000). Why this nostalgia for fruits of chaos? *The New York Times* (Arts and Leisure) October 29.

34. Kouwenhoven, Frank and Schimmelpenninck, Antoinet (1997). Guo Wenjing — a composer's portrait. *Chime*. Spring/Autumn: 19.

"For the first three years at the conservatory," Tan Dun told an interviewer, "I was totally involved with Western classical music, forgetting what I had done, the Peking Opera, shamanistic music, whatever." [35]

Some members of the older generation of composers started to use 20th-century Western technique in their work. Luo Zhongrong, the resident composer at the Central Philharmonic, began to write 12-tone and serial music in 1981 — his *Picking Lotus* is considered the first 12-tone composition in China.[36] Zhu Jianer, the Shanghai Symphony's Soviet-educated resident composer, then sat in on classes in contemporary technique taught by Chen Mingzhi and Yang Liqing and used 12-tone technique in his *Fourth Symphony*.

But in adopting modern technique, these composers still remembered their roots. In *Picking Lotus*, Luo Zhongrong used Chinese poetry as a text and combined 12-tone serialism with the traditional pentatonic system. Zhu Jianer's *Fourth Symphony* had no descriptive title or tonality, but it was based on Daoist thought — from nothing to something, from something to nothing.

And, though contemporary technique created excitement because it was being taught for the first time, the formal study of China's own music still occupied a considerable portion of the composition curriculum in these early years after the Cultural Revolution.

"In the first year, we were taught Chinese folk songs from different provinces and minorities; we had to memorize about four a week, in the proper dialects," Chen Yi explained to a journalist. "During the holidays we had to do fieldwork. In the second year we learned the different Chinese vocal forms, *quyi, pingtan, tanci*, etc. We even had to write compositions in these different genres. In the third year, the operatic tradition was taught: *bangzi, jingju*, etc. In the fourth year, Chinese instrumental music was taught." [37]

Although the Conservatory was hardly flush with money, enough was set aside for students to take year-end field trips to distant rural areas where they were able to collect folk songs and study the local music, which then often found its way into their compositions.

"Nearly all Chinese composers in the 1970s happened to write folklore-inspired compositions," explained Guo Wenjing. "But most of them used 19th-century Western harmonies which did not necessarily retain the spirit of the original melodies."[38]

These diverse studies in contemporary Western and Chinese traditional music began leading many composition students to experiment with a merger of Chinese themes, Chinese music, and Western technique. Tan Dun's 1979 symphonic work *Li Sao*, or *Encountering Sorrow*, incorporated Chinese music and instruments, used

---

35. Clements, Andrew (1995). Notes on white paper. *The Guardian* August 4.

36. See Mittler: 393. Mr. Luo had been at the National Conservatory in the late 1940s, where he was influenced by Wolfgang Fraenkel and Julian Schloss.

37. Mittler: 147. *Quyi* is story-telling music; *pingtan* and *tanci* are forms of accompanied story-telling; *bangzi* is a form of local opera popular in Hebei; *jingju* is Peking opera.

38. Kouwenhoven and Schimmelpenninck: 20.

polytonality and clustering sounds, and was based on a quintessential Chinese theme, the poetry of Chu Yuan.[39] Guo Wenjing's 1983 *Suspended Ancient Coffins on the Cliffs in Sichuan* is written for two pianos and orchestra. It incorporates the nasal glissandi of the *erhu* into the string parts and takes its strange title from the mysterious ancient coffins that hang suspended on poles above a gorge in the Yangzi River. Zhou Long's 1983 *Valley Stream* is a quartet written for traditional Chinese instruments, the *di, guan, zheng* and percussion. Chen Yi, Qu Xiaosong, Ye Xiaogang, Yang Liqun and other young composers made similar musical explorations and soon their work began to draw attention, both individually and collectively.

Commenting on *Valley Stream*, the ethnomusicologist Qiao Jianzhong said that "Zhou Long has dealt a deathblow to the established formulas of Chinese music of the last thirty years." Tan Dun's *Li Sao* was awarded a prize in the 1981 First National Competition of Orchestra Works and his *Feng-Ya-Song* took a prize in the 1983 Carl-Maria-von-Weber Music Contest in Dresden, making it the first Chinese composition to win an international prize in PRC history. The Central Philharmonic devoted an entire program to a concert of Chen Yi's orchestral works in 1986.

Within a few short years of the Cultural Revolution, a new form of musical nationalism had begun emerging to replace the government-mandated version of the 1950s and the discredited revolutionary version of the 1960s and 1970s. It was not a nationalism of politics or ideology, but of "spirit and emotion," like that once envisioned by Xiao Youmei. It was natural and individual, springing from each composer's experience and background rather than political precepts. It included a far wider swathe of China's culture — regional, minority, religious, musical — than ever before. And, it was musically far more sophisticated than previous efforts, which had often been little more than orchestrating folk songs.

Writing that same year, the music critic Li Xian noted that Tan Dun, Ye Xiaogang, Qu Xiaosong and many of their contemporaries in composition,

> have three basic characteristics in common. They are tenacious about expressing their own personalities in their music — something rare before and during the Cultural Revolution. They strive to combine traditional music with modern treatments. And they want their works to be understood.[40]

39. A deputy prime minister in the ancient Kingdom of Chu, Chu Yuan is best remembered today for drowning himself in despair because the king he served would not follow his well-intentioned advice. However, he was also an outstanding poet whose work has been admired and imitated by Chinese intellectuals for more than 2000 years. *Li Sao* is his lament for his country and his people, ruled by "That band of fools [who] enjoy their careless pleasures..." Chu denounces the possibility of compromise with his enemies and vows never to forsake his ideals: "Deep is the road and long; Everywhere I continue my search." Chu Yuan and his poetry are a favorite subject for Chinese composers; Tan Dun's *Nine Songs* is also about Chu Yuan. Wang Xilin's *Zhao Hun, Tian Wen* and Jin Xiang's *Tian Wen* are both also based on the poetry of Chu Yuan. For quotes, see Lu Yungpin (1978). Chu Yuan, Poet and patriot. *Chinese Literature* 5: 115-116.

40. Li Xian (1986). New wave in Chinese music. *China Reconstructs* December: 16.

But, if sensitive critics like Li Xian understood and valued the young composers' efforts, most arbiters of what was good and bad in Chinese music did not. Instead of seeing a new musical nationalism of "spirit and emotion," they heard "unintelligible" sounds devoid of national character — and became increasingly upset.

"In 1982, there was criticism of young composers like Tan Dun," explained Zhu Jianer. "So I went to Beijing to explain that the roots of their music are in the nationalities of China." [41]

Mr. Zhu's efforts may have helped calm the waters temporarily, but the criticism soon revived. The veteran music bureaucrat Lu Ji continued to insist that the development of music should come under the leadership of the Communist Party. Even his longtime opponent He Luting was apparently upset by the work of some of the young generation of composers.

"Melody is important: if there are national characteristics, then our music will be liked internationally. Modern music, on the other hand, is unintelligible, it has no national characteristics. The beauty of China's nature cannot be expressed in this monotonous atonal music." [42]

Another critic argued that the work of some of these young composers was only imitative nationalism — it may have had a Chinese composer and theme, but it sounded like it was written by a European student of Schoenberg, Stravinsky, or Bartok.[43]

Tan Dun's music continued to receive particularly harsh attention. One critic wrote that "Many Chinese listeners can understand Schoenberg's *The Warsaw Survivor* but cannot understand *Feng-Ya-Song*. This means that content and technique are not connected in the latter piece."[44]

The criticism of *Feng-Ya-Song* escalated in the anti-spiritual pollution campaign of 1983-84. That the Weber prize-winning string quartet was singled out for attack while *Li Sao* was awarded a prize in China is both ironic and revealing. As Barbara Mittler writes in *Dangerous Tunes*, *Li Sao* is "radical in its critique of the detrimental state of his country's government of bribery and sycophancy... but it never met with direct and harsh criticism. *Feng-Ya-Song*, on the other hand, which was never envisaged as a direct political statement, a composition which was honored with an international prize, always an important asset in Communist China, was condemned as decadent and anti-socialist."[45] In fact, that *Feng-Ya-Song* won a prize outside China is undoubtedly part of the reason it was so harshly criticized. Certainly the government was happy when its young instrumentalists won prizes for playing Chopin. But individualistic and experimental music — even if it was also national —

---

41. Quote is from Sheila Melvin's October 1999 interview with Mr. Zhu at his Shanghai home.

42. Mittler: 283. Mittler also states that He Luting considered the compositions of Xu Shuya to be proof that she had learned nothing while at the Shanghai Conservatory. (See Mittler: 270).

43. Mittler: 355.

44. Ming Yan (2002). *Ershishiji Zhongguo Yinyue Piping Daolun*. [A Guide to 20th-Century Music Criticism in China]. Beijing: Renmin Yinyue Chubanshe: 355.

45. Mittler: 120 and 124.

was not the image that Chinese officialdom wanted to present to the outside world, and many bureaucrats no doubt considered the prize to be an embarrassment.

The general disagreement over the works of these young composers was highlighted in 1986 when the China Record Company held its first composition contest. Although many were impressed by the quality of music in the competition, the jury presided over by Ding Shande was so divided that it awarded no first prize. Instead, it gave two second prizes, to Guo Wenjing for his *Suspended Coffins* and to He Xuntian for his *Sounds of Nature*.

But, the bright side of the criticism meted out to these up-and-coming composers was that it was part of a true debate. With the exception of the anti-spiritual pollution campaign, there was no broad official attempt to stop them from composing as they wished or to prevent their works from being performed. Indeed, no matter what Lu Ji and other members of the old guard musicians may have hoped, there was to be no turning back. As the music critic Li Xian wrote in his prescient 1986 essay,

> In the past five years, Chinese music has gone from seclusion to interchange with the outside world and from stagnation to creative proliferation. It's still to early to classify modern Chinese music, but the new wave is changing the structure, concept and course of the country's music — and perhaps also music abroad.[46]

In fact, right around the time Li penned these words, an exodus of the young composers whose work would indeed change music abroad was just beginning. Tan Dun, Zhou Long, Chen Yi, Qu Xiaosong and Ge Ganru went to Columbia University in New York; Bright Sheng went to Queens College and Columbia; Ye Xiaogang went to the Eastman School; Xu Shuya and Chen Qigang went to Paris, the latter to study with Messiaen; and Su Cong went to Freie University in Berlin.

Re-establishing themselves overseas was a tremendous challenge for most of these composers, who simultaneously had to learn foreign languages, support themselves, complete their degree work or other studies, and then find jobs or commissions. To make ends meet, Tan Dun played his fiddle on the streets of New York. Zhou Long found life in New York so overwhelming that he stopped composing for two years and delivered newspapers to make a living. Chen Yi struggled to keep her eyes open as she taught piano and violin.

However, slowly but surely, they and their compatriots began to break into the international world of classical music. By the 1990s, many were beginning to receive recognition, and the prestigious awards and commissions that come with it — Tan Dun received a Grawemeyer Award and an Academy Award, Bright Sheng a MacArthur Foundation grant, Chen Yi a Charles Ives Living Award, and so on. Indeed, as a group, the composers from the first post-Cultural Revolution classes at the Central and Shanghai Conservatories have received virtually every prestigious international award and commission that it is possible to get.

---

46. Li Xian: 16.

In the process of maturing, whether at home or abroad, many have found themselves becoming even more "national" in their approach to composition.

"I've begun to explore more Chinese elements. I mean, Chinese ways of expression..." Guo Wenjing explained. "I believe I've definitely grown more Chinese."[47] Qu Xiaosong similarly volunteered that he has become "more Chinese" than in his earlier operatic works.[48]

But becoming even "more Chinese" had little impact on the acceptance of these composer's works back home. As Guo Wenjing wrote in 1994,

> I believe that, right now, more new Chinese music is being played in the West than in China. And Western musicians play these works better than their Chinese colleagues. This is a big problem for China. I wonder whether all the new Chinese music of the final years of this century is going to be premiered in the West, and published by Westerners. [49]

The tide finally began to turn as a new wave of Chinese nationalism that began in the early 1990s grew stronger. Some China watchers attribute this resurgent nationalism to the Communist Party's efforts to find an alternative to its own bankrupt Marxist ideology. But, nationalism is also growing from the grassroots as the increasing economic prosperity of young Chinese makes them more confident about their own prospects, and those of their nation. It is once again accompanied by a measure of disillusionment with the West, spurred on by such events as the early 1990s opposition to China's bid for the 2000 Olympics by the US Congress and the American military's accidental bombing of the Chinese embassy in Yugoslavia in 1999. This reinvigorated nationalism is perhaps most noticeable in China's international relations, but it has also affected many aspects of domestic life and culture, including the study and performance of music.

Beginning in the early 1990s, academic proponents of a new music nationalism began to critically reevaluate the contributions of Xiao Youmei, Huang Zi, and the school-songers Shen Xingong and Li Shutong. They pointed out that all four were educated in the West or Japan and suggested that under the influence of their foreign studies and the May 4th movement, they had become convinced of the inferiority of Chinese music. They had then spread this belief so convincingly that it had corrupted music and musicology up to this day. Cultures cannot be compared in such a way that one is labeled progressive and the other backward, these new nationalists argued. Nor should Western classical music be seen as the general standard for all people — for China, the most important task should be to revitalize its own traditional music.[50]

Arguments such as these are confined to the ivory towers of academia, but the growing nationalism has contributed to a renewed interest in Chinese traditional

---

47. Kouwenhoven and Schimmelpenninck: 48.
48. Kouwenhoven, Frank (1997). New Chinese operas by Qu Xiaosong, Tan Dun and Guo Wenjing. *Chime.* Spring/Autumn: 113.
49. Kouwenhoven and Schimmelpenninck: 33.
50. Ming Yan: 446.

music and instruments that is played out in many different ways. It is, for instance, quite common now for a pop star to play an *erhu*; the pop group *12 Girls Band*, which is made up of classically-trained *erhu* and other traditional instrument performers, is popular in China and even in Japan where its first album sold more than two million copies.[51] The Chinese government has put more effort into promoting traditional instrument orchestras, including the China National Traditional Orchestra's 2000 US tour under the baton of Shanghai Symphony conductor Chen Xieyang. But even as the government tries to raise the profile of China's own music through such tours, a movement has grown up in traditional music circles that is critical of the artificial nature of the big orchestras and urges a return to a more authentic performance style and repertoire.

An interest in the music of contemporary classical composers has developed in tandem with these trends in traditional music. It has been further spurred on by the mounting acclaim bestowed on Chinese composers overseas. The increasingly sound economic footing on which Chinese orchestras now stand is also important since it enables them to present more diverse programs and commission more works. It also permits them to go on international tours more frequently and, as Guo Wenjing put it, "You can't go to Germany and just play Brahms."

Thus, beginning in the mid-1990s orchestras began performing more works by Chinese composers. Various government bureaus and agencies also began increasing the number and value of the commissions they offered. When the Chinese government was making its plans for the 1997 ceremonies marking the return of Hong Kong, it turned to Tan Dun, the composer whose works had been banned and labeled "poisonous weeds" just over a decade earlier. Tan composed a symphony called *Heaven, Earth and Mankind* which was broadcast repeatedly throughout China during the replays of the ceremony. In the years since, the works of Chinese composers have been performed with increasing frequency. "Chineseness" was the theme of the fifth Beijing International Music festival, in 2002, which included two separate concerts devoted to the works of Ye Xiaogang and Chen Qigang. When the China National Symphony Orchestra went to Australia that same year, its program was dominated by the works of Chinese composers, including three pieces by Tan Dun.[52] In 2003, the festival featured the China premieres of two operas by Guo Wenjing, *Night Banquet* and *Wolf Cub Village*.

In acknowledgement of the improving situation, some composers, including Ye Xiaogang and Qu Xiaosong, decided to return to China to compose and to teach.

"My music is played everywhere and my commissions are very high," said Ye Xiaogang. "There are so many opportunities here. I'd never have these opportunities in America."[53]

---

51. See (2004). 12 Girls rock the classics. *cnn.com* February 4.

52. See (2002). Chinese orchestra to perform in Australia. *China Daily* September 23. The pieces were *Death and Fire: Dialogue with Paul Klee* (1992); *Orchestral Theater II: Re* (1993); and *Out of Peking Opera*.

53. Interview with authors in Beijing, December 2000.

Composers who still live outside China also return with greater frequency. Tan Dun now conducts his own pieces in China several times a year and has given the Asia premieres of some of his works there. In March of 2004 he even conducted *The Map: In Search of Disappearing Roots* — a concerto for cello, orchestra and video which premiered in Boston in 2003 — in an ancient village in his home province of Hunan. *The Map* was inspired by the village music and folk traditions of Hunan and more than 30,000 villagers turned out to hear it performed by the Shanghai Symphony. For many, it was their first time ever to hear a live symphony concert.[54]

But even as China's hydra-headed nationalism leads to more pride in the success of Chinese composers overseas and more acclaim for them at home, it also leads to more criticism and carping. Sometimes it seems that the general rule among culture critics in China is that if foreigners like it, it can't be any good and it most certainly can't be authentic because a foreigner could never understand anything that is truly Chinese. Thus do some Chinese critics make the claim that composers use their music to trick foreigners, who are naturally assumed to be dumb enough to fall for this.

Unsurprisingly, it is Tan Dun who continues to be the lightning rod for much of this criticism — his music is the most experimental, his commercial success is the greatest, and he has been a favored target of critics for a quarter of a century. Perhaps best representative of his detractors is the conductor and critic Bian Zushan, who has written dozens of articles attacking Tan's music which he variously describes as "more concept than music" and "the emperor's new clothing."[55] The two had a showdown of a sort in 2001 when Tan Dun was discussing his music on a popular television talk show and Bian Zushan was suddenly escorted onto the stage. Tan Dun, who had not been informed that his chief critic would be appearing, listened to Mr. Bian's lengthy attack on his music and then politely excused himself and walked out in the middle of the show. Once the shocked TV hosts had recovered, the discussion was opened up to audience members, one of whom commented that "Tan's music has won an Oscar for its Chineseness, not its composition techniques. This shows once more that only things that are national will be accepted by the world."[56]

"Chineseness" is certainly an important element of the international success of Tan Dun and his contemporaries. The fact that so many Chinese composers from the same generation have become successful in the concert halls of the US and Europe brings them all more attention than they would otherwise be likely to receive. In 2001, for instance, *The New York Times* ran two front page Arts & Leisure stories about Chinese composers, headlined "The sound of new music is often Chinese," while in 2003, *The Financial Times* called Chinese composers "a huge phenomenon in the US."[57] The "Chineseness" of their music — perhaps better phrased as a shared capacity for plumbing the limitless depths of Chinese culture, musical and otherwise — is also certainly much of the reason for their success as individuals. Tcherepnin's long-ago

---

54. Account of concert comes from personal correspondence with Jane Huang.
55. See, Is It Music? www.bjreview.com.cn/2001/200150/Forum-200150
56. *Ibid.*

prediction that the value of Chinese composers' work would increase as it grew more national has proved absolutely right. But this "Chineseness" is as much a double-edged sword abroad as it is at home.

Indeed, while the music of many of these composers is criticized in China because it is deemed too individualistic and not national enough, outside China it is all lumped together as "Chinese" music. The composers, too, are permanently labeled as Chinese composers, even though their music is as different from one another as that of any randomly picked group of European composers. As James Oestreich wrote in *The New York Times*, "all of these composers tend to be marginalized, their cross-cultural works treated as novelties rather than a part of the contemporary-music mainstream (if mainstream there be anymore)."[58] Critics searching for a way to explain or describe their music tend compare it to that of Western composers, thus implying that their works are imitative, or at least derivative.

"It's quite a frustration that so many Westerners perpetually identify Chinese composers with Western ones," complained Guo Wenjing. "They will say: this is Cage, this is Ravel... I remember one older Conservatory teacher getting very angry when a visiting musicologist from the USA identified one of his pieces as Debussy. He cried out, 'No, this piece doesn't resemble Debussy! Not at all! Debussy resembles me! Debussy resembles China!'"[59]

The assumption among Western critics seems to be that it is natural for the work of a Western composer to be influenced by that of other Western composers, but when a Chinese composer displays the same influence in his work, he is copying. The truth, of course, is that Debussy and Ravel are as much a part of a conservatory-educated Chinese composer's heritage as they are of a Western composer's. Perhaps the most basic trait shared by the first post-Cultural Revolution generation of composers is that they have two musical foundations to draw upon, that of the West and that of China, in all its vast diversity. But ultimately, their success must be attributed neither to the "nationalness" nor the Chineseness of their music, but to the individual artistry of each composer.

As Tan Dun put it, "Ideally, every artist must be regarded, first and foremost, as an individual.... To a certain extent it is important to be aware of a composer's cultural background. But you wouldn't want to care too much about it, either. In the end, it's the composer's music which speaks when it sounds, and which explains everything that needs to be explained."[60]

---

57. The two *New York Times* articles are Oestreich, James R. (2001). A new contingent of American composers, April 1: 1; and Melvin, Sheila and Cai Jindong (2001). The offspring of a grim revolution, April 1: 1. *The Financial Times* article is Clark, Andrew (2003). An exotic mix: Bright Sheng and Tan Dun are leading composers of Chinese-American music — the latest cultural revolution to sweep New York. *The Financial Times* March 22.

58. Oestreich, James R. (2001). A new contingent of American composers. *The New York Times* April 1: 1.

59. Kouwenhoven and Schimmelpenninck: 22.

60. Utz, Christian (1998). Extreme cross-over, extremely personal music. *Chime* Spring/Autumn: 143-4.

POSTLUDE

Xiao Youmei believed that music was an international language — where foreign languages required interpreters, music needed no translation because it belonged to the world. Mao Zedong, on the other hand, believed that all the arts, including music, were inseparable from the customs, feelings, language, and history of a nation.

Xiao Youmei's admirable idealism notwithstanding, it does seem that Mao's view is closer to the mark. Classical music spread to China not because it is intrinsically international, but because it had missionaries like Matteo Ricci and musicians like Mario Paci to spread it. It took root there not because this was inevitable, but because it was nurtured, promoted, adopted and eventually transformed by generations of talented Chinese musicians, music educators, and music lovers. Some of these men and women were devoted to classical music because they believed it served a higher cause — like religion, modernization or revolution — and some believed that the music itself was the higher cause.

The story of classical music's transmission and transformation in China is at its heart a story of heroes. Their quest may be variously seen as noble, quixotic, even misguided, but their dedication cannot be questioned. All of us who enjoy classical music today — in China, or by way of Chinese orchestra musicians, singers, soloists, composers and conductors around the world — are in some measure beneficiaries of their devotion, determination, and sacrifice.

Three of these heroes, of course, are He Luting, Li Delun, and Tan Shuzhen and it is only fitting that we tell you how each completed his life's work.

***

He Luting relinquished most of his official Shanghai Conservatory responsibilities in 1984 so he could expand his efforts to promote music education.

335

He travelled around the country to meet with music teachers in elementary, middle, and high schools and then wrote music education proposals for local governments. He also started to compose again, including the score for a movie about Marshall He Long, a charismatic fellow Hunanese who had died during the Cultural Revolution — allegedly after Jiang Qing ordered doctors to give him glucose injections instead of the insulin he needed to control his diabetes.

Unsurprisingly, He Luting also continued to fight good fights. For instance, when a regulation was passed stating that only the Central and Shanghai conservatories could use foreign textbooks, it caused consternation in music circles nationwide. Although it did not affect the Shanghai Conservatory, Mr. He nonetheless led the battle to get the regulation rescinded.

He Luting's wife, Jiang Ruizhi, died in 1997. Mr. He himself passed away on April 27, 1999 at the age of 96. The death of "the hard-boned musician" known throughout the country for his stubborn adherence to principle was major news. More than a thousand people attended his funeral and floral wreathes were sent by the nation's top leaders, including then-president Jiang Zemin and then-premier Zhu Rongji. On the first anniversary of Mr. He's death, the Shanghai Music Publishing House released a collection of essays in his memory written by a variety of friends, students, colleagues and relatives. They are a testament to Mr. He's force as a composer, an educator, an inspiration, and a friend.

"When I heard the news of Director He's death," wrote Tan Shuzhen, "I first felt shocked and then numb. That afternoon I stayed alone in my room at sunset, but I felt strangely uneasy. And then I thought, 'Director He has gone,' and I could not stop myself from sobbing. Since that day, when dusk falls, I cry. Then I pick up a pen, but I don't know what to write."[1]

Li Delun considered Mr. He's loss from a broader perspective.

"Old He has gone far away," he wrote. "A great person respected by everyone has gone forever. But he will always be the conscience of the music world. He will always be watching over us."[2]

***

Li Delun made his last push to implement his plan for professionalizing the Central Philharmonic in the first half of the 1980s and accomplished his goal of seeing a new Beijing Concert Hall built. Then, like He Luting, he gradually began to step back from his work to devote more time to music education. He travelled around the

1. See Tan Shuzhen (2000). Huainian He Luting Yuanzhang [Remembering He Luting]. In, He Yuanyuan and He Yiqiu (eds). Yongyuan de Huainian: renmin yinyuejia He Luting de shishi zhounian jinian wenji [*Lasting Memories: a collection of articles about the people's musician He Luting on the first anniversary of his death*] Shanghai Yinyue Chubanshe: 23.
2. See Li Delun (2000). Wo suo renshide He Luting [The He Luting I knew]. He Yuanyuan and He Yiqiu (eds). [Lasting Memories]: 37.

country conducting regional orchestras *pro bono* and giving lectures on symphonic music that were filled with jokes, but also with much serious information.

In 1984, the Ministry of Culture sent Mr. Li to Moscow together with the composer Zhu Jianer, his first trip back since his student days. The visit was like a homecoming — he even remembered the bus routes and when he found himself at the Moscow Conservatory at lunchtime, he was delighted to find that he remembered how to get to his favorite restaurant, which was still there. Some of his former schoolmates were now running the Moscow Conservatory and as he visited with them, he reflected on how important his time as a student there had been, the key experience that transformed him from an amateur to a professional conductor.

Mr. Li's physical health worsened as the years went on and he found it increasingly difficult to get around. But even as he was forced to forgo most conducting opportunities, he became a mentor to many young conductors and helped more than a few to go overseas for study. He lobbied the bureaucracy on important musical issues and was instrumental in preventing the disbandment of the Beijing Symphony. Now and then he spoke out on other issues — like the practice of orchestras playing pop music in tee-shirts, of which he did not approve. He had many visitors who came to his home for good food and conversation, among them Seiji Ozawa, Yehudi Menuhin and even friends from the long-ago past, like Walter Joachim, the cellist from the Shanghai Municipal Orchestra, and his brother Otto, who had run the music store across from the Lyceum Theater.

In 1999, Isaac Stern returned to China for a gala concert with Li Delun and the China National Symphony to mark the 20-year anniversary of their 1979 performance and the making of the film *From Mao to Mozart*. It was Stern's first trip back to China since his original visit — a fulfillment of the promise he and Mr. Li had then made each other — and he once again had a camera crew in tow to document it. Li Delun was by then largely confined to a wheelchair and four of his students carried him on stage so he could lead the orchestra as it accompanied Stern in Mozart's *Violin Concerto in G-Major*. The concert also featured performances by several of the children (now grown up) whom Stern had heard on his first visit and later helped study abroad, including the cellist Wang Jian, the pianist Pan Chun and the violinist Vera Tsu.[3]

Mr. Li's reunion concert with Stern proved to be his last time at the podium. The China National Symphony held a special concert to honor his 55-year career as a conductor in the spring of 2001, but he was too ill to leave the hospital to conduct it. Even so, he listened to the performance on a transistor radio and occasionally "conducted" parts of it from his sick bed. He died later that year, on October 19, 2001, at the age of 84.

Mr. Li's career had not turned out as he hoped. He had not been able to conduct much of the music he loved and he had not been able to build the Central

---

3. Footage of Li Delun and Stern's reunion concert can be seen on the 2001 DVD version of *From Mao to Mozart*, which includes a postscript called Musical Encounters that covers Stern's 1999 return visit to China.

Philharmonic into the quality orchestra that he envisioned. As he told us, rather sadly, "From 1957 when I returned [from Moscow], there was the anti-rightist movement, the Great Leap Forward, the 'three -izes,' the Cultural Revolution — we couldn't do anything. Nobody really cared about art — it was all politics. I only want to do art, not politics."

But if Mr. Li did not achieve all he hoped, he never stopped trying. His determination to prove that one could love classical music and still be a revolutionary were instrumental in preserving his own orchestra and in spreading classical and orchestral music to millions of people. Still, Mr. Li downplayed his own achievements.

"I have done what I should over the years," he told the *China Daily* in March of 2001. "In comparison to what the pioneering Chinese musicians did since the 1920s, I have done very little. To me, popularizing classical music is not for the sake of the music alone. It is for elevating the spirit of society. It will not be done by a few people alone."[4]

***

Although Tan Shuzhen gladly forgave his Red Guard tormentors and resumed his position at the Shanghai Conservatory, his Cultural Revolution experiences left him so drained that he decided to leave China for a time. Three of his four children had become professional musicians and two of them lived in the US. Mr. Tan therefore spent much of the 1980s and 1990s in New York, teaching music, going to concerts, visiting museums, painting, reading, and generally immersing himself in the city's rich cultural life.

But, as he grew older, Mr. Tan's yearning for China grew stronger. "I wanted to see America. I wanted to understand. But still, I want to live in China. It's like an animal — you always go home."

Mr. Tan returned to the third-floor flat of the old house in Shanghai's former French concession that he and his family had lived in for many decades. He spent most of his time in a sunny room that brimmed with a long lifetime's love of music, art and literature. Violins were piled high and music always stood open on a stand near the center of the room. "I still keep working and practicing every day to keep my promise to myself to be a violinist," he would say.

Mr. Tan also continued to make violins, including a copy of Paganini's instrument for his daughter and a child-size violin for a great-grandson who is a prodigy currently studying at Julliard. He painted, too. As a 70th wedding anniversary gift to his wife, he made a portrait of her as she was in the early days of their love, a beautiful young woman in a blue cheongsam and bobbed hair with a languid look in her eyes.

He read voraciously and scrupulously, with a pencil in hand to carefully circle and correct the grammatical errors or factual mistakes that he was certain to find. He also bought more books, even though there was no space to put them. His bookshelves

---

4. See Li Xing (2001). Mission to Elevate Human Spirit. *China Daily*, March 27.

had long ago been filled by his pre-liberation collection of works about music and the tables spilled over with piles of new books — *The Kissinger Transcripts*; a French dictionary of the violin, together with the French language tapes he was studying so he would be able to read it; Mozart's letters; biographies of Paganini, Salti and Berlioz; and works on acoustics, art, and architecture.

In addition to all his artistic and literary pursuits, Mr. Tan remained a consultant to the Shanghai Conservatory. He continued to weigh in on important musical issues in Shanghai, like his fervent belief that the city should have a true concert hall and not just an opera house that doubled as a concert hall. He also wrote many letters about music to friends in China, the United States, and Europe in which he discussed such topics as his pet peeve, the poor intonation of Chinese musicians. What Mr. Tan did not write was a book, even though he was frequently asked to do so. He would not write a book about how to play the violin because, he said, he was still learning how himself; and he refused to write an autobiography.

"I don't want to write an auto-biography — if I write it, I don't want to change a word. I want to tell the truth. I have spent much of the past 20 years in America, where people speak their minds. Most people here don't speak freely, but I'm old, so I'm not afraid of saying anything."

Mr. Tan did not get out much because his legs were too weak, but he had many visitors — former students, famous artists, researchers and reporters, government officials, fellow musicians, children, grandchildren, and great-grandchildren. "When you get to be 90, you are like a Buddha — you never have to go out, you just stay home and people come to visit you."

Tan Shuzhen intended to live to be at least 100. He was determined to care for his wife, who had been ill for some years — but he died on November 28, 2002 at the age of 95.

In China, the funeral of someone who has made it to 80 or beyond is supposed to be considered a happy occasion rather than a sad one. But Tan Shuzhen was so young in his passion for music and enthusiasm for life that his funeral felt like that of someone taken away too early. Tears flowed as a string orchestra played Schubert's *Ave Maria* and the hundreds of mourners, Sheila Melvin among them, took turns bowing one last farewell.

The memory booklet handed out at Tan Shuzhen's funeral bore on its cover a testament that he had penned in 1997:

> Throughout my life, I have not been separated from music even for a moment. Without a life of music, I would lose the interest and the energy to carry on. Music is like air and water — I cannot imagine life without it.

In the week following Mr. Tan's death, Jindong Cai conducted the Shanghai Symphony Orchestra in a concert that he dedicated to Tan Shuzhen, its first Chinese musician. He spoke to the audience — which included Mr. Tan's son and a grand-daughter — about Tan Shuzhen's life-long dedication to music, and then led the orchestra in playing Barber's *Adagio for Strings* as a final salute to an honored musician, and valued friend.

BIBLIOGRAPHY

BOOKS

Allan, C.W. *Jesuits at the Court of Peking*. Shanghai: Kelly and Walsh, Limited. (Reprint edition by University Publications of America, Inc. 1975).

Anderson, Mary M. (1990). *Hidden Power, The Palace Eunuchs of Imperial China*. Buffalo, New York: Prometheus Books.

Arias, Enrique Alberto (1989). *Alexander Tcherepnin: A Bio-Bibliography*. New York: Greenwood Press.

Attwater, Rachel (1963). *Adam Schall: A Jesuit at the Court of China, 1592-1666*. Milwaukee: The Bruce Publishing Company.

Avshalomov, Jacob & Aaron (2001). *Avshalomov's Winding Way: Composers out of China — A Chronicle*. Xlibris Corporation.

Bangert, William V., S.J. (1972). *A History of the Society of Jesus*. St. Louis: The Institute of Jesuit Sources.

Bickers, Robert (2001). "The Greatest Cultural Asset East of Suez": the history and politics of the Shanghai Municipal Orchestra and Public Band, 1881-1946. In Chi-hsiung Chang (chief ed.), *Ershi shiji de Zhongguo yu shijie* [China and the world in the twentieth century] Taibei: Institute of History, Academia Sinica: Vol 2., 835-875.

Blom, Eric (1958). *Stepchildren of Music*. London: G.T. Foulis & Company, Ltd.

Bodde, Derk (1950). *Peking Diary, a year of revolution*. New York: Henry Schuman, Inc.

Brauchli, Bernard (1998). *The Clavichord*. Cambridge: Cambridge University Press.

Carl, Katherine A. (1986). *With the Dowager Empress of China*. London and New York: KPI.

Chang Shouzong (chief ed.) (1997). *Shanghai Yinyue Xueyuan Da Shiji Mingren Lu* [A record of major events and famous people at the Shanghai Conservatory]. Shanghai: Shanghai Yinyue Xueyuan.

Chen Lingqun, Qi Shuyi, Dai Penghai (eds)(1990). *Xiao Youmei Yinyue Wenji* [Collected music essays by Xiao Youmei]. Shanghai: Shanghai Yinyue Chubanshe.

Chen Xieyang (chief ed). (1999). *The 120th Anniversary Album of Shanghai Symphony Orchestra (1879-1999)*. Shanghai: Shanghai Symphony Orchestra, 1999.

Chen Ying (ed) (2002). *Ma Sicong Memorial Hall*. Guangzhou Museum of Art.

Chen Zhenduo (1997). *Liu Tianhua de Chuangzuo he Gongxian* [Liu Tianhua's compositions and achievements]. Beijing: Zhongguo Wenlian Chuban Gongse.

Cheng, Nien (1986), *Life and Death in Shanghai*. New York: Grove Press.

Chow, Tse-tung (1960). *The May Fourth Movement*. Cambridge: Harvard University Press.

Collar, Hugh (1990). *Captive in Shanghai*. Hong Kong: Oxford University Press.

Cray, Ed (1990). *General of the Army: George C. Marshall, Soldier and Statesman*. New York: W.W. Norton & Company.

Cronin, Vincent (1955). *The Wise Man from the West*. New York: E.P. Dutton & Co. Inc.

Dai Jiafang (1995). *Yangbanxi de Fengfeng Yuyu* [The Trials and Tribulations of Model Operas]. Beijing: Zhishi Chubanshe.

Dai Penghai (1993). *Ding Shande Yinyue Nianpu* [A Musical Chronicle of Ding Shande]. Beijing: Zhongyang Yinyue Xueyuan Xuebaoshe.

Dai Penghai, Huang Xudong (eds). (1993) *Xiao Youmei Jinian Wenji*. [Collected Articles on Xiao Youmei]. Shanghai: Shanghai Yinyue Chubanshe.

Debussy, Claude (1962). Monsieur Croche the Dilettante Hater. In *Three Classics in the Aesthetic of Music*. New York: Dover Publications.

Dong, Stella (2001). *Shanghai: The Rise and Fall of a Decadent City*. New York: Perennial.

Dunne, George H., SJ. (1962). *Generation of Giants: The Story of the Jesuits in China in the last Decades of the Ming Dynasty*. Notre Dame: University of Notre Dame Press.

Editorial Committee (1987). *Shanghai Yinyue Xueyuan Jianshi, 1927-1987* [Shanghai Conservatory of Music]. Shanghai: Shanghai Yinyue Xueyuan.

Fairbank, John King; Bruner, Katherine Frost; and Matheson, Elizabeth MacLeod (eds.) (1975). *The I.G in Peking, Letters of Robert Hart, Chinese Maritime Customs 1868-1907*.

Fang, Percy Jucheng and Fang, Lucy Guinong J. (1986). *Zhou Enlai – A Profile*. Beijing: Foreign Languages Press.

Feng Wenci (1998). *Zhong-Wai Yinyue Jiaoliushi*. [A Chinese-Foreign Exchange History of Music]. Hunan: Hunan Jiaoyu Chubanshe.

Ferris, George T. (1895). *Great Italian and French Composers, Palestrina to Massenet*. New York: D. Appleton and Company.

Gamewell, Mary Ninde (1916). *The Gateway to China: Pictures of Shanghai*. New York: Fleming H. Revell Company.

Han Guohuang (1995). Shanghai gongbuju yuedui yenjiu. [The Shanghai Municipal Orchestra]. *Yishuxue* 14: 143-205.

Harich-Schneider, Eta (1973). *A History of Japanese Music*. London: Oxford University Press.

Harrison, Frank (1973) (ed). *Time, Place and Music. An anthology of ethnomusicological observation c. 1550 to c. 1800*. Amsterdam: Frist Knuf.

He Luting (1999). *He Luting Quanji* [The Complete Works of He Luting]. Shanghai: Shanghai Yinyue Chubanshe.

Heppner, Ernest G. (1993). *Shanghai Refuge: A Memoir of the World War II Jewish Ghetto*. Lincoln: University of Nebraska Press.

Holm, David (1991). *Art and Ideology in Revolutionary China*. Oxford: Clarendon Press.

Howe, Sandra Wieland (1997). *Luther Whiting Mason, International Music Educator*. Warren, Michigan: Harmonie Park Press.

Hsu, Immanuel (1975). *The Rise of Modern China*. Oxford: Oxford University Press.

Hu Zhihui (Exec. Ed.) (1994). *A Biographical Dictionary of Modern Chinese Writers*. Beijing: New World Press.

Huang Renke (2001). *Luyi Ren* [The people of the Lu Xun Academy of Arts and Literature]. Beijing: Zhonggong Zhongyang Dangxiao Chubanshe.

Huang Xudong (ed.) (2000). *Lishi bu hui wangji tamen* [History will not forget them]. Beijing: Zhongyang Yinyue Xueyuan Xuebaoshe.

Huang, Ray (1981). *1587: A Year of No Significance*. New Haven and London: Yale University Press.

Jiang Ruizhi (chief ed.) (1995). *Lun He Luting* [On He Luting]. Shanghai: Shanghai Yinyue Chubanshe.

Johnston, Tess and Erh, Deke (1993). *A Last Look: Western Architecture in Old Shanghai*. Hong Kong: Old China Hand Press.

Jones, Andrew F. (2001). *Yellow Music: Media Culture and Colonial Modernity in the Chinese Jazz Age*. Durham and London: Duke University Press.

Kishibe, Shigeo (1980). Court traditions – Banquet music (China, II,3). In, Stanley Sadie (ed). *The New Grove Dictionary of Music and Musicians*, Vol. 4. London: Macmillan Publishers Limited.

Kissinger, Henry (1979). *White House Years*. Boston: Little, Brown and Company.

Kranzler, David (1988). *Japanese, Nazis and Jews: The Jewish Refugee Community of Shanghai, 1938-45*. Hoboken: KTAV Publishing House, Inc.

Kraus, Richard C. (1991). Arts policies of the Cultural Revolution: the rise and fall of culture minister Yu Huiyong. In William A. Joseph, Christine P.W. Wong, and David Zweig (eds.) *New Perspectives on the Cultural Revolution*. Cambridge: Council on East Asian Studies/Harvard University: 219-241.

Kraus, Richard Curt (1989). *Pianos & Politics in China: Middle-Class Ambitions and the Struggle over Western Music.* New York: Oxford University Press.

Lai, T.C. and Mok, Robert (1981). *Jade Flute: The Story of Chinese Music.* New York: Schocken Books.

Latourette, Kenneth Scott (1967). *A History of Christian Missions in China.* New York: Russell & Russell.

Lee, Leo Ou-Fan (1999). *Shanghai Modern: The flowering of a new urban culture in China 1930-1945.* Cambridge: Harvard University Press.

Lesure, Francois (1977). *Debussy on Music.* (Trans. and edited by Richard Langham Smith). New York: Alfred A. Knopf.

Li, J.D., trans. (1969) *China in Transition, 1517-1911.* New York: Van Nostrand Reinhold Company.

Li Zhisui (1994). *The Private Life of Chairman Mao.* New York: Random House.

Ling, Pan (1991). *In Search of Old Shanghai.* Hong Kong: Joint Publishing Co. Ltd.

Liu Bai (1983). *Cultural Policy in the People's Republic of China.* Paris: Unesco.

Liu Qiong (2002). *Nie Er.* Zhengzhou: Daxiang Chubanshe.

Liu Xingzhi (ed.) (1995). *Li Ling Yenjiu Wenji* [Collected articles about Li Ling]. Guangdong: Gaodeng Jiaoyu Chubanshe.

Liu Xinxin and Liu Xueqing (2002). *Haerbin Xiyang Yinyueshi* [The history of Western music in Harbin]. Beijing: Renmin Yinyue Chubanshe.

Lochner, Louis P. (1950). *Fritz Kreisler.* New York: The Macmillan Company.

Luluzhengyi [*The True Meaning of Pitch Temperament*]. National Library of China, Rare Books Collection.

Luo Junjun (2001). *Li Delun Zhuan* [A Biography of Li Delun]. Beijing: Zuojia Chubanshe.

Ma Lu Yawen (2001). (Trans. Chen Shanwei.) *Wode Erzi Ma Youyou* [My son Yo-Yo Ma]. Beijing: Renmin Yinyue Chubanshe.

Macartney, Lord George. *An Embassy to China, Being the journal kept by Lord Macartney during his embassy to the Emperor Ch'ien-lung, 1793-1794.* Ed. J.L. Cranmer-Byng, London: Longmans, 1962.

MacFarquhar, Roderick (1974). *The Origins of the Cultural Revolution, Volume 1: Contradictions Among the People, 1956-57.* New York: Columbia University Press.

MacFarquhar, Roderick (1997). *The Origins of the Cultural Revolution, Volume 3: The Coming of the Cataclysm, 1961-66.* Oxford University Press and Columbia University Press.

Mackerras, Colin (1975). *The Chinese Theater in Modern Times: From 1840 to the Present Day.* Amherst: University of Massachusetts Press.

Mackerras, Colin (1997). *Peking Opera.* Hong Kong: Oxford University Press.

Mai Zi and Ma Ruixue (eds.) (2002). *Ma Sicong Zui Hou Ershi Nian* [Sitson Ma's Last 20 Years]. Guangzhou: Guangdong Renmin Chubanshe.

Mao Zedong (1977). Talks at the Yanan Forum on Literature and Art. *In Mao Tse-Tung on Literature and Art*. Peking: Foreign Languages Press.

Mao Zedong (2002). *Mao Zedong Wenyi Lunji* [Mao Zedong's Writings on Literature and Arts]. Beijing: Zhongyang Wenxian Chubanshe.

Meisner, M. (1986). *Mao's China and After, A History of the People's Republic*. New York: The Free Press.

Menquez, Alexander (pseudonym) (2000). Growing up Jewish in Manchuria in the 1930s: Personal Vignettes. In Jonathan Goldstein (ed.) *The Jews of China, Volume Two: A Sourcebook and Research Guide*. Armonk: M.E. Sharpe.

Menuhin, Yehudi (1996). *Unfinished Journey: Twenty Years Later*. New York: Fromm International Publishing Corporation.

Miao Tianrui, Ji Liankang and Guo Naian (chief eds.) (1984). *Zhongguo Yinyue Cidian* [Dictionary of Chinese Music]. Beijing: Renmin Yinyue Chubanshe.

Miao Tianrui, Ji Liankang, Guo Naian and Li Quanmin (chief eds.) (1990). *Zhongguo Yinyue Cidian Xubian* [Continuation of the Dictionary of Chinese Music]. Beijing: Renmin Yinyue Chubanshe.

Ming Yan (2002). *Ershishiji Zhongguo Yinyue Piping Daolun*. [A Guide to 20th-Century Music Criticism in China]. Beijing: Renmin Yinyue Chubanshe.

Mitamura, Taisuke (1970). *Chinese Eunuchs, The Structure of Intimate Politics*. Rutland, Vermont; Tokyo, Japan: Charles Tuttle.

Mittler, Barbara (1997). *Dangerous Tunes: The Politics of Chinese Music in Hong Kong, Taiwan, and the People's Republic of China since 1949*. Wiesbaden: Harrassowitz Verlag.

Nichols, Roger (1988). *The Life of Debussy*. Cambridge: Cambridge University Press.

Nixon, Richard (1978). *The Memoirs of Richard Nixon*. New York: Grosset & Dunlap.

Pfister, Louis, S.J. (1932). *Notices Biographiques et Bibliographiques sur Les Jesuites de L'Ancienne Mission De Chine 1552-1773*. Shanghai: Imprimerie de la Mission Catholique.

Pogue, Forrest C. (1987). *George C. Marshall: Statesman*. New York: Viking.

Pott, F.L. Hawks (1928). *A Short History of Shanghai*. Shanghai: Kelly & Walsh, Limited.

Qi Teng Xiao Zhi (2003). (translated from the Japanese by Zhuang Li). *Nie Er: Shanguangde Shengya* [Nie Er: a shining life]. Shanghai: Shanghai Yinyue Chubanshe.

Qian Renkang (1997). *Huang Zide Shenghuo yu Chuangzuo* [The Life and Music of Huang Zi]. Beijing: Renmin Yinyue Chubanshe.

Ribeiro, Alvaro, S.J. (Ed.) (1991). *The Letters of Dr. Charles Burney, Vol. 1 1751-1784*. Oxford: Clarendon Press.

Ripa, Matteo (1844). (Trans. Fortunato Prandi) *Memoirs of Father Ripa during Thirteen Years Residence at the Court of Peking in the Service of the Emperor of China*. London: John Murray.

Ripin, Edwin. M. (1980). Clavichord. In, Stanley Sadie (ed). *The New Grove Dictionary of Music and Musicians*, Vol. 4. London: Macmillan Publishers Limited.

Ristaino, Marcia R. (2000). New Information on Shangehai Jewish Refugees: The Evidence of the Shanghai Muncipal Police Files, National Archives and Records Administration, Washington, D.C. In Jonathan Goldstein (ed.). *The Jews of China, Volume Two: A Sourcebook and Research Guide*. Armonk: M.E. Sharpe.

Roots, John McCook (1978). *Chou: An Informal Biography of China's Legendary Chou En-lai*. New York: Doubleday & Company.

Rosenson, Harriet P. (1999). Jewish musicians in Shanghai: bridging two cultures. In Jonathan Goldstein (ed.) *The Jews of China, Volume One: Historical and Comparative Perspectives*. Armonk: M.E. Sharpe.

Ross, Andrew C .(1994). *A Vision Betrayed: The Jesuits in Japan and China, 1542-1742*. Maryknoll, New York: Orbis Books.

Ross, James R. (1994). *Escape to Shanghai: A Jewish Community in China*. New York: The Free Press.

Rowbotham, Arnold H. (1942). *Missionary and Mandarin: The Jesuits at the Court of China*. Berkeley and Los Angeles: University of California Press.

Rubinstein, Arthur (1980). *My Many Years*. New York: Alfred A. Knopf.

Saerchinger, Cesar (1957). *Artur Schnabel: A Biography*. New York: Dodd, Mead & Company.

Schoenhals, Michael (ed) (1996). *China's Cultural Revolution, 1966-1969, Not a Dinner Party*. Armonk, New York: M.E. Sharpe.

Scott, A.C. (1965). *Literature and the Arts in Twentieth Century China*. London: George Allen & Unwin Ltd.

Seagrave, Sterling (1992). *Dragon Lady: The Life and Legend of the Last Empress of China*. New York: Alfred A. Knopf.

Selden, Mark (1971). *The Yanan Way in Revolutionary China*. Cambridge: Harvard University Press.

Sergeant, Harriet (1991). *Shanghai*. London: John Murray.

Shi Zhongxin (2000). *He Luting Zhuan* [A Biography of He Luting]. Shanghai: Shanghai Yinyue Chubanshe.

Snow, Edgar (1962). *The Other Side of the River*. New York: Random House.

Snow, Edgar (1973). *Red Star Over China*. New York: Random House.

Snow, Lois Wheeler (1972). *China On Stage: An American Actress in the People's Republic*. New York: Random House.

Spence, Jonathan (1969). *To Change China: Western Advisers in China 1620-1960*. New York: Little, Brown.

Spence, Jonathan (1984). *The Memory Palace of Matteo Ricci*. New York: Viking Penguin.

Spence, Jonathan. (1990). *The Search for Modern China*. New York: W.W. Norton & Company.

Stern, Isaac (with Chaim Potok) (1999). *My First 79 Years*. New York: Alfred A. Knopf.

Stoler, Mark A. (1989). *George C. Marshall: Soldier-Statesman of the American Century*. Boston: Twayne Publishers.

Strong, Anna Louise (1949). *The Chinese Conquer China*. New York: Doubleday & Co.

Tao Yabing (1994). *Zhong-Xi Yinyue Jiaoliu Shigao* [The History of Musical Exchange Between China and the Western World]. Beijing: Zhongguo Dabaikequanshu Chubanshe.

Terrill, Ross (1984). *The White-Boned Demon: A Biography of Madame Mao Zedong.* New York: William Morrow and Company.

Trigault, Nicola, S.J. (Gallagher, Louis J., S.J (trans.) *China in the Sixteenth Century: The Journals of Matthew Ricci: 1583-1610.* New York: Random House.

Tuohy, Sue (1999). Metropolitan sounds: music in Chinese films of the 1930s. In Yingjin Zhang (ed.) *Cinema and Urban Culture in Shanghai, 1922-1943.* Stanford: Stanford University Press.

Varg, Paul A. (1958). *Missionaries, Chinese and Diplomats: The American Protestant Missionary Movement in China, 1890-1952.* Princeton: Princeton University Press.

Wakeman, Frederick Jr. (1995). *Policing Shanghai 1927-1937.* Berkeley, Los Angeles, London: University of California Press.

Wang Ningyi and Yang Heping (chief eds.) (1999). *Ershi Shiji Zhongguo Yinyue Meixue* [Music Aesthetics in Twentieth Century China]. Beijing: Xiandai Chubanshe.

Wang Renyuan (1999). *Jingju Yangbanxi Yinyue Lungang* [A Brief discussion of the music of model Peking operas] Beijing: Renmin Yinyue Chubanshe.

Wang Yuhe (1987). *Nie Er Pingzhuan* [A critical biography of Nie Er]. Beijing: Renmin Yinyue Chubanshe.

Wang Yuhe (1998). *Zhongguo Jinxiandai Yinyuejia Pingzhuan* [Biography and analysis of contemporary Chinese musicians]. Beijing: Wenhua Yishu Chuban She.

Wang Yuhe (2002). *Zhongguo Jinxiandai Yinyueshi* [A history of modern Chinese music]. (3rd edition) Beijing: Renmin Yinyue Chubanshe and Huale Chubanshe.

Wiant, Allen Artz (2003). *A new song for China.* Victoria, Canada: Trafford Publishing.

Wilson, Dick (1984). *Zhou Enlai: A Biography.* New York: Viking.

Witke, Roxanne (1977). *Comrade Chiang Ch'ing* [Jiang Qing]. Boston, Toronto: Little, Brown and Company.

Wong, Isabel F. K. (1984). Geming gequ: songs for the education of the masses. In Bonnie S. McDougall (ed.) *Popular Chinese Literature and Performing Arts in the People's Republic of China, 1949-1979.* Berkeley: University of California Press.

Wong, Isabel F.K. (1991). From reaction to synthesis: Chinese musicology in the twentieth century. In Bruno Nettl and Philip Bohlman (ed.). *Comparative Musicology and Anthropolgy of Music: Essays on the History of Ethnomusicology.* Chicago and London: The University of Chicago Press.

Xiang Xiyuan (2002). *Zhong-Xi Yuelun* [A Study of Chinese and Western Music]. Beijing: Renmin Chubanshe.

Xu Buzeng (1999). Jews and the musical life of China. In Jonathan Goldstein (ed.) *The Jews of China, Volume One: Historical and Comparative Perspectives.* Armonk: M.E. Sharpe.

Ye Yonglie (1999). *Hei Hong Nei Mu* [The colors behind the curtain]. Beijing: Zuojia Chubanshe.

Ye Yonglie (2000). *Jiang Qing Zhuan* [A biography of Jiang Qing]. Ulumuqi: Xinjiang Renmin Chubanshe.

Ye Yonglie (2000). *Ma Sicong Zhuan. Aiguode panguozhe.* [A biography of Ma Sicong, patriotic traitor]. Urumqi: Xinjiang Chubanshe.

Zhongguo Yinyuejia Xiehui (1964). *Shiwu Nianlai de Zhongguo Yinyue* [Fifteen Years of China's Music]. Beijing: Zhongguo Yinyuejia Xiehui.

Zhou Weishi (chief ed.) (1989). *Xian Xinghai Quanji* [The Complete Works of Xian Xinghai]. Guangdong: Guangdong Gaojiao Chubanshe: Vol. 1.

Zhu Yongzhen (1997). *Zhou Xiaoyan Zhuan* [A Biography of Zhou Xiaoyan]. Shanghai: Shanghai Yinyue Chubanshe.

Zhuang Yongping (2002). Yinyuede bainian huixiang. [Looking Back at a Century of Music]. In *Shanghai Bainian Wenhuashi* [Shanghai Cultural History of the 20th-Century]. Shanghai: Shanghai Kexuejishu Wenxian Chubanshe: 743- 800.

PERIODICALS

— (1997). Foreign audiences hail modern Chinese music. *China Daily* July 30.

— (1966). Decision of the Chinese Communist Party Concerning the Great Proletarian Cultural Revolution. *Chinese Literature* 10, 1966: 53-66.

— (1968). A new form of proletarian art. *China Reconstructs* October: 19.

— (1969). Mao Zedong thought forever sheds its radiance. *Chinese Literature* 6: 94-101.

— (1973). Music for friendship. *China Reconstructs* July: 41-42.

— (1979). Virtuoso Isaac Stern charms Chinese audiences. *China Reconstructs* October: 33-34.

— (1980). The homecoming of pianist Fou Tsong [Fu Cong]. *China Reconstructs* May: 49-52.

— (1999). Guangzhou's quest for cultural refinement set back after night of musical chairs. *South China Morning Post.* February 22.

— *Liberation Army Daily* Editorial, April 18, 1966. Hold high the great Red Banner of Mao Zedong's Thought and Actively Participate in the Great Socialist Cultural Revolution. *Chinese Literature* 7: 3- 20.

— *People's Daily* Editorial, June 1, 1966. Sweep away all monsters. *Chinese Literature* 7:65-70

— The Tiananmen Poems (A Selection) (1979). *Chinese Literature* 3: 3-15.

Austin, Anthony (1939). Under the baton of Maestro Paci, director of Shanghai's symphony orchestra reviews his career as a music 'dictator.' *The China Press Sunday Magazine* May 7: 5-6.

Cameron, Lindsley (1997). A Marco Polo Going Backward at Full Tilt. *The New York Times* November 2.

Chang Feng (1962). Biggest Shanghai Music Festival. *Peking Review* June 8: 18-19.

Chang Keng My recollection of the production and first performances of *The White-Haired Girl* *Chinese Literature* 9: 99-105.

Chen Jie (2003). Curtain falls on musical showcase. *China Daily* November 7.

Chen Xing (1973). The Philadelphia Orchestra Performs in China. *Chinese Literature* 7: 104-107.

Frisch, J.C. (trans. Mary Pardoe) European Music in China, 17th and 18th centuries. In, *Baroque Concert at the Forbidden City* (compact disc liner notes). Astree Records.

Fu Hu (1980).Yehudi Menuhin's Chinese debut. *Chinese Literature* April:121-124.

Gild, Gerlinde (1998). Early 20th-century 'reforms' in Chinese music. *Chime* Spring/Autumn: 116-123.

Harris, E.F. (1942). The story of the Municipal Orchestra. *Souvenir Programme of Farewell Concert*, Shanghai Municipal Orchestra. May 31.

Ho Chia-Shui (1946). Paci gives highlights of life in last interview. *The China Press* October 20.

Hsia Lin-ken (1968). Literature and art must serve proletarian politics. *Chinese Literature* 10: 93-95.

Hua Wenying (1977).The 'Gang of Four's' revisionist line in literature and art. *Chinese Literature* 7: 88-96.

Huang Kang (1977). An unforgettable night in Yanan. *Chinese Literature* 9: 91-98.

Jiang Ning (2000) Chen Xieyang: Yinyue yu Yinyue Zhiwai de Huati [Chen Xieyang: Thoughts on Music and Beyond]. Arts Today.com. September.

Jiang Qing (1967). On the revolution in Peking Opera: speech made in July 1964 at forum of theatrical workers particiapting in the Festival of Peking Operas on Contemporary Themes. *Chinese Literature* Volume 8:118-128.

Kagan, Alan L. (1963). Music and the Hundred Flowers Movement. *The Musical Quarterly*: 417-430.

Kouwenhoven, Frank and Schimmelpenninck, Antoinet (1997). Guo Wenjing — a composer's portrait. *Chime*. Spring/Autumn: 9-49.

Lee, Joanna C. (2002). International gathering in Beijing. *Gramophone* www.gramophone.co.uk, October 14.

Li Delun (1973). Symphonies for the workers, peasants and soldiers. *China Reconstructs*. May: 10-14.

Li Xian. New Wave in Chinese Music. *China Reconstructs*, December 1986.

Li Xing (2000). Passion, professionalism make for great music. *China Daily* December 18.

Li Yeh-tao (1962). Chinese orchestral music. *Peking Review*. June 29: 14-16.

Li, Gang (2001). Jiangshu Yanan [A story of Yanan] *Arts Today. Com.* January: 15-18.

Lu Kungda (1967). A revolution in symphonic music. *China Reconstructs* September: 17-20.

Ma Ko (1965). Hsien Hsing-hai [Xian Xinghai] the composer. *Chinese Literature* 12: 110-116.

Ma Sitson [Ma Sicong] (1967). Cruelty and insanity made me a fugitive. *Life Magazine* June 2.

Mao Jingbo (1993). One note of sympathy for Central Symphony readout: good promotions, carefully chosen pieces and devoted musicians are the keys to the revival of symphony. *China Daily* April 23.

Mao Jingbo (1996). Classical music strikes the right chord. *China Daily* January 18: 9.

Mao Zedong. (1980). A talk to music workers. *Chinese Literature* January: 82-91.

Mass Criticism Group of the People's Literature Publishing House (1977). Chiang Ching [Jiang Qing], the Political Pickpocket. *Chinese Literature* 2: 109-120.

Melvin, Sheila (1997). Shanghai bids for culture with a grand theater. *The Asian Wall Street Journal* November 7:13.

Melvin, Sheila (1999). A Chinese violinist's voyage through the century. *International Herald Tribune* December 3: 20.

Melvin, Sheila (1999). A rage for opera houses (Oh, and opera, too). *The New York Times* May 30: 21.

Melvin, Sheila (1999). Of war and opera: a life on both fronts. *International Herald Tribune* July 1: 20.

Melvin, Sheila (1999). On a golden anniversary, a leaden yoke of ideology. *The New York Times* September 26: 1.

Melvin, Sheila (2000). Battle of the orchestras in Beijing. *International Herald Tribune* September 13: 12.

Melvin, Sheila (2000). Can a Frenchman inspire the heart of Beijing? — Forty years in coming, a theater still arouses fierce passions; is it a pearl or a duck egg? *The Wall Street Journal* September 6: A24.

Melvin, Sheila (2000). Music: eye on China — Chinese "Traditional" Orchestra: Westernizing the *erhu*. *The Wall Street Journal* August 31: 18.

Melvin, Sheila and Cai, Jindong (2000). An orchestra with a political accompaniment. *The New York Times* March 5: 39.

Melvin, Sheila and Cai, Jindong (2000). Why this nostalgia for fruits of chaos? *The New York Times* October 29.

Paci, M. (1942). Maestro Mario Paci (born 1878), Conductor Shanghai Municipal Orchestra 1919-1942. *Souvenir Programme of Farewell Concert*, Shanghai Municipal Orchestra. May 31.

Page, Frederick (1963). A musician's journal. *Arts and Sciences in China*: 9-16.

Propaganda team of Dazhai Brigade (1977). An exposure of Jiang Qing. *Chinese Literature* 2: 118-120.

Schimmelpenninck, Antoinet. & Kouwenhoven, Frank. (1993). The Shanghai Conservatory of Music. *Chime*, No. 6, Spring.

Schonberg, Harold C. (1973). Philadelphians a "Big Success" in their first concert in China. *The New York Times* September 15.

Schonberg, Harold C. (1973). Ormandy, unexpectedly, leads Peking Orchestra. *The New York Times* September 16.

Schonberg, Harold C. (1973). Philadelphians play committee music. *The New York Times* September 18.

Schonberg, Harold C. (1973). U.S. group plays for Mao's wife. *The New York Times* September 17.

Schonberg, Harold C. (1973). Yin spoke only Chinese, Ormandy only English. *The New York Times* October 14.

Shu Haoqing (1970). The stagecraft of a model revolutionary opera. *Chinese Literature* 6:119-125.

Sun, Claudia (2000). "Aristocratic" piano scales new heights of popularity. *Shanghai Daily* March 3: 9.

Tan Aiqing (1979). Music and friendship – the Boston Symphony Orchestra in China. *China Reconstructs* July: 6-8.

Tan Aiqing (1980). The homecoming of pianist Fou Tsong. *China Reconstructs* May: 50.

Tcherepnin, Alexander (1935). Music in Modern China. *The Musical Quarterly*, Vol.XXI, No. 4, October: 391-399.

Tcherepnin, Alexander (1979). A Short Autobiography. *Tempo* 1979: 12-18.

Tu Ho (1978). A hundred flowers in bloom again. *Chinese Literature* 11: 105-108.

Utz, Christian (1998). Extreme cross-over, extremely personal music. *Chime* Spring/Autumn: 142-50.

Wan Kung (1977). How our revolutionary operas and ballets were produced. *Chinese Literature* 6: 66-72.

Wang An (1962). New orchestral sounds. *Peking Review*. December 14: 24-5.

Wang Ruoshui (1993). Mao, the great Machiavellian: Why Mao launched the Cultural Revolution. Presentation at Colgate University. (www.wangruoshui.net/beiyong/mach.HTM)

Wedemeyer, Dee (2001). A Chinese-born composer and her own long march. *The New York Times*, March 2.

Wu Xiaoqing (1969). A great victory in "making foreign things serve China." *Chinese Literature* 5: 578-86.

Xiao Xiao (1992). How a lack of interest and funds is hurting the classics. *China Daily* July 27.

Xin Hua (1976). Mass debate on revolution in literature and art. *Chinese Literature* 6: 102- 108.

Yang Chunxia (1976). What the revolution in literature and art has taught me. *Chinese Literature* 7:116-123.

Yen Liangkun (1979). Boston Symphony Orchestra in China. *Chinese Literature* 7:101-104.

Yin Cheng-chung (Yin Chengzong) (1974). How the piano concerto "Yellow River" was composed. *Chinese Literature* 11: 101-2.

Yin Cheng-tsung [Yin Chengzong] (1968). Be revolutionary cultural workers always loyal to Chairman Mao. *Chinese Literature* 9: 10-17.

Yu Hedeng (1986). Commemorating two top composers. *Beijing Review* Volume 29, No. 9, March 3: 30-1.

Zaharoff, F.P. *Adventures in China in the 1940s.* Unpublished speech.

Zhao Gang (1993). Classical musicians moonlight at hotels. *China Daily* March 24.

Zhao Hua (1974). Do musical works without titles have no class character? *Chinese Literature* 4: 89-94.

Zhao Jinglun (1980). Berlin Orchestra and von Karajan acclaimed. *China Reconstructs*, February: 42-43.

Zhu Lan (1974). A decade of revolution in Peking opera. *Chinese Literature* 9: 85-94.

INDEX

A

Abbado, Claudio, 268
Academy of Fine Arts, 96, 189
Alfven, Hugo, 40
All-China Federation of Literary and Art
    Circles, 184
Amiot, Joseph-Marie (Qian Deming), 75
Anosov, Nikolai, 201
Anti-spiritual pollution campaign, 314,
    328–329
Asahina, Takashi, 149
Ashkenazy, Vladimir, 203, 212
Aubin, Tony, 191
Auer, Leopold, 101
Avshalomov, Aaron, 119, 123–124, 126,
    152, 164, 168

B

Ba Jin, 154
Bach, J. S., 75, 98, 115, 118, 141, 144, 146,
    173, 175, 186, 202, 210–211, 268
Bahr, Father Florian (Wei Jijin), 74
Banquet music, 55
Bantock, Granville, 34
Barrow, John, 79
Bartok, Bela, 118, 291, 328
Batavia, 17, 30
Beethoven, Ludwig van, 20, 22, 26, 29, 34–
    36, 89, 91, 97–98, 113, 115, 118, 120,
    123, 127, 131, 139, 142, 144, 148,
    153, 156–157, 192, 194, 199, 201,
    203–204, 210–212, 215, 218, 221,
    223, 256, 266–270, 274, 278, 286,
    288–289, 291–292, 299, 304, 310–
    311, 313, 322, 325
    Appassionata, 29, 148

    Fifth Symphony, 34, 120, 157, 203,
    219, 267, 269–270, 286, 288

    Ninth Symphony, 89, 156, 218, 291
Beijing Concert Hall, 216, 291, 302–303,
    318–319, 336
Beijing Culture Bureau, 314
Beijing International Music Festival, 303,
    316
Beijing Symphony Orchestra, 314
Belgium Royal Conservatory, 186
Benois, Marie, 110
Benoist, Father Michel, 76
Berg, Alban, 23, 108, 202
Berlin Philharmonic, 289–291, 317
Bian Zushan, 332
Big Brother, 198, 219
Black Gang, 247
Borodin Quartet, 310
Borodin, Alexander, 199
Boston Symphony Orchestra, 286, 288
Boulanger, Nadia, 186, 191
Bouvet, Father Joachim (Bai Ji), 70
Boxer Rebellion, 108, 186
Bridge House, 148
Bright Sheng, 329, 333
Broadway musicals, 312
Brother Sebastian, 52
Bruch, Max, 37
Buck, Rudolf, 26
Buddhism, 72, 298
Buffalo Boy's Flute, 125, 209, 294
Butterfly Lovers, The, 210–211, 219, 256–
    257

C

Cai Yuanpei, 95, 100, 110, 112–113
Cao Peng, 291
Cao Shijun, 174
Carl, Catherine, 85
Carreras, 311
Casals, Pablo, 174

269, 288, 296, 299, 307, 311, 313, 337, 339
   Coronation Concerto, 34, 117
Music Monthly, 137
Music Research Society, 87
Musical Quarterly, The, 111–112, 143, 210, 307
Muslims, 74
Mussorgsky, Modest Petrovich, 40, 103, 139, 271

N

Nanjing, 32–33, 45, 47, 54, 56, 83, 100, 119, 134–135, 139, 145, 156–157, 189, 246, 302
Nanjing Massacre, or the Rape of Nanjing, 136
Naples, 27, 38, 66, 70
National anthem, 126–127, 187, 231, 281
National Conservatory of Music, 100, 112, 117
National Defense Song Movement, 126
National Grand Theater, 186, 302–303
National Library of China, 69, 74
National music, 94
National Salvation Song Movement, 126
Nationalism, 321, 324
Nationalist Party (Nationalists), 41, 110, 136, 154–155, 170, 172, 176, 178, 180, 183, 203, 232, 238, 240, 250, 253, 324
Nepridi, Sonatas for solo violin with bass, opus 3, 69
New China Arts University, 90
New Fourth Route Army, 170
New Haven Symphony, 109
New Music Movement, 126
New York, 18, 36, 46, 49, 55, 59, 72, 77, 84–85, 92, 97, 105, 108, 111, 115, 117, 120, 125, 133, 160, 166, 169, 173, 175, 193, 195, 197, 202, 221, 233, 244, 267–268, 270, 273–274, 285, 289–290, 294, 305, 329, 333, 338
New York Times, The, 263, 267, 269–272, 274, 301, 314, 332–333
Nie Er, 126–131, 165, 174, 198, 280–281, 321, 324
Nixon, Richard, President, 265
North China Daily News, The, 22, 42, 119, 135

O

Oberdorfer, Paul, 122–123
Oberlin College, 109

Oestreich, James, 333
Ogdon, John, 212
Oistrakh, David, 187, 212, 215, 246
On the Docks, 252
One in, one out, 138
Opium War, 19, 82–84, 301
Ormandy, Eugene, 268–271, 274–275, 278, 299
Orphaned island, 136, 140
Ouyang Shanzun, 156
Ozawa, Seiji, 286, 337

P

Paci, Mario, 17–18, 27–28, 37, 40, 45, 117, 134, 144, 148, 151, 153, 192, 204, 231, 322, 335
Padushka, Josef, 127, 142, 185
Page, Frederick, 212, 322
Palace Hotel, 32, 135
Pan Chun, 337
Pantoia, Diego, 47
Parennin, Dominique, 68
Paris, 23, 25, 44, 72, 75, 111, 116–117, 122–123, 140, 184, 186–187, 191, 220–221, 288, 329
Paris Conservatory, 122–123, 191
Paris of the East, 23, 25, 44, 117
Pavarotti, Luciano, 310
Pavlova, Anna, 111
Peace Hotel, 102
Pearl Harbor, 147
Pedrini, Teodorico (De Lige), 66
Peking Academy, 44
Peking Opera, 248–250, 252, 262, 312, 326, 331
Peking Opera, Festival of, on Contemporary Themes, 248
Peking University, 95–96
Peng Dehuai, 227
Philadelphia Orchestra, 119, 268–269, 271–272, 274, 276, 278, 288, 299
Piano, 22, 28, 117, 142, 148, 153, 203, 223, 260, 262, 270, 274, 288, 290, 308
Piano fever, 308
Piccini, Nicola, 75
Pines of Rome, 270–271, 275–277
Pioneers, The, 280
Pope Clement XI, 72
Prince Yinzhi, 66, 68
Pritchard, John, 268
Prokofiev, Sergei, 23, 110, 123, 218
Protestants, 82–83
Prout, Ebenezer, 117
Puccini, Giacomo, 29–30, 148, 290, 292
Pugni, Caesar, 103
Pushkin, Alexander, 103